Social Capital and Poor Communities

Social Capital and Poor Communities

Susan Saegert

J. Phillip Thompson

Mark R. Warren

Editors

A VOLUME IN THE FORD FOUNDATION SERIES
ON ASSET BUILDING

Russell Sage Foundation ◆ New York

The Russell Sage Foundation

The Russell Sage Foundation, one of the oldest of America's general purpose foundations, was established in 1907 by Mrs. Margaret Olivia Sage for "the improvement of social and living conditions in the United States." The Foundation seeks to fulfill this mandate by fostering the development and dissemination of knowledge about the country's political, social, and economic problems. While the Foundation endeavors to assure the accuracy and objectivity of each book it publishes, the conclusions and interpretations in Russell Sage Foundation publications are those of the authors and not of the Foundation, its Trustees, or its staff. Publication by Russell Sage, therefore, does not imply Foundation endorsement.

Library of Congress Cataloging-in-Publication Data

Social capital and poor communities / Susan Saegert, J. Phillip Thompson, Mark R. Warren, editors.
    p. cm.
    Includes bibliographical references and index.
    ISBN 0-87154-733-3
    1. Social capital (Sociology)—United States. 2. Urban poor—United States. 3. Community development—United States. 4. Economic development—United States. 5. United States—Social policy. 6. United States—Economic policy. I. Saegert, Susan. II. Thompson, J. Phillip. III. Warren, Mark R., 1955-

HM708 .S64 2001
307.1'4'0973—dc21   2001041779

Text design by Suzanne Nichols

RUSSELL SAGE FOUNDATION
112 East 64th Street, New York, New York 10021
10 9 8 7 6 5 4 3 2

To community builders and organizers

Previous Volumes in the Series

Contents

Contents

Contributors

SUSAN SAEGERT is professor of environmental psychology and director of the Center for Human Environments and the Housing Environments Research Group at the City University of New York Graduate School and University Center.

J. PHILLIP THOMPSON is associate professor of political science at Columbia University.

MARK R. WARREN is associate professor of sociology and director of service learning at Fordham University.

MARK CHAVES is professor of sociology at the University of Arizona.

CATHY J. COHEN is professor of political science and African American studies at Yale University.

CYNTHIA M. DUNCAN is director of community and resource development at the Ford Foundation.

MICHAEL W. FOLEY is associate professor of politics at the Catholic University of America.

ESTER R. FUCHS is professor of political science and public affairs at Barnard College and Columbia University and director of the Center for Urban Research and Policy.

ROSS GITTELL is associate professor of management and department chair at the Whittemore School of Business and Economics, University of New Hampshire.

SHERMAN A. JAMES is the John P. Kirscht Collegiate Professor of Public Health and director of the Center for Research on Ethnicity, Culture, and Health at the School of Public Health, University of Michigan at Ann Arbor.

LANGLEY C. KEYES is the Ford Professor of City and Regional Planning in the Department of Urban Studies and Planning, Massachusetts Institute of Technology.

MARGARET LEVI is Jere L. Bacharach Professor of International Studies in Political Science at the University of Washington at Seattle.

M. LISETTE LOPEZ is a research consultant to the Aspen Institute's Roundtable on Comprehensive Community Initiatives, Project on Race and Community Revitalization, and is codirector of California Tomorrow's Project on Equity and Access in After School Programs.

JOHN D. MCCARTHY is professor of sociology at the Pennsylvania State University.

LORRAINE C. MINNITE is assistant professor of political science at Barnard College, Columbia University.

PEDRO A. NOGUERA is the Judith K. Dimon Professor in Communities and Schools at the Graduate School of Education, Harvard University.

MELVIN L. OLIVER is vice president of the Ford Foundation. He is responsible for overseeing the Asset Building and Community Development Program.

ROBERT D. PUTNAM is the Peter and Isabel Malkin Professor of Public Policy at Harvard University.

ROBERT J. SAMPSON is the Lucy Flower Professor of Sociology at the University of Chicago and senior research fellow at the American Bar Foundation.

AMY J. SCHULZ is assistant research scientist and associate director for qualitative methods at the Center for Research on Ethnicity, Culture, and Health, School of Public Health, University of Michigan at Ann Arbor.

ROBERT Y. SHAPIRO is professor and chair of political science at Columbia University.

CAROL B. STACK is professor of social and cultural studies in the Graduate School of Education, University of California at Berkeley.

JULIANA VAN OLPHEN is assistant professor in the Program of Urban Public Health at Hunter College, City University of New York.

Preface

Melvin L. Oliver

This book edited by Susan Saegert, J. Phillip Thompson, and Mark R. Warren is the third volume in a new series funded by the Ford Foundation and published by the Russell Sage Foundation. The series provocatively explores the strengths and policy relevance of the asset-building approach to poverty alleviation; at the same time, it points to areas in which the shortcomings of the approach may require further work. In this preface, I would like to introduce the concepts embodied in the asset-building approach and describe how it is being incorporated into the grant-making of the Ford Foundation.

In 1996 the Ford Foundation entered an era of new leadership. Susan Berresford succeeded Franklin Thomas as the foundation's president, and I became the vice president of a newly expanded program to advance the foundation's goal of reducing poverty and injustice. I was given the task of uniting within a single program all of the foundation's work on urban and rural poverty, sexual and reproductive health, and program-related investments. After long consultation and much discussion with the foundation's staff in New York and in our thirteen international offices, we decided to organize our efforts around the theme of asset-building. Reflecting on the work in which we had been engaged worldwide, we felt strongly that the most successful work—and the work most needed—is that which empowers the poor to acquire key human, social, financial, and natural resource assets. So empowered, the poor are better able, in turn, to reduce and prevent injustice.

The focus of the Ford Foundation Asset Building and Community Development Program is a departure from the conventional wisdom in several ways, both within the foundation and in the broader development community. Antipoverty policy in the United States and in international development programs worldwide has tended to emphasize efforts to increase income to some predetermined minimum level as the "magic bullet" that will solve poverty problems. But that approach builds on the common misconception that poverty is simply a matter of low income or low levels of consumption. Several critiques of this approach to poverty alleviation have pointed out that its emphasis on income ignores key causes of inequity, overlooks the consequences of low asset accumulation, and fails to address long-term stability and security for individuals, families, and communities.

The Nobel laureate Amartya Sen foreshadowed this approach in his 1985 Hennipman Lectures in Economics (Sen 1999), and he discussed it again in his 1999 volume *Development as Freedom*. For him, poverty is a function not of low income but, among other things, of "capability deprivation," where capability refers to the whole range of civil and financial abilities or entitlements as well as to human development. Michael Sherraden appears to have reached similar conclusions quite independently in his pathbreaking 1991 work *Assets and the Poor*. Thomas Shapiro and I provided further support for the importance of the concepts of asset-building for urban poverty alleviation in the United States in our volume *Black Wealth/White Wealth* (Oliver and Shapiro 1995). And more recently, Anthony Bebbington developed an application of the approach to rural areas in his essay *Capitals and Capabilities* (1999).

An "asset" in this paradigm is a special kind of resource that an individual, organization, or entire community can use to reduce or prevent poverty and injustice. An asset is usually a "stock" that can be drawn upon, built upon, or developed, as well as a resource that can be shared or transferred across generations. Because in all societies assets are unevenly distributed, their distribution is highly related to both public policy decisions and cultural traditions and forces. These policies and traditions have affected the ways in which society structures ownership of assets and investments in assets. These structures have often affected women and members of racial and ethnic minorities in particular by excluding them from asset-building activities. As the poor gain access to assets, they are more likely to take control of important aspects of their lives, to plan for their future and deal with economic uncertainty, to support their children's educational achievements, and to work to ensure that the lives of the next generations are better than their own.

Over the last four years the staff of the Ford Foundation's Assets Program have been reexamining its grant-making initiatives and asking hard-hitting questions about how they fit within an asset-building strategy. This evaluation has required considerable analysis of the essential attributes of assets, the strategies needed to build them, and the methodology that will help us assess progress in asset accumulation. We have tried to see how we can best support asset-building organizations and bring an assets perspective to the various fields of work we support in what are primarily nonprofit and governmental organizations.

As our colleagues among practitioners and policymakers have witnessed our struggle to develop the asset-building approach, they have become very enthusiastic about it. This approach, they note, avoids the traditional focus on the "deficits" or "deficiencies" of the poor and disempowered and does not treat them as impassive subjects of external forces who are incapable of affecting their own future. It recognizes that injustice is as much a determinant of poverty as the vagaries of individual and community histories. The assets approach builds instead on the innate ability of all human beings to develop their skills and on the near-universal desire to create a better life for oneself and one's progeny. We have also found that some researchers are interested in advancing work on specific interventions to build assets. We therefore thought that the paradigm and the practice could be advanced further by a broad and deliberate examination of asset-building concepts and strategies across a range of disciplines.

Bernard Wasow of the Assets Program's Community and Resource Development Unit developed a series of conferences whose papers would be published as edited volumes exploring these themes. He sought to bring together researchers who are concerned with various types of asset development, even those who may not have been accustomed to calling it such. He invited them to explore:

- The state of current knowledge about the links between poverty and the various kinds of assets that might affect it

- The policy implications of an asset-building approach, particularly with respect to improving support for poor people and communities

- Further related research questions that will assist practitioners and policymakers in developing more effective strategies to alleviate poverty and reduce injustice

The first two conferences led to the publication of *Securing the Future: Investing in Children from Birth to College*, edited by Sheldon Danziger and Jane Waldfogel (2000), and *Assets for the Poor: The Benefits of Spreading Asset Ownership*, edited by Thomas M. Shapiro and Edward N. Wolff (2001). Both volumes were published by the Russell Sage Foundation. The third national conference on social capital and the reduction of poverty, coordinated by Mark Warren, forms the basis of this volume; and a fourth conference on building natural capital assets as a mechanism for alleviating poverty and increasing environmental justice was organized by James Boyce. Each of these four conferences brought together some of the nation's best and most provocative academic thinkers and leading practitioners from both the public and private sectors for what proved to be highly animated discussions of the topics at hand. Each of the conferences provided foundation staff with important new insights into the links between asset-building and the foundation's goals. We believe that these insights, as well as the new research themes identified, are now reflected in the work that we support. We hope that the volumes in this series will also stimulate the development of other approaches to alleviating poverty and injustice among many other institutions worldwide.

This series represents one of many ways in which we at the Ford Foundation are engaging our academic and practitioner colleagues and encouraging discussion of the concepts that guide our grant-making in the Assets Program. We congratulate Susan Saegert, J. Phillip Thompson, and Mark R. Warren for the excellent volume they have produced, and we welcome further commentary on these themes.

REFERENCES

Bebbington, Anthony. 1999. *Capitals and Capabilities: A Framework for Analysing Peasant Viability, Rural Livelihoods, and Poverty in the Andes.* London: International Institute for Environment and Development.

Danziger, Sheldon, and Jane Waldfogel, eds. 2000. *Securing the Future: Investing in Children from Birth to College.* New York: Russell Sage Foundation.

Oliver, Melvin L., and Thomas M. Shapiro. 1995. *Black Wealth/White Wealth: A New Perspective on Racial Inequality.* New York and London: Routledge.

Sen, Amartya K. 1999. *Commodities and Capabilities*. New York and London: Oxford University Press. (Originally published in 1985 as *Commodities and Capabilities: Professor Dr. P. Hennipman Lectures in Economics*, vol. 7 [London: Elsevier Science]).

———. 1999. *Development as Freedom*. New York: Alfred A. Knopf.

Shapiro, Thomas M., and Edward N. Wolff. 2001. *Assets for the Poor: The Benefits of Spreading Asset Ownership*. New York: Russell Sage Foundation.

Sherraden, Michael. 1991. *Assets and the Poor: A New American Welfare Policy*. New York: M. E. Sharpe.

Foreword

Robert D. Putnam

The most urgent moral problem in contemporary America is the persistence of poverty and growing inequality in the midst of unprecedented affluence. Over the last three decades or so, the gap between haves and have-nots has grown steadily and alarmingly, a sharp reversal of previous trends. Too few Americans on the comfortable side of that gap have been outraged by this mounting deficit in social justice.

At the same time, Americans of all classes and races, and in all sections of the country, have become increasingly disconnected from their communities and from one another. In the language of social science, we have incurred a growing deficit in "social capital," the bonds of community that in myriad ways enrich our lives.

What is the connection between these two worrisome trends? How are social capital and social justice related? Many observers have assumed that these concepts represent, in effect, competing approaches to the problem of poverty. Some on the political right have argued that private philanthropy among the rich and moral uplift among the poor are measures that by themselves can solve persistent poverty. Some on the political left have feared that talk about social capital is merely the latest version of blaming the victims, an easy way of avoiding conflict and economic redistribution. Both sides, ironically, assume that we can choose—that we must choose—between a social capital agenda and a social justice agenda. The central merit of this volume is that, in exploring some of the many complementarities between social capital and social justice, it contests that false choice.

Ironically, the concept of social capital itself first emerged from practical concerns about overcoming poverty in rural Appalachia. Nearly a century ago, L. Judson Hanifan, a young Progressive educator and social reformer working in rural West Virginia, concluded that the grave problems of those communities could be solved only by strengthening the networks of solidarity among their citizens. "The individual is helpless socially, if left to himself," Hanifan argued (1916, 130). "If he comes into contact with his neighbor, and they with other neighbors, there will be an accumulation of *social capital*, which may immediately satisfy his social needs and which may bear a social potentiality sufficient to the substantial improvement of living conditions in the whole community."

The concept of social capital has been revived, extended, and contested in recent years through the contributions of a large number of social researchers and policy activists. The editors of this volume summarize and integrate many of those insights at the same time that they make some important new conceptual contributions—for example, in their elaboration of the distinction between "bonding social capital" and "bridging social capital." Above all, however, they focus the conceptual apparatus of social capital theory on the urgent issues of poverty and inequality in America. The editors' introduction to this volume should be required reading for anyone concerned about *either* social capital or social justice in America.

Drawing on an impressive array of case materials, the contributors to the volume highlight the important social capital assets within poor communities, and they consider how those assets can be deployed most effectively. They underline the powerful constraints on social capital within poor communities that derive from both broader structural conditions and misguided public policies. Like other social capital researchers, they stress that social capital (like other forms of capital) can be put to bad purposes as well as good, that social capital can have a "dark side." They clarify the incomplete fungibility of various forms of social capital: bonding social capital, for example, is important for some purposes, while bridging social capital is crucial for other purposes. Nonpolitical forms of social capital have important uses, but explicitly political forms are required for policy reform.

Social capital promises no "magic bullet" for solving problems of poverty and social injustice, for this theory is an analytic lens, not a package of policies. Indeed, some forms of social capital may be obstacles in the struggle against poverty, racism, and injustice. Social capital is not an easy alternative to social justice. In fact, in my view, stronger ties within and among America's communities are a prerequisite for politically sustainable policies aimed at greater social justice. In particular, comfortable Americans must summon up a more capacious sense of "we," an interpretation of "our" communities and "our" children that extends beyond the neat front lawns of suburbia. In that way too, as well as in the many ways explored in this volume, attention to social networks and norms of reciprocity is an essential ingredient in the urgent struggle for social justice in contemporary America.

REFERENCE

Hanifan, Lyda Judson. 1916. "The Rural School Community Center." *Annals of the American Academy of Political and Social Science* 67: 130–38.

Acknowledgments

The chapters in this volume were originally presented at the conference "Social Capital and Poor Communities: Building and Using Social Assets to Combat Poverty," held in March 1999. The editors would like to thank the Ford Foundation for its sponsorship of the conference as one of a series devoted to combating poverty through asset-building strategies. We benefited from the support and advice of a number of individuals at Ford, including Melvin Oliver, Betsy Campbell, Bernard Wasow, Roland Anglin, and Michael Conroy. We would also like to thank the other cosponsors of the conference: the Graduate School of Arts and Sciences of Fordham University, the Graduate School and University Center of the City University of New York, and Columbia University's School of International and Public Affairs.

The discussions at the conference were unusually lively and productive. All participants seemed to feel the urgency of the issues we addressed and were excited about the new possibilities for improving the lives of families and their communities that might come through building social capital. The editors and the contributors to this volume, the collective result of the conference, benefited from conversations among each other as well as with panelists and members of the audience. We would particularly like to thank the discussants of the papers: Philip Kasinitz, Michael Dawson, Ashutosh Varshney, Robert Crutchfield, Walter Stafford, Kenneth Jackson, Jennifer Hochschild, Aida Giachello, Victoria Hattam, Frederick Harris, and Sally Covington. We would also like to thank three who served as rapporteurs for the conference: Xavier de Souza Briggs, Angela Blackwell, and Marilyn Gittell.

Many people active in the practical work of community building took the time to serve on panels at the conference and share lessons from their work. These included Julie Thomasson of MDC, Inc., in Chapel Hill, North Carolina; Monifa Akinwole of the Malcolm X Grassroots Movement; Nancy Biberman from the Women's Housing and Economic Development Corporation; Lee Farrow from Rheedlen's Community Pride; Aida Giachello of the Midwest Latino Health Research, Training, and Policy Center; Nicholas Freudenberg of Hunter College; Miriam Thompson of the Office of Worker Education at Queens College; and the Reverend Adolphus Lacey from Grace Baptist Church in Mount Vernon, New York. Thoughtful and challenging comments from the diverse group of panelists and audience members at the conference helped enrich this book. The excellent organizing work of James Dobson helped make the conference such a success.

Finally, we would like to thank Eric Wanner and Suzanne Nichols from the Russell Sage Foundation, as well as two anonymous reviewers, for their assistance in the difficult task of editing conference papers into a coherent volume. We would also like to thank our families who have helped and encouraged us to find new strategies to fight poverty.

Acknowledgments

This volume is the fruit of an intellectual collaboration among the editors. We should be considered equal coeditors and have listed ourselves alphabetically. We hope this book contributes to our understanding of the causes of poverty and social deprivation. More than that, we hope the volume will help advance the work of policymakers and activists struggling to develop new strategies in community building and development.

Chapter 1

The Role of Social Capital in Combating Poverty

Mark R. Warren, J. Phillip Thompson, and Susan Saegert

As the third in a series of books about building assets in poor communities, this volume examines the contributions that social capital can make to combating poverty and fostering the development of poor communities. Social capital refers to the set of resources that inhere in relationships of trust and cooperation between people.[1] These kinds of social assets do not alleviate poverty directly; rather, they leverage investments in human capital and household financial resources. Poor people rely on the support of extended family relationships and of more formal organizations like churches to survive. Scholars have long recognized the importance of these community support structures, and in that sense, social capital is not an entirely new notion for understanding the dynamics of poor communities. But recent scholarly work on social capital has served to renew interest in how social organization and norms of cooperation, both within a community and in its relationships to outside institutions, affect its development. In particular, this work has stimulated new thinking about the role that social capital can play not just in helping families survive but in advancing public policy that seeks to combat poverty.

Making use of social capital as an analytical construct requires a shift from the individual to the community as the unit of analysis for strategies to combat poverty. Social capital is a collective asset, a feature of communities, rather than the property of an individual. As such, individuals both contribute to it and use it, but they cannot own it.[2] Because it is a "common good," social capital plays a particularly important role in ensuring those aspects of personal welfare that the individual alone can rarely provide (for example, security from crime and public health). In the last ten years, evidence has been mounting that social relationships and community action matter for family well-being, even where communities lack many financial resources.[3]

The chapters in this volume provide a fairly comprehensive assessment of the contributions that social capital can make to combating poverty. They marshal impressive evidence that a community's social assets can improve the health, safety, education, economic well-being, political participation, and quality of life of residents in poor communities. Yet these chapters also demonstrate that strengthening the social capital of poor communities and, just as important, making effective use of those assets to foster community well-being are no easy tasks. Important obstacles exist, and social capital rarely works on its own. Nevertheless, social capital matters, and it may be the most promising starting point for new directions in combating poverty.

This volume was assembled to foster better understanding of the contributions that social capital can make to combating poverty and of the important obstacles to building and using social capital. With these considerations in mind, the contributors were asked to identify strategies that show promise for developing and using social assets to improve the lives of families in poor communities. Our premise is that, within the constraints of social organization, economics, politics, culture, and history, people can act collectively to change their circumstances. We seek to direct our attention to how this can be done.

SOCIAL CAPITAL IN CONTEXT

Social capital is not an alternative to providing greater financial resources and public services to poor communities. Rather, it constitutes an essential means to increase such resources and to make more effective use of them. This perspective differs from one that counterposes community self-help to government action.

In the self-help view, the problems of poor communities lie in their weak internal organization and social norms. A decline in social capital here represents a collapse in a community's ability to solve its own problems.[4] Public support can be seen as a contributor to undermining community responsibility. The answer, then, is to decrease government assistance and instead foster community self-help and private, charitable support. Such thinking, in part, has served as a foundation for the charitable choice provision in recent welfare reform. This provision liberalized the rules allowing religious institutions to provide publicly funded services to local communities so that they could replace direct government provision.

Recent social welfare reforms have been premised on the moral deficit argument that poor people lack a proper work ethic and sense of responsibility for their children. Many scholars have criticized this "blaming the victim" approach (for example, Kelley 1997). In this light, we must be careful not to replace the moral deficit argument with a social deficit argument: that is, if poor communities just got their social capital "act together" so that they could be like middle-class communities, then the problems of poverty could be solved.

The essays in this volume reflect an understanding that the causes of poverty do not lie primarily within the weak social fabric of poor communities, no matter how problematic that is. Instead, the causes of poverty lie in the broader economic, political, and racial structures of American society. Although some social capital enthusiasts ignore this reality, these processes are well known. Our urban communities have experienced the decline of good-paying jobs for low-skilled workers and an exodus of more middle-class residents, processes that have concentrated poverty in the inner city (Wilson 1996). Practices of systematic racism and segregation trap African Americans in these neighborhoods and block avenues for socioeconomic advancement (Massey and Denton 1993). Numerous studies show how government policies, like the siting of public housing in already poor neighborhoods, have concentrated the most disadvantaged in our inner cities (Judd and Swanstrom 1994; Goering, Kamely, and Richardson 1997). Our reliance on the property tax system leads to great disparities in the financing of schools and contributes fundamentally to the inadequate provision of education to youth in poor communities (Kozol 1991).

What is perhaps less appreciated is the impact of external processes on the social organization of poor communities. According to William Julius Wilson (1996), the flight of jobs destroys businesses, social institutions, and youth socialization processes, leading to a condition that he characterizes as social isolation. Youth lose ties to job networks as well as to a stable community where good work habits are instilled as the norm. Other studies have also documented the decline of the rich social fabric and mutual support networks that used to characterize poor, black communities (Drake and Cayton 1945; Ehrenhalt 1995). Elijah Anderson (1992) shows how "old heads"—older African American men with stable jobs—used to help young black males grow to adulthood, accept social responsibility, and get jobs. With the rise of crime and drug abuse, these old heads are now too afraid to intervene with youth. Their role has also lost legitimacy because they often lack the necessary job connections to back up their advice with practical help.

Government policy has also contributed to social disorganization. Although the idea of "maximum feasible participation" by the poor was an explicit part of some 1960s social policy, for the most part, since then, the poor have been seen as the passive objects of policy. Moreover, the social capital of the poor was never considered an important asset to sustain, let alone expand. Consequently, many public policies were adopted that undermined community social capital. For example, public housing policies produced concentrations of very poor tenants in buildings that promoted anonymity. At the same time, tenant selection procedures made it difficult or impossible for tenants to choose housing near friends and relatives (Goering, Kamely, and Richardson 1997).

Although these considerations suggest that social capital has declined in the inner city, there is little systematic evidence that the decline is greater than in more affluent communities. To the extent that these connections may have been declining in recent decades, evidence from the chapters in this book as well as from a recent review of national data sources (Wuthnow 2001) suggests that exclusionary processes and behaviors by mainstream institutions and organizations may be more to blame than social processes within marginalized populations.

More affluent communities do have greater financial and human capital resources, and their public institutions, like schools, are stronger. Their social capital can be more effective because it is reinforced by these other resources. For example, residents of poor communities may be friends with their neighbors, but those neighbors cannot provide them with connections and references to high-paying jobs. PTA members in an affluent community can discuss the latest curriculum innovations with schoolteachers. PTA members in an inner-city school can work together too. But instead of using their social capital to advance pedagogy at the school, they must discuss how to get an unresponsive central bureaucracy to fix the ceiling that has been falling down in the school auditorium for the last ten years.

In other words, the main problem for poor communities may not be a relative deficit in social capital, but that their social assets have greater obstacles to overcome, and are constantly under assault.

Poor communities cannot solve their problems on their own, no matter how strong and well organized their internal social capital becomes. They require greater financial resources and better public services. Their residents need better education and human capital development.

Nevertheless, social capital can play an essential role in strategies to combat poverty in several ways. First, it can help make investment strategies work. The chapters in part 2 of this volume examine the contributions of social capital in a range of policy areas: public health, safety, housing, economic development, and education. These chapters explore the ways in which strong community organization can enhance the effectiveness of public institutions and revitalization strategies. Second, to the extent that the poor can act collectively and forge alliances with outside actors, they stand a better chance of commanding the greater resources that are necessary for combating poverty. A number of the volume's chapters focus on the conditions under which social capital can provide a foundation for political power for the poor. More broadly, social capital strategies suggest a shift toward seeing the poor as active agents in the betterment of their communities. Through strengthening and expanding social connections, poor people can become partners in community development programs while building the political power needed to increase America's commitment to combating poverty.

The broad set of community building, community organizing, and community development efforts that have arisen across the United States have shown an ability to build affordable housing, foster micro-enterprise development, promote neighborhood safety, improve schools, and, more generally, take steps to reweave the social fabric of torn communities.[5] While working to strengthen local institutions and collective efficacy, these community-based initiatives bring new resources into poor neighborhoods and draw upon local knowledge to advance fresh ideas. In the context of the limitations of market and state action, such civil society initiatives promise some significant new directions in combating poverty.

The authors in this volume examine the role of social capital in policy domains and institutional settings critical to community revitalization. They seek to identify the ways in which social capital matters to the well-being of families and communities. And they highlight the processes central to the development and use of social capital for combating poverty. This task involves the identification of important obstacles to building social assets in poor communities. The rest of this chapter summarizes a number of the lessons learned from these explorations.

POWER AND CONFLICT

Policymakers have sometimes narrowed the implications of social capital for antipoverty strategies to the relatively apolitical and unthreatening idea of community self-help. This reflects a broader weakness in the understanding of social capital. Some theorists of social capital have stressed the benefits of cooperation and have little to say about how to deal with the conflicts of interest that are part of any society. Michael Foley and Bob Edwards (1996) have characterized this approach as representing a wish for consensus, an "escape from politics." But as students of social movements understand, power and conflict are central elements of any process of social change that involves collective action.

The chapters in this volume document the many ways in which more affluent Americans and dominant institutions have worked to undercut the social capital of poor communities when their real or perceived interests are threatened. The realities of power conflicts are revealed perhaps most clearly in the chapters by Cynthia Duncan and by Lisette Lopez and Carol Stack. Both chapters illustrate how political elites in the South used public offices and agencies to prevent benefits from reaching their intended recipients and to stop the efforts of poor, minority communities to organize to improve their own lives.

Duncan takes a close look at poor white communities in Appalachia and poor black communities in the Mississippi Delta, examining the effects of racism and class inequality on the social capital of rural communities. She forces us to confront the legacy of institutional oppression and the contemporary reality of localities polarized between affluence and poverty, a division that often follows racial lines in the Delta. Duncan argues that poverty is fundamentally a political issue in both places. In other words, the affluent use their power to keep people poor for the benefit of the privileged. The poor become trapped, and their incipient organizing efforts are defused by lack of internal trust and repressive efforts by the affluent elite.

Lopez and Stack begin their chapter by discussing how processes of economic decline, racial exclusion, and welfare retrenchment have worked to undermine the social capital of poor communities. The authors show how several African American women who returned home to a small southern town with skills and knowledge developed during their sojourn in the North recognized that the grinding poverty and absence of social support and integration into the larger community placed a heavy burden on the largely poor African American community. In response, they formed Helping Hands, a volunteer organization to help neighbors reach out to each other and offer assistance. Yet the local power structure moved quickly to try to block initiatives by the new group; for example, it refused to award federal funds for a day care center sponsored by Mothers and Children, Inc. The effort succeeded only when the group's leaders were able to circumvent local elites and appeal to state-level agencies for the necessary funds.

In addition to the more overt efforts of elites to block the social capital of the poor, Lopez and Stack document institutionalized racial and cultural practices that often result in the same thing. For example, many low-income families in rural areas of the South qualify for federally financed Farmers Home Administration (FmHA) loans. Many African Americans would benefit from housing designs suited to extended family living and shared financing arrangements. But the FmHA refuses to allow such arrangements, preferring a single-family, suburban look and individual household mortgages. Unable to share the liability collectively, many new homeowners default. The FmHA then resells the foreclosed houses to not-so-low-income families at bargain prices.

Recognizing the realities of conflict and power rooted in structures of inequality and institutional arrangements does not mean that differences are irreconcilable. It is useful to consider power in the context of social capital not just as the "power over" others but as the "power to" act together (Warren 1998). This kind of power can be transformative, creating new forms of cooperation and new solutions to the problems related to poverty. Power, in this view, is connected to responsibility and therefore to the fundamental idea of social capital as the resources that contribute to cooperative action. From this standpoint, we can conceive of building social assets as a way to empower, that is, to expand the capacities of poor communities to act to combat poverty and to win over new allies.

The political will to seek broader institutional transformation is likely to come, at least in part, from poor communities themselves. A social asset–building approach, in fact, may be the most promising strategy for generating the power necessary to demand such change. Social capital provides an important foundation to such strategies because it is through social relationships that individuals are constituted in their capacity to act in public life. Mediating institutions like families, schools, and congregations develop in each individual the understanding, skills, and knowledge for personal autonomy, a sense of moral justice, and efficacy. That is, people develop many of the democratic traits assumed by liberal theory only through their embeddedness in a vibrant civil society.

The congregation-based organizing groups discussed in the chapter by Michael Foley, John McCarthy, and Mark Chaves seek to use the social capital embedded in churches as a basis to build more overtly political interfaith organizations (see also Warren 2001). These groups pay attention to rebuilding the social fabric and institutional life of poor communities, while also engaging in political, albeit nonpartisan, activity. They explicitly seek to build the power necessary to command resources for affordable housing and job training programs and to stimulate change in public institutions like schools. The more successful initiatives seem able to manage conflict and consensus building both within poor communities and in their relationships to external institutions.

New forms of mediating institutions, like these congregation-based groups, play a particularly important role in connecting social organizations to political purposes. The chapter by Cathy Cohen highlights how social capital–based initiatives that originally sought to improve community life, like community policing bodies, can evolve into an organized power base for poor communities through what she calls intervening institutions. In New Haven, community management teams created to implement community policing developed into a mechanism to increase the influence of community residents in the city's enterprise community on economic development issues. Several community leaders used this emerging base as a platform to run successfully for local office.

The chapters by Cohen and by Foley, McCarthy, and Chaves suggest that social organization is a necessary, but not sufficient, basis for empowering poor communities. Instead, social capital can serve as an important foundation for more explicitly political institutions. Ester Fuchs, Robert Shapiro, and Lorraine Minnite take up this theme directly. They argue in their chapter that social capital cannot be a substitute for political organization in low-income communities. Political institutions are necessary to generate the power the poor need to command resources and favorable governmental policies. The authors examine data from a survey of New York City residents that includes information on their group memberships. The results show a social capital effect on political participation: that is, individuals who are members of purely social organizations are more likely to be politically active than those without such memberships. But the results also show that membership in a politically active organization has a far greater effect on an individual's level of political participation. The authors conclude that we must be concerned not just with building social capital but with rebuilding the kinds of institutions, like political parties, interest groups, and unions, that used to provide representation and political power for low-income communities. Congregation-based organizing groups and community management teams perhaps represent new forms of such institutions.

THREE LEVELS OF SOCIAL CAPITAL: AN INSTITUTIONAL APPROACH

As a structural feature of communities, social capital is fundamentally rooted in the cultural traditions and institutional forms of those communities, as well as in the physical spaces that they occupy. In other words, the concept of social capital loses its meaning and effectiveness the further removed it becomes from specific kinds of institutions, like churches, schools, and tenant associations. People who trust each other and cooperate within a group for a specific purpose may have a general resource available for some other cooperative endeavor. But social capital, unlike money, is not a universal resource, anonymous and fungible. It is tied to specific organizational forms and to specific purposes.[6] The transfer from one purpose to another is by no means automatic. In a classic study, Aldon Morris (1984) shows how activists worked to transfer the trust, cultural traditions, and networks of followers and leaders embedded in southern black churches to support the emerging civil rights movement. But not all churches made that transition; some refused to join the movement. And even for those churches that did participate, it took effort on the part of activists to transfer social capital from church to movement. It was not automatic.

Moreover, the purposes to which social capital is put, or for which it was formed, affect whether and how easily it is used for individual and community economic advancement. Some forms of social capital are highly exclusionary, narrow in group orientation, or in other ways contrary to community well-being and the public good (Portes 1998). Robert Putnam (2000, 350–63) has also recognized this problem, calling it the "dark side" of social capital. The Mafia contains social capital but directs it illegally and toward narrow group gain at the expense of others. Members of racially exclusive resident associations trust each other and work together, but against the common good more broadly conceived. Gangs may offer important benefits to their members, but hardly represent a net gain for communities.

Most forms of social capital within poor communities represent at least potential contributors to economic advancement and community revitalization strategies. But the potential of different forms of social capital can vary, or they might contribute in different ways. For example, the personal-familial ties of some immigrant groups contribute to family survival and advancement but have been largely disconnected from action in the public realm. Certain forms of social capital, like some churches, may make critical contributions to community development because they engage trusted leaders motivated by religious commitment to act to support their communities. Yet such forms of social capital may not be available to address certain critical needs, like birth control or the health issues of gay residents.

An institutional and process-oriented approach allows us to move from a discussion of the potential of various forms of social capital to an examination of their actual practice. We need to look at norms of cooperation and trust not as a general resource, but as they affect what people actually do—for our concerns, the processes of community building and collective action. Consequently, the authors in this volume attempt to specify the key elements to building and using social capital, that is, to processes like leadership development, will formation, and relationship building. Whether they are examining religious institutions, labor unions, or voluntary community improvement associations, these authors work to deepen our understanding of the organizational forms and key actors critical to social capital building.

The social capital of poor communities is not limited to their internal relationships. The concept of social isolation (Wilson 1987) has unfortunately been interpreted to mean that the poor are entirely cut off from the outside world. Yet residents of poor communities are also members of other collectives and communities. African Americans, for example, share a history, a tradition, and an identity that cut across local territorial units. In addition, through their activities in churches, unions, social clubs, and political organizations, residents of poor communities are sometimes connected across poor communities and to the more affluent. Furthermore, poor people have numerous connections to the public institutions, like schools, hospitals, and the police, that operate within their communities.

Thus, there are three analytically distinct levels at which social capital operates: within communities, across communities, and through ties with financial and public institutions. The following three sections explore what we can learn from this volume about how to build and use social capital at each of these levels to combat poverty. The first section considers the foundational role of what we and others have called bonding social capital. The second looks at the challenges to the formation of "bridging" social capital across communities.[7] And the third articulates the possibilities for poor communities to create synergy, that is, cooperative relationships with private and public institutions to foster community building and development.

Within Communities: Bonding Social Capital

Strong social bonds and effective organizations within communities provide the foundation on which poor people can develop the capacity to address the problems of poverty, to rebuild their communities, and to achieve a measure of control over their lives. Strong community institutions, like churches, schools and PTAs, fraternal orders, and small-business associations, are essential to integrating individuals into society. And people, especially those lacking other resources, can rely on the social support and solidarity of immediate communities to develop their capacities as public leaders. Local communities can also provide the primary arena for the kind of face-to-face interactions critical to building trust and common understandings. For many reasons, then, poor communities require strong local institutions if they are to develop the leadership of their members in external institutions in the broader society. In that sense, strengthening "bonding" social capital within communities helps provide a foundation for developing social capital at the other two levels.

Ethnographic studies of poor communities have shown that poor people have historically relied on their social capital to aid in survival when other forms of capital have been lacking (Stack 1974; Edin and Lein 1997). More than the affluent, poor people often rely on social relationships for assistance and have networks of relationships in which access to aid is relatively prevalent (Boisjoly, Duncan, and Hofferth 1995; Stack 1974). Although the social fabric of poor communities has been under assault, as discussed earlier, numerous studies confirm that survival-oriented social capital persists in poor communities, the kind of social capital that helps people "get by," as Xavier de Souza Briggs (1998a) so aptly puts it.[8]

If we want to make headway in combating poverty, if we want people to "get ahead," survival is not enough. The chapters in this volume demonstrate the need for communities to make the transition from survival to broader collective action. In his chapter on public safety, for example, Robert Sampson shows that low-income communities of similar race and socioeconomic characteristics exhibit different levels of the kinds of social organization necessary to achieve social order. According to Sampson, "local communities high in social capital are better able to realize common values and maintain the social controls that foster public safety." All other things being equal, communities with greater social capital experience less crime. But some kinds of social capital appear critical. Sampson notes that many communities exhibit intense private ties yet still lack the capacity to achieve social control because of an institutional deficit. Informal ties—such as support networks in health and informal social control in public safety—matter. But more formal institutions appear to be critical to the ability of community residents to act collectively, particularly in the broader public sphere. Consequently, Sampson is led to emphasize the importance of neighborhood organizations within poor communities as sites for the regulation of public space.

In his chapter on school reform, Pedro Noguera shows that internal organization can serve as a source of power for those made powerless in their interactions with public agencies as isolated individuals. Alone, poor, minority parents have little input into the ways in which public schools educate, or fail to educate, their children. They can be easily marginalized by administrators. Working together, they can develop the confidence and capacities to work as partners with educators. Moreover, Noguera argues, urban schools offer a critical site for building social capital because they are increasingly the most reliable source of stability and social support for children, and one of the very few stable institutions through which parents can connect with each other.

Building local institutions capable of public action for community advancement is no easy task. Several chapters in this volume analyze efforts by the poor to build and sustain local institutions in the face of a sometimes hostile society. At times the grinding nature of poverty, combined with the efforts of some elites, as described earlier, to keep the poor "in their place," can lock people into a survival mode. It may prove critical for poor residents who find themselves trapped in this way to have experiences outside of their community. Lopez and Stack show how African American women who returned home to a small southern town with skills and knowledge developed during their sojourn in the North sparked Helping Hands, a volunteer support-oriented organization, and then transformed the group into a broader public force for change. Duncan shows how poor people in Appalachia and the Mississippi Delta remained trapped when their incipient organizing efforts were undermined by lack of internal trust and the repressive actions of local elites. Duncan emphasizes the critical role that education can play in broadening the outlook of indigenous leaders. In fact, new leaders are beginning to emerge in these communities, and many of them are younger, college-educated residents who have had some experience living and working outside of their home communities.

Religious institutions represent the most pervasive kind of civil society institution in low-income communities. They have historically helped sustain family and community life, that is, they have helped people survive under very adverse conditions. Many have sometimes played a broader public role in providing services and advocating for the needs and interests of their communities. The chapter by Foley, McCarthy, and Chaves demonstrates that, in fact, poor communities are heavily populated by religious institutions, and that a high proportion of them play a broader social role beyond fostering the spiritual life of their members. The authors describe the variety of ways in which churches work to improve community life, foster civic engagement, and increase political participation. As noted earlier, para-church organizations, like the congregational-based community organizing networks of the Industrial Areas Foundation in Texas (Warren 2001), have been particularly effective in bringing congregations and their social networks into a more active public role to revitalize low-income communities. But the authors document a wide range of other activities as well. These kinds of community mobilizations, as well as those discussed by Lopez and Stack, Duncan, and Noguera, increase the participation of indigenous residents and develop leaders among them.

At the same time, there are important obstacles and limitations to the role of the church. As Foley, McCarthy, and Chaves show, churches in poor communities suffer from limited finances. Moreover, churches can exclude nonbelievers, have historically limited the leadership roles of women, and find it difficult to address community needs when they conflict with traditional church teaching.

Other authors in this volume also warn that social networks and institutions can be exclusionary and sometimes corrupt. Langley Keyes develops this theme as it applies to the provision of housing. A genuinely open and representative organization of tenants at the grassroots level was one of the factors that Keyes found to be critical for successful cooperation with mainstream institutions in improving low-income housing. But participation in some tenant groups can become too narrow, causing them to lose their accountability to the community. Keyes labels as "amoral familism" the absence of accountability that came to characterize an otherwise powerful tenants' association in Boston. Eventually, the association alienated both the residents of the housing project and the public authorities on whom their housing development relied.

The chapters in this volume indicate that the creation of bonding social capital is critical to any effort to engage poor people to improve their communities. But they offer no magic bullets to use in building this form of social capital. Taken together, however, they offer important lessons about such processes. First, stable institutions, like churches and schools, as well as more fluid support groups like Helping Hands, provide an essential foundation for bonding processes. Second, those who emerge as key leaders in these groups are likely to have had the opportunity to gain education and experience that go beyond daily survival in a poor community. And finally, any long-term effort to combat poverty must pay particular attention to cultivating broad participation from the community and fostering accountability.

Bridging Social Capital Across Communities

Poor communities cannot address the problems of poverty simply by building internal social capital, as important as such bonding capital is. At their best, strong local institutions provide a foundation for binding individuals together and directing them toward the pursuit of collective needs and aspirations. To the extent that poor communities lack broader connections, however, they remain isolated and weak. "Bridging" ties can help bring greater resources and opportunities into poor communities. And in the long run, building trust and cooperation across communities can help provide the basis for strengthening the social fabric of the whole society and creating a national consensus for combating poverty.

Strongly bonded communities can be closed-minded, hostile to others, and possibly even corrupt (Portes 1998). White ethnic Americans, for example, have sometimes relied on the strong social capital of their urban communities centered in the Catholic parish to block attempts by African Americans to integrate their neighborhoods (McGreevy 1996). By sharing limited resources and pooling labor, some immigrant groups have used their strong internal social capital as a basis for economic development. But when some of the more successful businesspeople want to expand beyond the immigrant community to do business with and hire non-immigrants, the normative demands of the community often hold them back (Zhou 1992). To be effective, then, community revitalization efforts must balance the "bonding" social organizations they build with "bridging" ties to other communities.

Although the issue of bridging social capital has been discussed primarily in relation to the connection between poor and affluent communities, there are four types of bridging ties, each important in its own right. First of all, within a poor community itself, we need to consider bridging across different forms of social capital. Even a small geographically defined community has many different institutions and networks within it. We cannot assume that one form—for example, a church community—can speak for the whole. Moreover, different community institutions often do not cooperate with each other and can sometimes be in open conflict. To expand the basis of support for community initiatives and broaden the distribution of their benefits, we need to consider ways to build new and cooperative connections across local institutions—for example, across churches, between churches and PTAs, or between churches, tenant associations, and local community development corporations.

The second type of bridging connection occurs between different low-income communities or neighborhoods. Poor communities do not always, or evenly normally, cooperate with each other in the development and pursuit of initiatives that would be of mutual benefit. In fact, neighborhoods are often divided against each other, for complex historical reasons related to different interests and identities. These divisions are particularly acute when they fall along racial or ethnic lines, and they often lead to competition between neighborhoods and racially defined communities for limited public resources or economic opportunities.[9]

The third type of bridging is the one most commonly discussed, although seldom practiced: forging connections between the poor and more affluent communities. Scholars have explored the importance of bridging ties for the socioeconomic advancement of individuals and families (see, for example, Briggs 1998a). At the community level, bridging social capital can help build allies for strategies to combat poverty. Moreover, cooperative relationships across communities cultivate a sense of common identity that can sustain a national commitment to alleviate poverty.

Connecting people and communities nationally is the fourth type of bridging social capital. Building social capital at the local level is a necessary part of any strategy for combating poverty, since local roots provide intimate knowledge, trust, and a respect for the diverse needs of communities. Cooperation finds an important foundation in the face-to-face interactions, and in the socializing institutions, that operate best at the local level. But effective strategies at the national level will also be necessary to generate power and change. Community is not limited to the local level, nor should it be. Yet most community-building efforts with strong local roots lack much national coherence (Stoecker 1997; Dreier 1996). Strategies to combat poverty, then, need to build social capital locally yet connect it regionally and nationally.

A number of the chapters in this volume demonstrate that there is a significant institutional basis for creating the several types of bridging social capital just discussed, particularly in such fields as religion, education, labor, and economic activity. Although there are many obstacles to the building of bridging social capital, successfully doing so, the volume's authors suggest, can bring important gains.

While religious institutions help strengthen the bonding social capital of poor communities, they also offer an important institutional bridge to outside networks and organizations that can help overcome the limitations of isolated congregations. As Foley, McCarthy, and Chaves show, congregations located in even the poorest neighborhoods provide opportunities for the development of social capital between neighborhood residents and the majority of congregants who are not themselves poor. The national denominational structures of most religious institutions can offer outside resources and political advocacy for the poor. Foley, McCarthy, and Chaves review a number of promising faith-based initiatives—including para-church organizations and interfaith coalitions like Habitat for Humanity—that combine congregations within and across denominational lines. These coalitions play important roles in providing services and working as collective advocates for poor communities. Additionally, congregation-based community organizing networks knit congregations within and across low-income communities, and often link them to more affluent congregations within a metropolitan area. They consciously work to build leadership to advocate for greater public services, more financial resources, and new policy initiatives.

Pedro Noguera's chapter on public schools shows their potential to connect parents across neighborhoods, especially if a locality's school administration will support such an effort. A yearly parent empowerment conference organized in the San Francisco Unified School District brings together eight hundred parents from neighborhoods across the city. Parental organizing efforts developed by the Industrial Areas Foundation show the benefits of coordinating school-based projects across city and state levels: they can bring extra resources, new ideas, and outside political support to each school effort and together help to rebuild a political constituency for the support of public schools (Shirley 1997).

Despite the opportunities afforded by churches and schools, obstacles persist. The poorest or most marginalized people may not be part of the extended networks and activities sponsored by these institutions. And although they are growing, so far these efforts and the power they have generated have remained fairly small in relation to the scale of economic disinvestment and public neglect that plague poor communities.

In her chapter, Margaret Levi examines the potential for labor unions to work collaboratively with community-based organizations in poor communities. According to Levi, in earlier years labor unions represented members of poor communities. But as they were successful in raising their members' incomes, they lost accountability to those left behind, that is, low-wage workers in poor communities. Organized labor has a lot to offer these communities. Their pension funds could be used to finance affordable housing, as has been piloted in some cities. Their political clout could support public policies to help the poor, like increases in the minimum wage. Labor also has something to gain from such cooperation: it might help the newer efforts by labor to build its membership among an increasingly female and nonwhite labor force.

Levi argues that collaborative efforts will have to address the divisions that have arisen between unions and the poor. White male union leaders, particularly in the building trades unions, have developed a reputation for insensitivity, or even hostility, to the needs of people of color and women. Open hostility has broken out over hiring practices on construction projects, for example. Levi identifies the inclusion of women and members of racial minorities as one of the biggest challenges facing labor unions. When labor-organizing campaigns are successful, they increasingly require the development of multiracial and multiclass alliances, as has occurred, for example, in several "living wage" campaigns and in the Justice for Janitors campaigns.

More generally, in order to build trust across lines of division, labor must make credible commitments to institutional allies in poor communities. These commitments, which must ensure that the benefits of cooperation accrue to both sides, will require unions to use their resources in money, people, and reputation to support specific projects and campaigns. Usually these projects, like the living wage and affordable housing efforts, fall outside of labor's traditional focus on member services. Levi notes that the survival of the labor movement may well rest on balancing the trade-off between traditional service to members and winning jobs and living wages for those previously excluded from union membership. Union leaders who partner with community institutions do seem to advance a broader understanding of labor's identity and interests.

Cathy Cohen's chapter is particularly instructive in showing how real or perceived conflicts of interest can block cooperation between organizations that ostensibly represent low-income communities, people of color, and workers. In New Haven, the enterprise community management teams that originally emerged out of community policing efforts came to clash with civil rights and union organizations over hiring policies at a newly built hotel. The community groups wanted jobs for residents of their neighborhoods, while labor was most concerned with its right to organize newly hired workers, and the NAACP focused on opportunities for people of color to get high-end jobs. Each group construed its interests narrowly and failed to establish a process in which trust and cooperation could be built.

The chapter by Ross Gittell and J. Phillip Thompson shows the potential power of bridging ties for economic development. They argue that, while individual families in poor communities typically have low incomes, the purchasing power of the whole community can often be quite significant. Social capital can therefore provide an avenue for demanding market response when individuals lack the financial clout to do so alone. Moreover, Gittell and Thompson point out, market failure in poor communities is often not the result of a lack of profit potential. Instead, entrepreneurs from outside fail to see market potential because of lack of knowledge or racial stereotypes. To the extent that the poor can organize themselves and build relationships with entrepreneurs, they can help address these failures and create new investment in their communities.

In addition, Gittell and Thompson highlight the ability of social capital to serve as a basis for the political power necessary to affect market operations through public policy. In the late 1970s, community development corporations and other local community groups across the country joined forces to help get the Community Reinvestment Act (CRA) passed by Congress. The CRA required financial institutions to reinvest in poor communities. A wide variety of local community groups across the country made use of its provisions to pressure their local banks. Yet it has proved difficult to sustain national-level connections between local groups, and the CRA remains one of the very few fruits of bridging social capital at the national level.

Creating Synergy with Financial and Public Institutions

The social assets of poor communities may be ineffective because they are isolated from, or undermined by, mainstream economic and political institutions. Scholars studying the role of social capital in developing countries have used the term "synergy" to characterize the opposite situation in which local organizations, economic actors, and state institutions work together for positive developmental outcomes (Evans 1997; Woolcock 1998). These scholars show that development is most successful when governments cooperate with, rather than repress or ignore, initiatives and participation by local community networks. Such cooperation can flow from social connections. According to Peter Evans (1997), embeddedness occurs when public officials share social ties and trust with community residents across the public-private divide. As Evans (1997, 1122) argues, "Social capital inheres, not just in civil society, but in an enduring set of relationships that span the public-private divide. . . . [I]t is social capital built in the interstices between state and society that keeps [economic] growth on track." When public officials work to establish cooperative ties and efforts, they are able to "coproduce" the desired outcome, whether it is economic development, improved public health, or the education of children (Evans 1997; Tendler 1997).

In the American context, we can think of coproduction as occurring when synergy is created between community-based activities, economic organizations, and public institutions. Synergy demands the creation of constructive connections, a form of social capital, between organized residents of poor communities and the officials and staff of public and private institutions.

This perspective differs from that of those who see social capital, or the civil society sphere, existing independently of, even a priori to, economic and political institutions. The voluntary sector appears in that view as the "core" of society, and voluntary action is to be preferred to government provision. Yet there is considerable evidence that the civil sector is closely tied to government, as well as to economic action. To counter the claims of some conservatives that there is a zero-sum relationship between government and voluntary civic action, Theda Skocpol (1996) has shown the reciprocal relationship between many important federal government programs and civic associations, like the American Legion. Government policy, in fact, can help build social capital by encouraging the formation of associations like PTAs.

But public institutions do not always work to build social capital when it comes to poor communities. Efforts to establish coproduction often run up against widespread indifference or even opposition to cooperation with the poor by dominant institutions. Historically, the power of the state has been used for surveillance and supervision of the poor. To receive basic benefits, welfare recipients have to reveal the most intimate details of their personal lives. The police treat many residents of poor communities, particularly (but not only) young men of color, as suspects rather than citizens deserving of respect. Public institutions often contribute to the grinding quality of life in many poor communities that makes the task of personal survival difficult enough, let alone the building of social capital and the construction of a rich public life.

Public institutions have sometimes gone further, working to crush autonomy and the collective action of individuals and groups in poor communities when they perceive them as too threatening. During the last period of widespread community action in America's inner cities, the 1960s, many initiatives met with opposition and repression. As Noguera discusses in his chapter, the effort to establish community control of schools in New York City faced strong opposition from the largely white teachers' union and ultimately failed (see also Berube and Gittell 1969; Ture and Hamilton 1992 [1967]). Meanwhile, local police and the FBI worked to disrupt and repress more militant organizations in the black community. The distrust and fear spawned by the activities of the police, the FBI, and militant groups obscured the progress some of these groups made in building social capital and providing services for poor families.

Even when dominant institutions do not directly oppose the residents of poor communities, they may fail to serve them well because their staff are so disconnected from residents of the local community.[10] There are a number of ways in which detached public institutions undermine the social capital of poor communities or render it ineffective. First, they can make rules or institute practices, particularly nonresponsiveness, that create community instability or disrupt social ties. Nonresponsiveness works to undermine collective efficacy because it renders collective activity useless. One of the elemental lessons of efforts to organize in any community is that victories are needed to sustain and build collective action. If institutions refuse to respond, or delay ad infinitum, activists become discouraged and support withers. Social capital may continue to be latent in the community, but it will be even more difficult to use that capital to attempt to improve conditions in the future. Public institutions can also adopt practices that prevent communication or make it one-sided. They can provide information that demeans, demoralizes, or makes invisible the recipient poor community. Or they can fail to provide information that would be substantively useful to understanding community conditions. Geographic, bureaucratic, and technological buffers can prevent direct contact with poor communities. Even when government or nonprofit agencies attempt to bring poor neighborhood residents into planning and decisionmaking processes, different norms for communication and the formal structure of meetings can silence residents or lead professionals in charge to disregard their input (Briggs 1998b).

The chapters in this volume discuss a number of promising initiatives that have worked to overcome these obstacles to synergy. Pedro Noguera begins his chapter with a frank discussion of the resistance that public institutions can offer to working collaboratively with poor people. To the extent that school personnel lack any meaningful knowledge of and connection to the communities in which their students live, they will not understand local culture or serve their students well. To the extent that school personnel assume an air of superiority over parents, along racial and class lines, those parents will not be heard and they will be excluded from meaningful participation in the school community. Noguera argues that parent organizing can work to overcome these obstacles and play a decisive role in reforming failed schools. Organization serves as a source of power for those made power-less in their interactions with public agencies as isolated individuals. It turns out that many school administrators, facing the widespread failure of inner-city schools, welcome parental involvement. Synergy, then, seems to work best when there is support and action from the "bottom up" and from the "top down." Drawing on case studies, Noguera shows how organizing for parental and community control of schools, in conjunction with a broader effort to expand the resources available both to failing schools and to poor communities, can result in real improvement in the education of poor children.

Other chapters in the volume document the possibilities for synergy across a range of policy areas. Robert Sampson discusses a number of initiatives, like community policing, through which local residents, indigenous associations, and police can create synergistic partnerships to reduce crime and social disorder. Sampson shows that these initiatives can improve the accountability of the police, a public agency that has historically been one of the most repressive to poor communities.

Sherman James, Amy Schulz, and Juliana van Olphen identify new collaborative arrangements in the area of public health. Using a case study of the successful Village Health Worker Partnership in East Detroit, this chapter illustrates the kind of policy initiative that can build community capacity and synergistic relationships with public health agencies. The authors first articulate the multiple pathways through which social capital operates to affect the health status of communities. They show how such strong bonding forms of social capital as support networks are associated with better health outcomes. But they also show that factors associated with bridging forms, like mutual respect and low inequality across American states, are also powerfully associated with better health outcomes for *all* residents. The authors argue that differentials in social power between communities are related to the distribution of health problems within communities. Efforts to build social capital, they point out, must succeed in commanding real access to political power since the health problems of poor communities derive from institutional arrangements that lie beyond their immediate geographical boundaries. The chapter then illustrates how the Village Health Worker Partnership in East Detroit builds community capacity, brings needed resources into the inner city, and forges partnerships between residents and public health agencies that begin to change the institutional arrangements that undermine the health status of the poor. Its success is due in part to the organizers' conscious effort to deal with power differentials between community residents and health professionals.

In economic development, Gittell and Thompson discuss a number of initiatives that seek to create collaborations between private and public institutions and poor communities. Here again, initiatives can originate from either the bottom up or the top down, or from some complicated relationship between the two. New York City's Neighborhood Entrepreneur Program (NEP), for example, was initiated when neighborhood residents demanded a role in the privatization of city-owned housing. Through a collaboration between a range of city agencies, nonprofit organizations, and community groups, NEP was established to give resident, mostly nonwhite, entrepreneurs a chance to own and manage this housing. Tenant organizations in the buildings originally clashed with the entrepreneurs over some policies, but Gittell and Thompson point out that most entrepreneurs eventually came to see tenant groups as assets for their business, and they even funded resident organizing in some cases.

Drawing from a framework developed by Michael Woolcock (1998), Langley Keyes's chapter on public housing compares a range of cases that represent different arrangements of social capital both within communities and in their relationships to public authorities. He shows that lack of trust in public agencies or direct conflict with them makes housing initiatives fail, even when communities are well organized internally. The optimum arrangement is strong internal social relationships combined with cooperative ties to public agencies. As a good example of synergy, Keyes offers the community development system in Cleveland, where city agencies, community development corporations, and financial institutions work together to build affordable housing. But Keyes also shows that both community groups and public agencies need to be accountable to their constituencies and maintain standards of professionalism if positive outcomes are to be sustained.

Keyes alerts us to the danger presented by embeddedness, that is, to close ties between public officials and local communities. These ties can become corrupt, serve the interests of a narrow group, or lead to nepotism. Keyes offers the example of an apparently well-run housing project in Boston with a strong tenant leader. It turns out that she shielded her nephew who ran a drug-dealing operation out of the project.[11]

Synergy, then, needs to be balanced with a degree of autonomy and integrity on the part of public institutions (Woolcock 1998). In addition to being accountable to the local community, public institutions must be accountable to higher public authorities as well as to the standards of their professional communities. Evans (1995) refers to this balance as "embedded autonomy"; he argues that successful industrial development occurs when state authorities develop independent and efficient bureaucracies while working cooperatively with private economic actors. Ideally, there are coherent and relatively autonomous organizations in each sector (social, political, and economic) with connections between them that foster cooperation and mutual accountability.

Cooperative initiatives among these sectors can, as noted earlier, come both from the bottom up and from the top down. From the bottom up, communities need to develop effective strategies to encourage or compel public or private institutions to cooperate with their initiatives. From the top down, public institutions themselves can initiate reforms to encourage and collaborate with community-based efforts. Cathy Cohen shows how community management teams created by government action "at the top" have opened up opportunities for organizing "at the bottom"; the result has been greater political power and representation for poor communities. As we see in her chapter, synergistic partnerships between public, private, and community organizations require new forms for the institutionalization of political power. To be successful, however, cooperative relationships must incorporate both strong community organizations and professional public agencies with real accountability to local communities.

BUILDING SOCIAL CAPITAL AT THREE LEVELS: TOWARD SOCIAL TRANSFORMATION

Those designing strategies that seek to build and use social capital to combat poverty need to consider all three levels of social capital. Acting at one level alone will be insufficient. This process can be seen as a cycling through, from the micro level to the macro, then back to the micro. Action at one level can stimulate and sustain progress at another level.

Nevertheless, bonding social capital in poor communities appears to be foundational for effective action at other levels. Activities at higher levels assume and rely on a certain degree of coherence and support at the within-community, foundational level. Incoherence at the first level almost always leads to misrepresentation and resentment at other levels. As Margaret Levi discusses in her chapter, some trade unions would like to work with poor communities but often cannot find an organization that represents community residents. When banks, under pressure to comply with Community Reinvestment Act provisions, decide to lend to low-income neighborhoods, they search for knowledgeable and legitimate community organizations with which to partner.

Public institutions and more affluent communities are not always so ready to collaborate with the organizations of the poor. Another reason that bonding social capital is foundational, then, lies in the structural sources of poverty. To the extent that poor communities use their social capital to address their problems, they may be led to confront economic and political structures in which others have a vested interest. Bonding social capital provides a foundation for the political power needed in these conflicts.

Efforts to build and use social capital in poor communities, especially efforts that seek to stimulate political action, can contribute to a broader transformation of American civic and political life as well. Community revitalization initiatives have been one of the primary ways in which the social fabric of American communities has been repaired and democratic participation has been rejuvenated. Historically, the social movements of the poor and excluded have been some of the most important forces for democratic change in America. The contemporary period is ripe for equally broad transformation, one that begins to address the root causes of poverty.

Taken together, the chapters in this book bring into focus the cultural aspects of the structural divisions that must be confronted to create social change broad enough to reduce the burden of poverty on individuals and communities and revitalize democratic participation. The first division is blindness to the uneven division of labor along gender lines in the development of social capital in poor communities and elsewhere. The reality is that women play the central role in social capital processes, yet their leadership often lacks visibility and legitimacy. The second division is prominently discussed in many of the chapters in this volume: the persistence of a racial hierarchy, which resists social capital strategies because it draws such firm lines around groups and yokes them to historically cumulative differences in wealth and power. A concern with the third division, the prevalence of a punitive cultural image of the poor, which is often confounded with racial and gender stereotypes, also pervades the volume's chapters.

These divisions provide a rationale for economic inequality and reinforce patterns of social relationships that ensure that the social capital of those who are more privileged will have higher value. Nevertheless, even though they represent strategic resources for those who benefit from the status quo, they also point to arenas of potential transformation. The next three sections discuss each of the arenas.

Recognizing the Leadership of Women

The chapters in this volume demonstrate the leading role that women play in building and using social capital in low-income communities. Lopez and Stack discuss the African American women who run Holding Hands in the rural South. Cathy Cohen documents the leading role of women in the community management teams of New Haven. These women are all challenging the historical dominance of men as political leaders and community spokespersons. But in another sense they are continuing what has long been women's work: bringing together neighbors and relatives to support each other and to provide for the needs of daily life that are not met through the economic or political system. Lopez and Stack recount women's efforts to organize to assist families in making ends meet, to provide child care, and to support teenagers in their development into productive adults and citizens, and the resulting struggles with the dominant powers.[12] Cohen remarks on both the strong neighborhood roots of the women who go on to attain political office and their confinement to the "women's slots" on the ballot.

Some of the chapters in this volume do not identify the gender of the actors they discuss who are building social capital. To the extent that these omissions keep women's leadership invisible, it is harder to understand the organic connections between the different kinds of social capital needed to combat poverty. It turns out that approaches to generating and using social capital in poor communities are often gendered. Marilyn Gittell, Isolda Ortega-Bustamante, and Tracy Steffy (2000) have documented the distinctive characteristics of community-based organizations led by women that seem essential to using social capital to leverage investments in poor communities. According to these authors, such characteristics include "the comprehensive approach to community development, the concern with the process of community development, the focus on community participation, the human-centered and needs-centered programs, [and] the open style of leadership" (130). In contrast, community development organizations that lack significant numbers of women in leadership positions tend to focus solely on jobs, economic development, and housing construction. The processes related to these priorities are more often concerned with developing contacts and power positions vis-à-vis mainstream institutions rather than nurturing broad-based ties within the community and investing in human development at all levels. The gender gaps in priorities were especially pronounced when there were also few men of color involved in the male-led organizations.

If poor communities are going to develop effective power in the public realm, the roles of women as community leaders must be fully developed and appreciated. Yet the chapters in this volume demonstrate that this remains problematic. When community organization remains small or informal, women have freer rein. But in more formal settings where greater power and resources are at stake, men still seem to predominate. The pastors of the congregations that structure so much of life in poor communities are almost entirely men. And men still control many of the party organizations that nominate candidates for political office from poor communities.

There is cause for optimism that the emergence of leadership by women in more public-oriented social capital initiatives could translate into formal power. But such a change will require that we appreciate the strengths of women's leadership. In other words, our public life can be transformed in a positive direction by learning from women in the community-building movement. The strategies and approaches women have developed are diverse. In general, however, they emphasize relationship building, holistic approaches that integrate public and private spheres, and efforts to strengthen families and communities (Naples 1998; Stoecker and Stall 1998). Such approaches can help us find a greater sense of common purpose with which to temper the clash of interests that dominates in the political realm.

Confronting the Racial Order

A second arena of transformation concerns racism and racial inequality. Discussions about poverty and social capital take place in an America structured by what Michael Dawson (1994) has called a racial order. Developing effective strategies to combat poverty requires confronting the structures of racial inequality because they constitute a fundamental aspect of the generation of concentrated poverty in communities of color (Massey and Denton 1993; Sampson 1999). This point is amply demonstrated in the chapters by Duncan, Lopez and Stack, and Sampson. Moreover, narrowly racialized perceptions of the interests and identities of communities complicate efforts to develop the kind of bridging social capital and sense of common purpose necessary to combat poverty. The chapters by Noguera and Levi, among others, make this point clearly.

The concept of a racial order highlights the fact that many racial injustices are institutionalized, that is, the normal operations of dominant institutions create and reinforce racial inequality. Among other things, this means that no one needs to be intentionally racist to cause or sustain racial inequality, although some may be. The institutionalized nature of racism places a tremendous additional burden on social capital–based initiatives. At the same time, social capital formation can lead to group consciousness, solidarity, and political agendas that can begin to confront institutionalized racism.

How capable social capital–based initiatives are in addressing institutionalized structures of racism remains to be seen. Certainly, most of the initiatives discussed in this volume work to reduce inequality and improve the lives of people of color in housing, education, health, public safety, and economic development. At the same time, these initiatives remain localized and, in that sense, incapable of generating the political power that will be necessary to address broader structures of inequality.

Research on social capital could benefit from an effort to learn from the community-building traditions in communities of color. Although public attention is usually drawn to the problems of poor black communities, African Americans, despite facing adverse conditions, maintain some of the strongest forms of social capital in the country. For example, African Americans have the highest rates of church membership and participation. Rather than being inwardly focused, black churches are some of the most involved local institutions in providing services and support to the broader community and in initiating economic development and political participation (Lincoln and Mamiya 1990). African Americans also demonstrate a broad commitment to the whole community, demonstrated by their consistent support for the public provision of a broad range of social services (Bobo and Gilliam 1990).

Other ethnic minorities also offer lessons in the development and use of social capital to combat poverty. To name but two examples, theories of social capital as an aid to economic development have drawn from the experiences of Chinese, Cuban, and Korean communities (Portes 1995). And the remarkably healthy babies of Mexican immigrants in the United States have led to interest in the social supports for childbearing and healthy behavioral practices in which these women are embedded (Williams and Collins 1995).

Challenging the Cultural Consensus on Poverty

A fully developed social capital–building strategy requires challenging the nation's cultural consensus on poverty. Blaming the poor for their poverty has become the foundation for welfare retrenchment in the 1990s. Moreover, poor and marginalized people have been literally vilified by the media and public officials. For example, public housing tenants have been systematically represented in the media and in more scholarly publications as humanly as well as financially destitute, destined for lives of unemployment, dysfunction, and crime (Kotlowitz 1991; Rainwater 1970; Reingold 1997). People who have been arrested for committing crimes (including nonviolent "victimless" crimes) have been portrayed as morally and socially deficient and incapable of rehabilitation. In a number of states this moral censure has gone so far as to legitimize the permanent denial of the right to vote to convicted felons. Thirteen percent of all African American men are disenfranchised in this way; in Florida almost one-third of black men have permanently lost the right to vote (Sentencing Project 1998).

Many of the chapters in this volume show how social capital processes are infused with cultural meanings. Cultural understandings and biases affect social capital–building processes because they play such an important role in group identity. Lopez and Stack develop this theme perhaps to its fullest, but Noguera and Gittell and Thompson speak to the issue in a central way too. Lopez and Stack end their chapter with a call for transforming our notions of cultural citizenship to make them more inclusive of the poor and marginalized.

Such a transformation is important because civil society, far from exemplifying the communitarian ideal of harmony, is often the site where social groups vie for hegemony culturally as well as politically. A social capital–building strategy involves developing the capacity of poor people to engage in public discourse and contest popular cultural stereotypes. For example, if women of color are to emerge as leaders not just of poor communities but of the broader society, mainstream representations of them as dysfunctional (Kelley 1997) must be challenged. The terms of participation in civil society must be altered to better address informal inequality, and that requires contesting popular attitudes toward the poor and people of color.

In the short run, as this volume shows, social capital–based strategies can offer immediate improvements to the quality of lives of people living in some of our poorest communities. In the long run, however, for social capital to be sustained and enhanced in poor communities it needs to become "hardened" into explicit sets of policy mechanisms and legal codes whose value can be measured, evaluated, contested, and thereby justified to a skeptical public. Herein lies a great challenge to research, policy, and practice. Social transformation capable of addressing the root causes of poverty requires a paradigm shift in public policy discourse from a view of poor people as the passive object of social policy to a view of them as equal participants and leaders in policy-making and implementation. A social capital building strategy therefore requires that public discourse about poverty be infused with new mechanisms that enable poor people to participate more fully in shaping their own destinies and the future of American society.

We would like to thank Philip Kasinitz and two anonymous reviewers for helpful comments on this chapter.

NOTES

1. According to James Coleman (1990, 302), "unlike other forms of capital, social capital inheres in the structure of relations between persons and among persons. It is neither lodged in individuals nor in physical implements of production." Robert Putnam (1995, 67) defines social capital as "the features of social organization, such as networks, norms, and social trust, that facilitate coordination and cooperation for mutual benefit."

2. In one of the earliest studies to use the concept of social capital, Coleman and Hoffer (1987) argued that Catholic schools do a better job than public schools of educating inner-city children because of the tight connections and shared norms that exist among and between parents, teachers, and students in the Catholic school community. Any child in such a school-community benefits from the collective's social capital, even if his or her own parent is not particularly involved. Moreover, a child who leaves that school cannot take the school's social capital to a new one. Ties back to the old school may continue to play some role in the child's life. But, fundamentally, the benefit of the original school's social capital to the child comes from its nature as a public good in that school, not as an

individual asset of the child. Social capital is inherently the property of a group or a network, even in cases where it is measured at the individual level and used to predict individual-level outcomes (for example, Boisjoly, Duncan, and Hofferth 1995). The measurement of social capital at the individual level has led to some conceptual confusion. If an individual's perceptions of trust and cooperation, or expectations that the other will respond helpfully to a request for assistance, are not anchored in actual relationships, they do not constitute social capital. Decisions to measure social capital at the individual level usually result from the limitations of existing databases rather than from an alternative conception of social capital. Data are usually available about individuals and not about the relevant collectivities. The proper unit of measurement in studies of social capital should be the collective involved in bringing about the outcome. Multi-level statistical models can discriminate between the level of social capital within the group and the differences among individuals that derive from their different levels of involvement, power, and centrality. Indeed, what we need are multi-level studies that measure social capital at the level of the collective, while taking into account individual characteristics (Saegert and Winkel 1996; Sampson, Raudenbush, and Earls 1997).

3. For example, among similar neighborhoods, those with high levels of collective efficacy, that is, social cohesion among neighbors combined with a willingness to intervene for the common good, demonstrate lower homicide rates than ones with lower levels of such social capital (Sampson, Raudenbush, and Earls 1997). And as Robert Sampson has argued elsewhere (1999), crime can destabilize neighborhoods; the resulting turnover and fear of neighbors also inhibit the development of social capital. On the benefits of social capital for the revitalization of inner city housing, see Saegert and Winkel (1998).

4. The Committee for Economic Development (1995, 10), for example, argues that distressed inner-city communities suffer from a social capital deficit: "Inner-city distress is about more than poverty or individual problems; it is about the collapse of a community's ability to cope with problems." To be fair, however, the authors of this report argue that external causes have created that deficit and that social capital must work hand in hand with government and other financial institutions.

5. No systematic study of community revitalization efforts has been made. For a history of neighborhood-based initiatives to combat poverty, see Halpern (1995). For an overview of community development corporations, see Vidal (1992). Peter Dreier (1996) discusses community organizing and empowerment initiatives. Examples of the work of religious institutions in community-based development can be found in Scheie et al. (1991) and Thomas and Blake (1996). Lizbeth Schorr (1997) discusses a range of comprehensive neighborhood-based initiatives involving partnerships between government, service providers, foundations, and community institutions.

6. Some studies, such as Robert Putnam's (1993) examination of Italy, have treated social capital as a universal cultural resource that transcends the concrete social institutions and relationships in which it is embedded. Putnam's study broke new ground by demonstrating the role that social capital can play in economic and political development. But these kinds of macro-level studies of social capital as a general cultural resource lack the specificity of studies that show how social capital actually operates. Moreover, they may mask important differences in the roles of various forms of social organization (Foley and Edwards 1999; on aggregate measures, see also Paxton 1999). Putnam's (2000) most comprehensive treatment of the decline of social capital in the United States does pay close attention to specific forms of social organization.

7. The terms "bonding" and "bridging" social capital have been used by Robert Putnam (2000) and others. See, for example, Gittell and Vidal (1998) and Warren (2001).

8. Briggs (1998a) distinguishes between "getting by" and "getting ahead" a little differently than we do here. He is referring to the kinds of personal connections an individual needs to survive versus those needed to improve his or her socioeconomic status.

9. Roger Waldinger (1997) discusses competition between African Americans and Latinos for jobs in Los Angeles. Barbara Ferman (1996) shows how the cooperation between African Americans and Latinos that proved crucial to the election of Harold Washington as mayor of Chicago in 1983 later collapsed when Latinos charged that they were not getting their fair share of municipal jobs.

10. By contrast, public institutions in the United States are more likely to be embedded in affluent communities. Teachers and police officers, for example, live in the more affluent areas they serve. Or even if they do not, they are more likely to be part of similar communities that share the commonalities of race, education, and class. These shared identities, interests, and perspectives allow public officials and community residents to work in tandem with each other. Public institutions do not simply deliver efficient public services according to professional standards. In fact, if we look below the surface, we can see the myriad ways in which effective public institutions are embedded in the communities they serve.

11. The dangers of embeddedness are not limited to housing. Public schools, for example, can hire less qualified but well connected teachers, give out contracts for building work to the members of the ethnic civic association that helped elect fellow ethnics as school board members, and direct public funds disproportionately to the schools in the neighborhoods where administrators have close ties. See, for example, Jean Anyon's (1997) discussion of the corruption of the Newark school system.

12. The role of women's leadership in helping groups move from informal social support to organizational development, and to political and economic legitimation of claims on public resources, has also been documented by Leavitt and Saegert (1990) in their description of how poor African American and Latino households in Harlem organized to save their housing during the crises of landlord abandonment.

REFERENCES

Anderson, Elijah. 1992. *Streetwise: Race, Class, and Change in an Urban Community*. Chicago: University of Chicago Press.

Anyon, Jean. 1997. *Ghetto Schooling: A Political Economy of Urban Educational Reform*. New York: Teachers College Press.

Berube, Maurice R., and Marilyn Gittell. 1969. *Confrontation at Ocean Hill-Brownsville: The New York School Strikes of 1968*. New York: Praeger.

Bobo, Lawrence, and Franklin D. Gilliam Jr. 1990. "Race, Sociopolitical Participation, and Black Empowerment." *American Political Science Review* 84: 377–93.

Boisjoly, Johanne, Greg J. Duncan, and Sandra Hofferth. 1995. "Access to Social Capital." *Journal of Family Issues* 16(5): 609–31.

Briggs, Xavier de Souza. 1998a. "Brown Kids in White Suburbs: Housing Mobility and the Many Faces of Social Capital." *Housing Policy Debate* 9(1): 177–221.

————. 1998b. "Doing Democracy Up-close: Culture, Power, and Communication in Community Building." *Journal of Planning Education and Research* 18: 1–13.

Coleman, James S. 1990. *Foundations of Social Theory.* Cambridge, Mass.: Harvard University Press.

Coleman, James S., and Thomas Hoffer. 1987. *Public and Private High Schools: The Impact of Communities.* New York: Basic Books.

Committee for Economic Development. 1995. *Rebuilding Inner-City Communities: A New Approach to the Nation's Urban Crisis.* New York: Committee for Economic Development.

Dawson, Michael. 1994. "A Black Counterpublic?: Economic Earthquakes, Racial Agenda(s), and Black Politics." *Public Culture* 7: 195–223.

Drake, St. Clair, and Horace R. Cayton. 1945. *Black Metropolis: A Study of Negro Life in a Northern City.* New York: Harcourt, Brace and Co.

Dreier, Peter. 1996. "Community Empowerment Strategies: The Limits and Potential of Community Organizing in Urban Neighborhoods." *Cityscape* 2(2): 121–59.

Edin, Kathryn, and Laura Lein. 1997. *Making Ends Meet: How Single Mothers Survive Welfare and Low-Wage Work.* New York: Russell Sage Foundation.

Ehrenhalt, Alan. 1995. *The Lost City: Discovering the Forgotten Virtues of Community in the Chicago of the 1950s.* New York: Basic Books.

Evans, Peter. 1995. *Embedded Autonomy: States and Industrial Transformation.* Princeton, N.J.: Princeton University Press.

————. 1997. *State-Society Synergy: Government and Social Capital in Development.* Research Series 94. Berkeley: University of California Regents.

Ferman, Barbara. 1996. *Challenging the Growth Machine: Neighborhood Politics in Chicago and Pittsburgh.* Lawrence: University of Kansas Press.

Foley, Michael W., and Bob Edwards. 1996. "The Paradox of Civil Society." *Journal of Democracy* 7(3): 38–52.

————. 1999. "Is It Time to Disinvest in Social Capital?" *Journal of Public Policy* 19(2): 141–73.

Gittell, Marilyn, Isolda Ortega-Bustamante, and Tracy Steffy. 2000. "Social Capital and Social Change: Women's Community Activism." *Urban Affairs Review* 36(2): 123–47.

Gittell, Ross, and Avis C. Vidal. 1998. *Community Organizing: Building Social Capital as a Development Strategy.* Thousand Oaks, Calif.: Sage Publications.

Goering, John, Ali Kamely, and Todd Richardson. 1997. "Recent Research on Racial Segregation and Poverty Concentration in Public Housing in the United States." *Urban Affairs Review* 32(5): 723–45.

Halpern, Robert. 1995. *Rebuilding the Inner City: A History of Neighborhood Initiatives to Address Poverty in the United States.* New York: Columbia University Press.

Judd, Dennis R., and Todd Swanstrom. 1994. *City Politics: Private Power and Public Policy.* New York: HarperCollins.

Kelley, Robin D. G. 1997. *Yo' Mama's Disfunktional!: Fighting the Culture Wars in Urban America.* Boston: Beacon Press.

Kotlowitz, Alex. 1991. *There Are No Children Here.* New York: Anchor Books.

Kozol, Jonathan. 1991. *Savage Inequalities: Children in America's Schools.* New York: HarperCollins.

Leavitt, Jacqueline, and Susan Saegert. 1990. *From Abandonment to Hope: Community Households in Harlem.* New York: Columbia University Press.

Lincoln, C. Eric, and Lawrence H. Mamiya. 1990. *The Black Church in the African American Experience.* Durham, N.C.: Duke University Press.

Massey, Douglas S., and Nancy A. Denton. 1993 *American Apartheid: Segregation and the Making of the Underclass.* Cambridge, Mass.: Harvard University Press.

McGreevy, John T. 1996. *Parish Boundaries: The Catholic Encounter with Race in the Twentieth Century*. Chicago: University of Chicago Press.

Morris, Aldon. 1984. *The Origins of the Civil Rights Movement: Black Communities Organizing for Change*. New York: Free Press.

Naples, Nancy A. 1998. *Community Activism and Feminist Politics: Organizing Across Race, Class, and Gender*. New York: Routledge.

Paxton, Pamela. 1999. "Is Social Capital Declining in the United States?: A Multiple Indicator Assessment." *American Journal of Sociology* 105(1): 88–127.

Portes, Alejandro. 1995. "Economic Sociology and the Sociology of Immigration: A Conceptual Overview." In *The Economic Sociology of Immigration*, edited by Alejandro Portes. New York: Russell Sage Foundation.

———. 1998. "Social Capital: Its Origins and Applications in Modern Sociology." *Annual Review of Sociology* 24: 1–24.

Putnam, Robert D. 1993. *Making Democracy Work: Civic Traditions in Modern Italy*. Princeton, N.J.: Princeton University Press.

———. 1995. "Bowling Alone: America's Declining Social Capital." *Journal of Democracy* 6(January): 65–78.

———. 2000. *Bowling Alone: The Collapse and Revival of American Community*. New York: Simon & Schuster.

Rainwater, Lee. 1970. *Behind Ghetto Walls: Black Families in a Federal Slum*. Chicago: Aldine.

Reingold, David A. 1997. "Does Inner-City Public Housing Exacerbate the Employment Problems of Its Tenants?" *Journal of Urban Affairs* 19(4): 469–86.

Saegert, Susan, and Gary Winkel. 1996. "Paths to Community Empowerment: Organizing at Home." *American Journal of Community Psychology* 24(4): 517–50.

———. 1998. "Social Capital and the Revitalization of New York City's Distressed Inner-City Housing." *Housing Policy Debate* 9(1): 17–60.

Sampson, Robert J. 1999. "What 'Community' Supplies." In *Urban Problems and Community Development*, edited by Ronald F. Ferguson and William T. Dickens. Washington, D.C.: Brookings Institution Press.

Sampson, Robert J., Stephen W. Raudenbush, and Felton Earls. 1997. "Neighborhoods and Violent Crime: A Multi-level Study of Collective Efficacy." *Science* 277(August): 918–26.

Scheie, David M., et al. 1991. *Religious Institutions as Partners in Community-Based Development: Findings from Year One of the Lilly Endowment Program*. Minneapolis: Rainbow Research.

Schorr, Lizbeth B. 1997. *Common Purposes: Strengthening Families and Neighborhoods to Rebuild America*. New York: Anchor Books/Doubleday.

Sentencing Project. 1998. *Losing the Vote: The Impact of Felony Disenfranchisement Laws in the United States*. Washington: Sentencing Project/Human Rights Watch.

Shirley, Dennis. 1997. *Community Organizing for Urban School Reform*. Austin: University of Texas Press.

Skocpol, Theda. 1996. "Unraveling from Above." *American Prospect* 25(March-April): 20–25.

Stack, Carol B. 1974. *All Our Kin: Strategies for Survival in a Black Community*. New York: Harper & Row.

Stoecker, Randy. 1997. "The CDC Model of Urban Redevelopment: A Critique and an Alternative." *Journal of Urban Affairs* 19: 1–22.

Stoecker, Randy, and Susan Stall. 1998. "Community Organizing or Organizing Community?: Gender and the Crafts of Empowerment." *Gender and Society* 12(6): 729–56.

Tendler, Judith. 1997. *Good Government in the Tropics*. Baltimore, Md.: Johns Hopkins University Press.

Thomas, June M., and Reynolds N. Blake, Jr. 1996. "Faith-Based Community Development and African-American Neighborhoods." In *Revitalizing Urban Neighborhoods,* edited by W. Dennis Keating. Lawrence, Kans.: University of Kansas Press.

Ture, Kwame, and Charles V. Hamilton. 1992 [1967]. *Black Power: The Politics of Liberation.* New York: Vintage.

Vidal, Avis C. 1992. *Rebuilding Communities: A National Study of Urban Community Development Corporations.* New York: Community Development Research Center, Graduate School of Management and Urban Policy, New School for Social Research.

Waldinger, Roger. 1997. "Black/Immigrant Competition Reassessed: New Evidence from Los Angeles." *Sociological Perspectives* 40(3): 365–86.

Warren, Mark R. 1998. "Community Building and Political Power: A Community Organizing Approach to Democratic Renewal." *American Behavioral Scientist* 42(1): 78–92.

———. 2001. *Dry Bones Rattling: Community Building to Revitalize American Democracy.* Princeton, N.J.: Princeton University Press.

Williams, David R., and Chiquita Collins. 1995. "U.S. Socioeconomic and Racial Differences in Health: Patterns and Explanations." *Annual Review of Sociology* 21: 349–86.

Wilson, William J. 1987. *The Truly Disadvantaged.* Chicago: University of Chicago Press.

———. 1996. *When Work Disappears: The World of the New Urban Poor.* New York: Alfred A. Knopf.

Woolcock, Michael. 1998. "Social Capital and Economic Development: Toward a Theoretical Synthesis and Policy Framework." *Theory and Society* 27: 151–208.

Wuthnow, Robert. 2001. "The Changing Character of Social Capital in the United States." In *The Dynamics of Social Capital,* edited by Robert D. Putnam. Princeton, N.J.: Princeton University Press.

Zhou, Min. 1992. *New York's Chinatown: The Socioeconomic Potential of an Urban Enclave.* Philadelphia: Temple University Press.

Part I

The Creation and Destruction of Social Capital

Chapter 2

Social Capital and the Culture of Power: Lessons from the Field

M. Lisette Lopez and Carol B. Stack

S ocial capital resists simplification. It does not make a conversation lifted above the fray of time and place. Instead, it must be heard in dialogue with local voices, seen against the background of individuals, families, and communities, a nation and world in motion. At the beginning of the twenty-first century, changing geographies of financial capital have hardened the urban core; global and interregional migrations of people have altered it. It has been reconfigured by ethnic and racial divisions, and destabilized by the erosion of public institutions and services. But studies of social capital have sometimes obscured the interconnections that make the concept a useful research tool (see Portes 1998; Woolcock 1998; Waldinger 1995; Gittell 1998b). The purpose of this chapter is to (re)weave the threads of social capital into patterns of agency and constraint that can help us articulate effective strategies for change on the ground of urban life.

As this volume itself suggests, practitioners, researchers, and community members alike look to social capital for solutions to persistent poverty in communities of color. It's a solution that may invoke our collective memories (perhaps inaccurate) of a golden age—the 1920s and 1930s for some, the 1960s and 1970s for others—when people who lived in the urban core seemed to possess "civic virtue" that built social connections and forged norms of trust. Hard realities challenge the reductionist view that a revival of cooperative norms can erase the living history of racial barriers, hatred, and disharmony that affect our cities. We can, however, discover how scaffolds of support were maintained among those who were excluded over decades, even as racial and cultural politics marginalized the social power and depleted the assets of low-income urban communities.

Many social scientists took up the lens of social capital to fill in gaps left by community development studies that employed market- or state-centered models of analysis (Woolcock 1998). Efforts to chart the connections between social organization, economic well-being, and political process, scholars speculated, would improve our capacity to understand and facilitate community change. Some of those efforts, however, have failed to ground social capital arguments in a sufficiently complex framework.[1] They would repair traffic jams at the crossroads of multiple highways (connected through a series of overpasses) by visualizing them as one-way streets. To use social assets effectively to combat poverty, we must look at all the directions in which resources and power and cultural meaning travel across social groups, the market, the polity, and civil society.

We hope to contribute to such a multifaceted, process-focused model by offering an analysis grounded in racial and cultural politics and based on overlooked or undertheorized characterizations of social capital that emphasize its flow and rhythm.[2] Double-sided, dialectic, multidimensional, historical, and intra- and extra-institutional, social capital unfolds in multigroup settings in which one social group, intentionally or not, may secure advantages that disable others. Our characterizations of social capital build on one another. If we see them steadily and in confluence, if we *attend* to the practices, policies, and power arrangements that have enhanced or undermined individual and collective agency in urban communities of color over time, we recognize, with Louise Lamphere (1992, 4), that social capital works through sites that "mediate or serve to channel larger political and economic forces into settings that have an impact on the networks of a community, where macrolevel forces are brought to bear on micro-level relationships."

These characterizations of social capital are informed by anthropological perspectives on *cultural process.* Indeed, a central theme of this chapter is that cultural process—understood as meaning and power-laden relations and practices constituted in the everyday interactions of historically formed communities (Lave and Wenger 1991)—is inherent to the workings of social capital. The double-sided, cultural, institutional view of social capital is central to the work of Pierre Bourdieu (Bourdieu 1986; Bourdieu and Passeron 1977). He argues that biases embedded in state-regulated cultural and educational institutions reflect and reward the social-cultural[3] capital of upper classes and devalue that of lower classes, thereby ensuring the reproduction of social inequality. Building on Bourdieu's formulation, we stress the need to assess how the social-cultural capital of different social groups interacts through state institutions. Our understanding of the many facets of social capital mandates a program of multidisciplinary research that incorporates both qualitative and quantitative data.

In the first section of this chapter, we sketch with broad strokes the historical trends that affect urban communities and social capital formation. We focus on the racial politics of dominant-mainstream[4] institutions whose decisions and policies, over the last few decades, minimized the positive social capital of poor and minority communities and segregated their inhabitants in resource-deprived urban enclaves, racializing poverty and producing institutional crisis. In the second section, we present ethnographic documentation (Stack 1996a, 1996b, 1998; Gregory 1998) of efforts by low-income families, friends, and community groups to use their social assets. Here we focus on the role of public institutions that, sharing bias toward the cultural worldview and skills of traditional power holders, tend to marginalize poor and minority communities. Lisa Delpit (1988) argues that this institution-based "culture of power" is critically important. Minority students in public schools, Delpit contends, are judged on their use of a white, male, middle-class linguistic style and culture, but because they are not taught how to decode that culture's standards, their chances for success are limited.

We argue that it is critical to map the social, cultural, and racialized pathways that (dis)connect poor communities from mainstream-dominant institutions and outside social groups. For example, a practice or policy that looks neutral to those from the culture of power may, in effect, be biased toward its own cultural practices and experiences. The consequences of cultural-racial biases in mainstream-dominant state institutions have been significantly negative for poor communities. Those negative impacts cannot be overstated considering the range and depth of state influence—the state regulates and provides health care, housing, mortgage loans, education, employment, and community development, while through its political structure and policies, it also encourages, assists, or represses community attitudes and collective organizing around these issues.

In section three, we suggest a series of steps that could be incorporated into a social asset- and community-building agenda. They build on the historical and ethnographic case-based analysis, recognizing that the racial and cultural politics of public institutions have long acted as barriers to community social capital. The first of these steps would help individuals and families develop a bicultural orientation that facilitates effective use of social capital to link with mainstream-dominant institutions (Stanton-Salazar 1997; Schneider 1998). We refer to this process as cultural bridging; it conceives a role that can be played both by individuals within mainstream institutions and by intermediary organizations. But cultural bridging cannot ensure the deployment of social assets in collective action. To overcome the collective-level barriers we identify, social capital must be translated into political capital (Stone 1998; Gittell 1998b). The second in the series of steps, civic capacity-synergy, is defined here as a synergy between civil society and governmental institutions (Warren, Thompson, and Saegert, this volume; Evans 1995; Woolcock 1998; Stone 1998). It addresses the need to use social assets to build coalitions that can change existing power arrangements.

The analysis presented in this chapter suggests that a third step is required to transform fundamentally the conditions that maintain barriers and poverty for urban communities. This step harnesses cultural citizenship (Rosaldo 1997; Flores and Benmayor 1997; Ong 1999), a concept that, according to Aihwa Ong, "denotes the contradictory and subjective experiences of citizenship or membership in society, and its implicitly cultural and racial restrictions" (1999, 263). Conceptual work in the area of cultural citizenship "offers us an alternative perspective to better comprehend cultural processes that result in community building and in political claims raised by marginalized groups on the broader society" (Flores and Benmayor 1997, 15). It is also an important basis for all forms of the social capital referred to in chapter 1 of this volume in that certain types of cultural citizenship strengthen bonds between community members, build bridges between low-income communities and affluent groups, and facilitate the synergy of civil and civic institutions on the local and national levels. Redefining cultural citizenship more inclusively is crucial if we hope to change the negative impact of cultural-racial politics on social capital in this country.

THE RACIAL POLITICS OF URBAN DECLINE

We call into question a commonplace scholarly assumption—that social capital has diminished in poor urban communities over the last few decades—and start our discussion in a different place by trying to identify barriers to the constructive use of social resources. Paradoxically, the story of the Great Migration north from the rural South provides us with a jumping-off point for our survey of some of the changes that have affected urban communities of color (Stack 1974), and the story of the return migration of African Americans provides us with the chance to explore the lessons learned in those northern cities.

When Viola Jackson finished high school in 1940, her graduation present was a one-way ticket from Mississippi to Chicago on the Illinois Central Railroad. She was sixteen, old enough to join the stream of family that flowed north along those tracks between the 1930s and the late 1960s, a time when Jackson counted ninety-eight relatives, in three generations, who had left the South in search of jobs and better lives. Pearl Bishop stayed behind in Burdy's Bend, North Carolina, when her ten children, her nieces and nephews, and her husband, Samuel, headed to Brooklyn, the Bronx, Philadelphia, Newark, or Washington, D.C., to find work. She might have gone herself if there had not always been children blocking the path between her front door and the road north.

The Great Migration scattered sisters and cousins and brothers and parents across hundreds and hundreds of miles. But it reflected a strategy that kept families together too. As the political economy of a troubled South pushed blacks north in search of jobs, struggling families established support networks across long distances (Stack 1970). Workers in the North sent money home to help those who had stayed on to farm family land in the devastated South. Although African Americans looked away from poverty and toward opportunity when they set out from their rural homes, the benefits of economic growth in the postwar boom would privilege whites. After the 1960s the industrial jobs that had drawn black folks north were downsized or relocated to the suburbs or abroad. Service-sector jobs that might have replaced them would prove unstable and poorly paid. The interaction of de facto racial segregation with economic restructuring would lay the foundation for the decline of urban minority communities, a decline that could hardly be forestalled by the limited mobility and political gains secured by the civil rights movement.

Scholars of urban change argue that during the postwar expansion many whites defined upward mobility through the consumption of racially segregated yet publicly supported services (Kelley 1997, 1994; Gregory 1998; Haymes 1995; Katz 1993). In *Black Corona* (1998), his study of race and the politics of neighborhood change in Queens, Steven Gregory asserts that for working- and middle-class white anti-integrationists in particular, segregated services represented what W. E. B. Du Bois called the "wages of whiteness." Communities worked to maintain these privileges through an array of formal and informal practices that maintained the color line around the urban core. Alice O'Connor (1998) refers to these practices as a policy of "racial containment": "organized violence, zoning regulations, racial covenants, mortgage lending practices, and block-busting were the most overt and direct of the practices devoted to creating and maintaining residential [segregation]." Equally powerful was the "whole series of race-conscious decisions about urban development and infrastructure building over the years, whether seen in public housing, urban 'renewal,' public transportation, highway and road building, and in most major cities, the construction of stadiums, urban shopping malls and other major 'public' spaces" (O'Connor 1998, 7).

As we look beneath their surface, we see that many public policies and institutions that claimed to be nondiscriminatory actually helped concentrate the benefits of postwar prosperity among whites, easing their movement (through federal social programs such as the GI Bill of Rights and home loan supports) into suburbs where the common feature, whiteness, effaced old divisions between ethnic groups. Investments in highway infrastructure extended the reach of the new white middle class; the booming economy put them into cars, enabling them to follow high-wage work wherever it led, most often away from the possibility of integration in the inner cities, which continued to receive minorities moving north. The racial containment practices that prohibited the vast majority of people of color from moving to the emerging suburbs and from benefiting from resources directed there were inseparable from and linked to the mobility sought and achieved by whites.

This process did not go uncontested by minority communities. Blacks challenged restrictions on their full participation in society through one of the largest political movements of the century. Community leaders built on embedded social institutions, the church, homeplace ties, work and kin relations, neighborhood organizations, and friendship, to transform the political landscape. Civil rights struggles in the South and in the North demanded formal legal equality for African Americans. In well-organized campaigns of public protest, black Americans pressed for legal protection, seized political power, gained access to public jobs, and secured the commitment of government resources through the War on Poverty's ambitious and progressive social policy agenda. But some policies of the War on Poverty served to impede deeper change; the movement could not overcome the web of cultural, political, and economic dynamics that maintained the racial order (Gregory 1998; Katz 1989, 1993; Kelley 1997).

Even at the zenith of politicization in Corona–East Elmhurst, the Queens neighborhood that was the focal point of Gregory's (1998) community study, other forces worked to limit the long-term power of black mobilization. Through antipoverty programs and newly created institutions of decentralized city government, activists were incorporated into state-managed and state-funded arenas of civic participation, where they addressed interrelated social and economic problems as discrete and depoliticized categories of bureaucratic service provision. Attention shifted from poverty to "community development," while the role of community groups in identifying problems and organizing residents to act on them was taken over by antipoverty organizations and public agencies, transferring power back to local bureaucrats and elites.

Gregory points out that newly created community service organizations were not only "dependent on government agencies for funding, but were also constrained to formulate and address neighborhood needs in ways that complied with the narrow program priorities, guidelines, and service delivery strategies of their sponsors. . . . [Moreover,] the viability of these organizations depended less on the political mobilization of residents than on the tactical support of local political elites" (1998, 98). The significant achievements of the civil rights era were "less the consequence of state largess than of the mobilization of black political power. And it was precisely this political capacity, nurtured through decades of struggle and institution building . . . that would fall victim to the state's war on poverty in Corona–East Elmhurst" (97). The political leverage of minorities in cities was further circumscribed by the shift of political power to white middle-class suburbs (Davis 1986; Anyon 1997; Haymes 1995).

The same demographic and political changes that meant mobility and movement to the suburbs for many working-class white Americans resulted in the concentration of blacks in cities where their significant efforts at contesting racial and economic disparity were eventually circumscribed (Massey and Denton 1993; Wilson 1996). This racial politics would leave poor communities extremely vulnerable when the scaffolding of jobs and recent public investment in urban areas collapsed in the late 1970s and 1980s. In the mid-1970s, stagnating productivity and decreasing competitiveness in global markets produced economic crisis in the United States (Storper and Walker 1989; Piore and Sabel 1984). In the transition from an industrial to a service-based economy, poor urban and minority communities lost out (Bluestone and Harrison 1982; Reich, Gordon, and Edwards 1973; Katz 1993; Moore and Pinderhughes 1993). Jobs were highly segmented, and compensation for work assumed an hourglass shape—high skills won high income, low skills earned minimum wage and, eventually, in the urban core, no wage at all.

This form of economic restructuring was not natural, inevitable, or necessary, as the conclusions of some analysts would seem to suggest (O'Connor 1998). Coupled with racial containment and the neutralization of minority political power, the calculated withdrawal of private and public resources from cities destroyed the viability of essential community institutions. As Loic Wacquant (1998, 29) points out, "Brutal cuts in federal funds for urban and community development, the reduction of welfare programs, the shrinking of employment coverage, increasingly regressive taxation schemes, and state and city policies of 'planned shrinkage' vitiated pivotal sources of support for the formation and deployment of integrative social capital in cities." In middle-class white communities, institutions are traditionally well run and funded, allowing for the relatively successful and smooth formation of social capital assets. Parallel institutions in low-income minority communities have been deprived of resources through outright discrimination, antagonism, or inefficiency. During periods of internal stability and support, some nonpublic community institutions were able to foster the development of constructive community bonds. But over the last few decades, the push to downsize, privatize, and devolve responsibility for services from the federal government to states and localities led to the degradation of public institutions—apparent in the breakdown of police protection, the criminal justice system, education, welfare support, and health care provision (not to mention the absence of financial resources and services and decent housing)—and crippled urban communities (Wacquant 1998).

As chances to earn adequate income in the legitimate workforce evaporated in the 1980s, a growing number of residents in the central cities turned to an illicit underground economy. Violence grew with the drug trade. Cities became heavily militarized zones of surveillance and incarceration as the War on Drugs replaced the War on Poverty (Gordon 1994; Gregory 1998). Increasingly intractable poverty and its many troubling consequences—single-parent families, reliance on welfare, substance abuse—devastated urban communities, dangerously stressing the networks, norms, and trust by which minority residents of the urban core had lived. Although few would deny that a ravaged local economy, overdependent on drugs, crime, or welfare, has destructive consequences for urban communities, it is important to recognize the roots of what has been seen as a pathological, isolated "underclass" in the historical and contemporary practices of economic marginalization and racial containment as well as in the misdeeds of public institutions (O'Connor 1998).

In *The Prosperous Community,* Robert Putnam (1993, 41–42) acknowledges that "social capital . . . works through and with states and markets, not in place of them." Studies of urban change also make it clear that the social capital that works through states and markets is not race-neutral. Enforcement procedures that maintain the color line and locate power in segregated suburbs sever almost all paths of positive association between minorities and whites, between poor and middle-class. People of color who live in the central cities now have less access than ever before to sources of economic and social power. Regional racial politics have affected a wide range of practices, formal and informal, public and private, warping the institutions so critical to mediating social capital for poor urban communities. How could these urban communities thrive? Economically abandoned, politically hand-tied, and institutionally degraded, they have been prevented from using their social assets. The significance of racial politics in producing the blight of many cities cannot be overlooked or understated.

Building on this brief historical account of race-conscious practices and social policies, we now turn to the workings of social capital on the ground in families and communities and explore the multiple strategies that people use to transform social capital into community well-being.

MINING ETHNOGRAPHIES FOR SOCIAL CAPITAL

Although we look to social capital as a resource to help communities, it can also serve to produce and maintain inequality. Urban history reveals racialized processes that neutralized the constructive power of minority social assets. Networks to assist white mobility did so through racial discrimination and segregation, and the "wages of whiteness" were linked to racial containment practices and the maintenance of racial order that concentrated wealth and whites in suburbs and poverty and minorities in cities.

Across the board, up through the 1970s and into the 1980s, social policies systematically undermined trust and shared rights and responsibilities in African American kin networks. Just as policymakers in the child welfare system formulate value judgments as they debate the "best interests" of children, families, and communities, social capital theorists may unknowingly invoke their own values when they examine the kind of "doing for yourself" that ought to be encouraged. Welfare policy typically disacknowledges or discounts the "work of kinship" in African American family life (Stack and Burton 1993). In the 1960s, before welfare reform and time limits, AFDC (Aid to Families with Dependent Children) incentives encouraged household formation, even by young mothers, to limit "dependency" on kin. Mothers received higher welfare stipends if they lived alone, or if they lived with a female friend or stranger, than if they chose to remain with their own mothers, their grandmothers, or other relatives. And in case we have forgotten, although some states offered unemployed fathers the option to remain in AFDC households, most threw jobless fathers out of such families. It took nearly three decades of activism in kin-care movements to reconfirm what was obvious and natural all along: low-income African American grandmothers, not just strangers, should be eligible to become legal foster parents for their own grandchildren.

We might conclude that the cultural politics of public institutions negatively valued intricately fashioned kinship ties (and low-income or unemployed fathers as well). From the dominant-mainstream viewpoint, the social capital that formed the basis of communities of concern and enacted meager protections against the despair of poverty among African American families looked like "bad" social capital. So welfare policies that belittle difference were developed to oppose the work of kinship, and those policies disabled efforts to capitalize on networks of social trust and norms of reciprocity that moved beyond family life into common goals, civic engagement, and a larger sense of community well-being.

Carol Stack's ethnographic study (1998) of the culture and politics of shelter in Farmers Home Administration (FmHA) homeownership programs reveals the interplay between goal-oriented collective action and the disturbing logic frequently evidenced in public institutions, and it discloses the egregiously destructive consequences of the underlying racial-cultural politics. In the southern rural communities where this research was carried out, a typical family compound comprises two to four acres of property with small houses, cabins, sheds, and mobile homes grouped together around a central courtyard. The housing stock, some of which has not been improved for fifty years, includes two-room, shed-style houses— a front room with half loft, and a kitchen. People enter the house through the kitchen, which has a wood-burning stove and a pump for water. From the kitchen, you can look through to the windowless second room filled with beds. A ladder leads to the sleeping loft. Fifty percent of these households earn less than $9,000 per year, and across three to four generations, households accommodate, on average, five children and three adults.

Families that earn from $7,000 to $14,000 a year are eligible to apply for a Farmers' Home loan, but FmHA reserves the right to define the terms. The agency does not make loans to "single heads of households." It labels as high-risk older women and even single female heads of households with sufficient income. Often, families informally select a young, double-income married couple to front the loan to build a house, which then becomes the domain of the extended family. (Indeed, FmHA architects note that young buyers often have to consult with their kin about every design detail.) The young people who are its owners in name are least likely to enjoy the privilege of living in the house. Instead, grandparents or great-aunts and great-uncles are given the chance to enjoy a bit of indulgence—safer porch steps, better-equipped kitchens, comfortable bathrooms—in their later years.

Those who cannot or do not want to front the loan may bundle their resources to apply for a "family mortgage." But few FmHA administrators are willing to endorse such an arrangement. When one kin network—a group of adults, their children, and their grandchildren, all of whom had good jobs in the Northeast—tried to help their "mama," who had raised them after their mother died, get a decent house, the FmHA officer informed them that "the paperwork was too complicated" and that he "did not believe in spreading the liability." "Buying a house is like a business," another FmHA administrator said. "It's not a social operation."

Family mortgages that spread financial liability across low- or multi-income kin networks could serve to cushion against default on these loans. But the FmHA official knew only one thing about mortgages, and sadly, the one thing he knew was wrong. For African Americans living on family land in the rural South, the building of a home is a profoundly social as well as economic undertaking. And although the concept may be unconventional in the context of federal housing policy for low-income people, shared liability and multiple investors characterize most of their financial enterprises.

FmHA guidelines on who can get a loan are certainly rigid, but the agency's specifications for how houses may be built—with standard heating equipment, carpets on floors, small kitchens that include washing machines and electric stoves, and one centralized bathroom—actually defy community wisdom and experience. Many applicants consider it unsanitary to cook and wash laundry in the same room. They know that overflowing, secondhand washing machines are best located in a storage or utility room outside the house. They know that there are other advantages to putting the washers outside. You can take off your work clothes before you go into the house, and your clean laundry is closer to the clothesline. People who live on dirt roads, who work the land, or who are employed in poultry processing plants or in lint-filled mills often prefer vinyl floors that can be swept. But they cannot have them. Seeking a suburban look, FmHA also requires that each home have its own driveway from the main road. The setting that many mortgage holders would prefer—homes placed around a courtyard—is forbidden. Like welfare policymakers, FmHA administrators want each house to stand on its own. Why is agency policy so inflexible? Because officials are thinking about foreclosures and the "recapture market," the resale value of their "product."

Foreclosures on FmHA homes provide a ready-made entry point into homeownership for not-so-low-income families. Thus, the home intended for the low-income buyer becomes reduced-cost housing for the first-time buyer who earns more than $15,000 a year. And thus, some observers argue, FmHA subsidizes the real estate industry. From Washington to local administrators, the bureaucracy is remote from the people it ought to serve. Until the first black housing official showed up in the near-black-majority nine-county area that Stack studied, for example, fewer than 5 percent of FmHA loans for low-income housing went to African Americans.

At the county level, administrators have considerable discretion (which they seem seldom to exercise on behalf of mortgage holders)[5] and often act as real estate brokers and bank officers, manipulating the flow of eligible applicants to stimulate building in slow periods and to suppress it again when the economy picks up. From outside, it looks as though FmHA is designed to guarantee work to private contractors. Certainly, many low-income families learn that homeownership is an illusion during FmHA foreclosures, which take place after a very short grace period, within three to six months of default. Because they will lose the land too if they have built their house on family property, many low-income landowners choose to buy mobile homes instead. Financing charges are very high, but the buyer retains autonomy and property rights.

Why do agencies and institutions end up fighting the people they were mandated to serve? The answer is simple: FmHA's guidelines are determined by notions of how such a system works for white middle- and business-class interests. The perspective of mortgage holders is left out of the equation as bureaucrats contemplate housing starts and resale markets. Families may marshal their social assets to buy houses, but their collective power is diminished by the bias of institutional logic and by the dominant-mainstream cultural politics that pervades these institutions.

Researching another story, the return migration to the South, Carol Stack (1996a) crisscrossed nine counties in the Carolinas from the 1980s through the 1990s. She talked with white public officials across the region, but her focus was on a broad cross-section of African Americans who had left northeastern cities and headed home: professionals, workers, landowners and people who had lost their land, Vietnam veterans, experienced but out-of-work bureaucrats, people who wanted to start small businesses. Some were propelled back to the rural South by joblessness or urban decay. Others, made stronger by the uncompromising demands of city life, were drawn home out of a sense of obligation or mission—to help their kin or to redeem a lost community.

Their destinations share a certain statistical profile. They are far from big cities, far from Sunbelt industry, way below national and even state averages for income, linked historically to the traditional southern cash crops, and skewed demographically by generations of out-migration. One such destination, Chestnut County, North Carolina, has some twenty thousand inhabitants, 60 percent of them black.[6] In 1980 census-takers counted fewer than 1,000 people in the county seat, Chowan Springs, and just 467 in Rosedale, the next-largest town. But those who returned to these rural communities understood that need defies numbers; they looked around them and saw need everywhere, and they saw neglect.

When they mustered their skills and experience to form vibrant voluntary civic associations, they encountered systematic, organized, structural resistance—call it stonewalling—through which local (white) government hoped to negate or at least diminish their growing stock of social capital. At a backyard barbecue in October 1981, Collie Mae Gamble, Isabella Beasley, and Shantee Owens, who grew up daughters of sharecroppers in and around Chestnut County, decided that the time had come to tackle Chestnut County's problems head-on, hands-on. With little or no opportunity at home, they had all moved north in the 1960s. Collie Mae Gamble got a job in Camden, New Jersey, processing bids on government contracts. Isabella Beasley worked in Newark for a state agency that administered federal funds for Head Start. Shantee Owens worked in public administration in the Bronx. In 1980 Isabella and her family moved back home. Collie Mae and her husband followed. Then Shantee returned too. As they looked for employment, they could hardly ignore the poverty that surrounded them. Holding Hands was born in a conversation out behind Collie Mae's house, but the seeds had been planted long before. The organization was rooted in the world the women had experienced in their youth, in the political skills they had honed in the cities as they raised families, ran neighborhood organizations, and worked in government agencies, and in the painful lessons they had begun to learn when they moved home again.

It would be an exaggeration to say that Holding Hands began with an agenda. The organization's aims could hardly have been more modest. If there was a family without heat, Collie Mae, Isabella, and Shantee would arrange to bring them a load of wood or find money to lend them a down payment for a tank of oil. If somebody's porch steps were broken, or if children needed coats, if a mother needed a ride to town to see whether she was eligible for food stamps, Holding Hands could help. If somebody needed a sack of groceries to get through until the end of the month, if somebody else wanted to learn how to write his name, if a little old lady couldn't get around without a walker anymore, well, Collie Mae and Isabella and Shantee could help with that too.

By the end of 1981, Holding Hands was registered as a tax-exempt, nonprofit corporation. At the end of 1982, the women had reached their goal of one hundred members in Chestnut County, and they had signed up fifty-eight people in Powell County and thirty-one in Harden County. Several black churches honored the organization. But there were signs of hostility. A white reporter observed in the local newspaper that minding other people's business was not well received in Chestnut County. Others were more direct. "I got three phone calls in one day from people who would not identify themselves," Collie Mae said. "They threatened that we better watch out, we're asking for trouble. Instead of hanging up on them, I asked, 'Now, who is this *we* you're talking about?' And they said, 'You just keep your hands to yourself—keep your hands to yourself.'" "White folks don't want us organizing," Isabella observed, "but then they never stop talking how we can't do for ourselves. I say let's just keep going—cause we're helping" (Stack 1996a, 142).

Isabella's job search (and there were no jobs to be found that matched her qualifications) had taken her up and down enough rural roads to prove to her that Chestnut County had no projects funded by the kinds of federal programs she had helped to administer in New Jersey. Head Start did not exist here, nor did any subsidized day care. Even though many such programs were specifically designed for high-poverty areas (a description that fit Chestnut if it fit anywhere), the only federal social services dollars that came into the county went to food stamps and AFDC. Isabella had not yet heard all their explanations, but it was clear to her that local officials preferred not to provide the poor people of the county with such services as day care, even if those services could be offered without spending a penny of local money.

Isabella did some research on the employment picture in Chestnut and neighboring counties. Two food-processing plants in Chestnut County employed more than 1,000 workers, and three other such plants in nearby counties employed 2,000 more. A men's underwear factory employed 210 people, and a furniture-maker employed more than 400. Wages in these facilities averaged just over five dollars an hour, and employers offered nothing or next to nothing in benefits.

With such pay and benefits, day care services had to cost much more than most working people could afford. Isabella talked with parents, and she talked with public officials, who admitted to her what she had already suspected: year after year, they turned back federal funds available through programs such as Title XX. "One administrator told me she didn't believe in government subsidies at all, even though her office manages AFDC and food stamps. In another office the director said it was a point of pride for him that in his county they served very few of the eligible families . . . and he said that poor people have more dignity and self-regard for it" (Stack 1996a, 144–45).

Isabella Beasley did not believe that white bureaucrats should decide what constitutes dignity and self-regard for the near-majority black population of Chestnut County, and she thought she could organize a successful effort to bring Title XX day care funds there. Collie Mae would help, of course, and Eula Bishop Grant, who had become a vice president of Holding Hands; Menola Rountree and Maude Allen, director of another new organization, Chestnut Action for Teenage Students (CATS), would help too.

At their first meeting, Maude Allen asked a crucial question: How would they secure the necessary application forms? It would be foolish, self-destructive even, to approach area social service agencies. Someone would have to drive all the way up to the state capital and ask for the application packet in person. Isabella reminded the women that government bureaucracy moved slowly. But Mothers and Children, Inc. (MAC) set its own timetable for fundraising and site selection, and over the next several months Collie Mae and her committee prepared the old Shell gas station in Chowan Springs to house their demonstration project, a model day care center for several counties. The women kicked off a grassroots fund-raising effort from headquarters in the storage shed behind a produce stand on the highway outside of Chowan Springs. They bypassed obstructive social services agencies in Chestnut County as they wrote their grant applications and persuaded the chief deputy director in the Day Care Section of the Department of Human Services in the state capital to review their work, consulting him on every detail. After eighteen months, the day care center passed the mandatory physical inspection, and MAC received official notification of its first grant award.

Because the funds would go through her office, notice of the grant was also sent to the county director of social services in Chowan Springs, Mrs. Beard.

When Mrs. Beard announced her intention to return every penny of the money to the state, Isabella Beasley went straight past her to MAC's new friend in the capital.

> I worried the chief deputy director to death trying to find out what happened to our funds. We had renovated the building and completely furnished it. There were all the little tables and chairs, and the mats, the toys, the playground. We had interviewed day care teachers and assistants, and we had begun training. We had checked eligibility and assembled a group of children—not all black children either—it was strictly on income. We had everything but the funds. (Stack 1996a, 147)

Once again, the state official sent notice of the grant to Chestnut County. This time the social services department presented the matter to the county commissioners, most of whom were thought to agree with Mrs. Beard. But Maude Allen had successfully secured funding for CATS by overpowering the commissioners with her ordered, logical, and exhaustive presentation of facts and figures, and she made a suggestion: pack the meeting room with the children who would attend the new day care center. Supporters of the project never had to say a word; the commissioners approved the funding with a murmured voice vote.

From then on, opposition to MAC came in guerrilla-style skirmishes. Bureaucrats stalled, politicians filed to reduce the allocation, clerks said they could not find the funds, and officials forgot appointments, forgot to file papers, forgot how to write checks. But the funding was secure. Mrs. Beard could (and did) obstruct and delay, but she could not destroy what the women had built. After three years, Mothers and Children, Inc., was able to change funding protocols so that money could be allocated directly to their projects. Nevertheless, attempts at sabotage continued. "Our saving grace was that we created alliances across at least three counties," Shantee Owens said.

> When this all got started we could have been in, you know, competition. But then we started helping one another out. If one group was having trouble getting the money—political problems—well, one of us from another county would call the state capital for them, help them out with our direct contacts. We began to train board members in how they could help. We approached our state representative. Only the strong survive. (Stack 1996a, 149)

And only the strong have direct contacts in the state capital. The cross-county alliance of women succeeded in bringing federal child care funding to the region by creating their own syndicate of influence, their own structure of local power, and by forging independent associations with the North Carolina Department of Human Services. By 1986 MAC was operating six clean and safe day care centers that enrolled more than three hundred children in three different counties, creating fifty new full-time jobs and a couple of dozen part-time positions. By 1995 enrollment and staff had doubled again.

Just as MAC emerged from the training ground of Holding Hands, other groups began to make a difference in the 1990s. New leaders who had learned political skills in established organizations went on to develop advocacy groups and worker cooperatives; coalitions for economic justice and small businesses sprang up on the same ground. Feeding on the help that flows from one organization to another, they formed networks that enhanced civic life in predominantly African American communities in the rural South. But each modest success, each assault on vertical privilege, provoked resistance from white bureaucrats.

In response to a talk that Stack gave on this subject at Harvard's John F. Kennedy School of Government, Robert Putnam pointed out some of the similarities between the feudal Mafia in southern Italy and local white structures of power in rural North and South Carolina. Distrust between whites and blacks in these rural communities may indeed share some of the drama of arbitrary Mafia power in southern Italian communities. But as this story unfolds in the American South, the threat to organizing efforts comes from institutionalized state power and privilege; the adversary, we argue, is lodged deep in public-sector decisionmaking, in a living legacy of old southern race relations.

White Americans in particular continue to experience difficulties with seeing the institutionalized nature of racial barriers in the public sector as well as the private. Instead, whites tend to fault individual behavior or group culture for persistent inequality and to reduce racism to individual prejudice (Bobo 1998). An analysis that identifies pervasive institutional barriers to the deployment of social assets by minority groups runs against prevailing public discourses about race and poverty. Even when it is acknowledged that larger economic and political changes created the conditions for urban poverty, the dominant-mainstream story is that the ongoing concentration of poverty within minority urban communities is now due to pathological behavior and values in those neighborhoods (Bobo 1998).[7] Scholars of American history point out that discourses about an "undeserving poor" emerge or evolve in each era and help maintain racial and class disparities (Katz 1989; Gans 1995). Stereotypes of African Americans, and to some degree Latinos, as dangerous and likely to commit crimes influence policymaking and serve as constraints under which people of color live and work (Gordon 1994; Bobo 1998).

This sad reality motivated Steven Gregory's (1998) research on the impact of discourses about race, poverty, and black identity on heterogeneous black communities during periods of neighborhood change in Queens, New York. In his study of the Lefrak City housing complex in the southern part of Corona, Queens, Gregory tracks the impact of whites' perceptions of lower-income black neighborhoods and finds that many whites rush to conflate deteriorating urban space, black crime, and dysfunctional black families. "In public forums ranging from the monthly meetings of the Neighborhood Stabilization Committee Board 4 to the mass mediated reports of journalists, Lefrak City was viewed as a threat to the quality of life of surrounding neighborhoods; a potent symbol linking anxieties about urban decline and crime to ideologies of black welfare dependency and family pathology" (110–11).

Members of surrounding communities perceived residents of Lefrak, particularly African American men, as threatening in a physical sense, despite assertions by local security and police officers that such perceptions were inaccurate.[8] Inaccurate assumptions and overblown anxieties about Lefrak residents spurred those who perceived them as threatening to call for increased policing of those communities, a response that warps intercommunity relations and undermines the ability of Lefrak residents to link effectively to mediating institutions. Gregory's case study demonstrates "the concrete political and material stakes that are at issue in struggles over 'representation,' and more widely, identity politics," by disclosing the links between discourses about blacks and the ways in which dominant groups and institutions seek to exert power over them (1998, 16).

Communities of color recognize the detrimental effects of discourses of black pathology and develop organizing strategies to combat them, a process evident in the grassroots mobilization of residents of predominantly African American Lefrak City. In response to assertions by mostly white members of the surrounding area that the black men and youth of Lefrak City were causing problems, an informal network of Lefrak tenants started to mobilize. Gregory (1998, 117) observes that the group they formed, Concerned Community Adults (CCA), sought to "disrupt this conflation of race, crime, and space in the discourse and practices of everyday politics." CCA designed strategies to contest the discourses that combined with a disempowering local political structure to limit the participation of Lefrak residents in neighborhood policymaking.

Paralleling the development of Holding Hands and MAC in rural North Carolina, CCA grew out of the "everyday networks of child care, communication, and exchange among women, linking households, floors, and buildings within the complex" (Gregory 1998, 117). Through the leadership of Edna Baskin, an elderly child care provider and Lefrak resident, these networks opened up space for development of a collective identity geared toward collective action; they "would provide the social base for the mobilization of Lefrak City tenants as a political force within the community" (117). In particular, the Concerned Community Adults wanted to counter negative portrayals of the youth in their complex through the organization of a youth forum in which teenagers could speak for themselves.

The Lefrak City Youth Forum was designed to counter negative images of black youngsters in the surrounding community and to build support for youth-centered activities. Gregory (1998, 123) observes that

> this intervention, like many of CCA's activities to follow, served to contest and rework the discursive field within which Lefrak City was constructed as a racialized and pathological place. . . . By inverting the familiar relation between black teenagers and security, so central to the ideology of black crime, the testimony (and Edna's marking its significance) raised the possibility that black teenagers who were often the targets of police action could play a constructive role in neighborhood stabilization.

The focus on reconstructing black identity was central to CCA's community mobilization tactics.

> For Edna Baskin and Concerned Community Adults, the "hard work" of community organizing rested less in mobilizing ready-made subjects in response to fixed grievances and ideologies than in constructing an alternative political space or public sphere in which the needs, interests, and identities of Lefrak City residents could be collectively contested, negotiated, and recast in empowering ways. (Gregory 1998, 137)[9]

Through their collective activities, the leaders of CCA were able to provide alternative images of Lefrak youth and to secure additional resources to help them. CCA also helped mobilize tenants to secure positions in local governing bodies and thus to emerge as a recognized force with area politicians. Like the women of MAC, CCA's leadership learned to negotiate the political structure and to alter the balance of power. But CCA's work also exemplified a cultural citizenship approach: the organization challenged the cultural misperceptions that had marginalized their community socially as well as politically.

In low-income neighborhoods across the country, the same dynamic repeats itself. Energetic, imaginative, and tenacious efforts to consolidate economic, social, and political power often, if not always, meet resistance. People outside of poor communities seem to say, "Do for yourselves," as if no one in those communities had thought of, or was in fact, already doing for themselves. Many, like the social service administrators in Chestnut County, believe that they are acting in the best interest of their clients when they deny them access to public resources: poor people have more dignity and self-regard, according to this belief, if they do for themselves. This rhetoric fuels the ideological fires of those who were never very concerned about the well-being of needy citizens in the first place. But the experiences of poor minority communities lay bare a dismal reality.[10] In poor communities, social-cultural capital is handcuffed to the racial and cultural politics of locality and public institutions.

DEVELOPING COLLECTIVE STRATEGIES

Our objectives in this chapter have been twofold: to see what we learn by mining history and ethnographies for lessons about social capital, and then to offer suggestions about how we might build better and stronger social capital in urban communities. Looking at social capital processes over time and on the ground, it is clear that its workings cannot be understood without situating it at the crossroads of politics, the market, racial struggle, and cultural conflict. In the first section, we followed the historical and multidimensional path of social capital. Rooting it in changing social landscapes, we confront the racial barriers, prejudice, and distrust that have eroded its power in largely minority urban communities in the last few decades. Distrust was forged not only by economic withdrawal and residential segregation but also by the very institutions that purport to serve the public good.

In the second section, we tracked the pathways and functioning of social networks in Stack's (1996a) study of African Americans in Chestnut County, North Carolina, and in Gregory's (1998) research in African American neighborhoods in Queens, New York, and saw how social capital plays out in a multigroup, cultural process across pivotal public institutions. For poor minority communities, whether they are rural or urban, the racial and cultural politics of the mainstream institutions that determine many opportunities in life frequently reproduce patterns of inequality. Institutional barriers that stem from racism, however implicit, block not only the use of social capital but also the ability to acquire resources that would make social assets a building block for prosperity.

Social capital never stands alone. In impoverished and privileged communities alike, it must work through the mediating institutions of the labor market, the polity, and the state. So how can we help make it more effective in poor communities? We find some answers by looking at the efforts and the organizing that take place daily in those communities. Families and community leaders rely on their networks, skills, and resourcefulness to overcome the dearth of funds and surplus of obstacles imposed on them by mainstream-dominant institutions. In the urban context, this is our starting point: frameworks for envisioning interventions to enhance the constructive use of social capital begin with frank acknowledgment of the powerful racial, political, economic, and ideological barriers that confront communities of color. Once we have acknowledged those barriers, we can devise means to overcome them, and eventually to dismantle them. Drawing out implications from our analysis in the first and second sections, this final section identifies three steps—cultural bridging, civic capacity-synergy, and inclusive cultural citizenship—that should be included in an agenda to enhance the use of social assets in poor communities.

Cultural Bridging

Across the ethnographic case studies we reviewed, the cultural politics of mainstream-dominant institutions threw up barriers that prevented members of needy communities from taking advantage of important social networks and public resources. Research in schools and workplaces has found that, for disadvantaged, working-class, minority youth, as for women moving from welfare to work, success depends on learning and performing cultural cues to win the trust of institutional actors (Schneider 1998; Stanton-Salazar 1997; Delpit 1988). The strategy of cultural bridging appears in Stack's (1998) research: sophisticated readers of the culture of power at FmHA figured out how to look like a mainstream nuclear family, the image the housing agency wants to see before it grants home loans. The objective of the cultural bridge is to facilitate the development of knowledge and skills that will help members of a marginalized community overcome social-cultural obstacles. Based on research in the context of education, Ricardo Stanton-Salazar (1997, 25) argues that young people of color must build what he calls a "bicultural network orientation"—that is, a "consciousness that facilitates the crossing of cultural borders and the overcoming of institutional barriers and thereby facilitates entrée into multiple community and institutional settings where diversified social capital can be generated and converted."

Cultural bridging can be facilitated by individuals within mainstream-dominant institutions or by organizations acting as intermediaries. Stanton-Salazar observes (1997, 3) that it is crucially important to develop ties with institutional actors such as teachers (or, in the arena of welfare reform, job-training facilitators) who can help working-class and minority students decode the culture of power and gain access to institutional resources: "Social antagonisms and divisions existing in the wider society operate to problematize (if not undermine) minority children's access to opportunities and resources that are, by and large, taken for granted products of middle-class family, community, and school networks," he asserts. Not only are the cultural, cognitive, and linguistic skills critical to competence and success in traditional academic tasks built on white middle-class language, knowledge, and cultural style (see, for example, Bernstein 1977; Bourdieu and Passeron 1977), but different cultural, linguistic, and behavioral styles are devalued and seen as pathological (Ogbu 1986). Thus, distrust and detachment are institutionalized "between child and institutional agents, between family and community and school" (Stanton-Salazar 1997, 17). The ability to resist the harmful effects of the devaluation of one's cultural background depends on "simultaneous embeddedness in family and community networks of support" (25), Stanton-Salazar claims. The most effective linking to mainstream institutions appears to require both socialization into the culture of power and maintenance of the cultural and social capital of the home community.

Jo Anne Schneider (1998) examines social-cultural capital processes in welfare-reform job training, including the ways in which intermediary organizations act as cultural bridges for women in welfare-to-work programs. Schneider observes that knowledge and performance of certain cultural codes are required in the workplace as well as in educational institutions, and she advocates a similar bicultural approach for intermediary organizations. She highlights, for example, the way in which one community-based organization (CBO) provided a "safe recognized environment to practice the social cues and work habits expected by other employers." CBOs, she argues, could serve "as trusted bridges between the recipient of government services and the wider community," enabling communities of color to acquire the social-cultural capital needed to link with mainstream-dominant institutions.

The cultural bridge has many functions: creating a safe space in which to decode and translate the culture of power; enabling members of marginalized communities to rehearse the unfamiliar codes of the culture of power; serving as a means to deploy personal and collective social capital to gain access to the networks of targeted mainstream-dominant institutions; and integrating and affirming community cultural values, resources, and rights. Affirmation of the cultural capital of the home community serves three purposes. First, it enables the bridging process to benefit from the cultural and social assets of marginalized communities to support learning, coping, and achieving. Second, it fights against the alienation that people of color may feel as they interact with mainstream-dominant institutions that devalue them. Stanton-Salazar argues that maintenance of the cultural and social capital of the home community helps sustain youth through difficult social and psychological processes as they learn to decode and function within the culture of power. Last, such affirmation builds trust and facilitates cooperation among members of marginalized communities toward the mainstream intermediaries, allies, or institutional actors who seek to work with them.

The biases of public institutions demand that communities of color acquire the cultural cues and knowledge of the culture of power, but bridging institutions must affirm the cultural assets of minority communities to gain their trust and forge constructive alliances. Bicultural mutuality is key to generating trust on all sides. The objective is not to assimilate outsiders into the culture of power, but to develop a bicultural (or in the context of our country's growing diversity, a multicultural) orientation. Nevertheless, cultural bridging is not truly a collective strategy. It does not challenge the existence of the culture of power but simply equips individuals and families to function and succeed within it. To contest racial and cultural politics on a collective level, we need a conceptual framework that goes beyond helping individuals or families succeed in the mainstream.

Civic Capacity-Synergy

The objective of the strategy that we describe as civic capacity-synergy[11] is to move toward the transformation of social capital into political capital, and toward public institutions that respond to the needs of marginalized communities. When Loic Wacquant (1998) writes about the disintegration of state institutions into punitive agencies that breed mistrust, we must remember that programs designed to serve unemployed and low-income families never really had a golden age, in rural or in urban areas. Even when money was allocated at the federal level for subsidized day care or for home loans, the policy was always to make it hard to get. MAC, Inc., succeeded because the women who founded the organization were themselves so well organized, so determined, so aware. And they had their cross-kin, cross-county connections, not to mention direct contacts in the state capital to help them (Wacquant 1998). Their uplink into the state power structure and the availability of federal funding guaranteed their success.

The new old South is not the old old South, but distrust, fear, and hostility persist. In the midst of bitterness and ill will, outside money remains a critical resource. Although MAC forged abundant horizontal ties across counties within public and private circles of influence and engaged an active coalition of citizens in building civic community, it took the women who founded the organization a long time to transform their impressive stock of social capital into fully functioning day care services. The cross-county alliance of women succeeded in bringing federal child care funding to the region by creating their own syndicate of influence and their own structure of local power and by forging independent associations with the North Carolina Department of Human Services.

Ideally, alliances create civic-governmental linkages that cross city hall with the institutional and political centers of power and with multiple sectors in the community.[12] In chapter 1, Warren, Thompson, and Saegert refer to such cross-sector linkages as synergy, a concept advanced in the literature of development studies (Evans 1997; Woolcock 1998). Synergy encompasses effective cooperation by local organizations, economic actors, and state institutions to achieve positive developmental outcomes. It exists when a community's social assets are working in unison with government action (Warren, Thompson, and Saegert, this volume). Synergy can be weak, based on complementarity between public and private action, or strong, based on the embeddedness of public officials in social networks of trust that cross public-private domains (Evans 1997).

Embedded synergy captures the process of building cooperative relationships and coproducing outcomes, but it is formulated in a way that may underestimate obstacles or reasons for conflict. Warren, Thompson, and Saegert point out that, for public officials, embeddedness is likely to be based on residence in the community or on shared race, education, or class background. Shared experiences establish common "identities, interests, perspectives [that] allow public officials and community residents to work in tandem with each other." In effect, then, embeddedness stands on cultural commonalities. Identities, interests, and perspectives are shaped by cultural meanings and practices. As we have argued, cultural difference can act as a barrier to the use of constructive networks of social capital between organized residents of poor communities and public and private institutions.

Resistance and conflict are consistent themes in analyses of school reform efforts by low-income minority communities (Stone 1998; Henig et al. 1999; Gittell 1998a, 1998b; Orr 1998). As with MAC and Lefrak City's CCA, community strategies had to be overtly political in order to overcome barriers to social linkages and resistance to community efforts. Embeddedness shines the light on a social foundation for synergy but may fail to articulate all the obstacles that stand in the way. Here the concept of civic capacity comes into play (Stone 1998; Henig et al. 1999). It is adapted from an implication of studies of large-scale urban education reform: fundamental change requires altering the balance of power that enabled marginalization. In his work on the reform of urban educational systems, Stone (1998) uses the term "civic capacity" to describe cross-sector mobilization and coalitions of stakeholders that can effectively press for the destruction of old political relationships and the establishment of a new equation that supports and sustains reforms. Success depends on the dimensions of conflict and cooperation among stakeholders both inside and outside the policy arena, and on the formal and informal means they can harness to define and pursue common goals (Stone 1998; Henig et al. 1999). In recognition of the inevitability of resistance, the civic capacity framework defines as its goal the achievement of sustainable reforms by mobilizing actors across sectors and across difference. A civic capacity approach mandates the creation of "web[s] of alliances and interactions" and the discovery of "obstacles to such alliances" (Henig et al. 1999, 137).

Cultural bridging is also critical to the development of civic capacity, as leaders of collective efforts forge links between dominant institutions and urban communities of color. Biculturalism empowered the founders of MAC and Holding Hands, for example, as well as some of the leaders of the Lefrak City CCA. The women of Mothers and Children, Inc., succeeded because they had had the opportunity to work in the public sector up north and could rely on their knowledge of the real rules of public agencies and grants to overcome the resistance of local officials. They could read and maneuver within the structure of power that confronted them to establish a new, local structure of power that better served their community's needs. Their common ability to cross worlds was critical to their effectiveness as leaders in the transformation of local Chestnut County politics.[13]

Inclusive Cultural Citizenship

Cultural bridging and civic capacity-synergy alone would not challenge some cultural mechanisms that marginalize the social capital of low-income and minority communities and inhibit the development of civic capacity. William Flores and Rina Benmayor (1997, 15) argue that conceptual work in the area of cultural citizenship "offers us an alternative perspective to better comprehend cultural processes that result in community building and in political claims raised by marginalized groups on the broader society." The concept of cultural citizenship developed by the Latino Cultural Studies Working Group (see Flores and Benmayor 1997) focuses on the process through which cultural practices and meanings define how and why different social groups possess legitimate rights and privileges in society. Cultural citizenship affects the legal, political, economic, and social claims of groups and has considerable material and psychological force. The concept builds from arguments that social groups operate "in an uneven field of structural inequalities where the dominant claims of universal citizenship assume a propertied white male subject and usually blind themselves to their exclusions and marginalizations of people who are different in gender, race, sexuality, and age" (Rosaldo 1997, 37). It helps "distinguish the formal level of theoretical universality from the substantial level of exclusionary and marginalizing practices," such as those underscored in our historical and ethnographic discussion (27). Cultural constructions have a profound materiality because they define claims that affect the resources available (or not available) to different members of society. There are restrictions on the degree to which marginalized communities have the freedom to assert their claims and their view of cultural citizenship.

This framework explicates what is at stake in struggles to contest discourses about racial inequality and poverty. As the case studies by Gregory and Stack show, dominant discourses about poor minority communities operate on at least three levels. First, they jeopardize the ability of poor neighborhoods to gain support from more affluent communities, what Warren, Thompson, and Saegert (this volume) view as a component of bridging social capital. Gregory (1998, 105), for example, argues that by "framing urban poverty and decline as a black problem and as an issue 'of needy places rather than faulty labor market structure' (see Smith 1988), the war on poverty discourse and practices served to conflate poverty, urban space, and black identity in the consciousness of many Americans." This conflation of poverty, city, and race limited political support for social programs targeted at the urban core and eventually exposed them to destruction as conservatives and neoliberals attacked what they called the welfare state and its special interests.

Discourses that paint low-income minority communities as pathological by conflating racial difference, moral and cultural deficit, and social deviance also devalue their cultural-social capital and undermine the ability of members of those communities to link effectively to mediating institutions (Warren, Thompson, and Saegert, this volume). Gregory (1998, 111) observes that "by constructing Lefrak City and its residents as objects of surveillance and law enforcement, this discourse of black crime and family pathology hindered, if not precluded, their participation as subjects in the process of neighborhood stabilization." Members of the Latino Cultural Studies Working Group propose a remedy for such discourses of marginalization and pathology in the development of an empowering cultural citizenship. In *Latino Cultural Citizenship,* they argue that "enduring exclusions of the color line often deny full citizenship to Latinos and other people of color. From the point of view of subordinate communities, cultural citizenship offers the possibility of legitimizing demands made in the struggle to enfranchise themselves. These demands can range from legal, political, and economic issues to matters of human dignity, well-being, and respect" (Rosaldo and Flores 1997, 57). "Cultural citizenship can be thought of as a broad range of informal as well as formal activities of everyday life through which Latinos and other groups claim space in society and eventually claim rights," the editors of the collection assert (Flores and Benmayor 1997, 15). They insist on "the right to be different (in terms or race, ethnicity, or native language) with respect to the norms and dominant national community, without compromising one's right to belong, in the sense of participating in the nation-state's democratic processes" (Rosaldo and Flores 1997, 57).

The research of the Latino Cultural Studies Working Group contributes to our understanding of the cultural dynamics of entitlement, privilege, and marginalization in the United States. Aihwa Ong (1999) suggests, however, that the theoretical framework developed by Renato Rosaldo and his colleagues overestimates the degree to which communities are able to challenge the cultural basis of the state and the power of dominant groups. In practice, she argues, cultural processes may lead to marginalization as often as to democratic inclusion. Thus, Ong rearticulates the concept of cultural citizenship in less optimistic terms. She argues that it is more accurately defined as "the cultural practices and beliefs produced out of negotiating the often ambivalent and contested relations with the state and its hegemonic forms that establish the criteria of belonging within a national population and territory. Cultural citizenship is a dual process of self-making and being made within webs of power linked to the nation-state and civil society" (264). Ong asserts that "cultural citizenship denotes the contradictory and subjective experiences of citizenship or membership in society, and its implicitly cultural and racial restrictions" (263). She reminds us that we must distinguish between marginalizing forms of cultural citizenship and those that are inclusive and empowering, just as it is important to distinguish between enabling and constraining forms of social capital.

The process by which communities contest dominant views of cultural citizenship helps overturn obstacles to the three types of social capital outlined in chapter 1. Assertions of inclusive cultural citizenship can rupture existing relations between state and society that benefit dominant groups and break down barriers to bridging social capital between members of marginalized communities and mainstream-dominant institutions, as well as barriers to bridging between poor and affluent communities. Furthermore, discourse that challenges traditional practices may improve a community's ability to bridge with outside organizations and groups as it strengthens bonds within the community and facilitates large-scale organizing beyond local or regional levels.

The development of a counterhegemonic view—MAC created a new vision of Chestnut County's entitlement to federal funds for day care, and Lefrak City youth and CCA members articulated a different view of the problems of young people in their community—helps to build solidarity within the group. Assumptions about people of color and ideologies about poverty and race influence politics and policy and themselves act as constraints under which people live and work; the cultural politics of state institutions affect explicit policies, as well as the construction of collective identities and "counter publics" (Fraser 1989). Thus, "a key element of cultural citizenship is the process of 'affirmation' as the community itself defines its interests, its binding solidarities, its boundaries, its own space, and its membership." (Inter-University Program for Latino Research Cultural Studies Working Group 1987, cited in Flores and Benmayor 1997, 13.) The importance of a community's ability to define its own needs and interests was also cited in the literature of development studies. Michael Woolcock (1998, 76) points out that "the developmental effectiveness of state-society relations therefore turns on the articulation of the interests, needs, and resources of both parties."

For Gregory (1998, 18), the articulation of collective needs and collective identities is important to community building but is also neither straightforward nor uncontested. "Social identities and community-based solidarities are not given ready made to politics; rather they are formed and reformed through struggles in which the 'winning of identification,' the articulation of collective needs, interests, and commitments is itself a key stake." Scholars who study collective action (for example, Escobar and Alvarez 1992) argue that "the process of forming collective identities is not only key to our understanding of how and why people collectively act; it is also a critical axis of conflict in struggles between the people, the state, and capital" (Gregory 1998, 14). However, Gregory's own research in Lefrak City shows that the process of building inclusive cultural citizenship can be nurtured through cultural practices that organize the daily life of a community, through creative linguistic and artistic expression, and through formal organizing. Struggles for inclusive cultural citizenship, carried out in daily life or in coordinated campaigns, can help construct political identities and social consciousness that empower community groups to act.

IN CLOSING

The objective of an inclusive cultural citizenship strategy is to alter the terms on which communities participate in civic life. Robert Putnam (1995) has proposed that participation in civic life is crucial to building the trust that fuels prosperity, and he argues that the decline in civic participation produces a range of social problems.

Participation in and of itself, however, does not build trust. It can be positive or profoundly negative. When communities are submerged in contexts of institutionalized racism and prejudice, participation breeds hostility and distrust. Building on research on participation in communities of practice, we point out that it is necessary to distinguish between modes of participation and to identify their political and cultural, as well as social, bases. Participation occurs in different ways with dramatically different outcomes (Lave and Wenger 1991; Wenger 1998). It can be marginal when dominant stakeholders or cultural mismatch obstruct mutual engagement and negotiation. Or it can be empowered, building common norms and identities that eventually lead to integration, mutuality, and accountability. In a context of mutual engagement and negotiation, founded in common cultural ground and respect, trust can be forged and society transformed.

Social capital always exists in some form as people find ways to work together and to support one another. But its power to enact desirable change, to promote community well-being, is subject to circumstances and can be severely and consciously limited. At the beginning of the new millennium, we stand at a crossroads. From this vantage point, when we look backward, we confront a history of marginalization that destroyed trust. But as we look forward, we can envision bridges that overcome marginalization. We must now take the steps to build the accountability and mutuality upon which full participation and trust are based.

NOTES

1. For example, see Alejandro Portes's (1998) discussion of Putnam (1993, 1995).

2. We offer a corrective rather than critical analysis of social capital and poor communities. We build on the range of strong critical reviews that already exist (especially Portes 1998; Woolcock 1998; Schneider 1998; Stanton-Salazar 1997; Wacquant 1998) and focus our efforts on an analysis that is more cognizant of racial and cultural politics.

3. We are borrowing Jo Anne Schneider's (1998) formulation of social-cultural capital to highlight the cultural nature of the social processes involved. Following from her research on welfare reform, Schneider views social capital as functional, in that it refers to the social relationships and trust that enable people to gain access to resources; building on Bourdieu (1986, 1996), Portes (1998), and Portes and Sensenbrenner (1993), however, she also contends that social capital not only includes the "relationships with people and organizations that have access to resources" but also entails the "knowledge of cultural cues which indicate that an individual is a member of the group and should be given access to those relationships" (Schneider 1998, 1–2). She points out that Bourdieu's notion of social capital as a culturally based process has been lost in prominent formulations generated in the United States (Coleman 1988; Putnam 1993, 1995).

4. The term "mainstream" is frequently used but usually only implicitly defined. It relies on implied reference to the existence of an alternative set of institutions, norms, practices, or groups that are considered nonmainstream. We feel, therefore, that it is a loaded normative term that does not make its parameters explicit—that is, who decides and what is considered mainstream, appropriate, or normal. Generally, and certainly historically, the

institutions, practices, or groups that are accepted and endorsed by those with power in society are considered mainstream. Generally and historically, these "mainstream" institutions are based on a culture of white middle- and upper-class society—the historically dominant group in society that has had the ability to define difference as deviant. Therefore, we choose to use the term "mainstream-dominant" to refer to the institutions that have been based on the culture, history, or practices of the historically dominant groups in society, such as public schools and child and family welfare agencies.

5. FmHA officials claim not to know whether more flexibility in client financing would increase or decrease the foreclosure rate, which, not surprisingly, appears to be tied to the economy, to plant closings, to poor crop yields, and to summer heat that kills chickens, rather than to the values and attitudes of local clients.

6. Pseudonyms are used for county names in the Carolinas, and for people referred to or quoted in this chapter.

7. The argument, as made by academics and most often attributed to Wilson (1987, 1996) and Massey and Denton (1993), is that while economic changes may have destroyed the social fabric of inner cities and isolated them from the mainstream, choices and conditions within those communities now trap members of those communities in poverty.

8. In responses to assertions by nearby white residents that Lefrak City kids were a security problem at the local library, the chief of investigation and security for the Queens Borough Public Library system responded that their concerns were exaggerated, remarking that "the mind conceives and the eyes perceive. Lefrak isn't so bad." Similarly, although members of the wider community were pressing local government for additional police presence, Lefrak's chief of security said that "Lefrak City has a lower than average crime rate," and in fact the housing complex had shown a decrease in violent crime in the past few years (cited in Gregory 1998, 109–10).

9. Gregory's analysis of the CCA builds on Nancy Fraser's (1989) interpretation of the politics of needs. Fraser takes "the politics of needs to comprise three moments that are analytically distinct but interrelated in practice. The first is the struggle to establish or deny the political status of a given need, the struggle to validate the need as a matter of legitimate political concern or to enclave it as a nonpolitical matter. The second is the struggle over the interpretation of the need, the struggle for the power to define it and, so, to determine what would satisfy it. The third moment is the struggle over the satisfaction of the need, the struggle to secure or withhold provision" (Fraser 1989, 164, cited in Gregory 1998, 263).

10. When local power holders try to subvert efforts by black communities to help provide obviously needed services—firewood, say, or safe child care—only fools would trust them to administer block grants. Block grants, lump sums of federal money transferred to the states for the general purpose of helping the poor, may be headed in the wrong direction as they percolate through the state capitals. Serious scholarly investigations have not yet wrestled with the political implications of local controls over these funds, especially in the rural regions of the Southeast that remained battlegrounds of distrust in the 1990s. There the people who proclaim most loudly the urgency and legitimacy of self-help—the bureaucrats and politicians—also work to thwart that independence when they are faced with actual self-help organizations in the home communities. Decentralization limits checks and balances on the implementation of social policy at local levels and imposes serious, often pernicious controls over access to public capital.

11. Clarence Stone (1998) and Jeffrey Henig and his colleagues (1999) formulated the concept of civic capacity on which we build. It originated in an urban-regime theoretical framework. Although we find their work on civic capacity very useful, we do not agree with all of the urban regime theory from which it evolved. Our use of civic capacity has a great deal in common with the concept of synergy (Woolcock 1998; Evans 1995), but as discussed in this chapter, we choose to reemphasize the propensity for conflict and the existence of barriers that will not be resolved by a social capital response alone. A political strategy is also needed in the urban contexts discussed in this chapter.

12. The Texas Industrial Areas Foundation (IAF) offers a compelling example of how civic capacity can be built by combining social capital and political organizing (see Shirley 1997; Cortez 1998).

13. It would appear that migration was an engine for change because it showed African Americans that things could be different and taught them skills in making it so. "If I had come back here with the same attitude that I left with in my twenties," Maude Allen says, "I would be just like the people who have lived here and never gone anywhere. But I came back different. I know when they are dumping on us, and I call their attention to it. I talk to them in a diplomatic way, but I say, 'Hey, this is not the way it's supposed to be.' And you know, they back off when they know you'll call them on it. . . . The only problem is that down here, nothing can be direct. I have found it a major challenge. . . . Down here, to get anything done, you have to go about it delicately, and a lot of times you have to be very innovative" (Stack 1996a, 164). She and Eula Bishop and Shantee Owens could not only look critically at the links between their community and county government but had learned to renegotiate relationships between people of color and white-dominated government and social service agencies. They were able to function in, finesse, and transform multiple worlds.

REFERENCES

Anyon, Jean. 1997. *Ghetto Schooling: A Political Economy of Urban Educational Reform.* New York: Teachers College Press.

Bernstein, Basil. 1977. *Class, Codes, and Control,* vol. 3, *Toward a Theory of Educational Transmission.* 2nd ed. Boston and London: Routledge and Kegan Paul.

Bluestone, Barry, and Bennett Harrison. 1982. *The Deindustrialization of America: Plant Closings, Community Abandonment, and the Dismantling of Basic Industry.* New York: Basic Books.

Bobo, Larry. 1998. [Untitled]. Paper prepared for the Aspen Institute Roundtable on Comprehensive Community Initiatives, Project on Race and Community Revitalization, November, Wye, Maryland.

Bourdieu, Pierre. 1986. "The Forms of Social Capital." In *Handbook of Theory and Research for the Sociology of Education,* edited by John G. Richardson. New York: Greenwood.

———. 1996. *The State Nobility.* Cambridge: Polity Press.

Bourdieu, Pierre, and Jean Claude Passerson. 1977. *Reproduction, Education, Society, and Culture.* Translated by Richard Nice. London and Beverly Hills: Sage.

Coleman, James S. 1988. "Social Capital in the Creation of Human Capital." *American Journal of Sociology* 94 (supp.): S95–120.

Cortez, Albert. 1998. "Power and Perseverance: Organizing for Change in Texas." In *Strategies for School Equity: Creating Productive Schools in a Just Society,* edited by Marilyn Gittell. New Haven, Conn.: Yale University Press.

Davis, Mike. 1986. *Prisoners of the American Dream: Politics and the Economy in the History of the U.S. Working Class.* London: Verso.

Delpit, Lisa D. 1988. "The Silenced Dialogue: Power and Pedagogy in Educating Other People's Children." *Harvard Educational Review* 58(3): 280–98.

Escobar, Arturo, and Sonia E. Alvarez, eds. 1992. *The Making of Social Movements in Latin America.* Boulder, Colo.: Westview Press.

Evans, Peter. 1995. *Embedded Autonomy: States and Industrial Transformation.* Princeton, N.J.: Princeton University Press.

———. 1997. *State-Society Synergy: Government and Social Capital in Development.* Research Series 94. Berkeley: University of California Regents.

Flores, William V., and Rina Benmayor, eds. 1997. *Latino Cultural Citizenship: Claiming Identity, Space, and Rights.* Boston: Beacon Press.

Fraser, Nancy. 1989. *Unruly Practices: Power, Discourse, and Gender in Contemporary Social Theory.* Minneapolis: University of Minnesota Press.

Gans, Herbert J. 1995. *The War Against the Poor: The Underclass and Antipoverty Policy.* New York: Basic Books.

Gittell, Marilyn J. 1998a. "School Reform in New York and Chicago: Revisiting the Ecology of Local Games." In *Strategies for School Equity: Creating Productive Schools in a Just Society,* edited by Marilyn J. Gittell. New Haven, Conn.: Yale University Press.

———. 1998b. "Participation, Social Capital, and Community Change." Paper prepared for the Aspen Institute Roundtable on Comprehensive Community Initiatives, Project on Race and Community Revitalization, November, Wye, Maryland.

Gordon, Diana R. 1994. *The Return of the Dangerous Classes: Drug Prohibition and Policy Politics.* New York: Norton.

Gregory, Steven. 1998. *Black Corona: Race and the Politics of Place in an Urban Community.* Princeton, N.J.: Princeton University Press.

Haymes, Stephan Nathan. 1995. *Race, Culture, and the City: A Pedagogy for Black Urban Struggle.* Albany: State University of New York Press.

Henig, Jeffrey R., Richard C. Hula, Marion Orr, and Desiree Pedescleaux. 1999. *The Color of School Reform: Race, Politics, and the Challenge of Urban Education.* Princeton, N.J.: Princeton University Press.

IUP Cultural Studies Working Group. 1987. "The Concept of Cultural Citizenship." Working Paper 1. Los Angeles: UCLA Chicano Studies Research Center.

Katz, Michael B. 1989. *The Undeserving Poor: From the War on Poverty to the War on Welfare.* New York: Pantheon.

———, ed. 1993. *The Underclass Debate: Views from History.* Princeton, N.J.: Princeton University Press.

Kelley, Robin D. G. 1994. *Race Rebels: Culture, Politics, and the Black Working Class.* New York: Free Press.

———. 1997. *Yo' Mama's Disfunktional!: Fighting the Culture Wars in Urban America.* Boston: Beacon Press.

Lamphere, Louise, ed. 1992. *Structuring Diversity: Ethnographic Perspectives on the New Immigration.* Chicago: University of Chicago Press.

Lave, Jean, and Etienne Wenger. 1991. *Situated Learning: Legitimate Peripheral Participation.* Cambridge: Cambridge University Press.

Massey, Douglas S., and Nancy A. Denton. 1993. *American Apartheid: Segregation and the Making of the Underclass.* Cambridge, Mass.: Harvard University Press.

Moore, Joan, and Raquel Pinderhughes, eds. 1993. *In the Barrios: Latinos and the Underclass Debate.* New York: Russell Sage Foundation.

O'Connor, Alice. 1998. "Historical Perspectives on Race and Community Revitalization." Paper prepared for the Aspen Institute Roundtable on Comprehensive Community Initiatives, Project on Race and Community Revitalization, November, Wye, Maryland.

———. 2001. Poverty Knowledge: Social Science, Social Policy, and the Poor in Twentieth-Century U.S. History. Princeton, N.J.: Princeton University Press.

Ogbu, John. 1986. "The Consequences of the American Caste System." In The School Achievement of Minority Children, edited by Ulric Neisser. Hillsdale, N.J.: Lawrence Erlbaum.

Ong, Aihwa. 1999. "Cultural Citizenship as Subject Making: Immigrants Negotiate Racial and Cultural Boundaries in the United States." In Race, Identity, and Citizenship: A Reader, edited by Rodolfo D. Torres, Louis F. Mirun, and Jonathan Xavier Inda. Oxford: Blackwell.

Orr, Marion. 1998. "The Challenge of School Reform in Baltimore: Race, Jobs, and Politics." In Changing Urban Education, edited by Clarence N. Stone. Lawrence: University of Kansas Press.

Piore, Michael, and Charles Sabel. 1984. The Second Industrial Divide: Possibilities for Prosperity. New York: Basic Books.

Portes, Alejandro. 1998. "Social Capital: Its Origins and Applications in Modern Sociology." Annual Review of Sociology 22(1): 1.

Portes, Alejandro, and Julia Sensenbrenner. 1993. "Embeddedness and Immigration: Notes on the Social Determinants of Economic Action." American Journal of Sociology 98(6): 1320–50.

Putnam, Robert D. 1993. "The Prosperous Community: Social Capital and Public Life." The American Prospect (Spring): 35–42.

———. 1995. "Bowling Alone: America's Declining Social Capital." Journal of Democracy 6(1): 65–78.

Reich, Michael, David M. Gordon, and Richard C. Edwards. 1973. "A Theory of Labor Market Segmentation." American Economic Review 632: 119–55.

Rosaldo, Renato. 1997. "Cultural Citizenship, Inequality, and Multiculturalism." In Latino Cultural Citizenship: Claiming Identity, Space, and Rights, edited by William V. Flores and Rina Benmayor. Boston: Beacon Press.

Rosaldo, Renato, and William V. Flores. 1997. "Identity, Conflict, and Evolving Latino Communities: Cultural Citizenship in San Jose, California." In Latino Cultural Citizenship: Claiming Identity, Space, and Rights, edited by William V. Flores and Rina Benmayor. Boston: Beacon Press.

Schneider, Jo Anne. 1998. "Social Capital and Welfare Reform: Examples from Pennsylvania and Wisconsin." Paper presented at the annual meeting of the American Anthropological Association, Philadelphia (December).

Shirley, Dennis. 1997. Community Organizing for Urban School Reform. Austin: University of Texas Press.

Smith, Michael Peter. 1988. City, State, and Market. Cambridge: Blackwell.

Stack, Carol. 1970. "The Kindred of Viola Jackson: Residence and Family Organization of an Urban Black American Family." In Afro-American Anthropology: Contemporary Perspectives, edited by Norma Whitten Jr. and John Szwed. New York: Free Press.

———. 1974. All Our Kin: Strategies for Survival in a Black Community. New York: Harper and Row.

———. 1996a. Call to Home: African Americans Reclaim the Rural South. New York: Basic Books.

———. 1996b. "Holding Hands: African Americans Reclaim the Rural South." Dissent (Spring): 85–91.

———. 1998. "The Culture and Politics of Shelter." Unpublished manuscript.

Stack, Carol, and Linda Burton. 1993. "Kinscripts." Journal of Comparative Family Studies 24(2): 157–70.

Stanton-Salazar, Ricardo D. 1997. "A Social Capital Framework for Understanding the Socialization of Racial Minority Children and Youths." *Harvard Educational Review* 67(1): 1–39.

Stone, Clarence N., ed. 1998. *Changing Urban Education.* Lawrence: University of Kansas Press.

Storper, Michael, and Richard Walker. 1989. *The Capitalist Imperative: Territory, Technology, and Industrial Growth.* Oxford: Blackwell.

Wacquant, Loic J. D. 1998. "Negative Social Capital: State Breakdown and Social Destitution in America's Urban Core." *Netherlands Journal of the Built Environment* 13(1): 25–40.

Waldinger, Roger. 1995. "The 'Other Side' of Embeddedness: A Case Study of the Interplay of Economy and Ethnicity." *Ethnic and Racial Studies* 18(3): 555–79.

Wenger, Etienne. 1998. *Communities of Practice: Learning, Meaning, and Identity.* Cambridge: Cambridge University Press.

Wilson, William Julius. 1987. *The Truly Disadvantaged: The Inner City, the Underclass, and Public Policy.* Chicago: University of Chicago Press.

———. 1996. *When Work Disappears: The World of the New Urban Poor.* New York: Alfred A. Knopf.

Woolcock, Michael. 1998. "Social Capital and Economic Development: Toward a Theoretical Synthesis and Policy Framework." *Theory and Society* 27: 151–208.

Chapter 3

Social Capital in America's Poor Rural Communities

Cynthia M. Duncan

Rural communities would seem to be the ideal setting in which to see social capital flourishing. Most often we think of a rural community nostalgically as a small, uncomplicated place where everyone knows everyone else, neighbors help one another, and close ties and cooperation are the norm. We envision a kind of classless, family-based social structure with Tocqueville-like civic engagement of essentially equal citizens—farmers, small-business people, skilled tradespeople. But we also know there are chronically poor communities. From photographs, stories, songs, and histories we have images of the other rural America—poor southern sharecroppers, Appalachian coal miners, Native Americans. This chapter examines social capital in that other America, focusing on Appalachia and the Mississippi Delta. I argue that the strong institutions, widespread participation, and cooperation for communitywide benefit that characterize places with effective social capital have long been thwarted in these rural settings by rigid stratification along lines of class and race. The haves distance themselves from the have-nots, blaming them for their own poverty, and live separate lives with their own churches, schools, and other community institutions. Family-level support can assist some have-nots in escaping poverty, but historically these upwardly mobile have chosen "exit" over "voice," to use the phrase of the development economist Albert Hirschman (1972) for out-migration and political activism. The communities do not change.

Fifty-four million Americans live in rural areas, about one-fifth of the total population. In 1900, 60 percent of Americans lived in rural areas. By 1920 the proportion was one-half, and by 1960 it was down to 30 percent. The clear historical trend has been out-migration to greater opportunities in dynamic, diverse metropolitan areas. For many, leaving a rural home meant escaping poverty. Nonetheless, in the early 1960s the majority of America's poor still lived in rural areas, toiling on hardscrabble farms or plantations, in mines or the woods, still untouched by the modernization sweeping urban America (Gilbert and O'Connor 1996; O'Connor 1992; Deavers and Hoppe 1992). In 1967 President Johnson's Commission on Rural Poverty decried the plight of "the people left behind" as postwar America experienced unprecedented prosperity. Mechanization in resource industries like coal mining and cotton forced many people to move to cities seeking jobs, and by the 1970s, as economic restructuring transformed the nation, the demographics of poverty shifted. The majority of poor Americans now lived in cities. In the early 1970s, 9.0 million people lived in poverty in rural areas, compared to 13.7 million in metropolitan areas. By the late 1980s, the number of poor in metropolitan areas had increased to 23.4 million, while the number of rural poor stayed at 9.0 million. Today about one-third of these 9.0 million poor live in persistently poor counties in Appalachia, the Deep South, and the Southwest.[1]

I examine the social structure and political culture in persistently poor communities in Appalachia and the Mississippi Delta—who has power, who participates in community affairs, and how people treat one another. Historical accounts of the 1930s through the 1960s have described the deliberate repression by the elite of both civic participation and social capital in order to maintain control over their labor force and preserve the social system that served their interests. Interviews in the 1990s show that these same communities are still rigidly stratified by class and race, with glaring inequalities. Like the urban poor, the rural poor are isolated and left out of mainstream opportunities. Life is family-based, and resources tend to be distributed through family ties and connections, reinforcing the privileges of the haves and the disadvantages of the have-nots. In poor rural communities, family-level social capital—the encouragement, discipline, emotional support, and financial sacrifice that make up social support—helps those lucky few who can draw on it. But the community-level social capital that should underlie the more "equal opportunity" public institutions and is essential for those whose families lack resources is weak or absent in these divided communities. Fundamental social change in America's poor communities requires a commitment to inclusive community institutions (Orfield 1999; Duncan 1999), which both sustain and are nourished by community-level social capital.

POVERTY AND POWERLESSNESS IN NINETEENTH-CENTURY RURAL AMERICA

Conditions in poor rural communities have their roots in historical social relations and their impact on the distribution of assets. Here I review studies that illustrate these social arrangements in the coalfields of Appalachia and the plantations of the Deep South.[2] Others have argued that similar class and power relations have perpetuated poverty in the mill towns in the Southwest (Maril 1989; Montejano 1979, 1987; Taylor 1930; McWilliams 1968), the Carolinas (Pope 1976 [1942]; Billings 1982, 1988; Mertz 1978), and, to some degree, among Native Americans (Snipp 1989; Sandefur 1989), farmworkers in the Southwest (Bradshaw 1993; Rural Sociological Society Task Force 1993; Taylor et al. 1997), and timber workers in the Northwest (Peluso, Humphrey, and Fortmann 1994). The strategies used by the powerful to control their labor have included deliberate efforts to thwart the acquisition of human capital and prevent the development of social capital.

Appalachia

The original non-native settlers in Appalachia were subsistence farmers and woodsmen who lived off the land in isolated hollows. Their daily lives and social institutions were family-oriented, and they did only a small amount of trading. But by the late 1800s, outside interests from the Northeast had bought and cut vast timberland in the region, and they were soon followed by others prepared to mine the rich coal reserves (Eller 1982). By the early 1900s, railroads reached even the most remote counties. West Virginia and Kentucky historians describe how these business interests seized control of political as well as economic power in the mountains, even in small communities:

> After the turn of the century the level of citizen participation declined, and the average farmer or laborer became isolated from the political process. . . . There emerged in Appalachia a constricted political system based upon an economic hierarchy—those who controlled the jobs also controlled the political system, and those who controlled the political system used their power to exploit the region's natural wealth for their own personal gain. (Eller 1982, 12)

From the beginning coal companies kept a tight rein on their workers, partly by establishing clear differences between management and labor and partly by denying them control over community institutions. The coal-industry analyst Curtis Seltzer (1985, 13) describes communities with no middle class and no public sector, places run by management and operators: "Self-imposed segregation was the norm," he says. "There were those who provided the opportunity to dig through their investment and expertise, and there were those who dug." The historian Ronald Eller (1982, 13) concludes that industrialization "fragmented the social structure, creating a great and growing gulf between the lower class laboring population and those above them." Miners had separate social institutions, and many "simply withdrew from active participation in local and county politics, leaving a truncated political system to be controlled by the managerial elite." Coal operators feared union organizing and labor unrest. According to Seltzer (1985, 13), "Companies frowned on miners establishing their own institutions, be they lodges, churches, or unions. They preferred to envelop miners in a total environment, the better to control their behavior." Operators also prevented miners from owning property because ownership would give them independence.

Thus, miners had no opportunity to participate in civic life or local governance, and worker-run organizations were discouraged. There was virtually no public sector or infrastructure, in part because local organizations were deliberately blocked and in part because the taxes to finance them would have had to come from the coal operators, who had the power to prevent costly public investment. "Public" aspects of community life were controlled by the operators, who seized control of local politics in the early 1900s to ensure order and guarantee that their own interests prevailed:

The abuses of the new order were apparent throughout local government. There had always been a degree of nepotism in mountain politics, but the traditional political culture had rarely been plagued with serious cases of graft or dishonesty. With power concentrated in the hands of the coal barons, however, reports of corruption, intimidation, ballot fraud, vote buying, and other scandals became widespread. (Eller 1982, 14)

Suspicion and distrust were deeply ingrained in communities from the earliest days of coal development. Bituminous coal operators were in bitter competition for distant industrial customers who played companies off one another, and to maintain their own share of that market, operators pressed miners hard. The exploitation and class segregation generated a deep mistrust and antagonism. Even after John L. Lewis, the powerful leader of the United Mine Workers of America (UMWA), crafted a solid contract with George Love of the Bituminous Coal Operators Association (BCOA) in 1950, lack of trust and long-standing habits of violent confrontation still characterized the industry and the region. The UMWA-BCOA agreement raised wages and provided benefits for those who stayed on at the mines, but it also permitted mechanization that led to massive layoffs. Those who stayed behind but did not have union mine jobs were desperately poor.

In this job-scarce environment, control over public employment became even more important as a source of power. School officials had historically been appointed by coal operators as part of their general control over county politics and community life, and from the beginning school personnel were appointed more often for patronage reasons than on the basis of merit. In the 1930s, public jobs and resources were frequently used by politicians to enhance their own political capital. Later, in the 1960s and 1970s, when jobs were declining in the coalfields, patronage politics became entangled with welfare. As one coal miner told the child psychologist Robert Coles (1971, 16–17) in the 1960s, "Welfare is a business here, not the right of a citizen who needs help and is entitled to it. No wonder a lot of our people have contempt for welfare, even if they'll accept the money. They know that the county officials use welfare to stay in power, to buy votes and to punish enemies." A frustrated organizer told Coles that people wanted change, but they justifiably feared repercussions:

They are former miners or people from up a creek who are fed up with things and want to see changes take place. You get talking with them, and they tell you they'll help, and they do. But after a while they find it hard to get other people to go along, because people around here are plain scared; they're afraid they'll be cut off from welfare, or their kids won't be picked up by the bus, or won't get their free lunch, or a hundred other things will happen that the courthouse crowd can do to you. (Coles 1971, 17)

The iron hand of the coal operators first established and then maintained a corrupt civil society in which neither trust nor cooperation was possible. Rather, fear, ruthless competition, and greed were the norms for behavior. As they had in the early farm subsistence economy, people came to rely on their families only. Inequality, exacerbated by racism, had the same effect in the Delta.

The Mississippi Delta

Mississippi's Yazoo Delta was settled in the 1830s by wealthy planters from other areas of the South. The historian James Cobb (1992, 90) describes ambitious planters whose lifestyle "was wholly dependent on their success in retaining and controlling a large supply of black labor," a pattern that continued after the Civil War. Between 1900 and 1930, the opportunities and options available to black workers in the Delta were further eroded by disenfranchisement. Most continued to live as laborers or sharecroppers on plantations where they were subject to economic and social controls. In arrangements virtually identical to those in the coalfields, workers were often required to buy supplies at the plantation commissary, and most needed a cash advance furnished by the planter during the winter months when there was no work. During the 1930s, the psychologist John Dollard (1957 [1937]) and the sociologist Hortense Powdermaker (1939) documented the complete domination maintained by planters over black laborers and sharecroppers, not only in the workplace but also in crucial social institutions. Planters controlled all credit, stores, and housing, just as coal operators did in Appalachia. They also opposed education for black workers because they feared that educated blacks might challenge their hegemony, but they tolerated black churches because they believed churches mostly reinforced, rather than challenged, the status quo.

Resistance among laborers or sharecroppers was blocked by outright intimidation and violence as well as blackballing, feeding distrust and uncertainty among the poor. Cobb (1992) recounts how, in the 1950s, all those who signed a National Association for the Advancement of Colored People (NAACP) petition in favor of school integration lost their jobs. The relentless and devastating punishment that white employers inflicted on blacks who supported civil rights forced the NAACP to be less outspoken in rural areas, and it adopted "a conservative, middle-class orientation" (Cobb 1992, 92).

In the 1960s, mechanization in the cotton fields replaced hand-picking, crop reduction programs of the Department of Agriculture further reduced the need for workers, and minimum-wage laws pushed the planters to introduce greater labor efficiency. As in Appalachia, the 1950s and 1960s were a period of great out-migration, but planters still kept tight control over those laborers who remained. Federal welfare programs were manipulated by the elite, who made federal assistance available to black families when there was no work in the field, and then withdrew it when they needed workers. "Although the cumulative influences of the New Deal and World War II brought dramatic changes to the Delta's economy, the transformation of Delta agriculture left the region's planter-dominated social and political framework fundamentally intact" (Cobb 1992, 92).

More recent work by Stanley Hyland and Michael Timberlake (1993) and Bruce Williams and Bonnie Thornton Dill (1995) describes a region with high poverty rates derived from the underdevelopment characteristic of particular class forma-tions. For example: "A political and economic elite emerged in the South whose interests were vested in maximizing the profitability of export agriculture.... [T]he wealth and power of the planter class relied for many decades on the reproduction of a large, economically weak, and politically compliant class of agricultural work-ers" (Hyland and Timberlake 1993, 79).

The remnants of a "paternalistic society" and the Jim Crow system that had kept poor African Americans dependent combined with "effective elite opposition to industrial development" to prevent upward mobility for the poor and block eco-nomic development in the region. Dill and Williams (1992) describe the conse-quences of this political economy for poor families who struggled to forge daily survival strategies. Unable to find steady work that would provide a working-class income, and living in rural communities with few community institutions, poor, single-parent families combined welfare, work, and support from kin to survive. But these strategies merely maintained the status quo. To achieve mobility, these poor women would have had to migrate outside these Delta communities and leave their families, who had made crucial contributions to their livelihood. With limited education from poor, segregated schools and few connections to people with jobs elsewhere, they would have had difficulty finding and holding a job in an urban area. The social stratification and control by elites had eroded social capital outside the family (Dill and Williams 1992, 104). Identifying the link between this oppression and lack of cooperation, Hyland and Timberlake (1993, 79) conclude that the "paternalism, fatalism, and factionalism—identified as undergirding social interaction and community organizational structures—are largely cultural responses to the divisive social relations that have long characterized the political economy in the region."

These analyses report the same class dynamics found in John Dollard's *Caste and Class in a Southern Town* (1957 [1937]), Paul Mertz's *New Deal Policy and Southern Rural Poverty* (1978), and Sidney Baldwin's *Poverty and Politics* (1968). Powerful landowners deliberately created divided, unequal social systems in which the poor were vulnerable, dependent, and suspicious. As Baldwin (1968, 25) put it:

> Tenant farmers and sharecroppers acted as economic shock absorbers for landowners and planters. Many tenants never made a profit and succeeded only in going deeper and deeper in debt from year to year. Landlords kept the books and managed the sale of crops. Opportunities for exploitation were increased by the high rate of illiteracy among tenants and sharecroppers.

In Appalachia any cooperation among subsistence farmers before coal develop-ment was deliberately destroyed to ensure control over labor, and in the Delta the white elite instilled fear and suspicion in dependent black workers from the begin-ning. The lack of trust and cooperation persists today, rooted in the insecurity and even jealousy that prevail when resources are scarce, and fanned by political cor-ruption and arbitrary power in fundamentally undemocratic communities.

CONTEMPORARY POOR RURAL COMMUNITIES: RELYING ON FAMILY SOCIAL CAPITAL[3]

Old Habits Prevail in Appalachia

Today poor Appalachian coal communities are rigidly stratified into haves and have-nots. The haves live in one world, controlling resources and enjoying a pleasant small-town life, while the have-nots inhabit another, either dependent on public assistance or working in low-wage jobs, subject to arbitrary firing, hostage to patronage politics, and distrustful of those outside their family networks. The poor say that rich people "try to keep you down," but they also often are suspicious of the motives and actions of other poor families as well. Political participation is faction-driven. The fierce competition that characterized coal operations in their early days has a modern face, and family rivalries rather than community responsibility preoccupy the elite. Cooperation among the poor is also rare, as scarce resources and unreliable institutions infuse community life with distrust and people decide it is best to look after their own families.

Life is family-based and church-based, and families and churches are grouped by social class. As one minister in an elite church tells it, "I see people very, very concerned about their own families, and their concern stops there." While most poor families live out in the country, in hills and hollows, the haves live in the county seat and attend the old, established churches and send their children to the city school, where they participate in the parent-teacher organization and school events. The professional- and business-class families who make up the haves are insulated from the poor who make up the majority in their county. "People tend to stay together by church. I don't think there's a whole lot of interaction between the social elite and others," a coal company manager observes.

Family reputation is all-important. A government worker described how it works:

> You can hear somebody's last name, and before you even meet them, you've already got the idea that they're either a good person or they're sorry as can be. Everybody knows everybody's family names. If you're a certain family, then you're this way. But if you're from that family, then you're that way. There are last names that you would just immediately associate with being trouble or lazy—they're immediately in a class.

Employers in the private sector agree, whether they are in the mines, stores, or fast-food restaurants. Even the manager at the Department of Employment says, "Those that have a family with a horrible name, when they come in, we know them, and they're not worth two cents. They're sorry as can be—stealing, selling dope, bootlegging, picked up for driving drunk, in and out of bankruptcy court."

The poor know how they are perceived by the haves. As one teenager from a family with a "bad name" describes the community, "There are the good rich people and the bad poor people, and they are segregated." Family background matters for housing: "Everybody around here knows everybody, and they know what family you come from. Now my family, they've always been a bad family. There are places we can't even rent a house because of our last name. And that's just the way it is. You can't change it." The same holds true for work: "You have to come from the right family around here. You gotta know people. It depends on what your name is. If you got a last name that is a rich name, they'll take you; otherwise, you can't find no work." Family reputation affects access to health care as well: "The hospital staff was snooty until they heard what my parents did for work, and I know it was just because she thought I didn't have any money. I had my hair down and no makeup on." In school, "they make their picks on the people that's got the most money up here. They try to say it's because they achieve more, but it's not. It's because they got more money. The teacher treats them with respect, treats them right, like they're supposed to be treated—like a human being."

For decades the school system has provided a large proportion of the jobs in these Appalachian counties. A community organizer explained:

> Thirty years ago school boards and school superintendents were bought. . . . So the school superintendent pretty well ran everything in these counties, and they were pretty well manipulated by those powers. Nobody would dare do anything that would upset the superintendent. Because if you did, they controlled the jobs—and they knew who your family members were, and everyone would feel it.

Teachers and business owners tell a similar story about the present. "The schools are full of politics, and it's according to who gets the most board members on their side. And of course there's jobs. People get good jobs for payoff when they go along and people get shipped to Timbuktu when they don't cooperate."

Such politics not only affects the poor and the institutions they rely on but it reflects the broader lack of community-level social capital that permeates the region. A business manager who had lived in Georgia for years observes:

> I come here, to a county of thirty-thousand-something people in it, and the county commissioners are some of the best-paid people in the county! And most of your county commissioners are people who come from large families—an average working-type class of people—not that there's anything wrong with them, but they'll go into that county government with no expertise, no sense of how to run a big business. So they sure in hell are not going to know how to run a county. It's like that all over the region. Politics is an end in itself.

He notes that community business leaders "support some guy who has a ninth- or tenth-grade education, but who has got a big family. They support him and get him elected. They're not really part of it. They're just behind the scenes trying to move and manipulate, and they're only doing it for their own benefit."

The powerful families take their power for granted, and those who live and work here fear them. A young miner says he hears that you have to vote "the right way" to get on at the bigger mines—"You gotta be fer who they're fer up there at the big 'uns." A public employee describes her own vulnerability. "You have to be very careful here. You have to be extremely careful. If you're not careful, you'll make enemies, and you don't want to make enemies—especially if you don't have importance. You can make some real bad enemies here, and you'll never get a job."

The effects of corrupt educational and judicial systems are deep and far-reaching. Teachers who are hired because of their political connections are often neither interested nor skilled in teaching. Indeed, the pattern of relying on power and politics rather than merit extends even to how students are evaluated and rewarded: teachers describe pressure from powerfully placed parents to give their children high marks. The disarray of the school system reflects a more general corruption and disorganization in the political system. People insist that votes are still bought: "There's no doubt there is vote buying. . . . It's been like that forever." People say that the corruption extends directly to the legal system: the ways in which the police and the courts handle traffic tickets, driving without a license or tags, drunken driving, drug offenses, child or spouse abuse, or littering depend on your reputation and your clout with the powerful. Even informal organizations like food banks and clothing giveaway programs are suspected of corruption and favoritism.

Those working to improve the community have to overcome more than corrupt county politics, bad schools, and isolation. They must also battle the inept, self-serving management of key community institutions like the schools and hospitals. As one activist put it: "People are selfish. They will not replenish the things that need to be done. Then it deteriorates down the line because you hire people, and they're there only for exactly what that job description says. They aren't accountable. . . . This is one of the things that fragments our community. All these organizations have their own internal politics in addition to the other politics."

Some community leaders, as well as social workers, believe that there must be political change before economic growth can occur, while others believe the reverse is necessary. A state legislator who worked at the state level to bring about school reforms that might begin to break the patronage system was not reelected. Community organizers say that economic diversity is the key to countywide change. Diversification itself is held back not only by isolation and poor transportation but also by the corrupt politics and lack of civic cooperation. Roads might be improved if the county's elite could come together for the common good, but each player wants the new roads to benefit his or her business or constituency, distrusts the other's motives, and is uninterested in compromise. Some say tourism offers a development strategy, perhaps combined with historical exhibits on the coal industry and its dramatic, colorful labor history. But promoting tourism would require cleaning up the litter and the coal camps where so many poor people live— and perhaps reforming the legal system as well. Litter, the law, the welfare system— all are entangled in corrupt factional politics, and until the many residents who are poor and uneducated acquire education and modest jobs, independent of controlling bosses, significant change seems unlikely.

When coal regions in the Appalachian Mountains experienced a boom during the 1980s, some migrants who had left the region in the 1960s for jobs in automobile factories in the industrial Midwest returned to take the new coal-mining jobs. They returned with higher expectations for their communities and their social institutions. They were prepared to hold public officials accountable, ready to run for the school board on a platform of improved education rather than jobs for their family members, ready to support candidates who would advocate a cleaner environment. Their experiences had given them independence from the power brokers in these coal communities, and they were ready for civic engagement. They became engaged in creating community-level social capital that could bring about change and development. But the coal market began to collapse again in the mid-1980s, and many of those with higher expectations and experience of a different civic tradition lost their jobs, having been "the last hired." They moved on, to Georgia or to Florida, where the economy was not collapsing. Old habits, and diminished social capital, prevailed in Appalachia.

Longstanding Racial Distrust in the Mississippi Delta

There are two separate social worlds in poor Delta communities as well, but here divisions are based on race as well as class. The counties I studied are primarily black and have had poverty rates over 40 percent for decades. More than 80 percent of blacks living in these counties are poor today. Fewer than half of the residents have graduated from high school. But there are also very wealthy farmers in these counties, and over the past thirty years farms have become larger and ownership more concentrated. These thousand-acre farms receive very large federal subsidies—as much as $20 million in some recent years, twice the amount of federal grants for the three thousand families on public assistance. There is great wealth for the few, deep poverty for most, and virtually no middle class, white or black. Per capita income for whites is nearly five times that of blacks. This inequality, with its glaring racial dimension, is the dominant factor shaping social capital and determining prospects for mobility and change.

The very wealthy planter elite and the comfortable, upper-middle-class whites who ally with them are the haves for whom the small-town contacts and friendly social life make the place like "paradise," as a local physician likes to describe it. The have-nots, who make up the great majority in each county, are blacks who struggle to provide for their families. Although a few working-poor whites still live here and a small, new black middle class is emerging, the social milieu continues to be defined by the large divide between the whites who have money and power and the very poor blacks who have long been dependent on them. Plantation owners with enormous wealth are still called "bossman" by the blacks who work for them and "farmer" by other whites. As in Appalachia's poor communities, power is concentrated in the hands of a few families who "run things." People say these powerful farmers can get you out of jail if they need you in the fields, have you permanently blackballed from work if you cross them, or make sure you and your family never get credit anywhere if you let them down.

Life is segregated. White families live in town, and their children attend a private academy founded in the mid-1960s when integration looked imminent. The academy absorbs the white community's volunteer resources. The weekly newspaper features a school event organized by the Mothers' Club in nearly every issue: an auction, a bake sale, a fashion show, a carnival. The school also runs an annual tennis tournament, combining fund-raising with socializing. Scholarships are made available through the churches, the Women's Club, and several wealthy farmers, ensuring that even the children of the few white truck drivers and waitresses can attend the academy so that segregation is maintained.

When black sharecroppers lived on the plantations and the bossman furnished everything from housing to medical care, black children attended one-room plantation schoolhouses. Until the 1960s, a complete high school education was available only to the handful of black children selected by their congregation to attend a church-sponsored school. Now education is available to all black children for the full nine-month school year, but the schools themselves are deeply troubled. The few black professionals worry about their children's education, and several families pay tuition so that their children can attend the Catholic school in the next county. Most black students attend the chaotic, troubled public schools outside of town.

A hard-pressed educator laments, "It's a free-for-all. It is unbelievable what those kids are doing—food fights in the cafeteria, holes in the walls, cutting class, laying out on the benches all day long." Some students say they come to school drunk or high, and even twenty-year-olds are punished with wooden paddles and may spend all day in detention rooms. Teachers as well as students report that knife fights are common. Low test scores have kept the public schools on probationary status for years. Some administrators strive to enforce discipline and to improve the schools, but scarce resources, destructive racial politics, and discouraged teachers make these goals hard to achieve.

Everyone describes distrust between blacks and whites. A white principal explains that hiring requires extensive interviewing because he has to be sure white teachers are not prejudiced against blacks and black teachers are not racist toward white teachers. For years white school officials avoided making investments in the black schools and did not apply for public programs available for schools with poor children. Keeping costs down and outside interference to a minimum have been the goals of school administrations and the elected school boards to which they report. "When we tried to get the free breakfast program implemented in the school system, we had opposition from the superintendent, who was white, and even from some of the teachers. It was seen as 'too much trouble,' [as something that] 'wouldn't really help kids.' 'It would be a wasted program.' 'They wouldn't eat their food.' 'It's a giveaway program.' 'We shouldn't be doing that kind of stuff.'"

In recent years more blacks have been elected to replace white school board members and superintendents, but these new officials have not been able to transform decades-old patterns overnight. Change comes slowly. A black activist explains: "Sometimes the elected black is more oppressive than a white can be. I believe it is a phase the community goes through. You elect the most electable person in your county . . . so you can break the barrier, and then the next time around you find someone who will be more representative of our constituents."

Today most blacks live off the plantation in neighborhoods outside the city limits surrounding the enclave where most whites live. There is an unincorporated area just outside of town where the more established black families live. A few well-kept houses with tidy yards are those of schoolteachers and small-store owners who have been able to buy homes here. The majority are clearly substandard, patched over the years with bits of plywood and roofing material, their yards cluttered with discarded chairs or appliances, old cars, and leaning outbuildings. Despite the presumably stabilizing influence of long-term residents and married couples, idle teenagers gather near the small cafés scattered throughout the neighborhood and worry older residents. A twenty-year-old Farmers Home Administration–financed subdivision of modest single-family tract homes for low-income blacks is made up of younger households, many headed by single parents, and young men in gangs are said to control some streets. It is a socially disorganized and even dangerous place to live, much like a tough inner-city neighborhood. Some community leaders work with young people to get them on softball and basketball teams, but the problems dwarf the resources available to meet them. Finally, even today there are some white-owned houses that a plantation owner makes available rent-free to the older black tractor drivers on whom he has come to rely. "The plantation owner built five or six pretty nice little brick houses, bathroom inside, all the conveniences. His guys live in those with their families, and they don't pay any rent. They don't pay any utility bill. So they own you already, okay?"

Socially, the white and black communities are distinct worlds with separate schools, separate churches, separate Christmas parades, separate activities for children. The weekly newspaper increasingly covers news of the black community, in part to sell more papers, but its articles and pictures invariably depict all-white or all-black events. "Everything here is segregated. There is no social interaction between the races, and no trust. Whites say you can't trust blacks, and blacks say the same thing about whites." The only exception to the rule of segregation is when the panel or group is federally funded; then whites, according to one white professional, seek someone "safe" from the black community who won't make too much trouble.

As in other poor rural communities, the haves and have-nots are segregated in social life but deeply intertwined economically. Whites own almost all the property and control all the jobs, but they depend on blacks for labor and often for business. Blacks must seek jobs, credit, and housing from whites, and sometimes from those blacks who act on whites' behalf. Blacks work for white families and farms as domestics, cooks, tractor drivers, and field hands, and for white-run businesses as factory workers, stitching at the apparel plant or cutting off fish heads at the catfish plant. Black workers have no recourse or rights on the plantations, according to both whites and blacks. One white truck driver's wife explains: "If one of the blacks was to piss Jimmy off—you know he drives for a farmer—he could make it hard on him if he said something to his boss. He could make it really hard on the boy, make him get fired. It's just over here the blacks don't have the opportunities that whites does. They're really disgraded."

For years farmers, like coal operators, made sure no new industry came into the area, thus ensuring their monopoly over employment and wages. Many people think they continue to obstruct new industry. Farmers' fears about losing their workforce continue to be well founded, according to black leaders, and they partly manage the problem by deliberately setting up dependency relationships. "Tractor driving is hard work, and it's really only summer work, with long hours then. But, see, the advantage that the white guy has right now is that they may only work five or six months out of the year. So what does a guy with a family do during the winter months? He has to go back and ask his bossman for an advancement or a loan, or whatever, to help him until he starts working again." The furnishing of advances, just like the coal company commissary's extension of credit, helps maintain the old system of dependency. As in Appalachia, local merchants' clientele for furniture and appliances is the poor community. Whites drive to nearby cities to shop, where they can pay less using their cash or credit cards. Blacks often lack transportation and usually need credit, which the local merchants provide after "checking with the bossman" and "getting their mama's okay."

Here too the elites who control economic resources in the county also control the political machinery. Even though blacks make up the majority, whites influence county politics, partly by exerting direct economic pressure or interfering in the process. But black leaders also lament the way dependency is ingrained among people with little education or experience outside the community. The poor vote with plantation owners out of habit and deference. "Uneducated people need to go through someone, they need to get help from Toms, and the whites have gained control of them. Since a lot of the people living here can't read and write, when they have a problem, they depend on those people for direction. The white power structure tells them what to say, and they go out and preach in their area." Whites also recount stories of vote buying, deliberate coercion to affect voting, and even ballot tampering. In the 1970s, whites who tried to help blacks living on the plantation get to the polls were told, "Do not come around our place. We will tend to our own blacks." In the 1990s, blacks and whites agree that control is sustained largely by long-standing habits of deference and fear of crossing whites, especially among older blacks who have always worked for white farmers.

White congregations see their church's responsibility extending only to the border of the white neighborhood. At Christmas and Thanksgiving, these churches traditionally prepare church baskets for "nice white families who are really trying." But even today, the charitable activities sponsored by the churches most often take place outside the county: sending volunteers to repair homes in Mexican villages, sending money to national programs that help foster children or the handicapped. White churches do not run food pantries or sponsor outlets for secondhand clothes in their own county. A lawyer explains that white farmers will sometimes help blacks. "We've had a child or two that's been run over out on the highway, across from the highway, and they wouldn't have anything to bury them with. You could go up to several big farmers, and they would let go of money to bury the child. When I told them, 'This is a worthy cause,' they'd hand over the money. They just wanted somebody to say this is not a hoax, that the money would not be used to buy a gallon of whiskey."

Social problems, especially among young people, plague the poor black community and are the top concern of black leaders. Poor young women often move as teenagers from a crowded plantation shack to a poor neighborhood where welfare dependency is high, more than half of the households are headed by single women, drinking and drugs are common, and stable work is rare. Their personal lives are chaotic, and many cannot trust personal relationships: their boyfriends or the fathers of their children "jump on them." Like their Appalachian counterparts, they stick with family members. When they have no work, they spend their days watching children and soap operas, visiting with a sister, their mama, a boyfriend, or one of their children's fathers. They distrust neighbors who gossip and whites who "try to keep us down." Like the poor in Appalachia, the disadvantaged hear about, and sometimes participate in, corrupt local organizations. Rumors run through the black community about leaders stealing public money that should have gone to the new cooperative community store, and about low-income blacks taking advantage of charitable donation programs. Those in charge of giveaway programs, the gossip goes, save the best clothes for their own families or sell the better food in the neighborhood food pantry to the highest bidder.

Black men have few options for employment because they are not seen as suited for production work in the apparel or catfish factories. "There's a few black males out there, but you have to be very docile, you gotta get stepping." Opportunities for legitimate work always depend on the white bossmen, either directly or indirectly. The pervasive lack of trust in the county extends to employment policies. It seems that getting a job depends on whom you know: "I tried at the factories downtown and all those places, and they weren't hiring. Then about two weeks later, they called my neighbor for the job but they didn't call me. . . . That's the reason I say they got their picks on who they hire here." As in Appalachian communities, blackballing is reportedly common and discourages efforts to speak out. "That's why you have a lot of them that back off, simply because, if you do have a job and you're outspoken, you can be blackballed. That's what happened to me."

Black leaders who work to improve conditions for the black majority have had to battle not only whites' efforts to retain control but also divisions and distrust within the black community. Many say that whites deliberately fan factionalism to prevent coordinated efforts to bring about change. "In this community, the white can put out a rumor to start a rumor, and there it go. Nobody checks on whether it's true." A black schoolteacher notes: "When you have ambition here, the whites are not the only ones who come out and attack you. They use blacks to do so. They get other blacks to come out and do it." The black community is divided, most agree, and old habits persist. "First of all, you go back to the plantation mentality. It's very much in evidence here. A leader, he's got to have some followers to make an impact. So they get to his followers. And it leaves him out there exposed, naked. He's ineffective."

Factionalism spawns suspicion of leaders' motives and undermines efforts to improve institutions in the black community. Distrust and lack of cooperation also spring from envy of those who do better given the uncertain environment where jobs and resources are scarce. Some whites call it "the crab syndrome": the ones below hang on to the legs of the ones scrambling higher. Most blacks see it as the jealousy that is inevitable when there is too little to go around. A black mechanic says: "You might just be a plain old person who gets up and works like hell for what you have, but people will tag you as a 'big shot.' It becomes a problem when people get satisfied with their condition, and resentful of those who are getting up every day working hard." Political distrust and resentment of those who better themselves make it hard to bring about change.

Building Community Social Capital: The Role of the "Good Middle Class"

Contemporary social patterns and norms in persistently poor rural communities are anchored in the way the economy was organized a century ago when powerful coal barons and plantation owners deliberately destroyed trust and participation in civil society to maintain control over their laborers. One day a coal operator set up a company store and required miners to shop there, or a plantation bossman told his workers that their children would continue to pick cotton, and miss school, even after the plantation schools were closed. Maybe during an election the owner of a coal company handpicked the sheriff, who then ran out "unruly" laborers interested in organizing a union. Maybe a sharecropper who questioned the bossman's handling of his account was evicted and blackballed from employment. Over time these decisions, rules, and experiences, which are grounded in the structure of class power and racial oppression and define how people relate to one another, became patterns that people expected, norms governing how things were always done. Distrust and competition rather than trust and cooperation came to dominate social relations.

While the poor are trapped in dead-end, part-time jobs and ignored in disorganized schools, vulnerable to the internal politics and personal whims of managers and school administrators, the haves live comfortably in a "rural suburbia." In the Delta they send their children to the private school; in the Appalachian coalfields the children of the elite attend the independent public school in the county seat. With their neighbors, the haves support school and church programs that benefit their own families. They know one another, look out for each other's children, and devote themselves above all to their own families and churches. In many ways their lives include all the good things we look for in small-town life— familiarity, neighborliness, safety, an unhurried pace. These professionals, small-business owners, government workers, and salespeople who have middle-class incomes or occupations hold themselves apart from the disadvantaged. They consciously put themselves in a group with the very wealthy, whom they emulate and often envy, and distinguish themselves from the poor, whom they deride as lazy and deviant. They do not want their children to associate with poor kids, and they deliberately maintain a two-class system.

When middle-income families ally themselves with the rich and powerful and safeguard their privileges and control, there is no group holding local politicians and private employers accountable for good, fair government and just labor practices. No group is investing time and money to build strong public institutions like schools, recreation facilities and programs, and libraries. Potentially middle-class families look out for their own interests, and they do so through separate institutions and activities. They accept the corruption and patronage, watch out for their own family's well-being, and do not challenge the status quo. Consequently, their alliance with the elite and deliberate segregation affect the whole community. The distrust and greed that people perceive in public and private life prevent cooperation. Participation and open politics are discouraged, sometimes in subtle ways, other times through deliberate punishment of activists and their family members. Investment in public, collective community goods is neglected or consciously eschewed. The poor are scorned and stigmatized, blamed for the failure of the public schools that supposedly serve them, and left vulnerable to the politicians and powerful families who control scarce jobs. They do not have the economic independence and political clout necessary to change the public schools and other public programs that can provide what their families need. When communities are rigidly divided by class, or by race and class, community-level social capital may exist in the haves' world, but not in the community as a whole.

Class and racial divisions, pervasive distrust, and patterns of corruption that destroy social capital emerged from the historical organization of local economies and from relationships evolving over time. In the early days of Appalachia's coal economy and the Delta's plantation economy, operators and bossmen maintained tight control over workers, not just in the workplace but in every dimension of social and political life. Community organizations were discouraged or actively repressed. Company and plantation stores held workers in debt. Education was given little support and meager resources. And corrupt politics, arbitrary law enforcement, and complete control were firmly established. Those who challenged the system were punished. Although these actions not only were illegal but ran counter to the American ideology of democratic rules and equal opportunity for all, no outside force effectively intervened.

The combination of ignorance and fear of repercussions made the poor prey to, and often participants in, a corrupt system. Those who did not accept the status quo found themselves ostracized or openly encouraged to leave, forced to choose "exit" over "voice." Most of those who gained an education had to migrate to find decent work and experience the independence to which they had come to feel entitled. Since those who control the resources in poor communities are well connected to powerful politicians at the state level, they are likely to prevail when changes in the social arrangements are proposed at the local or state level. School administrators in the Delta frequently bypassed opportunities to bring in federal programs to benefit the disadvantaged because they might increase costs or entail federal oversight. In Appalachia, public programs often were commandeered by local politicians and made part of the patronage system because there was little accountability.

What will it take to break this pattern? Can the cycle of poverty in poor rural communities be broken? The premise of much of the social capital literature is that good strong community organizations are the key. It argues that working together in churches or other community-based organizations, people who live in poor communities can begin to change their circumstances. While rural churches in Appalachian and Mississippi Delta communities provide social support, they have rarely had the clout to be vehicles for community change for poor families. There are, of course, examples of regional organizations that make a difference for poor families in these places—for example, the Federation of Southern Cooperatives, Highlander Center in Tennessee, Alabama Arise, and the Rural Community Assistance Programs. There have also been small, heroic, community-based efforts to implement change and improve conditions in both Appalachia and the Delta (Gaventa, Smith, and Willingham 1990; Suitts 1992), but they are fragile, and poverty persists.

Those who study the structural underpinnings of social change consistently find a relationship between greater economic development, equality, and democracy. In a review of development studies, Peter Evans and John Stephens (1988) found that nations where property is predominantly in small landholdings rather than large, concentrated estates are more likely to develop a democratic political system when they industrialize. Where democracy is stronger and there is a large, active middle class, the opportunities and benefits associated with development are more widely distributed. Similarly, studies of the industrial revolution in western Europe by Barrington Moore Jr. (1966) and Daniel Chirot (1986) show that democracy flourished early in places where there was a strong capitalist middle class whose well-educated members protected their own personal liberties and opportunities. These authors also found that societies with a large middle class were more likely to have open political institutions. In contrast, when the middle class was small, as in many peripheral societies with high inequality or, as Chirot points out, in the American South, political and social institutions tended to be closed and exclusive. Participation was limited to those at the top.

In both Appalachian and Delta communities, people say, "Our middle class are those who left." Change occurs only when middle-class men and women do not leave—when they can find work and stay. Such a halt to out-migration occurred in a rural farm area in Appalachia in the 1990s. When a large Toyota plant opened in Lexington, Kentucky, satellite plants providing auto parts opened up in surrounding counties. The rural farm area, a chronically poor county, was adjacent to one of the counties where employment growth occurred. Families who might have moved to an urban area for better jobs could stay and still be economically independent. Their work did not depend on the old elite who historically controlled jobs and politics. Mothers organized a chapter of Mothers Against Drunken Drivers (MADD) to oppose a corrupt judicial system in which drunken drivers were given light sentences because they came from families who delivered votes in the corrupt, patronage-driven system. As in the coal counties during the 1980s, parents ran for school board on platforms of improved education, not jobs for relatives and supporters. School reforms included efforts to develop inclusive curricula in schools long divided by class. The old factions were voted out of office, and new, civic-minded officials were elected. A growing middle class, as the changes in this area of Appalachia illustrate, can build community-level social capital that benefits the whole community and begins to break down stratification.[4]

In recent years, a new configuration of black leadership has emerged in some Delta communities. There has long been an older establishment with long-standing ties to the white community, the "Toms" who are criticized by some for being overly deferential. And for years there has also been an older "radical" group of blacks who challenged white authority during the civil rights movement and have continued raising social justice issues up to the present. These men and women have paid a high personal price for that resistance. But now there is a new group of professionals: some are children of the older establishment and the radicals, others scraped and scrambled their way out of poverty and returned. This new middle class bridges the two long-standing black leadership groups in Delta communities, and like the Appalachian return migrants in the early 1980s and the middle class who stayed in the farm county when the Toyota plant came, it offers a glimmer of hope for renewed social capital and change.

Like their Appalachian counterparts, Delta leaders talk about the need for economic diversity—of employers as well as types of industry: "A political base without an economic base is no good to you. You need to have an economic base in place before you get a political. You got to be able to give the people something to pull them away from the power structure." The odds are formidable. Some have tried to develop community-owned businesses that can hire blacks and be trusted, serving as alternative outlets for food, gasoline, and appliances at fair prices. But those working at a small store constantly battle suspicion and lack of trust from the black community:

> People will say, "Well, I'm not going to shop there. I'm not going to make *them* rich." They think we get the money off of it! They don't realize that we work for nothing. It's just run by volunteers. But you can't get a person to believe that. They think, "They probably get something out of it." But we are trying to show black people that you can do for yourself. They don't understand it, they just don't understand it. They think that everybody's out to benefit themselves, and that's the biggest problem we have here—jealousy.

In addition, the store organizers believe that white merchants prevent regional distributors from selling the new store the large appliances that local blacks buy on credit because then the store would challenge the white merchants' monopoly. The store fights for survival on both fronts, against the suspicions within the black community and against the power the white shopkeepers still hold over all economic activity.

The lack of trust is pervasive and destructive:

> You have fear in a lot of black people. Black people are afraid of white people. The whites control everything—everything that you do, everything that you

try to do. They control the banks, so you can't borrow anything. They control the jobs, control the businesses, everything. A person has to either fall in line or be willing to suffer the consequences of not being allowed to make a living here. So people fall in line.

Black activists say the leadership in the black community is both fearful and grateful in a way that undermines freedom. "I think some of your black leaders feel that they owe an obligation. They're indebted for life. Someone has given him a job where he can make a little more than the rest. He is willing to keep on doing whatever he's been doing, and some more, to keep what he's got."

Activists see this attitude extending to the political realm. "During the last election votes were going for five and six dollars. 'Mr. So-and-So gave me this, and I'm sure going to vote for him.' That's the way it goes." And they see the control of the elites reaching into law enforcement, just as it does in Appalachia. Those working in law enforcement told stories that corroborate this view:

The law is who you know. I could go out there in the street and stagger as though I was drunk or whatever, and a policeman would come by and put me in jail. You have a big-time farmer, he goes for a ride in his truck and runs into somebody and crashes the car and the truck, they'll take him home. It's who you know or who you are, you understand? The county itself has been run based on the little, little bits of fines that black people pay. Very few whites pay fines. I've never seen them paying. White people do not go to jail. Even when they do illegal things, they do not go to jail.

For these black leaders, lack of education and decades of dependency on plantation owners are the fundamental obstacles to change:

It's going to take years to change this. People don't understand that. When you've got people that have been in politics for years and years, you can't just come in and vote them out that easily just by having a black running. I mean, they're ingrained in the community, in the black community. They've got a large share of black people depending on them for housing, for jobs, for Christmas bonus. In other words, they provide things to these black people that they need. Black people figure if you put Mr. So-and-So out of office, you are cutting your own neck off. It's economic power. How can you defeat a guy that has got half of the people working for him or that benefit from him, whether through a job, living in one of his houses, or going through him to get loans? How are you going to defeat him? They feel obligated to him because they've worked for him or he's provided them jobs.

These activists believe that success in building a better community ultimately depends on larger political changes.

It's such a divided community. I mean, there are all the political factors. It was just really the last two elections that blacks have had any part of the government in this county. Before that you knew nothing about what was going on or how they let things go by—what opportunities you could have had, had somebody put forth a little effort. So those have been some of the barriers, or some of the things that probably held this community back for so long. But you know, education is one of them too. For a long time, the farmers just did not want industry in this county because they felt like it would take away all their farmworkers. Which, I'm sure, it would have. And so, they just never encouraged education and never even wanted it.

The Delta in the 1990s is still a world divided by race and class. A few whites are ready to move beyond the old habits and customs of segregation. A few blacks, through determination and often sacrifice on the part of their families, have escaped the poverty to which they were born. But just as in Appalachia, social isolation and corrupt politics perpetuate poverty and hinder efforts to strengthen local institutions and create a community receptive to change and development.

Those who escape poverty have certain resources in common. Their families sacrificed for them, urged them on, and provided stability even when resources were scarce. In addition, they often benefited from public programs and opportunities in distant cities like Chicago; these programs exposed them to a new world, giving them skills, experiences, and habits that shaped later decisions they made about school, work, and family. But those who seek to address the community's poverty point to the need for political change. Politically the black community has been divided into factions, and whites have effectively used the dissension about political goals and strategies to maintain their own control. Steadily employed members of both the establishment and the radical leadership groups are often derided, "labeled as uppity-ups," as they say, by the poor, uneducated majority. Deep-seated distrust and long-standing dependence on white planters have made organizing for social change a formidable task, even in a black-majority county.

Now more and more educated blacks are staying or returning, finding jobs as social welfare workers, health care professionals, and school personnel, as the benefits of the civil rights struggle finally reach even rural Delta counties. Like the return migrants to the coalfields in the 1980s, they have higher expectations of civic institutions and politicians. They are ambitious, conscientious members of the middle class, and their interests as professionals and as parents coincide with what their communities need to fight the isolation and dependency of the chronically poor. The majority come from families that had modest resources in a region where most black families had no resources at all. Their families scraped and saved to make it possible for them to get an education. They benefited from greater opportunities after the civil rights movement and the Economic Opportunity Act in the 1960s. As Carol Stack demonstrates in *Call to Home* (1996), black women and men who have worked outside the rural South can become a potent political force for change. They return home with a different vision of what is possible and with practical experience running the programs they use in their professional and volunteer work.

When social capital is weak at the community level, as it is in these rigidly stratified communities with large numbers of poor who are uneducated, families become even more important as a resource and support group. Family members can be trusted and counted on. In fact, emotional and material support from family members is often what holds people in these poor places or draws them back if they left (Dill and Williams 1992; Duncan 1999). When poor young women are vulnerable to threatening boyfriends or ex-husbands, they call their families, not the police or other authorities. When opportunities arise, as we have seen, they are made available to family members. This reliance on family extends to the challenge of escaping poverty. In Appalachia and the Delta, and in the rural Carolina communities that Stack describes, it is the support and encouragement of a family member, teacher, or coach that most often makes the difference for young people because the mediating institutions that might do so are weak or nonexistent.

Those who escape poverty in these poor places are the ones who complete their education rather than drop out or coast through school, and they learn enough in school to take the next step toward further education and a steady job. Invariably, it was someone in their family—mother, father, aunt, grandfather—or a favorite teacher or coach who pushed them to finish school. Often they also had an opportunity to see a world outside their poor home community that broadened their perspective and gave them a sense of another kind of life and another kind of community. For example, Joanne Martin grew up in extreme poverty in Appalachia in a small farm county, the daughter of illiterate parents in a large family that relied on subsistence farming. Joanne says that a neighbor who was a teacher "helped my mother understand what school was about, and the importance of my going." Once in boarding school, she found that the teachers there planned for her to go on to college. After college, she returned to the mountains to work in health and education programs with her husband, who had also grown up poor and benefited from being pushed by farsighted teachers. Now Joanne tries to encourage young people and prods parents to support them, in both her work and her church.

Marlene Combs, the daughter of an illiterate coal miner and his wife, also grew up poor. Although Marlene's parents had only gone through elementary school themselves, they believed in education and pushed her to finish school. In school she benefited from the guidance and confidence of one of the few nonpolitical principals in the county, and after a few ups and downs in a bad marriage, she became a social worker who encouraged poor young women to go back to school and get their general equivalency degree (GED).

Robert Wilson grew up on an isolated cotton plantation where his mother worked as a maid. As a child, he worked in the fields and attended a plantation school when the children were not needed in the fields. But he was a good ball player, and a coach who saw his potential encouraged him through school and college. Now he is back in his home county, encouraging young students, providing leadership in youth programs, and holding local politicians accountable. Charles Smith's father owned a few acres of land, so Charles worked his own family's cotton first and then helped out white farmers in the area. But his father, who had worked in the North and knew a world outside the county, encouraged him to finish high school and college. He is one of the first blacks in the county to hold office. With Robert Wilson and other black men in the county dedicated to change, he is working to bring more resources into the county to help poor black families—assistance that, as we saw, white leaders have resisted for years.

These stories are representative of dozens I heard in the farm and coal counties of Appalachia and the cotton and casino counties of the Delta. Poor families sacrifice and prod their children to finish school, in school these children benefit from the mentoring of a farsighted teacher, and then the children escape poverty. If they return to work in their home communities, often in health or education, they dedicate themselves to building a community both for their own children and for others. They become the "good" middle class, not selfish and exclusive, but generous and inclusive. Stack found similar stories in the Carolinas. There, women who had left their rural county for northern cities returned with professional skills, a broader view of the possibilities for their communities, and the confidence to work for change. They established a women's service organization and began to challenge the status quo, building social capital at the community level. Their vision of what is possible had been expanded by education and experience outside their rural county, and when they returned home for personal and family reasons, they were drawn into community action.

Each of these success stories came about through family-level social capital. Young men and women were pushed and encouraged by a combination of support, high expectations, and discipline to achieve more. But what they also have in common is a commitment to stay home or return home and build community–level social capital. Joanne has developed a nursing training program. Marlene was a leader in the new JOBS program developed under the Family Support Act; this program helps clients find education and work opportunities rather than just making sure they are still eligible for benefits. Robert and Charles work with about ten other black men in their poor Delta community as part of a men's club to develop recreational opportunities for the young people. These men and women who grew up in poverty benefited from family-level social capital and achieved upward mobility. They returned to their home communities as political activists, working deliberately to build community-level social capital. They are the lucky few, the exception in communities with high dropout rates and bad schools.

The old alliances and factions within the black community are being challenged and reorganized by this newly emerging middle class of schoolteachers and principals, coaches and counselors, nurses and even a black lawyer—men and women coming home again. They are deliberately working to bring about changes, to build social capital, and to expand opportunities. They want a community with good schools and safe neighborhoods where they can raise their own children and grandchildren. They want to build stronger institutions in the black community to battle the drugs, idleness, dependency, and violence they see destroying the young people in their neighborhoods and schools.

These leaders who escaped poverty and are now working to build community-level social capital in their home communities are a new middle class. They acquired their middle-class status through education. Others who have the independence and vision to work for change in these poor rural communities are economically independent, like Charles Smith's father; they may own a small farm, a grocery store, a funeral home business, or even a small church. Some have an extraordinary skill—a renowned carpenter or tractor mechanic, a good mine electrician—that is valued by whites and gives them independence and confidence.

These assets, both financial and human, give potential change agents in poor rural communities the independence they need to work for political change and challenge the status quo. But financial assets for the have-nots are rare, and providing more assets, whether through economic development or redistribution of assets, is an enormous task. When programs have transferred assets to the poor, as in the Farm Security Administration (FSA), economically independent men and women become free to work for change. Steve Suitts (1992) explains that civil rights leaders in Holmes County, Mississippi, were those who owned their own farms and were less vulnerable to economic repercussions from whites. FSA-sponsored cooperatives gave their leaders economic independence to challenge local racism and participate in politics. These are powerful examples. But policies to bring about this fundamental change are hard to implement in the rural South.

Education is always the first step for those who have moved from poverty and disadvantage in the lower class to stability and opportunity in the middle class. Everyone who has "made it" in the poor rural communities I studied had finished school, and everyone who finished school and went to college had left poverty behind. Education is, just as the American dream has always implied, an avenue for upward mobility for individuals. But most schools in America's poor communities do not offer that opportunity. The public schools used by the have-nots in Appalachia and the Delta are chaotic and ineffective because a bad form of local control goes unchallenged. No one holds accountable administrators and teachers who fail to do their jobs, and there is little support for principals and teachers who try to improve the schools. Petty patronage politics dominates decisionmaking, and school jobs are rewards for the loyal lieutenants who form the base of the pyramid of political power in the community. Everyone acknowledges the schools' failure, even the elite and other haves who blame the parents and "elected" school boards for these districts. Of course, everyone agrees that these school board seats can be won only with the acquiescence, if not the active support, of these same elite families.

Education is not only the key to individual mobility in these communities, but the necessary catalyst for political change. Coal operators and plantation bosses deliberately restricted access to education in the late 1800s and early 1900s because they recognized its potentially disruptive impact. Even now some plantation bossmen are said to resist the efforts of literacy workers to reach their employees. Local politicians say their communities need economic independence before there will be political independence and true democracy. They recall the economic sanctions leveled against those who sought change, and they see day to day how economic dependency translates into political dependency. They need a critical mass of people acting independently, and they believe that independence must have its roots in jobs that are not controlled by the elite. They know that in the past those who were educated left. Out-migration has always been, and continues to be, a component of maintaining the status quo. Indeed, the elites promote out-migration when they blackball troublemakers and resist diversification or job growth.

Those who are educated and do stay in or return to their home communities actively participate in political life and community institutions as critical, public-minded citizens. Those who work for change in Appalachia and the Delta, like community leaders across the nation involved in economic development efforts, see that economic diversity is the foundation of a vital and independent middle class. A community with a vibrant middle class is a developed community, as Putnam (1993) found in northern Italy; with a healthy middle class, a community's civic norms include trust and businesspeople can invest and grow their enterprises with confidence.

Although history has shown the accuracy of this analysis, it has also shown how hard it is to create jobs and new development, especially in remote places where workers lack skills and education. Homegrown businesses, while important and good, are fragile, and companies that can be attracted to these communities, even when the elite is open to new jobs, are generally footloose and show little commitment to community development. Thus, poverty and underdevelopment seem intractable, and the status quo firmly entrenched.

Still, people's ability to think and vote more independently holds promise for transforming the current structure. Critical thinking facilitates the ability to find better ways to make a living and create new social institutions. Effective schools, leadership programs, and youth community service programs that take people out of their home community can create these critical thinkers. And these individuals, like the emerging middle class in the Delta, can help to break down the walls that seal off these communities from the rest of the world. With more educated participants, more community groups and organizations would instill new habits of democratic participation, establish new civic norms of engagement, and build social capital.

Creating good schools in these communities that are worlds apart from the mainstream requires local participants and commitment—people who want to see change and will work for it. But these potential reformers are already there, working quietly in some cases, despairing about the prospects for change in others. A national program to create good public schools that are accountable, challenging, and available to all would unleash the energy of existing change agents as well as would-be activists. A vigorous, well-designed national education intervention could change the ways in which schools are run. It could be a vehicle for local community leaders to gain more power and unleash their energy and creativity.

The men and women who escaped poverty themselves are struggling to build social capital in their communities, partly to benefit their own children and partly because they feel a sense of responsibility to the broader community. They clearly benefited greatly from the opportunity to see other programs and other strategies outside their home communities. Similarly, when poor young people are exposed to other milieus through programs that take them to new places, their vision of what is possible for themselves and their communities is expanded. But when poverty is great and education levels are low, we cannot rely on social capital at the community level alone. Local community development efforts must be partnered with national policies that provide accountability and regional efforts that facilitate communication and the exchange of ideas. There are remarkable heroes and heroines in the poor rural communities I have come to know, but they need more than funds to build local programs. They need national commitment to ensure equal opportunity.

The changes needed in persistently poor rural communities are political changes—true democracy, as the regional development expert Amy Glasmeier (1999) puts it. But political change does not have to wait for a revolution or a new social movement on the scale of the civil rights movement. We can give opportunities to expand "bridging social capital" to places that do have community development activists working to build social capital and invest in their communities. But what they need most of all are more people like themselves, men and women who are independent of the powerful elite and prepared to construct community organizations. Investing in good public schools is the best way to meet their long-term needs for more social capital and to have a real impact on these pockets of poverty.

The research reported here was supported by the Ford Foundation. Some material previously appeared in *Rural Sociology* and in Duncan (1999). The editors, reviewers, and Kara Heffernan provided helpful comments.

NOTES

1. Poor counties tend to be small, very rural, and often remote (Cook and Mizer 1994). Over 80 percent are in the South, and over 80 percent of nonmetropolitan counties in Mississippi and Louisiana and 50 to 60 percent of nonmetropolitan counties in Alabama, Georgia, Kentucky, and South Carolina are persistently poor. Mississippi continues to lead the nation in poverty rates, and many of Mississippi's poor live in rural areas. The Southwest also has poor rural communities, primarily among Native Americans and Hispanic groups. Recent work on migrant workers in rural California by the Urban Institute suggests that poverty is being re-created there as Mexican immigrants from poor regions come to work as farm laborers (Taylor, Martin, and Fix 1997).

2. The preceding sections on Appalachia and the Delta draw from Duncan (1996, 1999). Permission to reprint adapted material was granted by the publishers.

3. The quotes in the following pages are pulled from over two hundred in-depth semi-structured interviews conducted by the author and her colleagues in the early 1990s (see Duncan 1999).

4. In rural California, some newly settled Hispanic communities are also experiencing this kind of civic engagement, as local storekeepers and teachers work to make their community better for themselves and for the poor who live there (Juan Palerm, 1999 personal communication).

REFERENCES

Baldwin, Sidney. 1968. *Poverty and Politics: The Rise and Decline of the Farm Security Administration.* Chapel Hill: University of North Carolina Press.

Billings, Dwight B. 1982. "Class Origins of the New South: Planter Persistence and Industry in North Carolina." *American Journal of Sociology* 88(supp.): S52–85.

———. 1988. "The Rural South in Crisis: A Historical Perspective." In *The Rural South in Crisis: Challenges for the Future,* edited by L. J. Beaulieu. Boulder, Colo.: Westview Press.

Bradshaw, Ted K. 1993. "In the Shadow of Urban Growth: Bifurcation in Rural California Communities." In *Forgotten Places: Uneven Development in Rural America,* edited by Thomas A. Lyson and William W. Falk. Lawrence: University of Kansas Press.

Chirot, Daniel. 1986. *Social Change in the Modern Era.* New York: Harcourt Brace Jovanovich.

Cobb, James C. 1992. *The Most Southern Place on Earth: The Mississippi Delta and the Roots of Regional Identity.* New York: Oxford University Press.

Coles, Robert. 1971. *Migrants, Sharecroppers, and Mountaineers.* Boston: Little, Brown.

Cook, Peggy, and Karen L. Mizer. 1994. *The Revised County Typology: An Overview.* Rural Development Research Report 89. Washington: Economic Research Service, U.S. Department of Agriculture.

Deavers, Kenneth, and Robert Hoppe. 1992. "Overview of the Rural Poor in the 1980s." In *Rural Poverty in America,* edited by Cynthia M. Duncan. Westport, Conn.: Auburn House.

Dill, Bonnie Thornton, and Bruce B. Williams. 1992. "Race, Gender, and Poverty in the Rural South: African American Single Mothers." In *Rural Poverty in America,* edited by Cynthia M. Duncan. Westport, Conn.: Auburn House.

Dollard, John. 1957. *Caste and Class in a Southern Town.* New York: Doubleday. Originally published in 1937.

Duncan, Cynthia M. 1996. "Understanding Persistent Poverty: Social Class Context in Rural Communities." *Rural Sociology* 61(1): 103–24.

———. 1999. *Worlds Apart: Why Poverty Persists in Rural America.* New Haven, Conn.: Yale University Press.

Eller, Ronald D. 1982. *Miners, Millhands, and Mountaineers: Industrialization of the Appalachian South 1880–1930.* Knoxville: University of Tennessee Press.

Evans, Peter B., and John D. Stephens. 1988. "Development and the World Economy." In *Handbook of Sociology,* edited by Neil Smelser. Newbury Park, Calif.: Sage.

Gaventa, John, Barbara Ellen Smith, and Alex Willingham. 1990. *Communities in Economic Crisis.* Philadelphia: Temple University Press.

Gilbert, Jess, and Alice O'Connor. 1996. "Leaving the Land Behind: Struggles for Land Reform in U.S. Federal Policy, 1933–1965." Paper 156. Madison: Land Tenure Center, University of Wisconsin.

Glasmeier, Amy. 1999. Online editorial. Available at: *www.psu.edu/ur/oped/glasmeier.html.*

Hirschman, Albert. 1972. *Exit, Voice, and Loyalty: Responses to Decline in Firms, Organizations, and States.* Cambridge, Mass.: Harvard University Press.

Hyland, Stanley, and Michael Timberlake. 1993. "The Mississippi Delta: Change or Continued Trouble?" In *Forgotten Places: Uneven Development in Rural America,* edited by Thomas A. Lyson and William W. Falk. Lawrence: University of Kansas Press.

Maril, Robert Lee. 1989. *Poorest of Americans: The Mexican Americans of the Lower Rio Grande Valley in Texas.* Notre Dame, Ind.: University of Notre Dame Press.

McWilliams, Carey. 1968. *North from Mexico.* New York: Greenwood Press.

Mertz, Paul E. 1978. *New Deal Policy and Southern Rural Poverty.* Baton Rouge: Louisiana State University Press.

Montejano, David. 1979. "Frustrated Apartheid: Race, Repression, and Capitalist Agriculture in South Texas, 1920–1930." In *The World System of Capitalism,* vol. 2, edited by William Goldfrank. Beverly Hills, Calif.: Sage.

————. 1987. *Anglos and Mexicans in the Making of Texas, 1836–1986.* Austin: University of Texas at Austin.

Moore, Barrington, Jr. 1966. *Social Origins of Democracy and Dictatorship.* Boston: Beacon Press.

O'Connor, Alice. 1992. "Modernization and the Rural Poor: Some Lessons from History." In *Rural Poverty in America,* edited by Cynthia M. Duncan. Westport, Conn.: Auburn House.

Orfield, Gary. 1999. [Comment on "Schools and Disadvantaged Communities: The Community Development Challenge."] In *Urban Problems and Community Development,* edited by Ronald F. Ferguson and William T. Dickens. Washington, D.C.: Brookings Institution Press.

Peluso, Nancy Lee, Craig R. Humphrey, and Louise Fortmann. 1994. "The Rock, the Beach, and the Tidal Pool: People and Poverty in Natural Resource–Dependent Areas." *Society and Natural Resources* 7: 23–38.

Pope, Liston. 1976. *Millhands and Preachers: A Study of Gastonia.* New Haven, Conn.: Yale University Press. Originally published in 1942.

Powdermaker, Hortense. 1939. *After Freedom: A Cultural Study in the Deep South.* New York: Atheneum.

Putnam, Robert. 1993. *Making Democracy Work: Civic Traditions in Modern Italy.* Princeton, N.J.: Princeton University Press.

Rural Sociological Society Task Force on Persistent Rural Poverty. 1993. *Persistent Poverty in Rural America.* Boulder, Colo.: Westview Press.

Sandefur, Gary D. 1989. "American Indian Reservations: The First Underclass Areas?" *Focus* 12(1): 37–41.

Seltzer, Curtis. 1985. *Fire in the Hole: Miners and Managers in the American Coal Industry.* Lexington: University of Kentucky Press.

Snipp, C. Matthew. 1989. *American Indians: The First of This Land.* New York: Russell Sage Foundation.

Stack, Carol. 1996. *Call to Home: African Americans Reclaim the South.* New York: Basic Books.

Suitts, Steve. 1992. "Empowerment and Rural Poverty." In *Rural Poverty in America,* edited by Cynthia M. Duncan. Westport, Conn.: Auburn House.

Taylor, J. Edward, Philip Martin, and Michael Fix. 1997. *Poverty Amid Prosperity: Immigration and the Changing Face of Rural California.* Washington, D.C.: Urban Institute.

Taylor, Paul. 1930. *Mexican Labor in the United States.* Berkeley: University of California Press.

Williams, Bruce, and Bonnie Thornton Dill. 1995. "African-Americans in the Rural South: The Persistence of Racism and Poverty." In *The Changing American Countryside: Rural People and Places,* edited by Emery N. Castle. Lawrence: University of Kansas Press.

Part II

Policy Arenas

Chapter 4

Crime and Public Safety: Insights from Community-Level Perspectives on Social Capital

Robert J. Sampson

R esearch has long shown that crimes involving interpersonal violence are more frequent in socially and economically disadvantaged neighborhoods. Drawing on the concept of social capital, recent work has attempted to unpack why this is so and what might be done to improve the level of safety in poor communities. In this chapter, I assess the state of current knowledge on the relevance of social capital to the known facts about crime and public safety, including theoretical formulations on what social capital means at the neighborhood level, criticisms of the concept, and proposed revisions. I then review research attempting to measure key aspects of social capital and related constructs such as informal social control, collective efficacy, institutional support, and intergenerational ties. I pay special attention to the role of local institutions in fostering public safety, especially the integration of formal institutions of social control like the police with informal actions by community residents. Finally, I discuss some promising research and intervention efforts that attempt to put social capital to work in reducing crime and disorder.[1]

FACTS ON CRIME AND PUBLIC SAFETY

The first thing to know about predatory crimes is that they are disproportionately concentrated geographically.[2] Earlier, in the last century, Clifford Shaw and Henry McKay (1969 [1942]) demonstrated that high rates of delinquency persisted in the same areas over many years, regardless of population turnover. More than any other, this finding led them to question highly individualistic explanations of delinquency and to focus on the processes by which criminal patterns of behavior were transmitted across generations in areas of poverty, instability, and weak social controls (see also Bursik 1988). To this day, research has demonstrated that crimes are not randomly distributed in space. Rather, they are disproportionately concentrated in certain neighborhoods and "places" (for example, taverns and parking lots). Ecologically oriented criminologists have dubbed these areas "hot spots" of predatory crime (Sherman, Gartin, and Buerger 1989; Sherman 1995).

It follows that the goal of community-level research is not to explain individual involvement in criminal behavior, but to identify characteristics of neighborhoods and places that lead to high rates of crime.[3] The neighborhood-level perspective that I explicate heeds this goal and in so doing emphasizes rates of crime *events* more than the production of offenders. The "routine activities" perspective in criminology (Cohen and Felson 1979) provides the insight that predatory crime requires the intersection in time and space of three elements—motivated offenders, suitable targets, and the absence of capable guardians to prevent the event. The underappreciated lessons from this perspective are that a motivated offender is not sufficient to produce a crime and that illegal activities feed on the spatial and temporal structure of routine legal activities (transportation, work, shopping, family household configuration). Routine-activities models thus train an analytic eye on the explanation of crime events, assuming a pool of motivated offenders. This approach may seem like a radical departure for those accustomed to thinking about individual offenders, but it makes sense when operating at the level of the community. Indeed, it is logically possible to have no variation across neighborhoods in the prevalence of offenders but a high concentration of the manifestations of their behavior (crime events) in a few neighborhoods (for example, because of low social control or opportunities).

I focus for the rest of this chapter on an *event-based, neighborhood-level* perspective on crime and public safety. I take seriously, in other words, how neighborhoods fare as units of control, guardianship, and socialization over their own public spaces with respect to crime. The unit of analysis becomes the neighborhood, and the phenomenon of interest the crime events within its purview. The policy implication, to be explored later, is that we can have some influence over the incidence of crime without necessarily changing the propensity of offenders (see also Stark 1987). From a sociological view, I would add that we should not be solely concerned with questions about individuals, such as whether it was Sally or Joe who committed a criminal act, but with the distribution of acts. Individuals, we should remind ourselves, are replaceable.

Defining Local Community

It is useful to begin by considering how neighborhoods have been defined for the purposes of empirical research. A traditional and well-worn definition of neighborhood is an ecological subsection of a larger community—a collection of people and institutions occupying a spatially defined area that is conditioned by a set of ecological, cultural, and political forces (Park 1916, 147–54). Robert Park claimed that the neighborhood was the basis of social and political organization, although not in a formal sense. He overstated the cultural and political distinctiveness of residential enclaves, but he recognized that neighborhoods are ecological units nested within successively larger communities (114). There is no one neighborhood, that is, but many neighborhoods that vary in size and complexity depending on the social phenomenon of interest and the ecological structure of the larger community.

For example, most cities contain *local community* or *city planning* areas that have reasonable ecological integrity. Although large, these areas often have well-known names and borders, such as freeways, parks, and major streets. Chicago, the site of much neighborhood research, has seventy-seven local community areas (averaging about forty thousand residents) that were designed to correspond to socially meaningful and natural geographic boundaries. Some boundaries have undergone change over time, but these areas are widely recognized by administrative agencies and local institutions. *Census tracts* refer to smaller and more socially homogeneous areas of roughly three thousand to five thousand residents; their boundaries are also usually drawn to take into account major streets, parks, and other geographical features. A third and even smaller area approximating the layperson's concept of a neighborhood is the *block group*—a set of blocks with approximately one thousand residents. Although each of these ecological units of analysis has been used successfully in empirical research, it remains the case that administratively defined neighborhoods offer imperfect and often artificial boundaries.

NEIGHBORHOOD DIFFERENTIATION AND CRIME RATES

After a hiatus in ecological research during the middle of the twentieth century, the past several decades have witnessed a sharp increase in research on variations in urban crime rates.[4] Although many factors have been studied, the following stand out on theoretical and empirical grounds.

Poverty, Inequality, and Residential Instability

Neighborhood-based studies have always been motivated by the concentration of violent crime in areas characterized by poverty and economic inequality. The majority of studies in recent years have attempted to estimate the explanatory role of economic structure independent of related factors such as population composition. Overall, the results are mixed: some studies show a direct relationship between poverty and violence, whereas others show a weak or insignificant independent relationship (Sampson and Lauritsen 1994). Some evidence also suggests that the effect of poverty is conditional on neighborhood instability. For example, Douglas Smith and Roger Jarjoura (1988) discovered a significant interaction between mobility and low income in explaining violence across fifty-seven neighborhoods in three cities. Mobility was positively associated with violent crime in poorer neighborhoods but not in more affluent areas. They concluded that communities characterized by both rapid population turnover and high levels of poverty have significantly higher violent crime rates than either mobile areas that are more affluent or poor areas that are stable.

Consistent with this finding, one of the fundamental claims made by Shaw and McKay (1969 [1942]) was that population turnover had negative consequences for the social control of delinquency. A high rate of mobility, especially in areas of decreasing population, was inferred to increase institutional disruption and weaken community controls. The research on mobility is not as extensive as that on economic status, but it has been revealing. Richard Block's (1979, 50) study of Chicago revealed large negative correlations between residential stability and the violent crimes of homicide, robbery, and aggravated assault. Nationally representative victimization data also show that residential mobility has significant positive effects on rates of violent crime (Sampson 1985). After adjusting for other neighborhood-level factors, rates of violent victimization for residents of high-mobility neighborhoods are at least double those for residents in low-mobility areas.

Ralph Taylor and Jeanette Covington's (1988) study of poverty, instability, and violent crime (murder and aggravated assault) paints a similar picture. They examined ecological changes in economic status and family status for 277 Baltimore neighborhoods in the period 1970 to 1980. These authors hypothesized that neighborhoods experiencing declines in relative economic status and stability should experience increases in violence (561). In support of this notion, they found that the increasing entrenchment of urban poverty among disadvantaged minority areas was linked to increases in violence. Especially in neighborhood contexts of poverty, then, residential instability appears to have important consequences for violence.

Heterogeneity and Racial Composition

Although race-ethnic heterogeneity has been accorded a central role in ecological theory (see, for example, Kornhauser 1978), rates of interpersonal violence are generally higher in predominantly black and foreign-born areas than in areas of maximum ethnic heterogeneity. For example, Shaw and McKay's early research (1969 [1942], 155) showed that the delinquency rate in areas with over 70 percent black and foreign-born was more than double the rate in more heterogeneous areas (for example, 50 to 59 percent). Later research on violence has thus tended to focus on racial isolation and segregation. A consistent finding has been that the percentage of blacks in a neighborhood is positively correlated with rates of violence. It is questionable, however, whether there is an *independent* relationship of racial composition with rates of violence, especially since in American cities the percentage of blacks in a neighborhood is strongly related ecologically to the concentration of poverty (Wilson 1987; Land, McCall, and Cohen 1990). Several studies find a sharply attenuated effect of racial composition on rates of violence once family structure and socioeconomic factors are accounted for (Sampson and Lauritsen 1994). Others have found that the percentage of black residents is so strongly associated with poverty that it forms part of an ecologically valid dimension of *concentrated disadvantage* (Land et al. 1990). By contrast, the concentration of Latino Americans is separable from a poverty dimension and is positively, although modestly, related to rates of crime and violence (Sampson, Raudenbush, and Earls 1997).

Housing and Population Density

Recent research has highlighted the role that the physical structure and density of housing may play in understanding patterns of violent crime. Dennis Roncek (1981) found that the percentage of units in multi-unit housing structures was a consistent and strong predictor of block-level variations in violent crime in Cleveland and San Diego. Land area in acres, population size, and the percentage of single-individual households also had significant effects on violence, despite age and race composition. As Roncek (1981, 88) summarizes: "The most dangerous city blocks are relatively large in population and area with high concentrations of primary individuals and apartment housing." He argues that as the number of households sharing common living space increases, residents are less able to recognize their neighbors, to be concerned for them, or to engage in guardianship behaviors (88). Relatedly, several studies report a significant association between population concentration (persons per square mile) and violent crime net of social and economic variables.

Family Structure

The community-level association between family structure and rates of crime, largely ignored in the early ecological research on delinquency exemplified by Shaw and McKay (1969 [1942]), has been the subject of many studies of late. A consistent pattern has emerged: there is a large and positive relationship between rates of violence and both the percentage of female-headed families and divorce rates (Land et al. 1990; Sampson and Lauritsen 1994). However, the percentage of female-headed families, like the percentage of black residents, is strongly correlated with poverty and has often been conceptualized as part of an underlying construct of concentrated disadvantage (Sampson et al. 1997).

THEORIES OF COMMUNITY SOCIAL ORGANIZATION

Although the empirical evidence summarized earlier points to a number of neighborhood-level correlates of crime, it does not answer what is potentially the most important question. Namely, *why* does local community structure matter? What are the mechanisms and social processes that help explain why factors such as concentrated poverty, family disruption, residential mobility, and racial segregation lead to higher rates of violence? How do we measure community processes? It is to these questions that students of crime have increasingly turned their attention, especially those working in the classic Chicago-school tradition of social disorganization theory and, relatedly, the more recent but conceptually linked social capital paradigm.

Community social disorganization has been conceptualized as the inability of a community structure to realize the common values of its residents and maintain effective social controls (Kornhauser 1978; Bursik 1988; Sampson and Groves 1989).

Social control refers to the capacity of a social unit to regulate itself according to desired principles—to realize *collective,* as opposed to forced, goals (Janowitz 1975, 82, 87). This conception is similar to Charles Tilly's (1973) definition of collective action—the application of a community's pooled resources to common ends. Common ends include the desire of community residents to live in safe environments free of predatory crime and in neighborhoods characterized by economic sufficiency, efficacious schools, adequate housing, and a healthy environment for children. The capacity to achieve such goals is linked to both informal role relationships established for other purposes and more formal, purposive efforts to achieve social regulation through institutional means (Kornhauser 1978).

Contrary to what is sometimes inferred, a social-control framework does not require population or cultural homogeneity. Diverse populations can agree on common goals, such as safety for children. Yet social conflicts can and do rend communities along the lines of economic resources, race, political empowerment, and the manner in which criminal justice agents control crime. It is around the distribution of resources and power, in other words, that conflict usually emerges, not the content of core values (Kornhauser 1978). According to Philip Selznick (1992, 369), the goal of community is therefore the reconciliation of partial with general perspectives on the common good. This conception of social control allows the analyst to problematize the internal homogeneity of a community and yet still focus on the variable forms of social organization, both formal and informal. Moreover, I focus on variations in social organization across ecological units of analysis rather than elevating solidarity or identity to the major definitional criteria. Like Tilly (1973, 212), that is, I "choose to make territoriality define communities and to leave the extent of solidarity problematic." In this framework, dimensions of local social organization are analytically separable not only from sources of variation (for example, racial segregation, concentrated poverty, instability) but also from possible social outcomes.

Networks, Social Capital, and Collective Efficacy

The social-control approach to community is related to what John Kasarda and Morris Janowitz (1974, 329) call the "systemic" model—a view of the local community as a complex system of friendship and kinship networks and formal and informal associational ties rooted in family life, ongoing socialization processes, and local institutions. The systemic dimensions of community social organization include the prevalence, interdependence, and overlapping nature of social networks (for example, the density of acquaintanceship; intergenerational ties; network overlap), local participation in formal and voluntary organizations, and the span of collective attention that the community directs toward local problems (Sampson and Groves 1989).

The systemic model of social control is compatible with recent formulations of social capital.[5] As elaborated in this volume, social capital is defined largely by its functions—it is created when the structure of relations among persons facilitates action, "making possible the achievements of certain ends that in its absence would not be possible" (Coleman 1988, 98). By contrast, physical capital is embodied in observable material form, and human capital is embodied in the skills and knowledge acquired by an individual. Social capital is less tangible, for it is a social good embodied in the relations between persons and positions (Coleman 1990, 304). Robert Putnam (1993, 36) defines social capital even more broadly as "features of social organization, such as networks, norms, and trust, that facilitate coordination and cooperation for mutual benefit." Whatever the specific formulation, social capital is not an attribute of individuals but rather a property of the structure of social organization (Coleman 1990; Bourdieu 1986).

The connection of social disorganization and control theory with social capital is thus clear: local communities high in social capital are better able to realize common values and maintain the social controls that foster public safety. For example, neighborhoods characterized by an extensive set of interlocking social networks and voluntary associations are facilitated in the informal social control of public spaces. The fact that juveniles commit much crime means that intergenerational networks are critical. When parents know the parents of their children's friends, they can observe the child's actions in different circumstances, talk to each other about the child, compare notes, and establish norms (Coleman 1988). Such intergenerational closure of local networks provides the parents and children with social capital of a collective nature. One can extend this model to closure among social networks involving parents and teachers, religious and recreational leaders, businesses that serve youth, and perhaps even juvenile court personnel (Sampson et al. 1999; Sampson 1999).

Social networks and closure are not sufficient, however, to understand local communities. Networks are differentially invoked, and dense, tight-knit networks may impede social organization if they are isolated or weakly linked to collective expectations for action. At the neighborhood level, the willingness of local residents to intervene on behalf of public safety depends in large part on conditions of mutual trust and shared expectations among residents. In particular, one is unlikely to intervene in a neighborhood context where the rules are unclear and people mistrust or fear one another. It is the linkage of mutual trust and the shared willingness to intervene for the common good that defines the neighborhood context of what my colleagues and I have termed *collective efficacy* (Sampson et al. 1997). Just as individuals vary in their capacity for efficacious action, so too do neighborhoods vary in their capacity to achieve common goals. Moreover, just as self-efficacy is situated rather than global (one has self-efficacy relative to a particular task or type of task), neighborhood efficacy exists relative to collective tasks such as maintaining public order.

I thus view social capital as referring to the resources or potential inherent in social networks, whereas collective efficacy is a task-specific construct that refers to shared expectations and mutual engagement by residents in local social control (Sampson et al. 1999). Moving away from a focus on private ties, the term *collective efficacy* is meant to signify an emphasis on shared beliefs in a neighborhood's conjoint capability for action to achieve an intended effect, and hence an active sense of engagement on the part of residents. As Albert Bandura (1997) argues, the meaning of efficacy is captured in expectations about the exercise of control that elevate the "agentic" aspect of social life over a perspective centered on the accumulation of "stocks" of social resources. This conception of collective efficacy is consistent with the redefinition of social capital by Alejandro Portes and Julia Sensenbrenner (1993, 1323) in terms of "expectations for action within a collectivity."

Institutions and Public Control

A systemic-based model of social capital and collective efficacy should not ignore institutions, nor should it overlook the wider political environment in which local communities are embedded. Many a community exhibits intense private ties (for example, among friends and kin) and yet still lacks the institutional capacity to achieve social control (Hunter 1985). The institutional component of social capital is the resource stock of neighborhood organizations and their linkages with other organizations, both within and outside the community. Ruth Kornhauser (1978, 79) argues that when the horizontal links between institutions within a community are weak, the capacity to defend local interests is weakened.

Vertical integration is potentially more important. Robert Bursik and Harold Grasmick (1993) highlight the importance of *public* control, defined as the capacity of local community organizations to obtain extralocal resources (such as police and fire services, or block grants) that help sustain neighborhood social stability and local controls. Albert Hunter (1985) identifies the dilemma of public control in a civil society. The problem is that public control is provided mainly by institutions of the state, and we have seen a secular decline in public (citizenship) obligations in society accompanied by an increase in civil (individual) rights. This imbalance of collective obligations and individual rights undermines social control and, by implication, social capital. According to Hunter, local communities must thus work together with forces of public control to achieve social order, principally through an interdependence between private (family), parochial (neighborhood), and public (state) institutions such as the police and schools.

Metropolitan-Wide and Spatial Inequality

Research on the political economy of American cities has shown that structural differentiation—related to vertical integration—is shaped, both directly and indirectly, by the extralocal decisions of public officials and businesses. For example, the decline and destabilization of many central-city neighborhoods have been facilitated not only by individual preferences, as manifested in voluntary migration patterns, but by government decisions on public housing that concentrate the poor, incentives for suburban sprawl in the form of tax breaks for developers and private mortgage assistance, highway construction, economic disinvestment in central cities, and haphazard zoning on land use (Logan and Molotch 1987; Massey and Denton 1993).

The embeddedness of neighborhoods within the larger system of citywide spatial dynamics is equally relevant (Sampson et al. 1999). Recent research on population change shows that population abandonment is driven as much by spatial diffusion processes (for example, changes in proximity to violent crime) as by the internal characteristics of neighborhoods (Morenoff and Sampson 1997). In particular, housing decisions are often made by assessing the quality of neighborhoods relative to what is happening in surrounding areas. Parents with young children appear quite sensitive to the relative location of neighborhoods and schools in addition to their internal characteristics. Spatial diffusion processes for dimensions of social capital are even more likely, mainly because social networks and exchange processes unfold across the artificial boundaries of analytically defined neighborhoods. A neighborhood-level perspective on crime cannot afford to ignore the relative geographic position of neighborhoods and how that bears on internal dimensions of social capital. The importance of spatial externalities is shown by the finding that ecological proximity to areas high in collective efficacy bestows an advantage above and beyond the structural characteristics of a given neighborhood (Sampson et al. 1999).

ASSESSING SOCIAL CAPITAL AND COLLECTIVE EFFICACY

A new generation of research has emerged in the last fifteen years that attempts to examine the community-level dimensions of social capital and collective efficacy just noted. I provide a brief review of studies that have focused on crime and public safety, especially those that have tried to connect aspects of neighborhood social capital to structural characteristics.

Ralph Taylor, Stephen Gottfredson, and Sidney Brower (1984) studied variations in violent crime (mugging, assault, murder, rape) across 63 street blocks in Baltimore. Using interviews with 687 household respondents, they constructed block-level measures of the proportion of respondents who belonged to an organization to which coresidents also belonged, and the proportion of respondents who felt responsible for what happened in the area surrounding their home (1984, 316). Both measures were significantly and negatively related to rates of violence, exclusive of other ecological factors (320). These results support the hypothesis, consistent with social capital theory, that organizational participation and informal social control of public space depress the incidence of violent events in urban areas. A similar pattern emerged in Ora Simcha-Fagan and Joseph Schwartz's (1986, 683) survey-based study of 553 residents of 12 neighborhoods in New York City during the mid-1980s. Although the number of neighborhoods was small, they found a significant negative relationship between the rate of self-reported delinquency and rates of organizational participation by local residents.

Drawing on data collected in Great Britain in 1982 and 1984, my colleague Byron Groves and I (Sampson and Groves 1989, 789) showed that the prevalence of unsupervised teenage peer groups in a community had large effects on rates of robbery and violence by strangers. The density of local friendship networks had a significant negative association with robbery rates, while the level of organizational participation by residents was linked to significantly lower rates of robbery and stranger violence. Central to present concerns, variations in community social organization were shown to mediate in large part the effects of community socioeconomic status, residential mobility, ethnic heterogeneity, and family disruption. Namely, mobility had significant inverse effects on friendship networks, family disruption was the largest predictor of unsupervised peer groups, and socioeconomic status had a positive effect on organizational participation.

In a more recent study from the United States, Delbert Elliott and his colleagues (1996) examined survey data from neighborhoods in Chicago and Denver. A multi-level analysis revealed that a measure of "informal control" was significantly and negatively related to adolescent problem behavior in both sites. As with the British results, informal control in neighborhoods in these two cities mediated the prior effects of neighborhood structural disadvantage: declining poor neighborhoods displayed less ability to maintain social control, and they in turn suffered higher delinquency rates.

A research program in Chicago (Project on Human Development in Chicago Neighborhoods) has as its primary objective the study of criminal behavior in local community context. A major component of this study was a community survey of 8,782 residents of 343 Chicago neighborhoods in 1995. My colleagues and I (Sampson et al. 1997) developed a two-part scale from this survey to examine rates of violence. One component was shared expectations about "informal social control," repre-sented by a five-item Likert-type scale. Residents were asked about the likelihood ("Would you say it is very likely, likely, neither likely nor unlikely, unlikely, or very unlikely?") that their neighbors could be counted on to take action if: (1) children were skipping school and hanging out on a street corner, (2) children were spray-painting graffiti on a local building, (3) children were showing disrespect to an adult, (4) a fight broke out in front of their house, and (5) the fire station closest to home was threatened with budget cuts. The second component was "social cohesion," mea-sured by asking respondents how strongly they agreed (on a five-point scale) that "People around here are willing to help their neighbors"; "This is a close-knit neigh-borhood"; "People in this neighborhood can be trusted"; and (reverse coded) "People in this neighborhood generally don't get along with each other"; and "People in this neighborhood do not share the same values." Social cohesion and informal social control were closely associated across neighborhoods ($r = .80$), suggesting that the two measures were tapping aspects of the same latent construct. We combined the two scales into a summary measure of "collective efficacy" with very good aggregate-level reliability (.85).

Using this measure, we found that collective efficacy had a strong negative rela-tionship with the rate of violence in the neighborhood, controlling for concentrated disadvantage, residential stability, immigrant concentration, and a set of individual-level characteristics (age, sex, socioeconomic status, race-ethnicity, homeowner-ship). The results showed that, whether measured by official homicide events or violent victimization as reported by residents, neighborhoods high in collective efficacy had significantly lower rates of violence. This finding held up even when controlling for prior levels of neighborhood violence that may have depressed later collective efficacy (for example, because of fear). In this model, a two-standard-deviation elevation in collective efficacy was associated with a 26 percent reduction in the expected homicide rate (Sampson et al. 1997, 922). Concentrated disadvantage and residential stability were also strongly related to collective efficacy in theoretically expected directions (t-ratios = −10.74 and 5.61, respectively), and the association of disadvantage and stability with rates of violence was significantly reduced when collective efficacy was controlled. Because of the cross-sectional nature of the study and the possibility of reciprocity (for example, crime may reduce collective efficacy), causal effects could not be determined. Nonetheless, the patterns are consistent with the inference that neighborhood structural characteristics influence violence *in part* through the social mechanism of collective efficacy.

Although there are serious methodological limitations to neighborhood-level studies (see Sampson and Lauritsen 1994, 75–85), their cumulative results support the notion that neighborhoods characterized by mistrust and perceived lack of shared expectations, sparse acquaintanceship and exchange networks among residents, attenuated social control of public spaces, a weak organizational and institutional base, and low participation in local voluntary associations are associated with an increased risk of interpersonal crime and public disorder within their borders. Moreover, the data are consistent in suggesting that these dimensions of community social organization and collective action are systematically influenced (although not determined) by neighborhood structural differentiation. In particular, social capital and collective efficacy appear to be undermined by the concentration of disadvantage, racial segregation, family disruption, residential instability, and dense population concentration.[6]

EFFECTS OF CRIME AND CRIME CONTROL ON SOCIAL CAPITAL

It is important to recognize that crime and its consequences—such as fear or reactionary crime control measures—may themselves have important reciprocal effects on communities. Wesley Skogan (1990) has provided an insightful overview of some of these "feedback" processes, including: physical and psychological withdrawal from community life; a weakening of the informal social control processes that inhibit crime; a decline in the organizational life and mobilization capacity of the neighborhood; deteriorating business conditions; and changes in the composition of the population. For example, if people shun their neighbors and local facilities out of fear of crime, local networks and organizations have fewer opportunities to take hold. Street crime may also be accompanied by residential out-migration and business relocation from inner-city areas. In these ways, predatory crime can lead to demographic "collapse" and a weakening of the informal control structures and mobilization capacity of communities, in turn fueling further crime and mistrust. The rapid increase in crime rates in the United States starting in the mid-1960s may therefore be one of the missed "suspects" in the concomitant decline of social capital (Sampson 1999).

Although the number of empirical studies is relatively small, there is evidence that crime generates fear of strangers and a general alienation from participation in community life (Skogan 1986, 1990; Rosenbaum et al. 1998). High crime rates and concerns about safety have also been linked to population out-migration. For example, Robert Bursik (1986, 73) found that delinquency rates are not only one of the outcomes of urban change but an important part of the *process* of urban change. Studying

Chicago neighborhoods, he observed that "although changes in racial composition cause increases in the delinquency rate, this effect is not nearly as great as the effect that increases in the delinquency rate have in minority groups being stranded in the community." In a study of forty neighborhoods in eight cities, Wesley Skogan (1990) found that high rates of crime and disorder were associated with higher rates of fear, neighborhood dissatisfaction, and intentions to move out. Because of its connection to the perceived inhabitability and incivility of urban neighborhoods, predatory crime thus bears rather directly on our understanding of social capital.

Is Crime Control *Social* Control?

I would be remiss not to underscore as well the unintended and possibly negative consequences of some crime control efforts with respect to the destruction of social capital in urban communities. Incarceration presents a particularly vexing dilemma. Although dangerous and violent offenders surely need to be removed from the community, the widespread increase (roughly a doubling) in the incarceration rate for nonviolent crimes in recent decades may turn out to be counterproductive over the long run. Prison admissions data also indicate that African American males have borne the brunt of increased incarceration, especially for drug crimes (see Tonry 1995; Sampson and Lauritsen 1997).

The removal of young males from vulnerable communities serves to undermine key aspects of local social capital. Elsewhere (Sampson 1995) I have gone so far as to argue that incarceration may *increase* violence through a negative feedback loop: the removal of young males decreases the sex ratio (males per female), and that decrease in turn indirectly increases violence through its effect on family disruption. As Dina Rose and Todd Clear (1998, 450–51) note, every person entering a prison is exiting a neighborhood. This removal may achieve a safety objective, but in the case of nonviolent prisoners (usually drug offenders), removal is not solely a positive act because it imposes losses on family and community networks. Contrary to what we often hear, most offenders have legal employment, and many are involved in the support of children and families. A record of imprisonment also has negative consequences for a released offender's employment prospects, and that negative impact, again, may indirectly serve to increase future crime. The available evidence estimates the costs of imprisonment in terms of earnings potential and employability to be quite large, even after controlling for individual characteristics (Freeman 1991; Western and Beckett 1999).

I am not suggesting that incarceration is always unnecessary, undeserved, and ineffective as a form of crime control, and I recognize full well that the romanticization of the criminal has led to serious intellectual errors among sociologists. I am simply arguing that we need to give equal consideration to the potential negative consequences of our current addiction to incarceration for employment, family structure, and ultimately the reserve of human and social capital in local communities. After all, most offenders will be released from prison (Rose and Clear 1998). Their stigmatization and marginalization from the very segments of society that sustain desistance from crime (such as the family and the labor market) are ignored at society's peril.

Perhaps the risk of undermining social capital through crime control is more apparent and immediate when we examine the police. Heavy-handed attempts by police to reduce crime (for example, through "zero tolerance," or aggressive search and frisk for weapons even in the absence of probable cause) may breed cynicism and alienation among local residents toward the idea of private-public cooperation. To the extent that trust in the police is undermined by the excessive use of force and a siegelike mentality, the ability of the police to work with the local community is undermined. For example, there is anecdotal evidence that a strict police crackdown on minor offenses and the apparently unjustified shooting of an unarmed (minority) civilian in New York City may have seriously jeopardized the ability of the police to work as an equal partner with many minority neighborhoods (Wilgoren and Thompson 1999). It is also reported that among marginalized groups in European cities, fear and alienation from police authority undermine the ability of the community to aid in its own protection through mutual cooperation (Body-Gendrot 1998).

The perceived legitimacy of law enforcement is thus crucial, for what citizens appear to want is not fewer police, *but police of a different kind.* The evidence has long shown that more than nine in ten police-citizen encounters derive from citizen calls (Reiss 1970). This is a fact with deep implications, for it exposes the myth of the police as proactive crime control agents. Moreover, it exposes the fact that citizens are behind the demand for police services, especially in low-income, minority neighborhoods where crime rates are high (Skogan and Hartnett 1997, 117). Yet residents of the inner city do not want racist police, or a hierarchical form of policing from the top down that treats residents merely as passive recipients of a "crackdown." The insight of social capital theory for crime control policy, to which I now turn, points to the need to proffer innovative strategies that increase true partnerships between the police and the public.

THEORETICALLY GROUNDED POLICY: CHANGING PLACES, NOT PEOPLE

The general implication of my analysis is that there is an important role for policy in trying to change the dynamics of places rather than people. By focusing on everyday events grounded in the ecological spaces of our local communities, I believe that a social capital perspective offers plausible and realistic insights. Perhaps the most important goal is bringing together resident-based informal social control, local institutions, and extralocal (public) control as equal partners, while at the same time ameliorating the constraints imposed by structural differentiation in the form of resource inequality, racial segregation, concentrated poverty, and residential instability (Sampson 1999). Because other chapters in this volume are focusing on ways to harness social capital to address the "structural inequality" part of the story (for example, through housing authorities, community development corporations

[CDCs], public health organizations, or organized labor), I limit my attention to policy-related ideas that are tied directly to crime and public safety and that do not rely excessively on formal mechanisms of control (such as incarceration and arrest) that may erode social capital.

It is important to begin, however, on a note of caution. The evidence shows that community-level interventions are notably hard to implement and have achieved only limited success in the areas that need them the most—poor, unstable neighborhoods with high crime rates (Hope 1995; Skogan and Hartnett 1997). "One-shot" or short-run interventions that try to change isolated or specific behaviors without confronting their common antecedents are highly susceptible to failure. Moreover, I have argued elsewhere (Sampson 1999) that community-level interventions to increase neighborhood "self-help" and local voluntarism have succumbed to the lack of organization they seek to supplant. The paradox is that self-help strategies for "community" give priority to the very activities made difficult by the social isolation of residents in unstable and economically vulnerable neighborhoods (Hope 1995, 24, 51). Thus, neglecting the vertical connections (or lack thereof) that residents have to extracommunal resources and sources of power obscures the structural backdrop to community social organization. The importance of institution-based approaches to social capital articulated by other authors in this volume should be seen as complementary rather than in opposition to the approaches explicated here.

Even if we fully account for the wider structural context within which local communities are embedded, neighborhood interventions will fail unless they pull the appropriate internal levers of change. Seeking to penetrate the private world of personal relations and re-create a mythical past when everyone knew their neighbors is a recipe for failure (Sampson 1999). In fact, community interventions seem to fail the worst when the major thrust is to change individual behaviors by promoting friendships among neighbors (Hope 1995). To focus on resurrecting local friendships reflects nostalgia for a village life that is long gone from most cities (Skogan 1990, 156). For better or worse, in many neighborhoods, neighbors are acquaintances or strangers rather than friends, living out what M. P. Baumgartner (1988) calls "moral minimalism." Where local friendship ties are strong, they result not from government intervention but from natural processes induced over time by factors such as residential stability and the density of families with children (Sampson et al. 1999). The policy framework I propose recognizes the transformed landscape of modern urban life, holding that while social capital may depend on a working trust, it does not require that my neighbor or the local beat cop be my friend.

Identify Neighborhood "Hot Spots" for Crime

A beginning area of promise is simple yet powerful. Drawing on community theory and advances in computer mapping technology, safety-enhancing strategies can be more effective if they are implemented using information on ecological hot spots (see also Reiss and Roth 1993, 17). In Chicago, for example, Carolyn Block (1991) has pioneered the use of what is termed an "early warning system" for gang homicides.

By plotting each homicide incident and using sophisticated mapping and statistical clustering procedures, the early warning system allows police to identify potential neighborhood crisis areas at high risk for suffering a "spurt" of gang violence. With rapid dissemination of information, police can intervene in hot spots to quell emerging trouble. Hot spots may also be modified or put under periodic surveillance to reduce the opportunities for crime to occur. Lawrence Sherman and his colleagues (Sherman et al. 1989, 48) have reviewed "hot spot" neighborhood interventions such as differential patrol allocations by place, selective revocation of bar licenses, and swift removal of vacant crack houses. The idea of hot spots suggests a neighborhood-level response that in the end may be much more effective than policies that simply target individuals or even families. By responding proactively to neighborhoods and places that disproportionately generate crimes, policing strategies can more efficiently stave off "epidemics" of crime and their spatial diffusion.

I would argue here, however, for a bolder and more comprehensive strategy. To date, information technologies have been used as tools mainly and perhaps only for the "experts"—namely, the police. True to the notion that social capital is fundamentally a leveling process that entails civic participation, I do not believe such information should be made available to the police alone. With the rapid spread of technology, crime data and even the mapping of hot spots could, in principle, be made available to local residents and community-based organizations. If residents knew when and where incidents were occurring, in more or less real time, I predict that they would mobilize to prevent further incidents in innovative and effective ways that go well beyond police power. Moreover, one lesson we have gained from the research is that residents consistently overestimate the incidence of crime and their chances of victimization. Even in a high-crime area, most of the area is safe most of the time (Sherman et al. 1989). As Shaw and McKay (1969 [1942], 180) long ago argued, "The dominant tradition in every community is conventional, even in those having the highest rate of delinquents." Knowledge about the realities of crime's distribution and frequency might be alarming to residents at first. But ultimately such knowledge could be empowering: by signifying to residents that they far outnumber perpetrators, the crime numbers could enhance local collective efficacy in responding proactively.

Reduction of Social Disorder

A concern with crime and public safety should focus not just on serious crimes but also on the visible symbols of disorder that generate fear among residents (Skogan 1990). To foster a climate of safety, public order, and social organization, we should consider a number of collective strategies: cleaning up physical incivilities such as litter, vandalized cars, broken windows, and drug needles; removing or rehabilitating abandoned housing; "picketing" or protesting unwanted public drinking, drug use, and prostitution; promoting neighborhood-generated referenda on bar licensing and other zoning issues; and creating "graffiti patrols" and "phone trees" whereby residents keep a log of new incidents of disorder and promptly report them to city authorities (see Carr 1998).

There is limited evidence on the effectiveness of these strategies, although neighborhood-based interventions that target physical signs of decay (abandoned buildings, graffiti) have been found to increase perceptions of safety and public order (Hope 1995, 59). The available evidence also suggests that neighborhood watch programs targeted specifically to crime are largely ineffective (Rosenbaum et al. 1998), and thus a broader focus on informal social control and public order seems warranted.

Changing Routine Activities

A concern with ecology and place suggests another frequently overlooked mechanism in discussions of neighborhood effects—how land-use patterns and the ecological distributions of daily routine activities bear on crime (Sampson, 2001). For example, the location of schools, the mix of residential with commercial land use (strip malls, bars), public transportation nodes, and large flows of nighttime visitors are land use patterns that organize how and when local youth come into contact with their peers, with adults, and with nonresident activity. As noted earlier, the routine-activities perspective (Cohen and Felson 1979; Felson 1987) assumes a steady supply of motivated offenders and focuses instead on how targets of opportunity and sanctioning mechanisms combine to explain criminal events. This strategy has appeal in crime control, for it does not force on the local community the burden (and misplaced hope) of changing offenders. Rather, it provides insights into how to organize activity patterns to reduce the probability of crime events.

For example, not only do mixed-land-use neighborhoods offer greater opportunities for expropriative crime, they offer increased opportunity for children to congregate outside their homes in places conducive to peer-group influence (Stark 1987). Seemingly prosaic, an intriguing finding from criminology is that the incidence of delinquency is predictable from proximity to a McDonald's restaurant (Brantingham and Brantingham 1984). Big Macs are not the problem, of course; the unsupervised activity space and peer contagion is (Sampson, 2001). Because illegal and deviant activities feed on the spatial and temporal structure of such routine legal activities (transportation, work, entertainment, and shopping), the ecological distribution of situations and opportunities conducive to crime offers a strategic site for intervention. In particular, neighborhood strategies to monitor the ecological placements of bars, liquor stores, strip-mall shopping outlets, subway stops, and unsupervised play spaces promise to play an important role in controlling the distribution of high-risk situations for crime events.

From Policing Community to Community Policing?

No discussion of social capital and public safety is complete these days without confronting the seemingly ubiquitous demand for, and consumption of, community policing. The theory of community policing emphasizes the establishment of working partnerships between the police and the community to reduce crime and enhance security. Most community-policing efforts have focused their attention on the problems that lie behind crime incidents (such as drug markets or disorderly bars) rather than on crime only (Moore 1992, 99). Although sparse, there is evidence that community-policing efforts to help residents solve local disorder and crime problems are working in many large U.S. cities. For example, Wesley Skogan and Susan Hartnett (1997) report large declines in social disorder and crime in a quasi-experimental evaluation of community policing in Chicago.

Community policing, at least in theory, is obviously relevant to our concern with social capital because one of its explicit goals is to foster greater civic involvement by residents in the general life of their neighborhoods. Indeed, one of the major goals of community policing is for the police to spark among residents a sense of local ownership over public space and a greater desire to exercise informal social control. The organizational strategy designed to accomplish this outcome is the "beat meeting"— a regularly scheduled meeting of the police with the residents of their beat. In the language of the Chicago Police Department, "Beat meetings ensure community input in the problem-solving process" (quoted in Skogan and Hartnett 1997, 110). Do they work? Early evidence from the Chicago Alternative Policing Strategy (CAPS) suggests that beat meetings are one of the most visible and unique features of community policing. About twenty-five residents and five officers attended per meeting, with attendance highest in African American and minority neighborhoods. Skogan and Hartnett's evaluation (1997, 160) estimated that residents turned up on almost fifteen thousand occasions to discuss local problems with the police.

To be sure, the news is not all rosy. Skogan and Hartnett (1997, 125, 130) also found that the police took the lead in almost all beat meetings. Despite much prodding, it was difficult to sustain resident input and to induce collective problem-solving among residents. Still, the representation of Chicago residents in local problem-solving increased overall. From my perspective, perhaps the most important finding in this regard was that participation increased most in areas that had previously been missing at the table—low-income, minority, and unstable areas. As Skogan and Hartnett concluded, "By creating relatively uniform opportunities for participation, CAPS took the first step toward mobilizing wider participation among all segments of the community" (160). The beat meeting is therefore of interest because it serves to trigger just the sort of civic involvement that social capital theorists promulgate for poor communities.

Co-Creating Legitimate Social Order

The evidence so far seems to show that community policing has had mostly beneficial consequences. Yet, from the perspective of social capital, we need also to consider the legitimacy of community policing and its specific means of enactment. As argued earlier, to the extent that the police are mistrusted, particularly in the predominantly minority communities that bear the brunt of violent crime, cooperative efforts will fail even though all residents share a desire for lower crime rates. It is a myth, for example, that African American mistrust of the police goes hand in hand with a tolerance of deviance and violence. In our study of 8,782 residents of

343 neighborhoods in Chicago, we found that, contrary to stereotypes, African Americans and Latinos are in fact *less* tolerant of deviance and violence than whites are (Sampson and Bartusch 1998). At the same time, neighborhoods of concentrated disadvantage displayed elevated levels of cynicism toward the criminal justice system, dissatisfaction with police, and toleration of deviance unaccounted for by sociodemographic composition and crime-rate differences. Because of the ecological concentration of blacks in poverty areas, concentrated disadvantage helps explain why African Americans are more cynical about law and dissatisfied with the police. Neighborhood context is thus important for resolving the seeming paradox that estrangement from legal norms and agencies of criminal justice, especially by blacks, is compatible with the personal condemnation of deviance.

An intriguing example of "inner-city" community partnerships with the police that address the legitimization role is found in Boston. Although not developed under the rubric of community policing, the Ten-Point Coalition was formed by a group of inner-city Boston ministers in the early 1990s to deal with a sharply increasing problem of youth violence. As Jenny Berrien and Christopher Winship (1999) observe, a long-standing problem in the minority communities of Boston (and elsewhere) was a lack of trust and working relationship between the police and residents. When violence began to rise, residents faced a profound conflict—they wanted safe streets for their children, but they also objected to having their sons hauled off to jail en masse. Heavy-handed police tactics (such as aggressive search and frisk procedures targeted at black males) only made matters worse. As a result, it became difficult in Boston and many other inner-city communities to reach a consensus on what constituted legitimate and constructive police activity.

The key to Boston's Ten-Point Coalition was to create what Berrien and Winship (1999) term an "umbrella of legitimacy" under which the police could work. Rather than shut out the police, religious leaders in Boston's black community demanded change and essentially became an *intermediary* institution between the police and the community, adjudicating between conflicting goals and providing legitimacy for proper police activities. They asserted that inner-city residents wanted not fewer police but a different kind of police (see also Meares and Kahan 1998). The ministers took responsibility by insisting on social order among local youth as well as non-abusive, non-racist methods on the part of the police; only with the latter came the former. No one but the religious leaders had the local social capital and legitimacy in the eyes of inner-city residents to lead this high-stakes effort. Evaluation of the success of the Ten-Point Coalition is still ongoing, but Berrien and Winship (1999) make a convincing case that much of the large drop in the youth violence rate in Boston in the mid-1990s was attributable to the working partnership between the police and the public that was brokered by local ministers.

A similar and equally intriguing example of police-church alliance is found on the West Side of Chicago, an area long characterized by high rates of violent crime, drug dealing, and physical decay. The traditional law enforcement response to crime on the West Side was the arrest, removal, and harsh sentencing of local offenders. Tracey Meares and Dan Kahan (1998) describe a recent shift in drug enforcement policy to one that is more sensitive to local norms of order. Drug markets flourish because of demand, much of which comes from outside the inner city—often from outside the city itself in the form of suburban white buyers. "Reverse stings" recognize this imbalance and take a more democratic approach to crime control by targeting the buyer as well as the dealer. As Meares and Kahan argue, the old "buy-bust" strategy limited sanctions largely to inner-city neighborhoods, whereas the reverse sting parcels sanctions out among numerous communities that are more likely to contain the social buffers that can blunt and absorb them (817). The high visibility of the reverse sting erodes the skepticism of residents and works toward breaking the stigmatizing connection between race and criminality.

Perhaps more central to the concerns of this chapter, Meares and Kahan (1998) describe the emergence of a "working trust" between the police and residents of Chicago's West Side in the creation of zones of safety. In addition to the reverse sting, residents supported juvenile curfews and the policing of minor disorders, largely because of the leadership role of the local police commander, who was a longtime resident. In fact, the police commander led a prayer vigil to protest the drug dealing and crime in the community. More than one thousand residents participated, and in groups of ten they marched and reclaimed the street corners where drug dealers had previously dominated. Following the prayer vigil, more than seven thousand residents retired to a local park for a celebration. Such a police-church event is surely controversial, but from the perspective of social capital theory coupled with the undisputed strength of the black church as a site for collective-action strategies (Pattillo 1998), the Chicago alliance is a fascinating development that bears watching. Note also how Meares and Kahan's (1998) main conclusion echoes that of the Boston case: participation by residents in a newly constituted and legitimized community policing effort was in itself an action that increased community solidarity.

> The road to institutional integration between the police and the church has been paved on Chicago's West Side. . . . The newly formed connection between the church and the police has produced new species of social capital that can be directed toward violence control: The police have access to new sources of information that can assist them in criminal investigations, and church leaders have been assured of greater police responsiveness to the crime affecting their congregants. Church leaders are now even playing an active role in recruiting and screening police academy applicants from their congregations. (Meares and Kahan 1998, 829)

It is difficult to imagine a more direct example of putting neighborhood social capital to work.

Building Intergenerational Ties

As described earlier, a major dimension of neighborhood social control is the ability of adults to supervise and support safe activity patterns of adolescent and child peer groups. In particular, creating safe spaces for youth to "hang out" and play is important for counteracting the fear and perceived vulnerability that leads many youths to join gangs for protection and flee whenever possible their neighborhoods of residence. Policies to encourage adult connections to peer groups include organized supervision of leisure-time youth activities, parent surveillance and involvement in after-school and nighttime recreational and educational programs for youth, and adult-youth mentoring systems. The key to these measures is positive intergenerational connections between youth and adults in the community through informal and volunteer efforts. Stricter sanctions, such as nighttime curfews for children in public areas and stricter enforcement of truancy and loitering laws, should be considered in concert, but I would stress the greater importance of the informal social controls that arise naturally and positively from ongoing social interactions.

The evidence on such "intergenerational" interventions is mixed, but a recent evaluation of youth-oriented development programs concluded that adult mentoring holds promise. Based on their review of the only "rigorous" evaluation of a youth mentoring program, Jodie Roth and her colleagues (1998, 436) argue that the evaluation "provided evidence for the value of caring relationships between adults and youth created and supported by programs." Mentors who did not attempt to change their mentee but rather attempted to build a trusting and supportive relationship that was driven by the interests of the youth were the most likely to be successful. This finding suggests how the juvenile court might better respond to wayward youth and is consistent with the emphasis in this chapter on social supports through intergenerational closure rather than punitive prison terms.

CONCLUSION: SOCIAL CAPITAL AND THE "GOOD" COMMUNITY

The promise of social capital, in my view, is that it reaffirms the importance of thinking about collective ways to approach social problems. Too often our policies and theories are reductionist in nature, looking to change only individuals. The neighborhood perspective presented here suggests nearly the opposite. It is not that individuals or individual characteristics are unimportant, but rather that much can be learned, and possibly changed, by focusing on *events* in their *community context*. I hope to have provided some new ways of thinking about crime and public safety from a neighborhood-level perspective on collective efficacy and social capital.

That said, I nonetheless think it is important to conclude by emphasizing caution in neighborhood-based policies. First, the evidence on neighborhood effects is mixed and complex (Mayer and Jencks 1989). Research has only recently begun to measure directly the social mechanisms hypothesized to explain neighborhood effects (Sampson et al. 1999). Methodological issues, such as differential selection or compositional effects, measurement error, shared method variance, and simultaneity bias, represent serious challenges to drawing definitive conclusions on the role of neighborhood context (Duncan and Raudenbush 1999). Neighborhoods are also more heterogeneous internally and thus less monolithic than commonly believed (see also Cook et al. 1997).

Second, I would caution against falling too far into the trap of local determinism. Part of the appeal of "community" is the image of local residents working collectively to solve their own problems. The ideal of residents joining forces in order to build community and maintain social order is largely a positive one, but this is not the only or even the most important ideal. What happens within neighborhoods is shaped by extralocal social forces, the wider political economy, and citywide spatial dynamics (Sampson et al. 1999). In addition to encouraging communities to mobilize through self-help strategies of informal social control, we need to propose aggressive strategies to address the larger social-ecological changes that have battered many inner-city communities. The specific nature of such efforts is beyond the scope of this chapter. Nevertheless, policies at the political and macrosocial levels are extremely important; recognizing that community social action is possible does not absolve policymakers of the responsibility for seeking equality of opportunities among neighborhoods (Sampson 1999).

Third, there are obvious limits to neighborhood-level social capital. As Portes (1998) notes, proponents of social capital tend to gloss over its potential downside—social capital can be drawn upon for negative as well as positive goals. Moreover, achieving common goals in a diverse society is not easy and has proven problematic in an age of individual rights (Selznick 1992). In the pursuit of informal social control and collective goods, there is the danger that freedoms will be restricted unnecessarily—that individuals will face unwanted and even unjust scrutiny. For example, surveillance of "suspicious" persons in socially controlled communities can become wholesale interrogation of racial minorities (Skogan 1990). Suppose further that a community comes together, with high social capital, to block the residential entry of a racial minority. As Thomas Sugrue's (1996) poignant research on postwar Detroit has revealed, neighborhood associations were the social capital vehicles exploited by whites to forcibly keep blacks from moving into white working-class areas (for example, by means of arson, threats, or violence). Such exclusion prompted Gerald Suttles (1972) to warn of the dark side of "defended neighborhoods."

We must therefore balance concerns for the collective with a concern for social justice and the realization of truly non-exclusive public goods. For this reason, I have focused on widely expressed and shared desires for neighborhoods—most notably, public safety and freedom from violent crime. My strategy relies on shared values for safe communities that are held by all race and class groups (Sampson and Bartusch 1998). Nonetheless, the pursuit of common goals must proceed cautiously and with respect for individual rights, diversity, and limits on state power. Fortunately, legal justice and community are not the antinomy that common wisdom suggests (Selznick 1992). The constitutional law tradition has long been concerned with balancing individual rights against the need to promote the health and safety of communities. The very notion of police power suggests the tension, long recognized by the Supreme Court, between individual rights and the pursuit of social order (Gillman 1996). Integrating the notion of social and legal justice with neighborhood social capital is a welcome and necessary move (Sampson 1999).

It seems fitting to close, then, by reflecting on the essential features of social capital that characterize the "good" community. I would argue that the good community, at least with respect to public safety, is one that is created not through domination, marginalization, exclusion of outsiders, and reliance on threat by agencies of formal control. Rather, the good community is one where the legitimacy of a just social order comes from the mutual engagement—indeed negotiation—of residents and local institutions with agencies of law enforcement (Meares and Kahan 1998). It is instructive in this regard to recall Albert Hirschman's (1970) classic work on the options available to persons in organizations—exit, voice, and loyalty. Residents of American neighborhoods have long employed the exit option, often to the detriment of social capital. Loyalty has been used as well, but often in an exclusionary manner (as in the racially defended neighborhood). The logic of this chapter suggests that the success of a social capital approach to community safety is tied ultimately to the equitable implementation of voice.

NOTES

1. This chapter draws on the detailed review of neighborhood-level studies in Sampson and Lauritsen (1994) and the theoretical framework presented in Sampson (1999, 2001) and Sampson, Morenoff, and Earls (1999). I focus primarily on studies that make inferences about "neighborhoods" or "local communities" within urban areas. Cities and metropolitan areas are large, highly aggregated, and heterogeneous units with politically defined and hence artificial ecological boundaries. Although the operational units typically used to represent neighborhoods (for example, census tracts, wards, block groups) are imperfect substitutes, they have more ecological and social integrity (for example, natural boundaries, socioeconomic homogeneity) and are more closely linked to the social processes theorized to produce crime than cities or metropolitan areas.

2. This statement does not necessarily apply to so-called white-collar crimes and organizational deviance. In a global world, an interesting question is where such acts may be said to occur. Perhaps even more interesting would be an inquiry into social capital "at the top of the firm" (Burt 1992) and the nature of its relationship with organizational malfeasance. Although such an intellectual undertaking merits attention, it is well beyond the scope of my charge.

3. This level of inquiry is often misunderstood as an assertion that individual characteristics are unimportant. Nothing could be further from the truth. The job of neighborhood-level theory is not to explain individual differences in crime, just as individual-difference theories should not be required to explain, say, cross-national differences in crime rates.

4. Most ecological research has been forced to rely on official statistics (such as police and court records) that may be biased because of nonreporting or discrimination by the criminal justice system. To address these problems, many studies limit the domain of inquiry to offenses reported rather than arrest data and to serious predatory crimes, such as homicide, robbery, and burglary, toward which police biases appear to be minimal. A wide-ranging body of research shows that, for serious crimes found in incident-level reports of offenses known to the police, police bias and underreporting are either small or unrelated to community variables of interest. Moreover, self-reported offense behavior and victim-

ization experiences have been brought to bear on the validity of official statistics. A general convergence of community-level findings has been achieved between official and unofficial rates of violence (Sampson and Lauritsen 1994).

5. It is tempting to argue that the current fascination in the social sciences with social capital has merely reinvented the urban sociological wheel. Indeed, the literature in urban sociology on voluntary associations, organizational participation, local social bonds, friend-kinship networks, and neighborhood activism is rich and voluminous (Fischer 1982). Similarly, although using different language, theorists of social disorganization have explored many of the processes emphasized by modern social capital theory. Still, there is something to be gained by a disciplined effort to explicate the neighborhood-level dimensions of social capital, especially the concepts of working trust and shared expectations for social control (as discussed later in this chapter).

6. Again, a neighborhood-level perspective does not assume homologous relationships at the individual level. High prevalence rates of female-headed families with children, for example, have been posited to facilitate crime by decreasing networks of informal social control such as observing or questioning strangers, watching over each other's property, and taking responsibility for supervision of general youth activities (Sampson and Groves 1989). This conceptualization focuses on the communitywide effects of family structure and does not require that it is the children of single parents that are engaging in crime. Similarly, a high level of residential instability and single individuals in a neighborhood has been hypothesized to undermine the closure of social networks and thus the ability for collective supervision of children—without a corresponding prediction of whom *within* neighborhoods is more or less likely to commit a crime.

REFERENCES

Bandura, Albert. 1997. *Self Efficacy: The Exercise of Control.* New York: W. H. Freeman.

Baumgartner, M. P. 1988. *The Moral Order of a Suburb.* New York: Oxford University Press.

Berrien, Jenny, and Christopher Winship. 1999. "Should We Have Faith in the Churches?: Ten-Point Coalition's Effect on Boston's Youth Violence." Paper presented at the Joint Center for Poverty Research, Northwestern University/University of Chicago, Evanston, Ill. (January 14).

Block, Carolyn. 1991. *Early Warning System for Street Gang Violence Crisis Areas: Automated Hot Spot Identification in Law Enforcement.* Chicago: Illinois Criminal Justice Information Authority.

Block, Richard. 1979. "Community, Environment, and Violent Crime." *Criminology* 17: 46–57.

Body-Gendrot, Sophie. 1998. *Les Villes face à l'insécurité.* Paris: Bayard Éditions.

Bourdieu, Pierre. 1986. "The Forms of Capital." In *Handbook of Theory and Research for the Sociology of Education,* edited by John G. Richardson. New York: Greenwood Press.

Brantingham, Patricia L., and Paul J. Brantingham. 1984. "Mobility, Notoriety, and Crime: What Can Be Done to Reduce Crime and Fear?" *Journal of Environmental Systems* 11: 89–99.

Bursik, Robert J. 1986. "Delinquency Rates as Sources of Ecological Change." In *The Social Ecology of Crime,* edited by James Byrne, and Robert J. Sampson. New York: Springer-Verlag.

———. 1988. "Social Disorganization and Theories of Crime and Delinquency: Problems and Prospects." *Criminology* 26: 519–52.

Bursik, Robert J., and Harold Grasmick. 1993. *Neighborhoods and Crime: The Dimensions of Effective Community Control.* New York: Lexington.

Burt, Ronald. 1992. *Structural Holes.* Cambridge, Mass.: Harvard University Press.

Carr, Patrick. 1998. "Keeping up Appearances: Informal Social Control in a White Working-Class Neighborhood in Chicago." Ph.D. diss., University of Chicago.

Cohen, Lawrence, and Marcus Felson 1979. "Social Change and Crime Rate Trends: A Routine Activity Approach." *American Sociological Review* 44: 588–608.

Coleman, James S. 1988. "Social Capital in the Creation of Human Capital." *American Journal of Sociology* 94(supp.): S95–120.

———. 1990. *Foundations of Social Theory.* Cambridge, Mass.: Harvard University Press.

Cook, Thomas, Shobaba Shagle, and Serdar Degirmencioglu. 1997. "Capturing Social Process for Testing Mediational Models of Neighborhood Effects." In *Neighborhood Poverty: Policy Implications in Studying Neighborhoods,* edited by Jeanne Brooks-Gunn, Greg J. Duncan, and Lawrence Aber. New York: Russell Sage Foundation.

Duncan, Greg, and Stephen Raudenbush. 1999. "Assessing the Effects of Context in Studies of Child and Youth Development." *Educational Psychologist* 34: 29–41.

Elliott, Delbert, William J. Wilson, David Huizinga, Robert J. Sampson, Amanda Elliott, and Bruce Rankin. 1996. "The Effects of Neighborhood Disadvantage on Adolescent Development." *Journal of Research in Crime and Delinquency* 33: 389–426.

Felson, Marcus. 1987. "Routine Activities and Crime Prevention in the Developing Metropolis." *Criminology* 25: 911–31.

Fischer, Claude. 1982. *To Dwell Among Friends: Personal Networks in Town and City.* Chicago: University of Chicago Press.

Freeman, Richard. 1991. "Crime and the Employment of Disadvantaged Youths." Working Paper 3875. Cambridge, Mass.: National Bureau of Economic Research.

Gillman, Howard. 1996. "The Antinomy of Public Purposes and Private Rights in the American Constitutional Tradition, or Why Communitarianism Is Not Necessarily Exogenous to Liberal Constitutionalism." *Law and Social Inquiry* 21: 67–77.

Hirschman, Albert O. 1970. *Exit, Voice, and Loyalty.* Cambridge, Mass.: Harvard University Press.

Hope, Tim. 1995. "Community Crime Prevention." In *Building a Safer Society,* edited by Michael Tonry and David Farrington. Chicago: University of Chicago Press.

Hunter, Albert. 1985. "Private, Parochial, and Public Social Orders: The Problem of Crime and Incivility in Urban Communities." In *The Challenge of Social Control,* edited by Gerald Suttles and Mayer Zald. Norwood, N.J.: Ablex.

Janowitz, Morris. 1975. "Sociological Theory and Social Control." *American Journal of Sociology* 81: 82–108.

Kasarda, John, and Morris Janowitz. 1974. "Community Attachment in Mass Society." *American Sociological Review* 39: 328–39.

Kornhauser, Ruth. 1978. *Social Sources of Delinquency.* Chicago: University of Chicago Press.

Land, Kenneth, Patricia McCall, and Lawrence Cohen. 1990. "Structural Covariates of Homicide Rates: Are There Any Invariances Across Time and Space?" *American Journal of Sociology* 95: 922–63.

Logan, John, and Harvey Molotch. 1987. *Urban Fortunes: The Political Economy of Place.* Berkeley: University of California Press.

Massey, Douglas S., and Nancy Denton. 1993. *American Apartheid: Segregation and the Making of the Underclass.* Cambridge, Mass.: Harvard University Press.

Mayer, Susan E., and Christopher Jencks. 1989. "Growing up in Poor Neighborhoods: How Much Does It Matter?" *Science* 243: 1441–45.

Meares, Tracey, and Dan Kahan. 1998. "Law and (Norms of) Order in the Inner City." *Law and Society Review* 32: 805–38.

Moore, Mark. 1992. "Problem-solving and Community Policing." In *Crime and Justice,* vol. 15, *Modern Policing,* edited by Michael Tonry and Norval Morris. Chicago: University of Chicago Press.

Morenoff, Jeffrey, and Robert J. Sampson. 1997. "Violent Crime and the Spatial Dynamics of Neighborhood Transition: Chicago, 1970–1990." *Social Forces* 76: 31–64.

Park, Robert. 1916. "The City: Suggestions for the Investigations of Human Behavior in the Urban Environment." *American Journal of Sociology* 20: 577–612.

Pattillo, Mary. 1998. "Church Culture as a Strategy of Action in the Black Community." *American Sociological Review* 63: 767–84.

Portes, Alejandro. 1998. "Social Capital: Its Origins and Applications in Modern Sociology." *Annual Review of Sociology* 24: 1–24.

Portes, Alejandro, and Julia Sensenbrenner. 1993. "Embeddedness and Immigration: Notes on the Social Determinants of Economic Action." *American Journal of Sociology* 98: 1320–50.

Putnam, Robert. 1993. "The Prosperous Community: Social Capital and Community Life." *The American Prospect* (Spring): 35–42.

Reiss, Albert J., Jr. 1970. *The Police and the Public.* New Haven, Conn.: Yale University Press.

Reiss, Albert J., Jr., and Jeffrey Roth, eds. 1993. *Understanding and Preventing Violence.* Vol. 1. Washington, D.C.: National Academy Press.

Roncek, Dennis. 1981. "Dangerous Places: Crime and Residential Environment." *Social Forces* 60: 74–96.

Rose, Dina, and Todd Clear. 1998. "Incarceration, Social Capital, and Crime: Implications for Social Disorganization Theory." *Criminology* 36: 441–80.

Rosenbaum, Dennis, Arthur Lurigio, and Robert Davis. 1998. *The Prevention of Crime: Social and Situational Strategies.* Belmont, Calif.: Wadsworth.

Roth, Jodie, Jeanne Brooks-Gunn, Lawrence Murray, and William Foster. 1998. "Promoting Healthy Adolescents: Synthesis of Youth Development Program Evaluations." *Journal of Research on Adolescence* 8: 423–59.

Sampson, Robert J. 1985. "Neighborhood and Crime: The Structural Determinants of Personal Victimization." *Journal of Research in Crime and Delinquency* 22: 7–40.

———. 1995. "Unemployment and Imbalanced Sex Ratios: Race-Specific Consequences for Family Structure and Crime." In *The Decline in Marriage Among African-Americans,* edited by M. Belinda Tucker and Claudia Mitchell-Kernan. New York: Russell Sage Foundation.

———. 1999. "What 'Community' Supplies." In *Urban Problems and Community Development,* edited by Ronald F. Ferguson and William T. Dickens. Washington, D.C.: Brookings Institution Press.

———. 2001. "How Do Communities Undergird or Undermine Human Development?: Relevant Contexts and Social Mechanisms." In *Does It Take a Village?: Community Effects on Children, Adolescents, and Families,* edited by Alan Booth and Nan Crouter. Mahwah, N.J.: Lawrence Erlbaum.

Sampson, Robert J., and Dawn Bartusch. 1998. "Legal Cynicism and (Subcultural?) Tolerance of Deviance: The Neighborhood Context of Racial Differences." *Law and Society Review* 32: 777–804.

Sampson, Robert J., and W. Byron Groves. 1989. "Community Structure and Crime: Testing Social-Disorganization Theory." *American Journal of Sociology* 94: 774–802.

Sampson, Robert J., and Janet Lauritsen. 1994. "Violent Victimization and Offending: Individual, Situational, and Community-Level Risk Factors." In *Understanding and Preventing*

Violence, vol. 3, edited by Albert J. Reiss Jr. and Jeffrey A. Roth. Washington, D.C.: National Academy Press.

———. 1997. "Racial and Ethnic Disparities in Crime and Criminal Justice in the United States." In *Ethnicity, Crime, and Immigration: Comparative and Cross-National Perspectives,* edited by Michael Tonry. Chicago: University of Chicago Press.

Sampson, Robert J., Jeffrey Morenoff, and Felton Earls. 1999. "Beyond Social Capital: Spatial Dynamics of Collective Efficacy for Children." *American Sociological Review* 64: 633–60.

Sampson, Robert J., Stephen Raudenbush, and Felton Earls. 1997. "Neighborhoods and Violent Crime: A Multi-level Study of Collective Efficacy." *Science* 277: 918–24.

Selznick, Philip. 1992. *The Moral Commonwealth: Social Theory and the Promise of Community.* Berkeley: University of California Press.

Shaw, Clifford, and Henry McKay. 1969. *Juvenile Delinquency and Urban Areas.* 2nd ed. Chicago: University of Chicago Press. Originally published in 1942.

Sherman, Lawrence. 1995. "The Police." In *Crime,* edited by James Q. Wilson and Joan Petersilia. San Francisco: ICS Press.

Sherman, Lawrence, Patrick Gartin, and Michael Buerger. 1989. "Hot Spots of Predatory Crime: Routine Activities and the Criminology of Place." *Criminology* 27: 27–56.

Simcha-Fagan, Ora, and Joseph Schwartz. 1986. "Neighborhood and Delinquency: An Assessment of Contextual Effects." *Criminology* 24: 667–704.

Skogan, Wesley. 1986. "Fear of Crime and Neighborhood Change." In *Communities and Crime,* edited by Albert J. Reiss Jr. and Michael Tonry. Chicago: University of Chicago Press.

———. 1990. *Disorder and Decline: Crime and the Spiral of Decay in American Neighborhoods.* Berkeley: University of California Press.

Skogan, Wesley, and Susan Hartnett. 1997. *Community Policing, Chicago Style.* New York: Oxford University Press.

Smith, Douglas R., and G. Roger Jarjoura. 1988. "Social Structure and Criminal Victimization." *Journal of Research in Crime and Delinquency* 25: 27–52.

Stark, Rodney. 1987. "Deviant Places: A Theory of the Ecology of Crime." *Criminology* 25: 893–910.

Sugrue, Thomas. 1996. *The Origins of the Urban Crisis: Race and Inequality in Postwar Detroit.* Princeton, N.J.: Princeton University Press.

Suttles, Gerald. 1972. *The Social Construction of Communities.* Chicago: University of Chicago Press.

Taylor, Ralph, and Jeanette Covington. 1988. "Neighborhood Changes in Ecology and Violence." *Criminology* 26: 553–90.

Taylor, Ralph, Stephen Gottfredson, and Sidney Brower. 1984. "Block Crime and Fear: Defensible Space, Local Social Ties, and Territorial Functioning." *Journal of Research in Crime and Delinquency* 21: 303–31.

Tilly, Charles. 1973. "Do Communities Act?" *Sociological Inquiry* 43: 209–40.

Tonry, Michael. 1995. *Malign Neglect: Race, Crime, and Punishment in America.* New York: Oxford University Press.

Western, Bruce, and Katherine Beckett. 1999. "How Unregulated Is the U.S. Labor Market?: The Penal System as a Labor Market Institution." *American Journal of Sociology* 104: 1030–60.

Wilgoren, Jodi, and Ginger Thompson. 1999. "After Shooting, an Eroding Trust in Police." *New York Times,* February 19.

Wilson, William Julius. 1987. *The Truly Disadvantaged: The Inner City, the Underclass, and Public Policy.* Chicago: University of Chicago Press.

Chapter 5

Making Social Capital Work: Social Capital and Community Economic Development

Ross Gittell and J. Phillip Thompson

T he discussion of social capital as it relates to economic development in low-income communities has been inappropriately narrow. It has focused on social ties and relations within and between firms in ethnic enclave economies without paying sufficient attention to how social capital can influence private market rules, individual preferences, and economic outcomes. We offer an alternative view, with social capital as a contributing factor in the shaping of economic markets through political and collective community action and in the actualizing of market potential in inner-city economies. Our view is that social capital can operate in concert with other important development assets and contribute to community economic development.

HOW SOCIAL CAPITAL INFLUENCES MARKETS

To appreciate the role of social capital in shaping markets and their outcomes, it is necessary to shed some popular understandings of markets. In a simplistic view offered by traditional economic theory, individuals have money and preferences that take the form of demand. Businesses respond to these demands and compete in quality and price; this constitutes supply. It is assumed that individuals have a priori and stable preferences. This assumption is an important fallacy that hides the role of social capital in setting market preferences. Businesses know that consumers do not necessarily know what they want a priori. Businesses thus spend significant resources on marketing to influence consumer preferences. Extensive research is conducted by business to understand the social and cultural attachments of various subgroups of the population. Often, a "star" from a subgroup is hired to help promote a product to that subgroup, so that the product becomes identified with the subgroup. This entire set of activities could easily be thought of as businesses building up social capital with various subgroups of the population.

For many if not most consumers, social connection (or "fashion") is as important a selling point as product quality or price. If consumers do not have predetermined or stable preferences and producers can shape consumer demand, then the distinction between supply and demand dissolves. It follows that the idea of a "natural balance," or equilibrium, between the distinct elements of supply and demand loses its foundation. If there is no rigid law of supply and demand, then we must ask again some old questions: How do suppliers and consumers come to know, understand, and interact with each other? How is economic success achieved and sustained in markets? It is in rethinking these old questions from a fresh perspective that social capital can become more analytically and practically useful in community economic development and other discussions.

At a micro level, we could explore how individual consumers come to choose one sneaker or another and the role that social attachments play in that decision. We are instead interested here in identifying how social capital affects a couple of *macro* issues: Why are market institutions (that is, market rules and regulations, consumer individual interests and incentives) shaped the way they are? Relatedly, why are consumer markets primarily oriented around *individual* demands versus group or social demands? We start with the question of how social capital structures markets.

Many have remarked on how U.S. citizens, businesses, and government all tend to defend the U.S. economic structure under the banner of freedom, or "free" markets (Ankersmit 1996). However, there is actually no such thing as a free market; there are only agreements and conflicts over the degree of regulation and types of structuring of markets (Block 1994). In making the argument that social capital influences the shape of U.S. markets, we need only show that free markets are themselves a social construct. That is, by disconnecting free markets from any notion of natural economic necessity, the only alternatives for explaining why the United States has a "free market" structure are social and political. In the United States, however, political battles over free markets have been comparatively rare. Coordination of production and services through markets has been socially popular.

Without social organization and government, neither individuals nor *private* businesses would survive for long. Markets are not natural systems. Rather, they are constructed by social agreements reinforced through law, government power, and social norms. Business conduct, far from being value-free and responsive only to objective market forces, is heavily value-driven (DiMaggio 1994) and affected by politics. Corporations attempt to put in place public policies that will structure the kind of markets they can thrive in. Corporations have championed the idea of freedom to defend their ability to move capital across national borders and regulatory domains with a minimum of governmental control (Albrow 1997). Unions and environmental groups have frequently called for government regulation of such market freedom to protect constituent interests in combating poverty, political repression, and environmental degradation.

In Arthur Okun's (1975) seminal view of market efficiency, market efficiency benefits the *whole* of society, but it is interrupted by various government requirements that promote equality for particular classes and groups—such as those represented by unions and environmental groups. Some government interference is necessary for market stability because too much inequality produces social disruption, protest, and even revolution. Too much equality, however, leads to serious disruption of market freedoms and stifles economic incentives and efficiency for everyone. The key to long-term growth is stability achieved through the "right mix" of equality and efficiency. In this view, private firms concentrate on efficiency (to serve the greater good), while government focuses on increasing equality for those weakened in the marketplace. Okun pushes the dichotomy between equality and efficiency too far, however.

For example, many government efforts made in response to demands for equality have generated economic growth that narrow views of efficiency do not recognize. This includes governmental programs such as public education and health insurance (Medicare), which help contribute to worker productivity. Also, some of the actions of major private corporations—such as the recent support of affirmative action by the General Motors Corporation—have suggested positive correlations between diversity in hiring and economic performance. The University of Michigan has an unusual ally in its effort to defend its affirmative action policies in admissions against two separate lawsuits in federal court. In a brief submitted in U.S. District Court, General Motors maintained that its interest in affirmative action legal disputes involving the university is substantial. The company, based in Detroit, employs a large number of graduates from the university, in particular from its business and engineering schools. The brief says: "In General Motors' view, only a well-educated, highly-diverse work force, comprised of people who have learned to work productively and creatively with individuals from a multitude of races and ethnic, religious, and cultural histories, can maintain America's global competitiveness in the increasingly diverse and interconnected world economy" (quoted in Schmidt 2000).

Another aspect of the efficiency-versus-equality paradigm deserves mention. This is the notion that markets pursue efficiency while government pursues equality. We noted earlier that government programs for equality can produce economic growth over time, that is, they can enhance efficiency in the long run. We also believe that markets can promote equality—for instance, through the diversity programs of many U.S. corporations. It is critical not to view markets as driven by individual economic self-interests only; we must also recognize the potential value of social ties and cooperation to individuals.

Social cooperation can take a variety of forms in economics, including customer loyalty, the sharing of information, and asset maintenance. Customer loyalty, for example, enables Nike to charge higher prices than competitors whose product is virtually identical. The sharing of information, such as a worker's willingness to inform employers of problems on the job, has been increasingly recognized as a key factor in business success. Asset maintenance, such as an apartment renter's willingness to help maintain leased property, has helped some low-income landlords to turn a profit and maintain housing; landlords lacking such cooperation have sometimes lost money and had to abandon property (as discussed later in this chapter).

Increasing equality can lead to greater social cooperation, lower costs, and improved economic efficiency: lower rents and better service for the poor, for example, can lead to timely rent payments, building preservation, and lower maintenance costs. In this example, the opposition between equality and efficiency fades. In short, there can be sound economic reasons to pursue equality and social justice as good business practice.

If this is so, however, why have not more businesses pursued equality and social cooperation? The answer does not lie, we think, in some inherent law of the market. There are numerous examples of businesses that utilize social cooperation toward economic ends. The answer, we suggest, has to do with the limited perspective of commercial capitalism-liberalism, which sees connections to consumers as something made through blind and anonymous interactions based on individuals' economic interests. Under this view, one understands universal needs only through their expression in individual buying habits, and then in the aggregation of individual desires and needs.

It is this "ideal" of commercial liberalism (that is, that progress is achieved through *individual* efforts rather than in cooperation with others), not a hidden economic law, that leads many businesses and entrepreneurs to underappreciate equality and social cooperation. Business managers and owners undervalue equality because, like consumers, they are overly enamored by the logic of commercial liberalism.

If it is disconcerting that business owners and managers have hung on to the competitive individualistic ideal, it is more disturbing and surprising that social capital and civil society advocates (who often decry the individualism of commercial society) have not been more engaged in applying social capital concepts to economic development. Some prominent "oversights" have contributed to this shortcoming in thinking about how social capital can aid in the process of economic development in poor communities. First is the long-standing view that market economies have an inherent and unalterable tendency to exploit the poor, undermine the environment, and exacerbate various inequalities. We do not want to argue that these evils have not happened and that markets have not contributed to them. However, we do not believe that the market must always serve neutral or morally repugnant ends. What is often considered to be an evil inherent in market structures is more accurately a criticism of bourgeois social values, or a "mis-education" of citizens on the role of social ties and cooperative action in the economic process.

An example may clarify this point. Imagine that a business executive encounters a large hardwood forest along a pristine river in Maine. When it occurs to the executive to buy the forest, she immediately puts her mind to work on how she might develop the property. She considers selling the hardwood to lumber companies for shipment to Japan. She thinks about damming the river to generate electricity that could be sold to nearby towns. Once the hardwood is cleared, she could replant fast-growing trees, subdivide the property, build luxury homes, and sell parcels as vacation getaway homes. Her imagination, structured entirely around the production of commodities that people could purchase and use, has led her to think about all of the useful products that could be developed out of the property.

Now imagine a slightly different scenario. An executive purchases the same piece of property, and rather than thinking of how it can be transformed into various types of commodities, she decides that the greatest value of the property is its beauty: the fauna and wildlife. The executive decides to build a network of trails through the property, along with a network of ecologically friendly hotel facilities on the outer edges. She advertises the property to environmentalists (a significant market segment) as a tourism site. The executive imagines that if she preserves the property in its natural state, the property will never lose value and will continue to generate income for her in perpetuity. In fact, because she has no trouble convincing investors that she has a secure income stream from the property, she has no trouble securing financing to acquire a similar property, even larger, in upstate New York where she plans to replicate the preservation model.

As shown in this example, there is nothing logically inherent in the notion of markets that prevents them from being used to preserve the environment rather than destroy it. The difference between the two examples is in the market *assessment* and social *values* the two entrepreneurs bring to their view of the property. In other words, the differences are human and aesthetic.

Another misunderstanding, also mentioned by Cathy Cohen (this volume), is the tendency of social capital theorists to define social capital in purely positive terms, or to define social capital as promoting the type of community values that they themselves wish to promote. Yet there is a negative side to social capital that has been too often ignored. For example, when businesses extensively promote youth interests in gangsta rap, smoking, and alcohol through mass media and direct marketing, they are not seen as building social capital. Similarly, suburban housing developers who build exclusive residential communities are criticized for destroying social capital in the communities from which residents are moving (often city neighborhoods with more diverse populations), but social capital analysts tend to ignore that developers are building social capital of another type in residentially exclusive neighborhoods. Such one-sided analysis of social capital often leads researchers to ignore the vast influence of businesses in organizing social groups and determining social trends, and it reduces the general understanding of how social capital connections affect markets.

Theoretical prejudices against markets and blindness to the influences on social capital formation that businesses already have in large part lead social capital researchers and advocates to overlook much of the practical value of social capital in economic development. Although these theorists and advocates sometimes make a connection between building social capital and group political organizing, on economic issues they tend to think of individuals as generally isolated from others. They rarely think about how mass economic preferences are generated or how they could be generated. The powerful effect that organizations and networks could have on both the supply and demand sides of the market is thus too often obscured from view.

For instance, although black communities in the United States are poor when black individuals' wealth is compared with white individuals' wealth, this way of thinking about wealth is one-sided and disempowering. African Americans in 1998 earned roughly $460 billion in income (Graves 1998). A single trade union of low-income, mostly black and Hispanic hospital workers in New York, local 1199, has a pension fund worth more than $6 billion. If blacks were half as unified in their economic preferences as they are in their voting patterns (they are overwhelmingly Democratic), they could make some markets flourish. They could force change in business practices that they do not like. They could require businesses that receive their investments and purchases to reinvest in their communities and make community members directors of the companies. Similarly, a union like 1199 could use its pension funds to establish a credit union and community investment fund that would significantly improve members' income and quality of life by offering low-interest credit cards and building day care facilities in underserved areas. In short, the economic power of African Americans exists *only* at a collective or *social* level, but their power at this level could be considerable. The relative lack of attention given to collective community economic power and assets in low-income and minority communities suggests the dominating prevalence of the ideology of individualism (embodied by commercial liberalism) even among its critics.

As in politics, social cooperation can generate new perspectives and opportunities that are often hidden from isolated poor individuals. A social capital approach to markets could emphasize such opportunities. By asking low-income citizens to consider the economic landscape from a social perspective, new appreciations of market power and opportunities (on both the supply and demand sides) emerge.

Another example has to do with energy privatization and its potential effect in poor communities. A number of community groups fear any form of privatization as a threat to guaranteed service, affordable prices, or the maintenance of quality jobs. And privatization has a well-established track record of leading to just these types of negative outcomes. Ironically, however, if poor urban communities form energy cooperatives for the purchase or supply of energy, they may be well positioned to exact leverage over (and benefit from) the privatization process. Poor communities have long been targeted as locations for the large, energy-consuming, and frequently noxious facilities (treatment plants, airports, hospitals) that are refused by more powerful and wealthy communities. By working cooperatively with large energy consumers to coordinate demand—for instance, by encouraging community residents to use energy when it is least needed by a local hospital—poor communities can minimize strains on the local utility system. As demand rises faster than the supply of energy in many areas, poor communities become critical leverage points in a utility company's efforts to provide reliable energy service. In this way, energy co-ops could broker reductions in energy prices or utility contributions to community improvement in ways that would be unimaginable for an individual consumer in a poor neighborhood.

As these examples illustrate, our thinking about community economic development often neglects the social capital concept, which is an important potential mechanism for accessing and leveraging economic and political resources.

SOCIAL CAPITAL AT THE NEXUS OF COMMUNITY ECONOMIC DEVELOPMENT

The Components of Economic Development

Social capital is just one of many assets important for community economic development. Financial capital, a skilled workforce, a physical infrastructure, organizational capacity, and supportive public institutions and policies are also important assets. These assets collectively are also important for the economic development of (rich and poor) cities (Gittell 1992), states (Osborne 1988), and nations (Thurow 1999; Reich 1991). Social capital is not magical, nor is it a special formula for developing low-income areas. All the development factors are important for all kinds of economic development.

A long-standing contribution to the understanding of the interrelationships between community development assets is the literature on black capitalism. Proponents of black capitalism stress that black businesses increase black employment, improve consumer welfare, stimulate community investment, reduce welfare dependency, and increase black political clout by strengthening black economic power. R. L. Boyd (1990, 269) suggests that black business presence grants the power and status necessary to reduce prejudice and break down barriers to black economic progress. He argues that black businesses can be important institutions at the community level (169) by catering to the low-income, nonwhite customers often neglected by major stores, providing initial employment experience to disadvantaged youth, and reinforcing the notion that community life is organized around work. Lending support to an African American business focus in inner-city development is evidence that black business owners are more likely than their white and Asian counterparts to employ black workers, thus generating greater employment and communitywide benefits in African American neighborhoods (Bates 1994; Porter 1997).

A major and all-too-common problem in low-income communities is a severe lack of one or more of the important development assets; thus, these communities must develop some combination of those critical assets before they can make any significant economic progress. The value of social capital in this context is that it can be generated internally through some form of community organizing or by leveraging organizational networks established for some other purpose (such as political campaigns or organized labor). The possibility that one or two of the development assets might fit together and the potential role of social capital in helping to blend the different development assets to the benefit of the broader community interest do not emerge often enough in thinking about community economic development. For example, an organized community with a large segment of workers in a particular union might press the union to invest in a community project and pressure local government officials to match the funds. Such assets are often not developed or deployed because community development efforts are driven by whatever external resources are available at the time, not by the local social assets available for economic development. It is well known that both government agencies and foundations fear that community organizing may cause them to lose control of community projects. Nonetheless, community organizing is critical to building social capital in neighborhoods (Gittell and Vidal 1998). Social capital for economic development can be built through community organizing that conducts strategic planning, identifies community assets and liabilities, and draws in community groups and residents to prioritize objectives and demands.

Community organizing is also important because of the disconnection between community assets in economic development perpetuated by the organization of many federal and state government programs meant to assist low-income communities. The programs often operate along traditional agency lines (education, labor force development, financial assets, and physical infrastructure) and tend to deliver resources narrowly targeted within agency guidelines. This leaves the task of integration—putting the development pieces together—to local communities, which must often develop the experience, operating capacity, and social cohesiveness to plan and operate effectively.

Poor communities have many internal deficits and require bridges to outside resources. However, our view is that they often also have many social assets and internal capabilities to develop additional assets. The capacity to combat poverty (and develop low-income community economies) can be enhanced by identifying and utilizing existing community social assets synergistically to create new economic assets. Communities that cooperate internally to make effective use of their own assets are more attractive to private investors and businesses and better partners for outside institutions.

In our view, the most effective way to foster community economic development is through a holistic approach that draws on the social capital assets of communities, such as churches, unions, fraternal organizations, political organizations, and child care networks. Although individuals in poor communities have little financial capital, when aggregated through networks, the social capital that these communities assemble can be powerfully leveraged to accumulate economic and political capital. Community residents can use social capital to ensure that economic development efforts improve their lives and strengthen their social, political, and economic networks.

The Role of Social Capital in Economic Development

A number of researchers studying ethnic enclaves have suggested that social capital accounts for the business success of these enclaves and the success of local enclave economies. These studies tend to focus on the role of social capital as an alternative to working through mainstream financial and political institutions rather than on how community and mainstream development assets might work in concert. The studies have focused on communities with concentrations of ethnic entrepreneurs—for example, Koreans in Los Angeles (Light and Bonacich 1991), Cubans in Miami (Portes and Rumbaut 1996), and Chinese and Dominicans in New York City (Portes and Zhou 1996). The main finding is that some immigrant groups are very effective in their use of social relationships (for example, in their ethnic solidarity) to achieve levels of economic growth independent of mainstream institutions.

Although they illuminate the potential economic role of social capital, the studies of ethnic entrepreneurs are generally limited by a lack of specificity about the other assets necessary for business success and community economic development. Timothy Bates (1994a), for example, in a critique of the literature on ethnic entrepreneurs, finds that ethnic entrepreneurs succeed for reasons applicable to any small business, including access to equity capital and the human capital of entrepreneurs. From our perspective, the two views (Bates's and the sociologists') on ethnic entrepreneurs need not be at odds. It is entirely conceivable that ethnic entrepreneurs need money, skills, *and* community support in order to succeed. Social capital can have positive direct economic effects in communities as well as important indirect effects by developing other community assets.

One of social capital's strongest indirect influences in community economic development is on political institutions, policymakers, and public policy. For example, social capital has contributed indirectly to financial asset enhancement by first affecting political discourse and policy, as with the organized community protests that led to the Community Reinvestment Act. Social capital can affect physical development, as it does with NIMBY efforts in both poor and rich communities. It can influence public policies related to wages and human capital development, such as living-wage legislation. And it can affect the market rules that govern entrepreneurial and business development opportunities. This was the case with New York City's Neighborhood Entrepreneur Program (discussed in detail later), in which neighborhood residents demanded that privatization of city-owned property in low-income neighborhoods include the condition that neighborhood residents be given priority (Gittell and Thompson 1999).

Nevertheless, it is important to recognize that social capital is no community development panacea. As mentioned earlier, social capital's effect on community economic development is not always positive. In enclave economies, neighborhood residents who are not members of the dominant groups can be excluded from financial resources and employment and market opportunities. In diverse neighborhoods, strong ethnic and racial groups can distract from the political capacity to act on communitywide issues. Old boys' networks in the construction trades can limit opportunities for women-owned businesses (discussed in more detail later in the chapter). Second, there is a concern that social capital may be lacking in low-income communities (Wilson 1987), and therefore that it may not be a promising community asset base for organizing development efforts. We are skeptical, however, about such conclusions: researchers may simply not be well trained in identifying social networks in low-income and minority communities. Not all communities have equal levels or the same types of social capital, but recent research suggests that even "abandoned" neighborhoods have some social organization and relations to advance their development prospects. Organizations that have often been described in purely negative terms, such as youth gangs, may also be utilized for positive social functions (Venkatesh 2000).

THE OTHER COMPONENTS OF ECONOMIC DEVELOPMENT AND HOW THEY RELATE TO SOCIAL CAPITAL

Financial Assets

Access to financial capital has been identified as one of the most significant factors contributing to the development of economies at all levels. Loans to developing nations are the dominant form of aid in international development. In developed countries, national, state, and municipal government bonds are used to fund a variety of economic development activities, ranging from physical infrastructure development and capital improvements to subsidized financing for start-up, relocating, and struggling businesses. Examples of how access to financial capital can contribute to community improvement and minority business success—such as South Shore Bank (Taub 1988) and immigrant groups arriving with "capital in hand" (Bates and Dunham 1993)—are used by policymakers to make the case for the importance of financial capital in community economic development. The significant growth in and support of microloan programs in the United States (and globally) also suggest the prevalence of the view that financial capital is important to community economic development (Servon 1995, 1999).

Ways in which social capital can enhance financial assets in community economic development include peer lending, credit unions and rotating credit associations, and union pension investments. These methods rely on social bonds and good relations among members and participants. Financial assets and relations can (in turn) enhance social capital within a community. This is apparently happening with union housing investment programs in New York (Greenhouse 2000). This also appears to be happening in high-technology centers such as Silicon Valley (Bronson 1999), where close social bonds are built from financial and business relationships.

Organizational Capacity

Perhaps the key asset in utilizing social capital for economic development is the organizational capacity of local community-based organizations, firms, nonprofit organizations, and public agencies. Community development corporations (CDCs) and other community-based organizations have played a prominent role in community development in many low-income neighborhoods across the country (Vidal 1992). Key factors contributing to CDC success (and the success of other community-based organizations) include management skills, technical planning, and the project development capabilities of board members and staff, as well as relations with community residents (Gittell and Wilder 1999).

A number of institutions with organizational capacity that operate in low-income communities may also play a leading role in organizing social capital or in community organizing. One of the most important research questions for using and developing social capital in poor communities is determining exactly which individuals build social capital, identifying their incentives, and tracing economic and social outcomes related to these and other factors. As discussed earlier, because CDCs and other community-based organizations tend to compete for governmental and foundation funding, their role in community organizing has been limited. Fortunately, there are other organizations that can play a significant role in community organizing and building social capital, including churches, cooperatives, labor unions, and environmental groups. Each brings different interests, incentives, and capacities to bear on building social capital. These organizations may initiate some of the community organizing that has been largely missing. Private entrepreneurs engaged in private market activities can also play a role in building social capital (in their private market self-interest, as we discuss in the next section).

Entrepreneurial Capacity

A final asset important for community economic development is entrepreneurship. In the traditional economic development literature, Joseph Schumpeter (1934) was the first to highlight the private profit-seeking entrepreneur as the key agent in economic development. Today it is hard to read an article about the U.S. economy without reference to entrepreneurs.

Ronald Burt (1992) provides a useful framework to discuss why there may be a paucity of private market entrepreneurial effort in low-income areas. Burt's framework suggests that such efforts fail in low-income communities as a result of a lack of social connections, what he calls "structural holes." In the inner city, private market entrepreneurs often fail to identify inner-city market opportunities and to link resources outside the inner city to take advantage of market opportunities in the inner city. We believe that some market opportunities are unrealized—and that structural holes are prevalent in the inner city—because of social disconnection between inner cities and outside business resources.

In a similar fashion, Mark Granovetter (1973), a sociologist focused on labor markets, recognized that most new opportunities (including jobs) come from weak ties—those ties that represent new relations linking individuals together in novel ways. Burt's and Granovetter's views together suggest that what may be most lacking in community economic development are the social ties and connections to move on market opportunities. Stated in different terms, social capital can be a key link to the actualization of market potential.

Michael Porter (1995) generated much interest in and attention to what he called the "untapped" potential in inner cities (low-income, inner-city neighborhoods) for business development. Porter highlighted the market potential of inner-city businesses supplying nearby large businesses, drawing on an available labor supply and serving underserved local demand for services and products. For Porter (as for Schumpeter and others), the main agent for change in the inner city (as in the market economy globally) is the profit-motivated entrepreneur. To realize inner-city market opportunities, we need entrepreneurs who effectively utilize existing human capital assets and connect them to outside resources and businesses.

In Porter's view, virtually any community has community assets and economic potential. The critical element is the private entrepreneur, who identifies the market opportunity and draws together the assets to realize the potential. It is social capital that helps to overcome the social disconnection that prevents outside entrepreneurs from understanding the economic potential of the inner city. Better connections can bring in outside entrepreneurs who would not even have considered the inner city—for example, a friend telling a friend to consider opening a new business in an inner-city community, or an MBA student who grew up in a low-income community connecting with Professor Porter in class.

Once entrepreneurs invest in the inner city, they have pecuniary incentives to build social capital, that is, to establish good relations with local residents and other businesses. Furthermore, when they invest in a community, they also bring in their human capital, access to financial and political assets, and a network of relations with outside resources. In Porter's framework, the community economic development pieces can be blended in inner cities, and social capital is one of the pieces. However, the entrepreneurs whom Porter talks about may not be strongly tied to the communities in which they operate, and they may also be unlikely to return the economic gains from their work to those communities. Community residents would therefore do well to develop their own bonding associations so as to be in a position to maximize economic benefits from Porter's entrepreneurs. For example, residents might join unions in order to increase their share of the benefits from profitable inner-city ventures.

What Porter's perspective highlights is that in low-income community economic development, Burt's spanning structural holes would require some bridging (connecting to and bringing in outside resources and expertise) targeted to business development. Social capital bridges into low-income communities can improve the prospects for inner-city entrepreneurship.

Successful inner-city entrepreneurs can give back to the communities in which they operate. They can use their social relations to garner outside resources for broader community benefit. They can also mentor others, including their employees, and serve as role models, making residents feel better about themselves and each other. This is most likely to happen, at least some research suggests, with entrepreneurs who are operating in strongly bonded communities (Gittell and Thompson 1999). The cooperative model may be interesting to study in this regard, as well as various other forms of community ownership, as a way of institutionalizing entrepreneurial accountability and connectivity in low-income communities.

"MODELS" FOR COMMUNITY ECONOMIC DEVELOPMENT

We now offer some models ("best practices" in operation or conceptually) for economically developing inner cities and critique them from our social capital perspective.

The Neighborhood Entrepreneur Program

There is evidence of the potential of social capital in community economic development in the Neighborhood Entrepreneur Program (NEP) in New York City (Gittell, Lawrence, and Thompson 1995; Gittell and Thompson 1999). In this novel, award-winning program (Innovations in American Government Award, 1999), inner-city entrepreneurs—the large majority of whom are minorities—are emerging as important local institutional foundations.

The Neighborhood Entrepreneur Program was established in 1994 by New York City's housing agency and a nonprofit private intermediary, the New York City Housing Partnership. It involves privatization of city-owned residential property in neighborhoods with high unemployment and poverty rates and concentrated minority populations. The program blends market incentives with community interests. By providing rent subsidies for low-income tenants and designing the rules for privatization, government plays an important role in the NEP in a way that complements local private entrepreneurial efforts. Political action by community groups also had a significant influence on program design—most specifically, the requirements that entrepreneurs have ties to low-income neighborhoods and that tenants not be evicted.

To participate in the NEP, entrepreneurs had to have had experience owning or managing property in the neighborhoods where program activity was concentrated. Geographic clusters of buildings were sold to entrepreneurs selected in a competitive process. Entrepreneurs had to agree not to evict existing tenants (except those guilty of destruction of property or nonpayment of rent), and they had to commit to not selling any buildings for eighteen years. Of the twenty-two entrepreneurs participating in the first two rounds of the NEP, nineteen were minorities, and most of these nineteen were living in, or had previously resided or worked in, inner-city neighborhoods.

Program experience indicates that the neighborhood entrepreneurs have profited and neighborhood residents have benefited. Entrepreneurs exercise control over the local environment and exert significant leverage in negotiating services from local governmental agencies. Because the market value of the buildings depends on the behavior of their tenants and on conditions in the neighborhood, the neighborhood entrepreneurs have an economic incentive to secure good long-term tenants by providing quality services and to improve the neighborhood. This motivates them to work with community-based organizations familiar with area residents and to increase their personal presence in the neighborhoods where they own property.

The neighborhood entrepreneurs operate more effectively than either large outside property managers or the city. They pay greater attention to cost issues than the city does, and unlike the city or large outside property owners, they help to build social capital by establishing personal relations with tenants. They are responsive to tenants' problems, and they insist that tenants reciprocate by paying rent and maintaining the buildings. For example, many neighborhood entrepreneurs indicated that they develop close relations with tenants so that they will be able to gain reliable and sensitive information about problems such as local drug dealing. These relationships facilitate their efforts to clear the buildings and surrounding neighborhood of drugs and related crime and protect their investments.

The NEP illustrates how leveraging development assets can work—in this case, the leveraging of entrepreneurial, political, and social assets in community economic development. It should be emphasized that the NEP was initiated only after six months of intensive community organizing by the city's Department of Housing, Preservation, and Development in conjunction with local officials, community groups, and a nonprofit intermediary, the New York City Housing Partnership.

Entrepreneurs in the program are building bridges to mainstream resources (for example, bank lines of credit) and new capabilities (connection to professional service organizations). They are earning profits, and community residents appear to be benefiting.

The NEP experience suggests that entrepreneurial opportunities in the inner city can be exploited in ways that benefit both private and community interests. This can be accomplished by aligning entrepreneurs' interests to the improvement of low-income neighborhoods through political action, public policy, and program design. But the key to having residents buy in to the program and cooperate in maintaining the buildings (which is the major source of the entrepreneurs' cost savings) was that they were organized to participate in the process from the beginning. This enabled residents' interests to be included in the design of the new privatized market. It was residents who insisted on anti-displacement language that prevented entrepreneurs from evicting existing tenants (except for serious offenses) and forcibly committed the entrepreneurs to working with the residents. The entrepreneurs initially resented the residents' organizations, but most soon came to recognize them as assets for their business, and in some cases the entrepreneurs eventually choose to fund resident organizing.

Women Business Owners

Based on growth statistics, there seems to be progress and significant potential for women business owners (WBOs) to play an important role in community economic development. WBOs are the fastest-growing business segment in the United States, both in the population as a whole and among all major minority groups. Among minority firms, between 1987 and 1992 (the year of the last available data), the number of minority female-owned firms increased by 85 percent, while the number of minority firms owned by males increased by just over 50 percent. Currently approximately 16 percent of all U.S. firms are female-owned, 62 percent are male-owned, and 19 percent are owned by both. At 37 percent, the percentage of WBOs among minority groups is even higher, suggesting the potential importance of WBOs in low-income areas with high concentrations of minority populations and female-headed households.

High proportions of WBOs are engaged in businesses that draw on social relations and ties to communities. A disproportionate percentage (twice as many as male-owned businesses) of WBOs provide personal services and retail to household clients: 35 percent of U.S. WBOs are in these industries, compared to 18 percent of male-owned firms (U.S. Bureau of the Census 1996). Some studies of women entrepreneurs suggest that they place more emphasis on social goals (such as helping family and friends) than on conventional measures of success (Godfrey 1992; Hagan, Rivchin, and Sexton 1989). However, low average receipts, low employment levels, and the type of industries in which WBOs are concentrated suggest limitations and barriers, as measured in conventional economic and business terms. With WBOs, gender and social roles appear to have motivated business ownership and created opportunities in particular market niches (such as personal services and retail), but discrimination against women appears to have also worked to limit market advancement in other areas.

Many WBOs complain that they are often not taken seriously when they seek customers beyond their traditional household clienteles (Brush 1997). Bates (1999) has documented how WBOs suffer from restricted access to government contracts and contracts with other businesses. Holding all things else equal—including industry, business size, equity investment, debt, and the education and experience of the business owner—being a woman owner translates into limited market access. The crux of the problem is that WBOs have to confront status quo networks that have traditionally not included them; those networks tend to be resistant to change (Bates 1999, 6).

From the standpoint of individual business ownership development, WBOs as many currently operate in the United States are not the ideal model for economic advancement and community economic development. However, data suggest that women are drawn to more cooperative relationships in business development. It is likely that cooperative business structures such as co-ops, trade associations, and sweat equity arrangements may attract women entrepreneurs and leverage their social networks in low-income communities. Women may then be better able to leverage their strong social ties to break into industry networks and enhance their financial and political assets.

Industry Associations

James Rauch (1996) suggests promising new strategies for minority businesses. He suggests that African American firms can benefit from affiliating with mainstream businesses and business associations. African American entrepreneurs working in such associations can learn the benefits of social networking and eventually form their own associations.

Rauch begins by critiquing international trade theory's treatment of differentiated products. He disputes the "black box" view that buyers and sellers are connected to an abstract international market that serves to match them without cost. In the alternative view he suggests, the more contacts you have with sellers and buyers who know what you are about, the better informed you are about opportunities for selling and buying without engaging in costly search. Using this concept, Rauch proposes to affiliate African American apparel and accessory retailers in Harlem with a large private independent buying office. For Rauch, there can be benefit in Harlem (and other African American communities) from the development of intermediary institutions that play the same role in facilitating trade as is played in other ethnic communities by preexisting intracommunity ties. The intermediary associations act in effect as community organizers whose base consists of small independent retail establishments.

A variant of the approach recommended by Rauch seems to have met with some success. Members of the National Minority Supplier Development Council

(NMSDC) have been able to work collectively to penetrate networks from which they have traditionally been excluded (Bates 1999). In 1997 the NMSDC had thirty-five hundred corporate members (most of the nation's large corporations) and over fifteen thousand minority business establishment (MBE) members. Large corporations seeking to expand their network of MBE suppliers use NMSDC as the vehicle for publicizing their desire to buy specific products from MBEs. The MBE members, in turn, use the NMSDC to publicize the products they would like to sell to business clients; they also use NMSDC information to seek out corporations offering specific goods and services that overlap with products they sell. Corporate members of the NMSDC purchased over $30 billion in goods and services in 1997 from MBE members (NMSDC 1998).

The NMSDC is an example of how a formal association can be used to establish new ties and open new market opportunities. From Rauch's perspective, it demonstrates that more information flows between buyers and sellers can facilitate market exchange. It also reinforces the important role of political capital in community economic development and minority business development. The effectiveness of the NMSDC is influenced by the preferential procurement programs of government agencies and corporations, which have been affected over the years by political action and public pressure (for example, Jesse Jackson's campaign with Corporate America). Political action in this case may have opened (even perhaps forced open) the opportunity for market exchange.

Cooperatives and Credit Unions

Since the founding of our nation, members of agricultural cooperatives have derived economic benefits from a mix of market, social, and political relations, including: collective buying of supplies; the sharing of equipment; common information dissemination on weather and agricultural conditions; collective control of pricing (and exclusion from antitrust laws); and using a collective political voice to influence public policies. Credit union members benefit from their affiliations (mostly workplace- or community-related) and their control of collective financial resources, deriving improved access to financing and lower credit costs.

In similar ways, community economic development efforts could benefit from the community-organized collective efforts of producers and consumers. Such efforts could draw on social capital to reduce business costs by collectively providing or purchasing property, casualty, and health insurance, goods and supplies, and health care and other services at reduced costs to community businesses and residents.

Another way the residents of low-income communities can collectively act to improve their economic situation is through protected or captive markets. Ethnic entrepreneurs have been described as benefiting from captive enclave economies. In enclave economies, the shielding of consumer and labor markets from outside competition gives businesses a captive market to charge prices above the competitive price and pay wages below the market wage. This can have both positive and negative market and community consequences. On the one hand, start-up firms can enter markets, develop basic business know-how, and get up on the learning curve. On the other hand, an enclave economy can lead to exploitation of consumers and local workers and market complacency.

Bringing Venture Capital Networks to Low-Income Areas

Venture capital and private angel investor networks (Freear, Sohl, and Wetzel 1995) have played a strong role in financing nontraditional business start-ups (that is, those without the collateral or cash flow on which banks rely). Even more than traditional sources of financing, venture capital and private angel investors draw heavily on social ties and business relations to identify investment opportunities. They then stay closely connected to their investments, adding value to their investments through personal advising and connecting the businesses in which they invest to each other and to other businesses to which they are connected. Because these investors rely on personal contact, most of their ties and subsequent investment are geographically bound and industry-focused (for example, Silicon Valley outside of San Jose; Route 128, the high-technology highway surrounding Boston; and New York City's Silicon Alley).

The U.S. Small Business Administration (SBA) has tried to extend some of the dynamics of the venture capital and private angel investor market. In April 1997, it established ACE-NET, an Internet-based service that attempts to extend the venture capital and private angel financial funding network to start-up businesses that are outside its traditional venues. The hope is that the Internet can help overcome the geographic and social disconnection between the venture capital and private angel investor markets and minority and other businesses. Overcoming this barrier has been difficult to achieve. Only eight "marriages" were made between funders and start-ups in the first two years of program operation. There is a paucity of evidence that venture capital and private angel investor ties can be created (and social capital constructed) through the Internet. This is of little surprise to experienced venture capitalists and private angels who highlight the value of frequent informal personal contact in guiding their investments.

The experience of ACE-NET reinforces the value of personal contacts and relations in economic ventures. A lesson for community economic development is that it will not be easy to transfer networks (and bridge), even with new information technology. This will still have to be done the old-fashioned way, with personal, face-to-face contact. In markets with a history of discrimination and exclusion, such as information technology, it is likely that political action will be necessary.

A Role for Political Action

Michael Porter (1995) takes the position that in community economic development there has been an overemphasis on politics and overreliance on public policies. We believe that, because of the long history of economic development benefits being siphoned from inner cities, politics cannot be ignored. We also think that residents, businesses, and labor groups can organize more effectively to affect market rules, and thus economic outcomes and the distribution of economic benefits. What is required is a new focus for politics and political action in community economic development.

In contrast to Porter's anti-politics view, there is the long history in the United States of business lobbying and (to a lesser degree) union organizing to affect market structures, trade policies, labor standards, and subsidies for research and development. There is also some history of community mobilization on these issues. The Community Reinvestment Act (CRA), for example, represented a significant political victory for the supporters of low-income communities. The success of CRA, however, might have inadvertently contributed to a slowdown in political activism in low-income communities and to disempowerment. Politics has been marginalized in community development theory and practice. For example, CDCs (one of the main beneficiaries of the CRA) have focused on increasing housing production and gaining access to traditional sources of financial capital, but they are not active in political organizing (partly because of their nonprofit tax status). This is unfortunate. Recently, the CRA has been weakened by Congress, and political mobilization on the issue has not been as strong as it was during the initial legislation.

The CRA also created a market for national community development financial intermediaries, such as the Local Initiative Support Corporation (LISC). These organizations provide important financial assets for low-income residents. The quarter-billion dollars of community development financial capital that LISC has contributed to more than thirty metropolitan areas across the nation has resulted in thousands of new housing units and the physical improvement of many low-income neighborhoods across the country. Yet LISC and other community development financial intermediaries could be criticized for furthering the dependency of the residents of low-income communities by focusing too narrowly on financing housing and failing to contribute enough to the enhancement of other community assets—in particular, human capital and social capital. The narrow focus on financial assistance and housing production can make residents heavily reliant on the service of the intermediary and its staff and the goodwill of business elites, and it can depoliticize community development, with negative consequences for the development of other important community assets.

Summary: Lessons from Models

Social capital's role in community economic development has too often been highlighted without adequate definition of its connection to political and financial institutions and other factors that shape local economies and business opportunity. We have presented an alternative framework that suggests how social capital can work in concert with other critical community economic development assets to serve the interests of both businesses and residents in low-income communities.

CONCLUSION

Social capital is a key resource for community economic development because it can be used to aggregate and leverage other development assets. Social capital is not a substitute for economic resources or political power. It may be a good starting point, however, for developing and leveraging other assets. Social capital is built by individuals and institutions with differing goals, incentives, prejudices, and dislikes. In the absence of strong community institutions, international and national corporations have utilized mass media and marketing techniques to affect social trends in low-income communities that end up being detrimental to these communities. Key questions include: Who builds up social capital in low-income communities? What is the nature of incentives to build social capital? And for what ends is social capital built? It is not easy to construct mechanisms that encourage individuals to organize in their communities, especially with the prevailing ideology of individualism, and there is no guarantee that social capital will be used to serve broad community interests.

A research agenda for inquiries into the role of social capital in community economic development should include a focus on how different institutions and entities (such as private entrepreneurs with strong social ties to low-income neighborhoods) affect social capital in poor communities. A goal should be to discern which approaches to social, political, and economic organization in a community inspire the greatest trust and commitment from its residents and contribute the most to the economic prospects of local businesses and residents.

REFERENCES

Albrow, Martin. 1997. *The Global Age*. Stanford, Calif.: Stanford University Press.

Ankersmit, Franklin R. 1996. *Aesthetic Politics: Political Philosophy Beyond Fact and Value.* Stanford, Calif.: Stanford University Press.

Bates, Timothy. 1994. "An Analysis of Korean-Immigrant-Owned Small-Business Start-ups with Comparison to African American and Non-Minority-Owned Firms." *Urban Affairs Quarterly* 30(2): 227–48.

———. 1999. "Restricted Access to Markets Characterizes Women-Owned Businesses." Unpublished paper. Wayne State University, Detroit, Michigan.

Bates, Timothy, and C. Dunham. 1993. "Asian-American Success in Self-Employment." *Economic Development Quarterly* 7(2): 199–214.

Block, Fred 1994. "The Roles of the State in the Economy." In *The Handbook of Economic Sociology,* edited by Neil Smelser and Richard Swedberg. Princeton, N.J.: Princeton University Press.

Bonacich, Edna, and Ivan Light. 1991. *Immigrant Entrepreneurs: Koreans in Los Angeles, 1965–1982*. Berkeley: University of California Press.

Boyd, R. L. 1990. "Black Business Transformation, Black Well-being, and Public Policy." *Population Research and Policy Review* 9: 17–132.

Bronson, Po. 1999. *The Nudist on the Late Shift*. New York: Random House.

Brush, Candida. 1997. "Women-Owned Businesses: Obstacles and Opportunities." *Journal of Developmental Entrepreneurship* 2(1): 1–24.

Burt, Ronald S. 1992. *Structural Holes: The Social Structure of Competition*. Cambridge, Mass.: Harvard University Press.

DiMaggio, Paul. 1994. "Culture and Economy." In *The Handbook of Economic Sociology*, edited by Neil Smelser and R. Swedberg. Princeton, N.J.: Princeton University Press.

Freear, John, Jeffery Sohl, and William Wetzel. 1995. "Angles: Personal Investors in the Venture Capital Market." *Entrepreneurship and Regional Development* 7(January): 85–95.

Gittell, Ross. 1992. *Renewing Cities*. Princeton, N.J.: Princeton University Press.

Gittell, Ross, K. Lawrence, and Phillip Thompson. 1995. "Neighborhood Entrepreneurs and Inner-City Employment." Report to the Rockefeller Foundation.

Gittell, Ross, and Phillip Thompson. 1999. "Inner-City Business Development and Entrepreneurship: New Frontiers for Policy and Research." In *Urban Problems and Community Development*, edited by Ronald F. Ferguson and William T. Dickens. Washington, D.C.: Brookings Institution Press.

Gittell, Ross, and Avis Vidal. 1998. *Community Organizing: Building Social Capital as a Development Strategy*. Thousand Oaks, Calif.: Sage Publications.

Gittell, Ross, and Margaret Wilder. 1999. "Community Development Corporations: Critical Factors That Influence Success." *Journal of Urban Affairs* 21(3): 341–62.

Godfrey, Joline. 1992. *Our Wildest Dreams: Women Entrepreneurs Making Money, Having Fun, Doing Good*. New York: HarperCollins.

Granovetter, Mark S. 1973. "The Strength of Weak Ties." *American Journal of Sociology* 78(6): 1360–80.

Graves, E. G. 1998. "The Black Wealth Imperative." *Black Enterprise* 28(11): 17.

Greenhouse, Samuel. 2000. "Labor Group Plans Housing for Workers." *New York Times*, August 29.

Hagen, Oliver, C. Rivchin, and D. Sexton, eds. 1989. *Women-Owned Businesses*. New York: Praeger.

National Minority Supplier Development Council (NMSDC). 1998. *Celebrating 25 Years*. New York: NMSDC.

Okun, Arthur. 1975. *Equality and Efficiency: The Big Trade-off*. Washington, D.C.: Brookings Institution Press.

Osborne, David. 1988. *Laboratories of Democracy*. Boston: Harvard Business School Press.

Porter, Michael E. 1995. "The Competitive Advantage of the Inner City." *Harvard Business Review* 73(May–June): 55–71.

———. 1997. "New Strategies for Inner-City Economic Development." *Economic Development Quarterly* 11(1): 11–27.

Portes, Alejandro, and Rubén Runbaut. 1996. *Immigrants in America, a Portrait*. Berkeley: University of California Press.

Portes, Alejandro, and Min Zhou. 1996. "Self-Employment and the Earnings of Immigrants." *American Sociological Review* 61: 219–30.

Rauch, James E. 1996. *Trade and Networks: An Application to Minority Retail Entrepreneurship*. Report to the Russell Sage Foundation.

Reich, Robert B. 1991. *The Work of Nations: Preparing Ourselves for Twenty-first Century Capitalism*. New York: Vintage.

Schmidt, Peter. 2000. "General Motors Joins University of Michigan's Defense of Affirmative Action in Admissions." *Chronicle of Higher Education* (July 28): A21.

Schumpeter, Joseph A. 1934. *The Theory of Economic Development*. Translated by R. Opie. Cambridge, Mass.: Harvard University Press.

Servon, Lisa J. 1999. *Bootstrap Capital*. Washington, D.C.: Brookings Institution Press.

————. 1997. "Microenterprise Programs in U.S. Inner Cities: Economic Development or Social Welfare?" *Economic Development Quarterly* 11(2): 166–80.

Taub, Richard. 1988. *Community Capitalism.* Boston: Harvard Business School Press.

Thurow, Lester. 1999. *Building Wealth: The New Rules for Individuals, Companies, and Nations in a Knowledge-Based Economy.* New York: HarperCollins.

U.S. Bureau of the Census. 1996. *Characteristics of Business Owners.* Washington: U.S. Government Printing Office.

Venkatesh, Sudhir A. 2000. *American Project: The Rise and Fall of a Modern Ghetto.* Cambridge, Mass.: Harvard University Press.

Vidal, Avis C. 1992. *Rebuilding Communities.* New York: Community Development Research Center, New School for Social Research.

Wilson, William J. 1987. *The Truly Disadvantaged: The Inner City, the Underclass, and Public Policy.* Chicago: University of Chicago Press.

Chapter 6

Housing, Social Capital, and Poor Communities

Langley C. Keyes

Given the current definitional controversy surrounding the term "social cap-ital," any discussion of its relationship to housing and poor communities can quickly become mired in theoretical and empirical debate.[1] Rather than curs-ing the definitional darkness, this essay seizes Michael Woolcock's (1998) framing of the term as the lens through which to view housing and poor communities.

In "Social Capital and Economic Development: Toward a Theoretical Synthesis and Policy Framework," Woolcock (1998, 184) throws down this gauntlet:[2]

> As arguably the most influential concept to emerge from economic sociology in the last decade, it behooves serious students to critique, clarify, and refine what they mean by this tantalizing term [social capital], lest it go from intel-lectual insight appropriated by policy pundits, to journalistic cliché, to even-tual oblivion.

Woolcock developed his theoretical synthesis and policy framework to look at issues of development in emerging countries, where the focus is on the nation-state and its relationship to local communities. When applied to the urban world of devel-oped countries, his terminology needs some reformulation. But when focused at the level of the city, the neighborhood, or the individual housing development, his model provides a disciplined way of looking at the relationship of social capital to housing and poor communities in American cities.

Woolcock's developmental world is one in which the legal, cultural, and institu-tional structures at the national and local levels of a nation both affect and are affected by the nature of the country's social capital networks. He posits four social capitals, each representing a unique kind of social network. Two of the networks are "bottom up," located at the local grassroots level. The other two are "top down," originating at the corporate and governmental levels. The first bottom-up social capital is con-cerned with "intracommunity ties"—the degree of *integration* of the community under consideration. The second bottom-up social capital focuses on *linkage*, the term Woolcock uses for extracommunity networks, that is, the degree to which the community is able to reach out to entities, organizations, and notables beyond itself. His underlying presumption is that the more integrated the community, the more readily it can successfully carry out such linkage.

The social capital "view from the top" approximates a mirror image of the two bottom-up networks. Parallel to community integration at the bottom, *integrity* is the term applied to intra-integration of individual top-down organizations. How efficient, well organized, and rational are they? *Synergy* is Woolcock's concept for extra-organizational networking at the top between state and economic institutions, that is, linkage between key public and private stakeholders.

Woolcock's schematic networked nation has horizontal linkages across "the top" and "the bottom." When spelled out in developmental terms, these four social networks present a two-by-two matrix of high and low degrees of social capital (see figure 6.1).

FIGURE 6.1   /   Woolcock's Four Social Networks

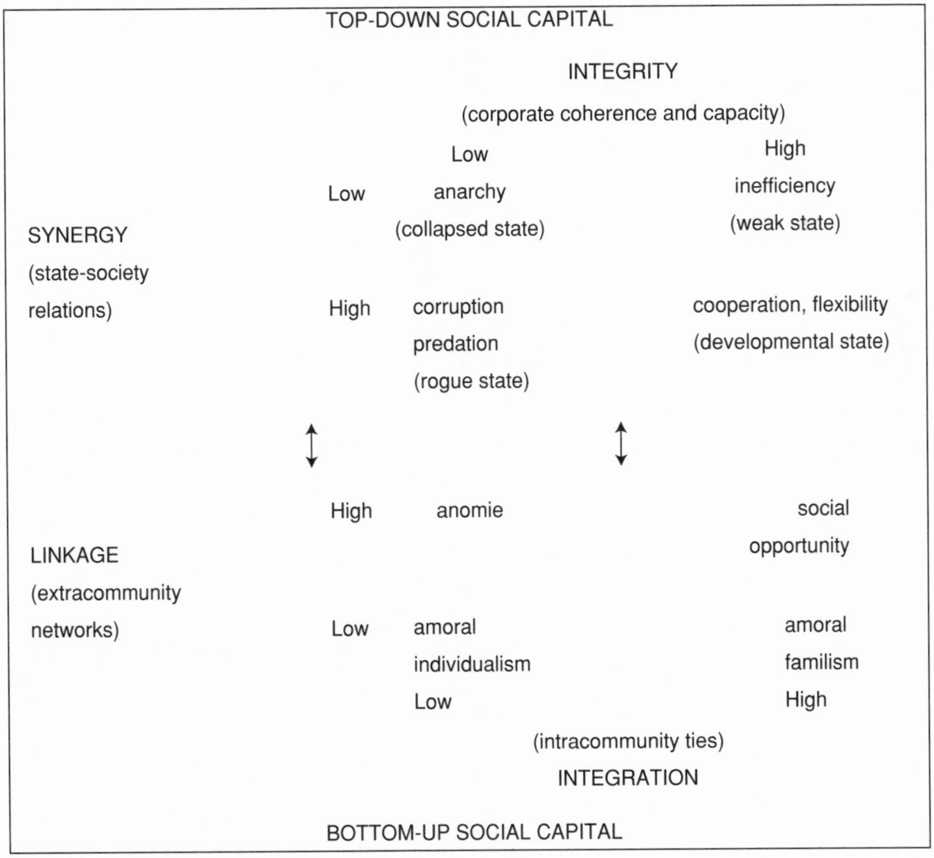

TOP-DOWN SOCIAL CAPITAL

INTEGRITY

(corporate coherence and capacity)

		Low	High
SYNERGY (state-society relations)	Low	anarchy (collapsed state)	inefficiency (weak state)
	High	corruption predation (rogue state)	cooperation, flexibility (developmental state)
LINKAGE (extracommunity networks)	High	anomie	social opportunity
	Low	amoral individualism	amoral familism
		Low	High

(intracommunity ties)

INTEGRATION

BOTTOM-UP SOCIAL CAPITAL

Source: Woolcock 1998.

After identifying the four types of social networks, Woolcock concludes that

the most pressing issues for development theory and policy—especially those concerned with poverty alleviation—emerge from *interaction between both realms.* . . . [T]he prospects of local-level development efforts very much turn on the extent to which both bottom-up and top-down dilemmas are resolved (179). . . . [T] *he interaction between "top down" and "bottom up" must therefore be a dynamic one.* (180, emphasis added)

The synergized-top should reach down, and the linkaged-bottom reach upward. There must be positive interaction between the two levels to achieve the ultimate "network of networks": the integrated and networked local community linked to a cohesive and civic-minded corporate realm that works synergistically with an equitable and efficient state.

Interactions between Woolcock's bottom-up and top-down "dilemmas of development" produce sixteen possible "performance outcomes." Performance outcome is defined in terms of the quality of social capitals. In the best of all worlds, all four forms operate in tandem. Woolcock's "beneficent autonomy" belies the immediate response to the term "autonomy" and represents a world in which the four are both individually highly functioning and mutually networked. At the other end of performance outcome, "anarchic individualism" is a world without meaningful social capitals at either the grassroots or upper level of the institutional system, nor in the interactions between the top and the bottom (table 6.1).

Woolcock's model defines social capital in terms of social relations (networks) within both the poor community (bottom up) and the larger society (top down), that is, it frames *opportunities and weaknesses at each level and in each direction.*

REFOCUSING WOOLCOCK'S MODEL: FROM ECONOMIC DEVELOPMENT TO LOW-INCOME URBAN HOUSING

Woolcock's vocabulary and framework can be used to build a model of social capital, housing, and poor communities. In the low-income housing world, "community"

TABLE 6.1 / Performance Outcomes

	Bottom-Up Social Capital		Top-Down Social Capital		
	Integration	Linkage	Synergy	Integrity	Performance Outcome
16	High	High	High	High	(Beneficent autonomy)
15	High	High	High	Low	
. . .					
3	Low	Low	High	Low	
2	Low	Low	Low	High	
1	Low	Low	Low	Low	(Anarchic individualism)

Source: Woolcock 1998.

can mean several things: neighborhood, housing development, or group utilization of a particular program or policy. It is critical to establish the "unit of community" under consideration because that unit then frames the meaning of the other three elements of the social capital matrix. The housing of low-income people in poor communities operates within a dynamic framework defined by top-down and bottom-up networks and the interrelationship both between and among the four.

Low-income urban households in subsidized and private housing stock maintain social relationships that range along a spectrum from low to high degrees of integration. Low-integration households often have little sense of embeddedness in their residential enclave—whether a development or a neighborhood—and thus may be trapped in a state of amoral individualism (Wilson 1987). High-integration households have developed intracommunity ties and are socially embedded in their housing development or neighborhood (Gans 1962; Gill 1977; Briggs and Mueller 1997). Low intracommunity integration results in little if any linkage that reaches beyond the bounds of the housing development or neighborhood to the broader society (Gans 1962; Warren 1963). But the presumption is that highly integrated residential developments have a greater likelihood of linkage to their surroundings.

Extracommunity linkages benefit the community as a whole. Linked housing entities, be they developments or neighborhoods, have a networked relationship with banks, police, and schools that represents an extracommunity network; for example, there may be a "trust-based" relationship between an individual (a housing manager or tenant leader) and the police department around issues of security (Keyes 1992). Some households, living with a high degree of intracommunity integration, may turn their backs on the larger social system as a way of reaffirming their "solidarity" as an integrated community. The result may be amoral familism: the norms and opportunities of the larger society are proscribed out of loyalty to intracommunity ties.[3]

At the conceptual level, Woolcock's discussion of community and the micro environment seems readily transferable to low-income neighborhoods and residential owners and renters. However, his macro concepts of collapsed, weak, and rogue states have an unfamiliar ring to the domestic ear. The parallels at the top (the macro level) become clearer if one thinks not in terms of military dictators and the grossest lack of corporate integrity but rather of ineffective mayors, weak community development departments, patronage-ridden housing authorities, and insensitive or absent corporate leadership, as well as hostility among the various stakeholders at the top.

Organizations and institutions that have an impact on the lives of poor people and their housing opportunities are found in all three sectors: public, private, and nonprofit. The corporate coherence, capacity, and professionalism of each determines how effectively public money, private loans, and nonprofit support flow into housing in poor neighborhoods. The network of players—public, private, and nonprofit; national, state, and city government; banks, corporations, and foundations—has a critical impact on the quality of housing production and maintenance (Keyes et al. 1996; Walker and Weinheimer 1998). No one sector has a monopoly on efficient housing provisions. The effectiveness of each in carrying out housing programs and strategies for and with low-income households is a function of: the competence and professionalism (integrity) of individual organizations; the ability of each to work synergistically with others across public-private-nonprofit lines; and the capacity to forge and sustain "social relations connecting top-down resources and bottoms-up capacity building" (Woolcock 1998, 179).

Woolcock's macro image of the state is focused on the central government of emerging countries. Viewing the top-down macro model through a domestic housing lens, the picture becomes more complex. Domestically, macro can refer to the three levels above the community, that is, the city, the state, or the federal government, as well as to their relationship to each other. For example, the macro environment in which a HOPE VI public housing development must operate to be successful at the micro level on the ground in the neighborhood cuts through all three public levels (city, state, and federal) and a range of institutional public, private, and nonprofit actors and their various degrees of integrity and synergy.

What seems most critical in Woolcock's presentation of macro is that the public and private actors networking *above* the community neighborhood or housing development have a key impact on how the bottom-up sector is able to perform. That impact is in part related to the *degree of integration and linkage* of the housing community at the grass roots.

A high level of professional competence on the part of individual top-down organizations combined with sustained inter-organizational networks provides a context for linking extracommunity individuals and organizations networking upward from the local residential community. Ultimately, where a development, residential enclave, or neighborhood stands along Woolcock's spectrum from "anarchic individualism" to "beneficent autonomy" is a function of the individual strength and integration of four forms of social capital, that is, the level of integration of horizontal and vertical networks related to the production, financing, affordability, and maintenance of housing for low-income people.

The top-down–bottom-up view of the world requires embedding any examination of housing and social capital in a framework larger than simply the development, the residential enclave, or the neighborhood. Social capital is dynamic not only at the bottom (integration and linkage) and at the top (synergy and integrity) but also, and perhaps most important, *interactively* between the top and the bottom. Woolcock's model poses a way of thinking about affordable housing in the community that requires analyzing the issues associated with the four social networks and how they impinge on that housing.

ISSUES WITH THE WOOLCOCK MODEL

Translating the Woolcock model from developing countries to the domestic urban world seems readily appropriate. But in making the transition, a few concepts need clarification, and others remain problematic at the conceptual level.

"Community" is critical in describing issues of transformation from the bottom-up perspective. Although community is a key word in Woolcock's use of the concepts of integration and linkage, he never defines this central term. Like many writing about its domestic counterpart, he assumes for the purposes of his model that the term "community" is sufficiently descriptive in and of itself. Recognizing that it is not self-defining, this chapter posits that the unit of analysis equivalent to Woolcock's "community" can occur at several levels: individual housing developments, whether rental, coop, condominium, public housing, or mixed-income; geographic residential neighborhoods, which can be of various sizes and housing mixes; and programs serving specified residential populations (potential homeowners, for example).

There are other conceptual difficulties with Woolcock's use of the term "community" when applied to the domestic housing context. Does community include not only households but also other institutions that are considered part of the neighborhood, such as schools, service organizations, and retail shops? What about horizontal ties between the community of residents and the institutions serving them? Are connections of this kind considered intra- or extracommunity networks? Where does "intra" end and "extra" begin within the horizontal and vertical worlds of potential networks? For purposes of clarification, this chapter assumes that bottom-up linkages refer to connections between the community, be it neighborhood, development, or a community housing entity, and other horizontal entities, that is, other organizations and stakeholders in the neighborhood at the grassroots level.

Woolcock presents a clear image of how communities at the bottom must reach out to form extracommunity networks with institutions "above" them. It is less clear how corporate, state, and nonprofit institutions "reach down" from above. The dynamic interaction between top and bottom "bridging down" as well as "bridging up" also remains somewhat mysterious.

Woolcock does not explore the role of political power in promoting or discouraging network formation, either horizontal or vertical. But power—definable as the capacity to enforce a decision—is a critical aspect of interactions between various actors and institutions, a point to be considered at length at the end of this chapter.

Whether in the homeownership or rental sector, housing in the United States is overwhelmingly dominated by the private market. Woolcock's model of the four social capitals does not readily provide a role for this most dominant factor in the housing world: the interaction of buyers and sellers, of supply and demand. Does the market encourage or discourage synergy and interaction between top-down and bottom-up social capitals? What is the interaction between the market and Woolcock's top-down–bottom-up networked world? Between the social capital and economic capital worlds? These questions are not dealt with in Woolcock's discussion.

FROM THEORY TO PRACTICE

Although it bypasses or leaves ambiguous significance issues, at a conceptual level Woolcock's framework provides an evocative way to look at the role of social capital in the dynamics of urban housing. But to truly test how well the framework works as a heuristic device for exploring housing, social capital, and poor communities, we must move from theory to practice.

How well does the framework hold up when reviewing specific housing policy issues and controversies in its terms? How useful is it as a heuristic device to frame and organize specific stories about housing, social capital, and poor communities? As a way of framing, does it help us move beyond description or analysis to a strategic framing of the issues of housing and poor communities that will be useful for practice and policy?

The remainder of this chapter provides three explorations of these issues and questions. It first presents seven case studies, each representing one of Woolcock's sixteen performance outcomes. Using his terminology to frame the stories, the exercise explores the relevance and utility of Woolcock's construct in presenting the narratives and understanding their content. Second, the chapter explores if and how Woolcock's mode of framing these narratives of housing, social capital, and poor communities has a utilitarian quality helpful in considering practice and policy. Finally, it addresses the housing issues of poor communities that are not sufficiently addressed by the Woolcock construct and the kind of research and thinking that would be necessary to integrate those concerns into Woolcock's framework.

THROUGH THE WOOLCOCK LOOKING GLASS: SEVEN STORIES OF HOUSING, SOCIAL CAPITAL, AND POOR COMMUNITIES

The following cases are presenting in rough order of performance—from examples close to "anarchic individualism," at one extreme, to "beneficent autonomy" at the other, as well as examples of variations along the way. They do not all neatly fit one of Woolcock's sixteen performance outcomes, but they come remarkably close. And their variance from his outcomes is in itself informative. Not all four social networks can be evaluated with equal accuracy in all seven of the cases (and in a few instances not at all). Two of the cases—community development in Cleveland and HOPE VI in Boston—are based on my own research. The other five stories are housing cases, researched by others, that I have reframed in Woolcock's terms. I chose them to test the degree to which Woolcock's model provides structure for their narrative line.

Anarchic Individualism: Rainwater's Pruit-Igo

Lee Rainwater's (1966) description of life in Pruit-Igo, a large public housing development in St. Louis, is a classic portrait of a residential development with low integration and lower linkage. The title of the article reporting his findings, "Fear and the House-as-Haven in the Lower Class," captures the sense of low performance outcome in both intra- and extracommunity social capital.

Bottom-Up Social Capital		Top-Down Social Capital		
Integration	Linkage	Synergy	Integrity	Performance Outcome
Low	Low	Unclear	Low	Modified anarchic individualism

In Rainwater's analysis, housing for a poor community is seen primarily as refuge "from a wide variety of human and nonhuman threats, from which [tenants] fear consequences that combine elements of physical threat, disruption of familial and other interpersonal relations, and threats of moral damage to the self" (23). Rainwater's lower-class world is one in which "people often seem isolated" and their "participation in a community of known and valued peers" seems "tenuous" (26). Given concerns for safety and fear of violence, the role of housing is to provide safe haven. "At the cost of perhaps increased isolation, lower class people in public housing sometimes place a great deal of value on privacy and on living a quiet life behind the locked doors of their apartment" (30).

Rainwater takes as given that life among the lower class in public housing is mean, unsafe, and isolating. In Woolcock's terms, the policy challenge is to provide a secure residential setting for a family whose intra- let alone extracommunity ties are a luxury. Viewed through the social capital lens, Rainwater's lower-class world is one in which the absence of social capital implicitly is taken as a given and the role of public policy is to make more secure a life of "amoral individualism."

The public housing tenants look to top-down organizations—the police and the housing authority—to make "their immediate neighborhood or the housing project grounds a more controlled and safe place" (30). But there is real concern lest those same top-down organizations "seem to demand and damn more than they help. . . . The crux of the caretaking task in connection with lower class people is to provide and encourage security and order within the lower class world without at the same time extracting from it a heavy price in self-esteem, dignity, and autonomy" (30). Thus, the lack of social ties, linkage, and networks between the top-down enforcing agency and the public housing community results in the possibility that the security cure is worse than the insecurity disease.

Compare Rainwater's description with Woolcock's presentation on organizational integrity without synergy. Woolcock points out that among weak states, where there is too much bureaucracy and too little civil society, "government may be committed in principle to upholding common law . . . but in practice . . . is largely indifferent to the plight of vulnerable groups (women, the elderly, poor and disabled) . . . [and] responds slowly if at all to citizen demands" (177).

The image is equally applicable to the St. Louis public housing development that Rainwater describes in the United States in the 1960s. Woolcock's model thus provides a useful way of framing the experience of Pruit-Igo and positing a performance outcome close to "anarchic individualism."

Moving Toward Integration: Halpern's Southgate Estate

David Halpern (1988, 50) presents a case study of a "problem" public housing development, the Southgate Estate in Runcorn, England, which he describes as a "notorious estate that . . . came out bottom out of 207 . . . [estates] in the region on six different measures of deprivation." As a result of extensive physical changes, the social atmosphere of the estate and the mental health of residents were vastly improved.

Bottom-Up Social Capital		Top-Down Social Capital		
Integration	Linkage	Synergy	Integrity	Performance Outcome
Moderate	Moderate	Moderate	Moderate	Increased integration

Although Halpern emphasizes that the impact of the physical changes "should not be underestimated," he sees the consultation with the tenants as the most critical element in changing the social atmosphere. "Ironically problems with the building . . . brought residents together. This semi-enforced social interaction broke down barriers giving residents opportunities to get to know one another and to establish trust" (52). His conclusion is that "a major casual factor in the improvement of problem estates is the increase in the social capital of the residents, and particularly levels of trust" (52). Greater intracommunity integration occurred because the housing agency, in a top-down effort that demonstrated some degree of corporate integrity, was able to work effectively with tenants working from the bottom up. Halpern cautions, however, that "this reinvigorated social trust inside the estate will not, by itself, reconnect residents to the wider community or greatly improve their economic well-being" (53).

But the obvious success of the connection between the tenants and the housing authority raises the interesting question of the significance of the source of the linkage connection. In this case, the successful linkage seems clearly to be the result of the "reaching out" (or down) of the authority rather than of the extracommunity efforts of the tenants. As Woolcock points out, integration without upward linkage has its limits. Through what process would successful linkage move beyond the connection with the housing authority to address the broader issues of economic well-being and connection to the wider community? Woolcock's model helps frame the question but does not point in the direction of an answer.

Integration with and Without Linkage: HOPE VI in Boston

In the mid-1990s, the Boston Housing Authority (BHA) won federal funding for two large HOPE VI developments, Mission Main and Orchard Park. In theory, the story of the redevelopment of these large, deteriorated family housing developments should have been similar: demolition of most if not all the units, replacement with lower-density housing, income-mixing, and an effort to integrate the

	Bottom-Up Social Capital		Top-Down Social Capital		
	Integration	Linkage	Synergy	Integrity	Performance Outcome
Orchard Park	High	High	High	High	Beneficent autonomy
Mission Main	High	Low	Low	Mixed	Inefficiency-amoral familism

new development into the surrounding neighborhood. Both projects were undertaken by the same housing authority, the same mayor, and the same representatives from the Department of Housing and Urban Development (HUD). Similar case studies should have emerged given that the only real variations were the tenant bodies and the developers. Yet the route taken by the planning and development processes were radically different.

At both Mission Main and Orchard Park, the espoused collective mandate has been the same: to produce an economically and socially viable mixed-income, mixed-finance development. Synergy between public, nonprofit, and private actors needed to occur in both cases. Demolition, relocation, and interim management had to be coordinated with issues of physical design, land assemblage and income mix. The demands for a successful outcome to the process were the same for each development: innovative and creative solutions to nonroutine procedures. The need for such decisionmaking placed a premium on coordination, open communication, and trust among the players. In Woolcock's terms, there was a need for high synergy, integrity, integration, and linkage. All four social capitals had to be operating if a successful HOPE VI initiative was to be achieved.

Observers of and participants in the two development processes agree that the nature of the relationship among three of the players—the BHA HOPE VI project team, the developer, and the tenants—is the key to understanding why Mission Main became mired in trouble and the development process at Orchard Park, by contrast, can be judged high in performance outcome.

At Orchard Park, major conflicts had to be resolved along the way. But the level of trust and mutual goodwill among the BHA project staff, the tenants, and the developers was strengthened over time as decisions were made and individual conflicts were resolved one at a time.

At Mission Main, the reverse was the case. Initial misunderstandings and miscommunication were exacerbated. In practice, collective trust and "shared vision" were scarce commodities among the players in the developer, tenants, and BHA project team triangle. Distrust was nurtured with each decision made or not made.

The interaction among the three players at Orchard Park was the mirror opposite of the experience at Mission Main. The first critical difference was the relationship between the tenants and the BHA team. At Orchard Park, the positive and long-standing connection with the BHA architect who had worked with the Orchard Park Tenants Association (OPTA) through an earlier lengthy and complex rehabilitation process established a trust-based relationship from the start of negotiations. The tenants had no deep regard for "the Authority" as such. But they did have confidence in the architect. Orchard Park residents were led by individuals experienced in working on development issues with the BHA. The tenants had preestablished linkage. Moreover, OPTA could speak with authority for the development, in which there was a significant degree of tenant integration in Woolcock's sense. Leadership was thus able to deliver the rest of the tenants at critical points in the development process.

From the start of negotiations, a sense of mutual interest existed among the BHA project team members, the tenants, and the developer. Whatever the disagreement and battles on individual issues, the players worked together and made the development a reality. The developer entered the opening round of discussions with the BHA with a view of the terms of agreement at odds with that of the BHA. However, the players reconciled those disparities without breaking down the fundamental goodwill among the players.

Woolcock's language appropriately describes the planning process at Orchard Park: "Top-down resources [HOPE VI funds] and bottom-up capacity building [OPTA] need to be in a dynamic and cooperative relationship in order to assemble the range of people and materials capable of overcoming problems or to take advantage of opportunities" (185). Orchard Park posed the difficult challenge of integrating into a battered neighborhood a residential project undertaken by a development team made up of tenants, a local community development corporation, and a private developer. This set of bottom-up and top-down actors successfully wove its way through the complex processes of demolition, land assemblage, public-private partnership, and tenant participation.

The HOPE VI at Mission Main, located in a community rich with institutions (Adams et al. 1995), was awarded to two private developers with long and successful track records. The initiative bogged down during the development process in recrimination and conflict. Mission Main has been an example of a fairly well integrated development that resisted linkage while dealing with a lack of synergy between the top-down players.

Before HOPE VI, Mission Main was a super-block surrounded on three sides by well-functioning institutions. The contrast between the income and social status of the public housing development and its neighbors was stark. It was a challenge to knit together the urban fabric given how different the uses outside Mission's footprint were from the development itself. Mission Main had always had a difficult relationship with its neighbors. Linkage through the vehicle of HOPE VI was not perceived by the Mission Main Tenant Task Force (MMTTF) as necessarily an opportunity. To the contrary, the MMTTF consistently fought to maintain the integrity of the original Mission Main space and to resist efforts to blend the new development into the larger community. The community outside the footprint of the development was viewed as "threat," not opportunity. The residents did not perceive linkage into the larger neighborhood as a benefit. They battled against making interior private roads public and putting a proposed community center on the edge of the site. Both physical changes were seen as providing linkage to the surrounding neighborhood, a virtue from the point of view of the BHA program team. In the tenant leaders' eyes, however, such changes threatened the integrity of the Mission Main community. At Mission Main, the benefits of linkage were in the eye of the beholder.

Orchard Park's physical relationship to its surroundings contrasted vividly with Mission Main's. The circle around Orchard Park, a ring of vacant, rubble-filled land and low-rent, deteriorated residential buildings, looked ripe for a planned urban renewal program. Whereas Mission Main was essentially a lower-class, minority, residential super-block surrounded by middle-class white institutions, Orchard Park was not radically different in income or ethnicity from its neighbors, who were also low-income minorities.

The BHA and the Orchard Park tenants worked hard to communicate their plans to the surrounding neighbors, who were delighted to know that vacant land was going to be put back to residential use. The neighbors' fears of public housing tenants were assuaged by the BHA staff, who indicated that the new units would be well managed and that the people living in them would be working-class.

We can use Woolcock's social capital vocabulary to explain the disparity in outcome at the two HOPE VI sites. The tenant population of Mission Main had a reasonably high level of intracommunity integration but very little linkage to or trust in top-down organizations, particularly the BHA. At the top, the two Mission Main developers showed little synergy between themselves and even less with the Boston Housing Authority and the other public actors trying to move the project forward. Conversely, Orchard Park had not only a high level of integration but also a capacity and willingness to reach upward (and outward) to link with both the top-down organizations and the surrounding residential area. In addition, the top-down institutions showed not only a high level of integrity and synergy among themselves but also a high capacity to interact positively with the Orchard Park community.

Although Woolcock is commenting on a vastly higher level of generality than the success or failure of public housing development projects, his language is applicable to the Boston situation: "It is impossible to understand the prospects of development policies and projects without knowing the characteristics of social relations at both the micro and macro level, whether and how these levels articulate with one another, and how this degree of articulation has emerged historically" (183).

The differences between the narratives at the two HOPE VI sites were fueled by differing levels of trust. The social networks at Orchard Park were strengthened by experience, and the potential networks at Mission Main were consistently weakened by events. Distrust reinforced distrust at Mission Main and grew as the development planning process proceeded.

Amoral Familism: Boston's Bromley Heath

A twelve-hundred-unit public housing development, Boston's Bromley Heath, has the longest record, twenty-five years, of tenant management in the United States. When the residents took over, "the place was so scary that ambulance drivers sometimes refused to pick up the sick and the wounded" (*Newsweek*, December 7, 1998). Today the development looks far better, delivers quality maintenance, is served by a modern health center, and scores higher than the Boston Housing Authority itself on federal housing performance audits. Over the years, the Bromley Heath tenant management corporation (TMC) has become a national symbol of public housing

Bottom-Up Social Capital		Top-Down Social Capital		
Integration	Linkage	Synergy	Integrity	Performance Outcome
High	Unique	Low	High	Modified amoral familism

residents taking charge of their lives and providing quality public housing even when the housing authority itself was mired in organizational problems. *Newsweek* reported that the leader of the tenant management corporation, Mildred Hailey, has been called "the Mother Teresa of public housing."

In Woolcock's terms, Bromley Heath is a setting of high integration in the face of a collapsed state—in this case, the Boston Housing Authority, which through much of the life of the TMC has been both inefficient and incapable of maintaining institutional synergy with other public and private actors.

In early November 1998, Bromley Heath was swept by a strike force made up of local, state, and federal law enforcement agents. Twenty-eight suspected drug dealers were arrested. BHA officials essentially took over the development when they "changed lock, secured records, and dismissed the tenant management team, the eight member police force, and maintenance workers," reported the *Boston Globe* on November 3. Although debate has abounded about the appropriateness of the BHA takeover and the basis for the authority's "coup," there is little contention about the following facts. Hailey's grandson was running a major drug operation out of the development, and often "right beneath Mrs. Hailey's window," *Newsweek* reported. The TMC-controlled housing police had ignored drug dealing for years and had been instructed by members of the board to keep the Boston police out of the development. "Housing police say board members turned a blind eye to drug dealing. . . . Unable to stir the tenant board to action, the frustrated housing police went to the Feds—who moved in with the . . . sting." Outside observers of the development have argued that both the project police and tenant leaders ignored drug dealing by residents of the development, "especially when the dealers were their own offspring," *Newsweek* reported. As the chief of the project police stated in the newsweekly, "It's hard for us [the police] when you have to answer to a board made up of parents of kids we're arresting." The *Boston Globe* reported that years ago the Boston police labeled Bromley Heath "New Jack City," a place where "crime was controlled by several drug families."

This short summary of the Bromley Heath drug bust omits the nuances and diversity of viewpoints on that event. Although there is disagreement about the legitimacy of the BHA takeover and the process by which it was engineered, there is little dispute that Bromley Heath had become a protected area for a significant amount of drug dealing. A high level of internal integration in the development and a set of broadly held norms created a setting of amoral familism "characterized by the presence of social integration but the absence of linkage" (Woolcock 1998, 171) in which, according to Jean-Phillippe Platteau, "codes of conduct are governed by a limited-group morality which emphasizes the strength of ties to close personal relations; procedural norms, when they exist, are particularistic" (quoted in Woolcock 1998, 171).

However, the linkage concept is complicated in the case of Bromley Heath. The development has historically had a strong linkage to the outside world beyond the Boston Housing Authority, in particular with the Washington headquarters of the Department of Housing and Urban Development. For years HUD had marketed the development and its leaders as models of what a tenant management corporation could be in practice. From the BHA's perspective, the TMC would end-run the authority and go to HUD for support when there was disagreement between the development and the authority. More often than not, Washington backed the TMC. In Woolcock's terms, a highly integrated community was able to bypass a weak state, the BHA, to get the support of a strong state organization, the Department of Housing and Urban Development. The case, like others we have reviewed, raises the issue of the relationship between social capital and power. Leveraging a strong extracommunity social network against a weak state (the BHA) has the feel of political power rather than social capital.

In addition, the Bromley case raises the important—and frequently mentioned—view that social networks may not always be beneficial to society as a whole. The assumption behind Woolcock's bottom-up linkage is that such connection is always a good thing for the integrated community. Yet, as with Bromley Heath, some networks provide opportunity for amoral familism. Others preserve the community for what might be called integration integrity, that is, supporting it against the inroads of gentrification and displacement. Again, the role of power in determining the relationship between integration and linkage surfaces as a critical factor not explored in the conceptual world of the four social capitals.

Top-Down Synergy: Saegert and Winkel's New York City Housing

Numerous subsidized housing studies have explored the relationship among ownership form, tenant satisfaction, and the economic efficiency of the development (Sadacca et al. 1974). The social capital construct has deepened the texture of such analyses, as indicated by Susan Saegert and Gary Winkel's study "Social Capital and the Revitalization of New York City's Distressed Inner-City Housing" (1998). The article

> presents evidence that social capital can be an effective component for locally sponsored low income housing programs. It provides a model for measuring social capital at the building level, where it may be effective in improving housing quality and security. Results of the analysis [487 buildings in Brooklyn] demonstrate that the positive effects of tenant ownership were largely mediated by the higher levels of social capital found in these buildings. (17)

The authors do a thorough job of reviewing the literature that relates ownership form, housing quality, and social capital. They point to concern with the definition and measurement of social capital in multifamily housing. "Building-level social capital is directly linked to actions tenants can take to keep up their property and combat crime in the building. However we believe that social capital at other levels would also contribute to improving building conditions in a variety of ways" (19).

Bottom-Up Social Capital		Top-Down Social Capital		
Integration	Linkage	Synergy	Integrity	Performance Outcome
High	?	High	Moderate	Beneficent autonomy

Saegert and Winkel frame their discussion of New York City's distressed housing from the "bottom up." The macro view, that is, the city and state of New York, the federal government, and private financial organizations, are "out there" but not linked to social capital as the authors define it. However, the degree to which the two forms of top-down social capital—cooperation and flexibility among professional organizations acting synergistically—might further promote development of integration at the building level is revealed in the authors' comment that

> reductions in housing subsidies make the future of all programs uncertain. At present, the reprivatization programs selling buildings to landlords or to community groups receive their major operating subsidy through tax credit financing. . . . These funds are supplemented by HUD rent subsidy or voucher programs. Thus far, the financial intermediaries responsible for most tax credit financing in New York have been reluctant to apply them to tenant-owned cooperatives. (54)

Cooperation between the top-down public (HUD) and private sectors (the financial intermediaries) is necessary to advance the micro agenda of integrating housing developments. Integration at the building level can be developed only if there is greater institutional flexibility at the top. The dynamic relationship, then, between social capital at the bottom (integration) and social capital at the top (organizational integrity) is clear if we stretch integrity in this instance to include imaginative investment on the part of the financial intermediaries.

This study of housing in New York poses the question: How is social capital at the top expanded? Framing the case within the Woolcock structure raises the critical issue of the relationship between integration and linkage at the bottom with capacity and synergy at the top, as well as how and whether they are dynamically interrelated. The issue of the capacity of the bottom to influence the top emerges in this case and again raises the issue of the relationship between social networks and political power.

Beneficent Autonomy: Cleveland and the Production of Affordable Housing

With some redefinition of terms, Woolcock's model provides a useful framework within which to analyze the subsidized housing production system in Cleveland's low-income neighborhoods. The unit of analysis in this bottom-up system is the community development corporation, not a specific housing development or residential area. "Integration" and "linkage" represent the degree to which the CDC has representative legitimacy for and is embedded in its neighborhood through connections

Bottom-Up Social Capital		Top-Down Social Capital		
Integration	Linkage	Synergy	Integrity	Performance Outcome
High	High	High	High	Beneficent autonomy

with other organizations and stakeholders. Upward linking (the push toward the top-down system) is the extent to which the CDC can reach beyond its neighborhood constituency to develop networks with citywide actors and institutions—for example, the banks, the police, and the building inspection department.

Viewing the top-down subsidized housing production system, "integrity" refers to the competence and professionalism of the public and private actors with whom the CDC must do business. "Synergy" identifies the networks of cooperation among those top-down actors.

Cleveland has a sophisticated, highly developed, and productive community development system that channels public, private, and nonprofit resources into CDCs in each of the city's twenty-one wards. Although the system's organization, participation, and output can be criticized, it remains nonetheless the standard by which other cities judge their progress. With strong commitment from the mayor and the city council, the corporate community, and the foundation world, the Cleveland CDC strategy has evolved into a complex but workable system for funneling public and private resources to the neighborhoods for one- and two-family houses and larger development using the Low-Income Housing Tax Credit.

The top-down level in Cleveland has strong indicators of synergy and integrity. Conversely, the bottom-up system is made up of CDCs with a mixed record of integration and a high level of linkage to the top-down actors.

The current housing system for poor neighborhoods in Cleveland, with its configuration of top-down and bottom-up players, is the outcome of a lengthy local evolution in community development. Throughout the 1970s, neighborhood organizing and advocacy planning was the order of the day for both Cleveland neighborhoods and the Cleveland Planning Commission, which worked in concert with the emerging small-scale housing producers and neighborhood advocates. The 1977 election of Mayor Dennis Kucinich was seen as a victory for neighborhood populism, but conflict quickly developed between Kucinich and his neighborhood base as well as with the business community. The "regime anarchy" (Woolcock's term) was symbolized by the fistfights that broke out between neighborhood activists and the city's Community Development Department at the second annual Neighborhood Conference held in November 1978. The organizational integrity of the state—in this case, the city—was low, and its synergy with the business community even lower.

Cooperation (synergy building) became a driving force in Cleveland after the "troubles" of the 1970s. The city looked over the brink of political and financial collapse and decided that public-private collaboration was critical. City hall could not afford to challenge the white corporate power structure, an "anti-synergy" move that Mayor Kucinich had attempted with disastrous results.

In 1979, tired of conflict, Clevelanders elected George Voinovich, a fiscally conservative Republican, who promised downtown development and a new image for the city. The Cleveland Foundation, a major and influential funding source for neighborhood advocates, moved away from support of organizing (which was seen as fracturing relationships between city hall and the neighborhoods) to focus on creation of the Cleveland Housing Network (CHN). City hall began to back neighborhood housing development. Top-down synergy and integrity became focused on Cleveland neighborhoods.

Throughout the 1980s, Cleveland's powerful and socially engaged foundations sought means of rationalizing housing production and neighborhood revitalization. Community organizing was out, but neighborhood revitalization—meaning housing rehabilitation and some new production—was in. Production proceeded at a slow pace: three or four houses per competent CDC per year.

By the late 1980s, the foundations and city hall were getting edgy with the informality of the process they were funding—its lack of structure, strategy, or significant production and its single-minded focus on low-income households. Top-down synergy cutting across the corporate, nonprofit, and public sectors was expanding. The Gund Foundation suggested a consolidated venture on the part of the corporate community, represented by Cleveland Tomorrow, a philanthropic organization made up of the forty CEOs of Cleveland's leading corporations. In 1987, with the backing of all the major philanthropic and corporate interests in the city, Neighborhood Progress Incorporated (NPI) was created to coordinate corporate, foundation, and city funding to the CDCs, a clear symbol of formalized synergy.

In 1989, George Voinovich was elected governor of Ohio. Mike White, a Democratic African American, became mayor of Cleveland. The CDCs supported his candidacy, and his commitment to the neighborhoods was symbolized when he appointed the highly respected and battle-tested head of the Cleveland Housing Network as director of the Cleveland Community Development Department. The bottom-up neighborhood actors, the CDCs, were developing stronger extra-community networks (linkage reaching toward the top-down system). The production capacity for affordable housing was increasingly enhanced by the mutually reinforcing development of four kinds of social capital.

The marriage among the public, private, and nonprofit sectors remains strong and perhaps the key feature of the Cleveland success story. There is a collective view in the city of all sectors pulling together to get out of the crisis, and there is pride in the good work done as the downtown booms and highly visible new construction goes on in key neighborhoods. This is not to say that each player is totally happy with the role it is being asked to play. But cooperation goes on nonetheless in a growing synergy of public and nonprofit organizations.

A critical aspect of the network structure and history in Cleveland is the extent to which the neighborhood advocates of the 1970s became players in the city hall world of the 1990s. Leaders in the different settings are both personal and professional colleagues. With so many individuals who have worked both in the neighborhoods and at city hall, Cleveland's housing system radiates an aura of shared vision and trust. The importance of the collective history among the players—Cleveland's equivalent of Mao's Long March—is critical.

There is little sense of "us versus them," of neighborhood leaders versus "the Hall." Mayor White is comfortable with the CDC players, and he has made them central in his administration. Not only has the bottom linked with the top-down organizations, but representatives from the grassroots community have joined them.

The "thickness" of the network ties between the neighborhoods and city hall (in Woolcock's terms, the growing linkage between top-down and bottom-up systems) has expanded over the past six years primarily because of Mayor White's open acceptance of CDC leaders as people with whom he can work and who he wants to work for him. One view of the phenomenon of bringing neighborhood leadership into city hall is that the traditional competence on community development issues in city hall is so limited that the mayor has had to rely on the competence from the neighborhoods. In Woolcock's terms, community competence makes for a greater capacity for integrity at the state (city) level.

It is also critical that many of the current players inside and outside city hall have worked together in Cleveland since the 1970s, when they were neighborhood activists fighting against city hall. The image of the Long March, which they shared, emerged to describe their collective experience over the past sixteen years in making the transition from advocacy roles to development and neighborhood strategy. At each point in that transition, the players have seen their roles expand and their connection to power and decisionmaking become stronger. The collective story, then, is one of relationships and outcomes getting better because of cooperation and a shared vision.

The Cleveland top-down–bottom-up system is a vivid example on the ground of the model that Woolcock (1998, 180) posits for sustained economic development (in the Cleveland case, affordable housing).

> For sustained development, then, the interaction between "top down" and "bottom up" must therefore be a dynamic one: in the case of bottom-up development, intensive intra-community ties (integration) must begin to coexist with more extensive albeit "weaker" extra-community networks (linkage), while at the same time top-down combinations of state-society-relations (synergy) must coexist with cohesive corporate ties (integrity).[4]

CDCs, bankers, and other major players in general marvel at the degree to which the city and the outside players have become part of one system. Obviously, there are exceptions to the sense of well-being. But as discussed, many players from outside are now in city hall, and the tradition of working together, expanding the pie, not worrying about turf, has become part of the common language in Cleveland. The perception of such cooperation has probably enhanced the fact of it.

Efforts have been made to shake out and consolidate the CDC system since 1991 under the leadership of NPI, with decidedly mixed results. Although some positive consolidation has occurred, CDCs see some such efforts as destructive, and those outcomes have given consolidation a bad name within the CDC world. Issues regarding the size and strength of the CDCs center on trying to consolidate them and to make the weak end of the collection of over thirty organizations function more like the strong end. High priorities of both the mayor's office and NPI are rationalizing the system and making the strong remaining CDCs even stronger organizations. But achieving these goals remains a huge challenge in the wake of the less-than-successful effort at consolidation several years ago under the former director of NPI.

With not only a politically sensitive system by which housing funds are allocated but the twenty-one "mayors" of Cleveland's wards with whom the mayor's office contends, targeting by neighborhood—that is, singling out a ward—is difficult. Targeting within neighborhoods has been a major preoccupation of NPI and the city. The city sees NPI as a key player in this effort: the private organization is better able to be tough with the CDCs because the mayor's office would be subject to political fallout with the city councilors if it took on that role.

The environment for community development and CDCs is overwhelmingly supportive. The neighborhood movement of the 1970s has evolved into the CDC system of the 1990s. The various historical and institutional strands have come together to produce an environment of deep commitment to the concept and practice of community development corporations as the key neighborhood actor in the community development system.

In summary, although blemishes in the Cleveland housing picture can be identified, all four types of social capital seem to be in remarkable synchronization. The issue for the future is whether the goodwill, shared vision, and high level of trust among the players in the system can translate into an environment with more competent, and fewer, CDCs. These would be characterized by their focus on targeted neighborhood revitalization, jobs and economic development, and their traditional role as producers of housing.

On the less positive side, there is concern about what will happen after Mayor White's term in office. There is no obvious successor, and long-term city council members are looking to get out. Cleveland's job-income issues remain a tough nut to crack, both locally and regionally. The decline of federal programs remains a constant worry. Finally, the potential for housing market growth is not distributed evenly in the city, and there is concern that some low-income neighborhoods will continue to decline in population, thus making the economic divisions in the city greater between the well-to-do and the poor.

There is a growing sentiment among some players in the system that housing production is overemphasized, that this priority has led to inadequate resources and planning for neighborhood development initiatives that are broader, integrated, and strategic. Such initiatives are more closely aligned with Cleveland's priority today—to go beyond building low-income housing to focus on building markets and neighborhoods.

Yet when all the concerns about the present and future of the Cleveland community development system are surfaced, the fact remains that it is the model that other cities look to with envy. From a conceptual perspective, Woolcock's four social capitals provide a rich vocabulary with which to describe the complexity of the Cleveland institutional ecology.

Creative Beneficent Autonomy: Income Mixing in Lake Parc Place

No recent housing policy issue has generated more debate than income-mixing: opening up public housing to higher-income groups and transforming public housing from shelter for solely the poorest of the poor to accommodation for a population

Bottom-Up Social Capital		Top-Down Social Capital		
Integration	Linkage	Synergy	Integrity	Performance Outcome
High	High	High	High	Beneficent autonomy

mix that includes the working poor and working-class. In 1998, the journal *Housing Policy Debate* featured a series of articles that focus on Lake Parc Place, a nationally known mixed-income development orchestrated by the Chicago Housing Authority.

The researchers agree that income-mixing at Lake Parc Place worked to promote a safer and more attractive development, which in turn created a supportive social environment. But there is great contention among these researchers as to *why* Lake Parc Place succeeded. They disagree, for instance, about the importance of working-class role models for lower-income tenants. Viewing the Lake Parc Place debate through the Woolcock lens, however, provides a visual vocabulary for appraising what happened and why the development was successful.

Prior to redevelopment, Lake Parc Place had been a public housing development characterized by low integration. Shaking up the resident population by screening former residents and adding working-class families from outside not only elevated the level of integration within the development but also brought households with extracommunity ties to the work world beyond the development into the population. As the authors of the central research on Lake Parc Place conclude: "At a time when policy analysts are seeking ways to increase the 'social capital' available to residents of public housing . . . the present results suggest that mixed-income housing by providing connections to neighbors who can provide information, resources, and constructive social norms, clearly has promise" (Rosenbaum, Stroh, and Flynn 1998, 736).

One of the challenges facing Lake Parc Place and other similar developments is that the surrounding neighborhood, which is itself low-income and devoid of much integration or linkage to the broader community, makes it difficult to create extra-community networks. Seen in the Woolcock framework, importing working-class households leapfrogs that "linkage desert" and provides residents who represent connection to the larger world. If public housing tenants cannot make those linkages themselves, bring the linkages to the public housing communities. Mixed-income developments, then, are less about role models and more about providing extracommunity linkage.

WOOLCOCK REVISITED: APPLICATION TO PRACTICE AND POLICY

The application of Woolcock's model to a range of social capital, housing, and low-income scenarios demonstrates that the language and the concepts can be used to describe settings in which social capital surfaces in different shapes and forms. As such, it provides a common mode of analysis for knitting together what otherwise appear to be widely diverse settings.

Woolcock's model works well for narratives in which the housing development or residential neighborhood constitutes the bottom-up community for which integration and linkage are issues. The concept of social networks at either the group (community) or individual level is a useful heuristic by which to frame such cases. Woolcock's emphasis on the role of top-down networks in what happens at the community or neighborhood level is particularly helpful in understanding the degree to which neighborhood affordable housing issues are embedded, not only in horizontal linkage issues but, equally important, in the quality of top-down public and private organizations.

Most of the examples explored in this chapter have been drawn from public housing or subsidized developments and thus low-income enclaves, but the model can also be applied to upper-income or highly organized working-class residential enclaves. Edward Blakely and Mary Gail Snyder's *Fortress America* (1997) tells a story that profits from such an analysis through the Woolcock lens, as does Herbert Gans's close look at the urban village of Boston's West End, *The Urban Villagers* (1962).

When focused on domestic, poor urban neighborhoods, does the Woolcock lens provide anything more than a common vocabulary and mode of analysis? However useful to researchers as a heuristic for framing "stories," does the Woolcock model help practitioners and policymakers? I think the answer is yes. Woolcock asks six important questions about a housing entity:

1. How well do the residents of the housing development work together? (integration)

2. Has the development made connections with other organizations and stakeholders in the surrounding neighborhood? What kind of connections are these, and how good are they? (linkage)

3. Has the development reached up to make connections with downtown stakeholders? How has it done so?

4. Flipping the angle of vision from the development to the institutional environment, which (if any) individual government body, private or nonprofit organization, or corporation impinging on the life of the development functions well as an organization? (integrity)

5. How well and in what combinations do the for-profit, nonprofit, and public sectors work with each other? (synergy)

6. Do these top-down organizations reach down to make connections with the housing entity? How have they done so?

These are questions that anyone working on issues of housing in poor communities must answer to be an effective practitioner. Rigorously exploring the quality of the four social networks for a given development or neighborhood identifies opportunities for enhancement as well as weaknesses to be overcome. How one goes about exploiting the strengths and correcting the weaknesses—building the four social capitals—is, of course, another story.[5]

A good community organizer, housing manager, director of a community development corporation, or tenant leader probably knows the answers to these six questions intuitively. It is critical, however, for practice and program development to move beyond tacit knowledge. Woolcock provides a mode of analysis for those who lack the intuitive skills.

SOCIAL CAPITAL AND POLITICAL POWER

Social capital has only recently joined the family of "capitals." Two others to be considered in relationship to it are economic and political capital. There is work to be done to further clarify the relationship between the world of social capital and the world of the market. There is as much if not more work to be done to clarify another relationship: between social capital and political capital or political power. Because the issue of power arises so often in the seven stories set forth in this chapter, it is important to explore this relationship.

Although it implicitly assumes a relationship between political power and social capital, Woolcock's model does not explicitly clarify the nature of the connection. The state is a major fixture in his top-down configuration, but he explores the integrity of the state and its potential for synergy with society, not its political power or influence.

We can make the case that political power is the eight-hundred-pound gorilla in the social capital garden. Who has power? How do they use it? How is it distributed, and how do individuals or groups get access to it? And most critically, *what is the relationship of political power (or perhaps political capital) to social capital?* To what extent do the multiple parsings of social capital ignore or fail to integrate the substance of urban power analysis, which so fascinated political scientists in an earlier era (Long 1962; Mann 1964; Yates 1977; Polsby 1963; Rossi and Dentler 1961; Banfield and Wilson 1963)?

Few commentators on social capital make the connection to power. Xavier Briggs is an exception. In "Brown Kids in White Suburbs" (1998, 178), he asks whether those focused on the

> collective dimension of social capital . . . will draw adequately on . . . research focused on interests and conflict in the domain of urban politics. Some of the latter . . . grapple with similar conceptual and empirical problems in the city-as-system vein but sometimes with quite different assumptions. In general, the risk in collective-good analyses of urban social capital is in reductionism. *Establishing patterns of trust and reciprocal obligation is critical not because it eliminates important conflicts of political interest but because the former makes it easier to reconcile the latter in creative ways. Social capital is a vital resource for cities, neighborhoods and individuals because of power and politics not in place of them.* (178, emphasis added)

Briggs takes as given the reality of interests and conflict "in the domain of urban politics" and sees social capital not as replacing or single-handedly solving those conflicts but rather as modifying or reconciling them. His analysis raises a conceptually important issue: Where does the political sphere of interests, factions, and power end and the social capital domain of trust, mutual obligation, and shared vision begin? Does the lion of politics ultimately lie down because of the lamb of social capital? Or rather, are today's power lions simply dressed up as social capital lambs by observers who are determined to find social networks where Edward Banfield (1965), for example, would have found political influence?[6]

To begin to address the question, we must first view affordable housing and poor communities through the conceptual lens of the political scientist. Margaret Weir (1996) does just that in her important study of community development and political power. She explores the strategies that community groups use "to win access to resources—protest, participation, and networking" (2), and she examines the historical linkages between those strategies and different urban policies.

Weir observes the urban housing saga through a lens very different from that of the social capitalists; she uses the term "network" to denote a "strategy to win resources for local development. Networks encompass a diverse set of ties to public, private, and nonprofit entities that provide access to resources and permit the leveraging of public resources" (15). Although framed through a political science lens, Weir's discussion of network building can be readily understood in terms of the structure of Woolcock's model. Community organizing, power, and politics fit readily into the interaction of the bottom-up and top-down sectors. Political networks can be substituted for social networks.

The critical difference is not in the framework but in the *content* of the networks and in their relationship to each other. Political networks deal with control, power, influence, leverage, positioning. Social networks are about trust, shared vision, reciprocity. We can conceptualize the differences, and we can also use Woolcock's model to accommodate both. Nevertheless, the critical issue raised in this chapter remains unanswered: What is the relationship between social capital and political power? Should we think of them as synergistic? As coexisting along a continuum? As cumulative? As in conflict?

A detailed analysis of the relationship between social and political capital is well beyond the scope of this chapter. However, an example that draws heavily on Weir's analysis evokes the two lens within one narrative and shows their relationship in practice.

Political Capital and the Community Reinvestment Act

How political action and social capital become interwoven can be seen in the evolution and implementation of the Community Reinvestment Act (CRA) of 1977 and the 1975 Home Mortgage Disclosure Acts (HMDA).

Bottom-up community forces consisting of integrated organizations linked together had the lead role in the passage of both acts "to prevent redlining and disinvestment by banks" (Weir 1996, 15). The CRA was not self-executing, and the federal government itself made little effort to enforce it. The top-down public actors were passive. It would take the grassroots efforts of community organizations "to mobilize, learn about the law, collect appropriate information and present their case to local banks" (15). National organizations emerged to help local grassroots coalitions understand and utilize the CRA.

The initial successes of the CRA cannot be understood in terms of social networks—the building of trust, linkage, integrity, and synergy between the bottom-up coalitions and the top-down banks. Rather, successful strategies put pressure on reluctant banks through protest and utilization of the media, "which . . . widened the scope of conflict" (16). Real and potential conflict, diverse interests, pressure, influence—this is the language of the political scientist, discussing the CRA story using Woolcock's framework but not his social network language.

The evolution of the CRA is a good example of Bob Edwards and Michael Foley's (1997, 677) insight that

> economic incentive structures, often implemented by state efforts to negotiate a political settlement to prior economic conflicts, are an important and beneficial source of cooperation in contemporary industrial democracies. Contrary to the neo-Tocquevillian presumption that trust is a prerequisite of cooperative relations, specific forms of government regulation produce economic cooperation independent of trust.

Community pressure and national mobilization resulted in the CRA, which regulated bank participation in inner cities. Political power (capital) roped economic capital into serving low-income communities.

But there's more to the story. There appears to be a *transition* from a political capital to a social capital story. Once pushed by regulation and economic self-interest into lending in low-income, inner-city neighborhoods, many banks found themselves building networks of trust with community groups. Pressure politics forced the initial linkage between the bank and the community group, but the productive political experience (not always the case, to be sure) resulted in the eventual development of a social network—the linkage between the community and the banking institutions. Political conflict and governmental regulation pushed the bankers and the community together. Good economics—that is, economically sound loans for mortgages—emerged from that linkage. Social networks sprouted from the realization that good business could be done and that each stakeholder, the banks as well as the community, was trustworthy. But the political pressure came first. Without it, there would have been no room for the mediating force of social capital to operate, or for the good business relationship to develop.[7]

Social capital in its collective form can help to reconcile conflicts of both political and economic interest and advance the "capital" of both. That's the good news. But there is reason to believe that those conflicts have grown in the past twenty years and that the mediating role of social capital in such reconciliation has become more challenging. Edwards and Foley make this point when they argue that "the source of our socio-cultural malaise lies in the political-economic trend of the past quarter century, which has been fed by three increasingly significant tributaries: economic restructuring, welfare state downsizing, and the devolution of government" (676). From the perspective of social capital, housing, and poor communities, the waters in these three tributaries can be seen in the following terms. Corporate leadership has abandoned cities as firms have consolidated and business elites have focused their interests on a national or international horizon. In Boston, for example, the strong leadership of the Metropolitan Boston Housing Partnership, an organization involved in the support of CDC-based affordable housing production, has disappeared as banks have consolidated and their leadership has been moved to other cities. Elsewhere, with welfare-state downsizing and devolution, there are fewer targeted public programs, less federal funding is available for low-income housing production and maintenance, and the potential for competition for the funds that are available has increased. To the extent that policy decisions around welfare and public housing are turned over to state and local government, there is concern that market-oriented solutions rather than mandated programs for low-income households will result.

Through the social capital lens, the new federal emphasis on income-mixing in public housing can be viewed as a way to expand linkage and develop extracommunity ties (à la Woolcock). Through the political capital lens, the same policy, seen as a diminution of resources, represents a political loss for the advocates of low-income housing.

AFTERWORD: COLLECTIVE VERSUS INDIVIDUAL INTEGRATION AND LINKAGE

The mandate to the authors of this volume was to focus on collective social capital. I have followed that directive, yet in closing I cannot resist pointing out the degree to which Woolcock's theoretical synthesis and policy framework for social capital can be used to shed light on what Xavier Briggs (1998, 178) defines as "the *individual dimension* of [social capital] and the multiple forms seen in that more micro-level dimension." It is to that "more micro-level dimension" that we now briefly turn.

Analyzing social capital in terms of individual social networks, Briggs distinguishes between networks that provide social leverage—that is, social capital that helps one "get ahead"—and social capital that produces social support that helps one cope with life situations. He then looks at housing through the individual social capital lens: "There is a vast social network literature, rarely used by housing researchers, which provides important clues about the processes and social structures *through which a move to more affluent neighborhoods might affect poor people and their stock of social capital*" (187, emphasis added).

At first blush, Woolcock's framework seems to apply solely to the domain of collective social capital, and thus Briggs's analysis of social networks and social ties would be undertaken at too individual a level to warrant inclusion in any discussion of Woolcock. But a more considered view shows that when Woolcock's lens is adjusted slightly, it provides a useful framework for exploring the world of individual social networks in poor communities. Substituting "household" for "community," Woolcock's model can accommodate Briggs's individual dimension of social capital as follows. The level of integration of a residential setting determines the degree of intracommunity ties available to a household. Such ties can provide both social support and social leverage. It is likely that households in poor communities have significantly less access to leverage ties (access to higher-paying jobs, for example) than to ties of social support. Only through extracommunity networks of some kind can such leverage ties be created. Leverage ties can be created for the individual in two ways: by linking the household to leverage ties (extracommunity ties) so as to gain access to job opportunities outside the individual's current residential setting (Harrison and Weiss 1998), or by moving the household to the environment where the leveraged tie can be made (Turner 1998). Which of these strategies is used (the policy question) is a function of the strategy and performance of the top-down system of synergy and integrity and the interaction between that top-down system and the bottom-up community.

Briggs makes the important point that a critical task of public policy is determining how to measure and track, and how to positively *shape*, the links between social capital, economic opportunity, and urban policy. From the Woolcock perspective, this task involves figuring out how the top-down organizations and their networks can best interact with, shape, and make choices among strategies to enhance extracommunity ties, whether in the form of housing mobility or dispersal strategies or through workforce strategies, such as transportation and bridging to distant job opportunities.

If extracommunity networks result in leveraged ties for households that remain in their community, individual social capital reinforces integration in the same way that income-mixing is argued to benefit housing developments (see the discussion of Lake Parc Place). Individuals who develop extracommunity networks can make them available to others at the community level. Individual social capital and collective social capital are then mutually reinforcing.

The real challenge for collective social capital, however, occurs when the "geography of urban opportunity" (Galster and Killen 1995) is defined in terms of housing mobility and dispersal. In that policy mode, the community is not strengthened; instead, the effort to create extracommunity networks on an individual basis requires that the household leave the community of origin. What strengthens individual extracommunity ties weakens the community of origin.

The perennial debate between dispersal, gilding the ghetto, or doing something for both, first conceptualized in the Kerner Commission Report some thirty years ago, is still with us. Strategies that improve the lot of individual households may in fact cut against the improvement of inner-city neighborhoods and vice versa. At the micro level, social capital as integration or "bonding" can enhance a neighborhood. Social capital as "bridging" may benefit households, but not the collective.

NOTES

1. "Social capital" is so freely and widely used that, as Robert Lang and Steven Hornburg (1998, 4) point out, "the concept . . . seems applicable to almost any social condition." In the same issue of *Housing Policy Debate*, Xavier Briggs (1998, 178) states that "social capital [has] a circus-tent quality: all things positive and social are piled beneath it." Kenneth

Temkin and William Rohe (1998, 63) go one step further and posit that "there is no agreement as to what, specifically, constitutes social capital."

2. Woolcock's critique of current uses of "social capital" and his "intellectual history" of the phrase make it clear why there is need for clarification. He points to four theoretical and empirical weaknesses resulting from "indiscriminate applications of social and other 'capitals' . . . [which are] part of . . . the recent emergence of 'a plethora of capitals'" (155):

  1. Social capital's "revisionist grounding in different sociological traditions risks trying to explain too much with too little" (155).
  2. It is not clear whether social capital is the infrastructure or the content of social relations (ties versus trust).
  3. Social capital seems to justify contradictory public policy measures and is claimed by both left and right. Does the state supplement or destroy social capital? Or is a society indifferent to governmental action?
  4. Social capital is not always an unqualified good. More is not always better, and the term can understate "corresponding negative aspects" (159).

3. South Boston ("Southie") is a highly integrated community that has historically used powerful and strategic political actors to protect the urban village from incursion from outside. The strategy has not always been successful, and it is in danger of unraveling at present because the top-down world has decided that Southie is too valuable a terrain to be left solely to the goals of the integrated and strategically linked community. But the old-guard, integrated "urban village" is fighting a dramatic rearguard action to preserve its right to link to the larger top-down world on its own terms.

4. Jordan Yin, a Ph.D. candidate at Cornell in the Department of City and Regional Planning, has written an interesting paper entitled "The Community Development Industry System: An Institutional Analysis of Community Development Corporations in Cleveland, 1967–1997." He looks at many of the same issues discussed here, but his lens of analysis is what might be called a post-Marxist power model. He conceptualizes a "network continuum" along which environments can be ranged as "cooperative" to "controlling." Applied to Cleveland, the continuum shows that a cooperative environment (from the perspective of the CDCs) was pushed toward the controlling end by powerful foundations, the corporate community, and the city, which wanted more moderate-income housing, more strategic neighborhood planning, and less organizing. The casual cooperation of the early 1980s was transformed into the NPI-driven scheme of bringing back the middle class. In Woolcock's terms, Yin describes a situation in which the top-down forces have essentially overwhelmed whatever equilibrium existed between them and the bottom-up forces of integration and linkage. Although his analysis is provocative and provides food for thought, its conspiratorial view of the Cleveland world is difficult to embrace.

5. See Robert Putnam's *Bowling Alone* (1995) for a serious effort to come to terms with the issue. Roland Burt's *Structural Holes* (1992) provides a way of thinking about "opportunity areas" among and within the four social capitals.

6. Nicholas Lehmann's (2000) review of Cohen and Taylor's *American Pharaoh: Mayor Richard J. Daley* paints a picture of a master of the political capital game. Daley could converse brilliantly about political power. If he had been asked about the role of social capital in getting things done in Chicago, the silence would probably have been deafening.

7. This transition view accords with interviews I have conducted with bankers in several cities. In talking about the CRA, they indicated that the loans they first made because they

were forced to turned out to be financially beneficial. As a consequence of their economic viability and their emerging positive relationships with the community development corporations receiving the loans, the bankers developed, in Woolcock's terms, a top-down connection with the community (the CDC). Political influence resulted in good economics, which produced social capital.

REFERENCES

Adams, Charles, et al. 1995. "HOPE VI Baseline Case Study: Mission Main; Boston, Massachusetts." Report to the Department of Housing and Urban Development. Cambridge, Mass.: Massachusetts Institute of Technology.

Banfield, Edward C. 1965. *Political Influence.* New York: Free Press.

Banfield, Edward C., and James Q. Wilson. 1963. *City Politics.* Cambridge, Mass.: Harvard University Press/MIT Press.

Blakely, Edward J., and Mary Gail Snyder. 1997. *Fortress America: Gated Communities in the United States.* Washington, D.C.: Urban Institute Press.

Briggs, Xavier. 1998. "Brown Kids in White Suburbs: Housing Mobility and the Many Faces of Social Capitalism." *Housing Policy Debate* 9(1): 177–221.

Briggs, Xavier, and Elizabeth Mueller, with Mercer Sullivan. 1997. *From Neighborhood to Community: Evidence on the Social Effects of Community Development.* New York: Community Development Research Center, New School for Social Research.

Burt, Ronald S. 1992. *Structural Holes: The Social Structure of Competition.* Cambridge, Mass.: Harvard University Press.

Edwards, Bob, and Michael Foley. 1997. "Social Capital and the Political Economy of Our Discontent." *American Behavioral Scientist* 40(5): 669–78.

Galster, George, and Sean P. Killen. 1995. "The Geography of Metropolitan Opportunity: A Reconnaissance and Conceptual Framework." *Housing Policy Debate* 6: 10–47.

Gans, Herbert. 1962. *The Urban Villagers.* New York: Free Press.

Gill, Owen. 1977. *Luke Street.* London: Macmillan.

Halpern, David. 1988. "Social Capital, Exclusion and the Quality of Life: Towards a Causal Model of Policy Implications." Draft 31.3.98, Nexus briefing document.

Harrison, Bennett, and Marcus Weiss. 1998. *Workforce Development Networks: Community-Based Organizations and Regional Alliances.* Thousand Oaks, Calif.: Sage Publications.

Keyes, Langley. 1992. *Strategies and Saints: Fighting Drugs in Subsidized Housing.* Washington, D.C.: Urban Institute Press.

———. 1998a. "HOPE VI in Boston." Draft report to the Department of Housing and Urban Development.

———. 1998b. "Networks and the National Community Development Initiative: The Cleveland Model." Cambridge, Mass.: Massachusetts Institute of Technology. Unpublished paper.

Keyes, Langley, Alex Schwarz, Avis Vidal, and Rachel Bratt. 1996. "Networks and Nonprofits: Opportunities and Challenges in an Era of Federal Devolution." *Housing Policy Debate* 7(2): 201–29.

Lang, Robert E., and Steven P. Hornburg. 1998. "What Is Social Capital and Why Is It Important to Public Policy?" *Housing Policy Debate* 9(1): 1–16.

Lehmann, Nicholas. 2000. [Review of Adam Cohen and Elizabeth Taylor, *American Pharaoh: Mayor Richard J. Daley*]. *The New Republic,* July 31.

Long, Norton. 1962. *The Policy.* Chicago: Rand McNally.

Mann, Lawrence. 1964. "Studies in Community Decision Making." *Journal of the American Institute of Planners* 30(1): 58–65.

Polsby, Nelson W. 1963. *Community Power and Political Theory.* New Haven: Yale University Press.

Putnam, Robert D. 1995. "Bowling Alone: America's Declining Social Capital." *Journal of Democracy* 6: 65–78.

Rainwater, Lee. 1966. "Fear and the House-as-Haven in the Lower Class." *Journal of the American Institute of Planners* 32(January): 23–31.

Rosenbaum James, Linda Stroh, and Cathy Flynn. 1998. "Lake Parc Place: A Study of Mixed Income Housing." *Housing Policy Debate* 9(4): 703–40.

Rossi, Peter H., and Robert Dentler. 1961. *The Politics of Urban Renewal.* New York: The Free Press of Glencoe.

Sadacca, Robert, Suzanne Loux, Morton Isler, and Margaret Drury. 1974. *Management Performance in Public Housing.* Washington, D.C.: Urban Institute Press.

Saegert, Susan, and Gary Winkel. 1998. "Social Capital and the Revitalization of New York City's Distressed Inner-City Housing." *Housing Policy Debate* 9(1): 17–60.

Temkin, Kenneth, and William Rohe. 1998. "Social Capital and Neighborhood Stability." *Housing Policy Debate* 9(1): 61–88.

Turner, Margery A. 1998. "Moving out of Poverty: Expanding Mobility and Choice Through Tenant-Based Housing Assistance." *Housing Policy Debate* 9(2): 373–94.

Walker, Chris, and Mark Weinheimer. 1998. *Community Development in the 1990s.* Washington, D.C.: Urban Institute and Weinheimer & Associates.

Warren, Roland. 1963. *The Community in America.* Chicago: Rand McNally.

Weir, Margaret. 1996. "Community Development and the Paradox of Decentralization." Paper presented at the Conference of the National Community Development Policy Analysis Network, Brookings Institution, Washington, D.C. (November 20).

Wilson, William Julius. 1987. *The Truly Disadvantaged: The Inner City, the Underclass, and Public Policy.* Chicago: University of Chicago Press.

Woolcock, Michael. 1998. "Social Capital and Economic Development: Toward a Theoretical Synthesis and Policy Framework." *Theory and Society* 27: 151–208.

Yates, Douglas. 1977. *The Ungovernable City.* Cambridge, Mass.: MIT Press.

Yin, Jordan. "The Community Development Industry System: An Institutional Analysis of Community Development Corporations in Cleveland, 1967–1997." Unpublished paper. Ithaca, N.Y.: Department of City and Regional Planning, Cornell University.

Chapter 7

Social Capital, Poverty, and Community Health: An Exploration of Linkages

Sherman A. James, Amy J. Schulz, and Juliana van Olphen

This chapter explores the degree to which the overall health of communities depends, at least in part, on reliable access to social capital among their residents. As discussed in chapter 1 by Mark Warren, Phillip Thompson, and Susan Saegert, social theorists (for example, Bourdieu 1987; Coleman 1988, 1990; Putnam 1993) have generally defined social capital as resources that inhere in social relationships. These resources include mutual trust, a sense of reciprocal obligation, and civic participation aimed at benefiting the group or community as a whole. As such, social capital is construed to be a property of groups or communities, not of individuals. Thus defined, social capital bears a strong resemblance to a number of other theoretical constructs (such as social integration, social support, and community capacity) that have been used with great success by public health researchers for many years. We examine the overlap between social capital and these analogous constructs in setting the stage for our review of the emerging literature on the relationship between social capital and the public's health. Following the review, we present a conceptual model outlining our own perspective on the pathways through which social capital may influence, directly and indirectly, the health of poor, inner-city U.S. communities. We illustrate several key points of our model through a case study of an ongoing, community-based, public health intervention in Detroit, Michigan. The chapter concludes with several policy recommendations designed to foster sustainable progress in building the capacity of poor communities to solve public health problems.

SOCIAL CAPITAL AS A CONSTRUCT IN PUBLIC HEALTH

The field of public health has a long-standing interest in the impact of socio-environmental factors on health (Yen and Syme 1999). Research dating back to 1854 has examined patterns of social behavior and social organization and their implications for understanding the differential distribution of diseases across communities (Snow 1936). Despite the fact that scientific paradigms and research methods emphasizing the individual as the unit of analysis have come to dominate public health in recent decades (Pearce 1996), a subset of researchers and practitioners continues to focus on the impact of community structures, broadly conceived, on the public's health. The latter emphasis includes the location and quality of housing (Saegert and Winkel 1998); patterns of residential segregation by race (Polednak 1996; Wallace 1990; Collins and Williams 1999; Fullilove 1998); membership in social networks and related perceptions of social support (House, Umberson, and Landis 1988; Heaney and Israel 1997); community and political participation (Wandersman et al. 1987; LaVeist 1992; Israel et al. 1994; Eng and Parker 1994; Goodman et al. 1998); and relative equity in gaining access to community-level economic resources (Wilkinson 1996; Kennedy, Kawachi, and Prothrow-Stith 1996; Kaplan et al. 1996; Lynch et al. 1998).

These aspects of the social environment are interconnected in complex ways. For example, the physical structure of communities shapes, and is shaped by, patterns of social interaction among residents. Those patterns, in turn, are strongly influenced by the economic resources of residents (Wallace 1990; Fullilove 1998) and by cultural values linked to race or ethnicity (James 1993; Lomas 1998). Over the years a substantial body of evidence has emerged attesting to the impact of these features of the social environment on the health of both individuals and communities (Cassel 1976; House et al. 1988; Wolf and Bruhn 1993; Aday 1994; Cohen et al. 1997; Israel et al. 1998). Importantly, this impact does not appear to be disease-specific; rather, the evidence suggests that it shapes a community's overall risk for being at risk (Link and Phelan 1995).

The growing interest in the relationship between access to social capital and community health (for example, Wilkinson 1997; Kawachi et al. 1997; Kennedy et al. 1996; Lomas 1998) is a potentially important elaboration on the ancient public health thesis that the manner in which social relationships are structured in a given society is a powerful determinant of the health status of all members in that society (Cassel 1976; Link and Phelan 1995). To paraphrase Bob Edwards and Michael Foley (1997), however, the question is, to what extent does the concept of social capital yield a distinctive analytic payoff above and beyond the analogous constructs used in public health for many years?

Despite unresolved theoretical and measurement challenges, the construct of social capital appeals to many public health researchers because of its potential to integrate complex, community-level economic and social processes in ways that could help explain variations in the general health status of communities across time and place (Wilkinson 1997; Kawachi et al. 1997). However, the construct's full research and policy potential can be realized only through its greater theoretical specification (see Warren, Thompson, and Saegert, this volume) and through improved operational measures for specific applications, including applications in public health.

To date, only a few empirical studies (Kawachi et al. 1997; Kennedy et al. 1997, 1998) have directly investigated the relationship between social capital, as defined here, and public health outcomes. Ichiro Kawachi, Bruce Kennedy, and their colleagues, the group that has pioneered this empirical work, have operationalized the construct in keeping with the framework provided by James Coleman (1990) and

Robert Putnam (1993). That is, they have emphasized mutual respect, social trust, and group membership (equating the last of these with civic engagement) as the key dimensions of social capital. Importantly, none of the potentially negative aspects of social capital, including its instrumental relationship to the abuse of social power (see Portes and Landolt 1996), have been investigated thus far, an issue we discuss in more detail later in the chapter.

Constructs like group membership, mutual respect, and trust appear to share much in common with constructs like social integration, social cohesion, and social support, all well-established predictors in the public health literature of both physical and mental health outcomes (House et al. 1988; Aday 1994; Heaney and Israel 1997). Indeed, the *positive* contributions to health made by social integration and social support are said to rival in strength the *detrimental* contributions of several well-established biomedical risk factors like cigarette smoking, obesity, elevated blood pressure, and physical inactivity (House et al. 1988). The mechanisms responsible for these "protective effects" are not well understood, but it is likely that several pathways are involved. In addition to buffering individuals against the harmful effects of daily stressors, for example, group membership (and related access to social support) could foster a sense of meaning and coherence for individuals, facilitate access to material aid or emotional comfort at critical moments, or promote adherence to healthy lifestyles (House et al. 1988). Hence, the health benefits derived from social integration probably result from the *cumulative* contributions of these varied, complementary pathways (see Cohen and Syme 1985).

Although public health researchers have not entirely neglected the theoretical relationships between social capital (group membership, mutual respect, and trust) and social power, neither have they satisfactorily addressed them. Kawachi and his colleagues (1997) and Kennedy and his colleagues (1998), for example, equate social capital with social cohesion and, evoking an hypothesis first formulated by Clifford Shaw and Henry McKay (1942), argue that

> inequality and the concentration of poor economic conditions lead to social disorganization through the breakdown of social cohesion and normlessness. It is hypothesized that communities lacking in social cohesion (social capital) are less effective in exerting informal means of social control through establishing and maintaining norms to reduce violence compared to communities with higher levels of social capital. (Kennedy et al. 1998, 8)

Temporarily setting aside the equation of concentrated economic poverty with social disorganization—itself an empirical question—this excerpt explicitly connects social capital (defined as social cohesion) with the mobilization and enforcement of community norms. In doing so, it emphasizes one form of social power—that exerted *within* communities by some individuals, or groups, over others. The role of power differentials *between* communities in producing and maintaining social inequalities in health, however, is not addressed. Thus, articulating the multiple pathways through which differentials in social power between communities are related to the distribution of health problems both within and between communities is, we believe, a largely unrecognized issue among researchers who are actively investigating the utility of the social capital construct for public health.

The importance of this point is underscored by noting that a variety of theoretically similar constructs that are widely used in public health research and practice explicitly address the issue of community power differentials. Examples of such constructs include community competence (Cottrell 1976; Eng and Parker 1994; Iscoe 1974), community capacity (Parker and Eng 1995; Thomas, Israel, and Steuart 1985; Clark and McLeroy 1995; Goodman et al. 1998), and community empowerment (Israel et al. 1994; Schulz et al. 1995; Zimmerman and Rappaport 1988; Wallerstein 1992; Wallerstein and Bernstein 1994; Patrick and Wickizer 1995). Each emphasizes the importance of a community's ability to identify collective concerns related to the health of residents and a corollary ability to mobilize resources to address those concerns effectively. Moreover, in varying degrees, the literature based on each of these constructs recognizes that while social norms in communities are often beneficial, they frequently reinforce ideologies that result in positive harm to individuals because of their race, gender, social class, or sexual orientation (Israel et al. 1994; Goodman et al. 1998). Finally, not only do the theoretical frameworks for these analogous constructs give explicit attention to the different meaning that the exercise of social power can assume, depending on the social, political, or economic context, but they also underscore the important mediating role of community organizations in amplifying or diminishing the effects of between-group differentials in social power on individuals' health and well-being (Berger and Neuhaus 1977).

We have three major concerns about how the construct of social capital has been conceptualized so far in public health. First, the functional definition of social capital as "whatever facilitates individual and collective actions" makes it difficult to separate what social capital *is* from what it *does* (Edwards and Foley 1997; Cohen 1996). Specifically, when defining the construct, it seems important to distinguish the group connections within which social capital inheres from the actual resources (social, economic, political) that these connections may contain. This point has relevance to the earlier quote (Kennedy et al. 1998, 8) regarding the alleged breakdown of social networks and resulting social disorganization in poor communities. Social networks in poor communities may be quite strong, but these networks may also have an undersupply of certain critical resources (such as political power) that could be mobilized to deal with a range of threats to community health, such as substandard housing, neighborhood violence, and a lack of jobs. In sum, social capital that involves real access to political power may be crucial when poor communities confront problems whose roots lie in institutional arrangements that go beyond the immediate geographical boundaries of the community itself (Stack 1974, 1996; Kaplan and Lynch 1997; Portes and Landolt 1996; Parker et al. 1998; Israel et al. 1994).

Second, it is important to be both critical and wary of conceptualizations of social capital as an unmitigated "good." A substantial literature suggests that social groups often go to considerable lengths to define preconditions for group membership. Individuals who belong to excluded categories may fall outside the "moral boundaries" established by the excluding group—resulting in acts motivated, for example, by racism, sexism, or homophobia (Cohen 1996; Cohen 1985; Frankenberg

1993; Almaguer 1994; Ferber 1998; Israel et al. 1994). It is clear, then, that the public health implications of access to social capital vary considerably, depending on who is mobilizing the social capital, and for what purposes (Kaplan and Lynch 1997; Portes and Landolt 1996; Foley and Edwards 1997).

A final observation follows closely on the preceding two. Although social capital inheres within social relationships and therefore is clearly linked to the structure of those relationships, an analysis of structural features alone is insufficient for understanding social capital as a construct and how it relates to community health. As Edwards and Foley (1997, 671) point out: "It is precisely [the] sociocultural component of social capital that provides the context within which it acquires meaning and becomes available to individuals or groups in a way that can facilitate individual or collective action not otherwise possible." A conceptual framework for understanding the conditions under which social capital can be effectively mobilized must therefore include an analysis of the systems of meaning, as well as the structures within which social capital is embedded and enacted (Warren, Thompson, and Saegert, this volume).

SOCIAL CAPITAL AND COMMUNITY HEALTH: THE EVIDENCE

In this section, we review the published evidence concerning the relationship between social capital and infant and adult mortality. Data on these health outcomes are widely regarded as key indicators of the overall health of communities; they have the added advantages of being routinely collected and easily aggregated at the level of cities or states. Our review includes U.S. studies that explicitly address health and social capital, the latter measured as the presence or absence of mutual respect, trust, and group membership (that is, the Coleman-Putnam perspective). In addition, we discuss studies that deal with how equitably economic and political resources are distributed among communities and with racial segregation and health, both of which we argued earlier are fundamentally linked to the construct of social capital. The literature on the positive effects of social integration on the health of individuals is both clear and convincing (House et al. 1988; Heaney and Israel 1997). Social capital, viewed at the geopolitical level (for example, cities and states), permits an examination of analogous protective effects that may operate at the community level.

Table 7.1 summarizes the characteristics and key findings of studies dealing with the respect–trust–group membership dimensions of social capital. Studies on income inequality are included in this table as well, since several authors (Kawachi et al. 1997; Wilkinson 1997) suggest that reduced social capital (equated here with reductions in social cohesion) could be both a cause and an effect of increasing income inequality. We begin with a study by Kennedy and his colleagues (1997) on the association between "collective (dis)respect" toward black Americans and state-level variations in all causes of mortality.

"Collective respect" displayed by one group toward another qualifies as a dimension of social capital because, as Kennedy and his colleagues (1997, 208) note, "a lack

TABLE 7.1 / U.S. Studies of Social Capital and Mortality: Disrespect, Trust, and Income Inequality

Authors	Study Design	Sample	Construct	Findings
Kennedy et al. 1997	Ecological; cross-sectional	39 states	Collective disrespect (percentage saying blacks are poor because they are less smart or motivated)	Higher disrespect associated with higher mortality for both blacks and whites, independent of poverty rates
Kennedy et al. 1996	Ecological; cross-sectional	50 states	Income inequality (Robin Hood Index[a] scores)	Higher income inequality associated with higher adult and infant mortality across states
Kaplan et al. 1996	Ecological; cross-sectional and longitudinal	50 states	Income inequality (percentage of total household income in each state received by poorest 50 percent of households)	Higher income inequality associated with higher mortality and smaller declines in mortality over time; inequality associated with low investments in human capital
Lynch et al. 1998	Ecological; cross-sectional	283 metropolitan areas	Income inequality (percentage of total household income received by richest 10 percent of households versus poorest 50 percent and 90 percent)[b]	Higher income inequality associated with higher adult and infant mortality, independent of per capita income
Kawachi et al. 1997	Ecological; cross-sectional	39 states	Income inequality (Robin Hood Index[a] scores); social capital (trust; group membership; perceived fairness and helpfulness)	Higher scores on social capital associated with lower state-level mortality; income inequality effects operate through social capital

Source: Authors' compilation based on data from cited works.
[a] The proportion of aggregate household income that must be redistributed from households above the mean to those below the mean in order to achieve perfect income equality.
[b] Additional indices, all showing associations in the expected direction, included the Gini coefficient, the Atkinson Deprivation Index, and the Theil Entropy Index.

of respect (that is, disrespect) is usually accompanied by a breakdown of social trust between members or groups within society, and a consequent disinvestment in social capital. Poor health status arises in such societies because the community fails to invest in, and assume responsibility for, the collective well-being of its members."[1] Collective disrespect toward black Americans ranges from negative media stereotyping, absence of representation in important spheres of public life, recurring exposure to prejudicial attitudes or even physical violence, and internalized oppression (that is, diminished self-respect among blacks as a consequence of the foregoing).

Archival data from the General Social Survey (GSS), a national representative survey of non-institutionalized, English-speaking adults conducted periodically by the National Opinion Research Center, were used to measure collective disrespect toward blacks. Respondents were asked to answer yes or no to each of four possible reasons why blacks have worse jobs, lower income, and poorer housing than whites: (1) racial discrimination, (2) less in-born ability to learn, (3) a decreased chance to gain the education it takes to get out of poverty, or (4) a lack of sufficient willpower and motivation. Responses to these questions over the five-year period 1986 to 1990 were averaged. For each state, the percentage of respondents who answered each question in the affirmative was calculated. Data from thirty-nine states were used because, "by chance, people residing in some of the less populous states were not picked up by the sampling scheme" (Kennedy et al. 1997, 209). Age-adjusted total mortality rates for 1990 constituted the dependent variable.

Results showed a significant, positive relationship between age-adjusted total mortality and the proportion of respondents in each state who attributed the economic problems of blacks to lack of motivation or intelligence rather than racial discrimination. Significantly, collective disrespect for blacks was associated with higher mortality rates almost as strongly for whites as it was for blacks.

Several groundbreaking studies on income inequality and community health have been conducted within the past decade, both in Europe (Wilkinson 1996) and in the United States (Kennedy et al. 1996; Kaplan et al. 1996; Kawachi et al. 1997; Lynch et al. 1998). These studies suggest that the wider the gap in income between the poorest and the richest members of a society, the higher the mortality among adults and infants in that society. Thus, gross inequalities in income appear to undermine the health of all members of the society, not just the poorest members.

Table 7.1 summarizes the key characteristics and findings from the five studies of income inequality conducted so far in the United States. The adverse effects of income inequality on overall community health were observed using a variety of approaches to measure income inequality. It should be noted, however, that the study by George Kaplan and his colleagues (1996) is the only one to date to include both a cross-sectional and a longitudinal component. Specifically, in 1980, states with higher levels of income inequality (see table 7.1 for a definition) reported higher age-adjusted total mortality rates. During the period 1980 to 1990, when total mortality rates continued to decline for the country as a whole, states with more income inequality showed significantly smaller declines in mortality. Interestingly, states with higher income inequality invested less in the development of human capital, as indicated by such measures as spending on education, library books per capita, and the percentage of the state population with health insurance coverage.

Kawachi and his colleagues (1997) examined more directly the hypothesis that income inequality undermines overall community health in part because it undermines the social capital of communities. Again, five-year (1986 to 1990) GSS data from thirty-nine states were averaged to produce measures of social capital. In addition to the number of group memberships per capita (civic engagement), three additional statements were presented to respondents for a yes-or-no answer: (1) most people can be trusted (social trust); (2) most people try to be fair (perceived fairness); and (3) most people try to be helpful (perceived helpfulness). Income inequality was measured by the Robin Hood Index (see table 7.1 for a definition). In general, high scores on the social capital variables were associated with lower age-adjusted total mortality rates, even controlling for the poverty rate in each state. Similarly, high scores on income inequality were also associated with higher mortality, controlling for state-level poverty rates. Subsequently, path analyses determined that the association between income inequality and mortality was almost completely explained by the strong, inverse association ($r = -0.73$) between income inequality and the social trust variable. There was no evidence, however, that income inequality mediated the strong protective association ($r = -0.64$) observed across states between social trust and all cause mortality rates.

The impact of institutionalized racial segregation on overall community health is a relatively new topic in public health research. Like income inequality, however, hyper-segregation of neighborhoods by race and the related underrepresentation of blacks in elected offices at the municipal and state levels have important implications for the kinds of life-enhancing resources to which black communities will be able to gain access. Since the hyper-segregation of neighborhoods by race usually reinforces the economic and political "dis-empowerment" of black communities (Wacquant and Wilson 1989), racial segregation in housing patterns and the underrepresentation of blacks in local elected offices are herein viewed as forms of community disempowerment.

Table 7.2 summarizes the characteristics and key findings from studies investigating community-level variations in infant and adult mortality in relation to residential segregation by race and the proportional representation of blacks on city councils in medium-size to large cities. Residential segregation was measured by the Index of Dissimilarity or by the Isolation Index (see table 7.2 for definitions). Anthony Polednak (1991, 1993) found that black excess infant and adult mortality (as indicated by age-standardized black-white mortality ratios) increased linearly with residential segregation across thirty-eight metropolitan statistical areas (MSAs). These adverse effects on black mortality relative to whites were independent of race-specific poverty rates. A similar study conducted several years later, however, failed to replicate these findings (Polednak 1996).

Thomas LaVeist (1989) found that black-white racial segregation in 176 central cities was associated with higher infant mortality among blacks, but not among whites. Using 1990 U.S. census and vital statistics data, Chiquita Collins and David

TABLE 7.2 / U.S. Studies of Social Capital and Mortality: Community Disempowerment

Authors	Study Design	Sample	Construct	Findings
Polednak 1991, 1993	Ecological; cross-sectional	38 MSAs	Racial residential segregation (Index of Dissimilarity)[a]	Higher segregation scores associated with larger black-white infant and adult mortality ratios, independent of poverty rates
Polednak 1996	Ecological; cross-sectional	38 MSAs	Racial residential segregation[a]	Segregation scores unrelated to infant mortality in both blacks and whites
LaVeist 1989	Ecological; cross-sectional	176 central cities (population 50,000 or more and 10 percent black or higher)	Racial residential segregation[a]	Higher segregation scores associated with higher infant mortality for blacks but not whites, independent of percentage of low-birthweight births, percentage of unwed mothers, and percentage of blacks in poverty
Collins and Williams 1999	Ecological; cross-sectional	107 cities (population 100,000 or more and 10 percent black or higher)	Racial residential segregation;[a] black social isolation (Isolation Index)[b]	Higher mortality observed for both whites and blacks under conditions of high residential segregation and high black social isolation
LaVeist 1992	Ecological; cross-sectional	176 central cities (population 50,000 or more and 10 percent black or higher)	Relative black political power[c]	Relative black political power associated with lower post-neonatal mortality[d] for blacks, independent of percentage of low-birthweight births; no association for whites

Source: Authors' compilation based on data from cited works.

[a] The proportion of a racial group (blacks, for instance) who would have to change neighborhoods in order to achieve an even racial distribution across neighborhoods in a given city.

[b] The probability that a randomly drawn black person in a city interacts with a nonblack person.

[c] The proportion of black city council members divided by the proportion of blacks in the voting-age population.

[d] Death of an infant between one and twelve months old.

Williams (1999) reported higher age-adjusted total mortality for *both* blacks and whites in cities with high levels of residential segregation as well as high levels of black social isolation. In other words, in urban areas where blacks and whites had little contact, mortality rates for both groups were elevated.

Finally, in a study of 176 central cities, LaVeist (1992) investigated the association between infant mortality among blacks and whites and the numerical representation of blacks on city councils in relation to the black voting-age population. LaVeist termed this ratio "relative Black political power." As scores for this variable increased from below 1.0 (indicating underrepresentation) to 1.0 or higher (proportional, or more, representation), post-neonatal mortality among blacks decreased in linear fashion. In this study, post-neonatal mortality rates among whites had no association with black political representation. Interestingly, while relative black political power was positively associated with municipal expenditures on public infrastructure (street repairs, public safety, and so on), differences in such expenditures did not explain the observed protective association. LaVeist speculated that a relatively high level of community organization may have been responsible for both the political success of certain black communities and their lower post-neonatal mortality rates. If true, this would underscore the potential importance of neighborhood levels of social capital in achieving a range of desirable outcomes in poor urban communities.

Collectively, the studies summarized in tables 7.1 and 7.2 strongly suggest that an equitable sharing of societal resources—social, economic, and political—translates into a lower burden of mortality for all members of the community. Even so, this body of research is characterized by a number of limitations, the first of which concerns the study designs. With only one exception (Kaplan et al. 1996), all of the studies employed cross-sectional designs, leaving unanswered the question of whether high mortality rates (especially among working-age adults) precede or follow high levels of inequality in access to community resources. Though limited by small numbers, data from the longitudinal component of the study by Kaplan and his colleagues (1996) suggest that high state-level inequality does in fact precede high state mortality. Studies using larger databases are needed, but this interpretation of the temporal relationship involved is clearly consistent with findings from a large number of longitudinal studies among *individuals* that provide convincing evidence that chronic economic and social deprivation are linked to early mortality in adults (Williams and Collins 1995; Link and Phelan 1995).

Second, the ecological measures of social capital are relatively crude. To a large degree, this crudeness is due to the newness of public health research on social capital per se and the exclusive reliance so far on state-level survey data that were collected for other purposes. Nevertheless, exploiting the full research potential of the social capital construct will require the development of improved measures, including measures that can be used with economically and culturally diverse populations (Kreuter et al. 1998; Goodman et al. 1998). In addition, more attention needs to be given to the theoretical and empirical relationship between social capital and social power. Social connections may exist in poor communities in abundance, but the resources that inhere in these connections may not be easily translated into social power. Again, LaVeist's (1992) work and recent theoretical distinctions between the "bonding" and "bridging" features of social capital (see Warren, Thompson, and Saegert, this volume) underscore the importance of this distinction.

Third, it is not clear how high levels of social capital at the community level actually work to promote health among all members in the community. It could operate by imposing limits on income inequality (Wilkinson 1997; Kawachi et al. 1997), on interpersonal and institutional expressions of racism (Kennedy et al. 1997; LaVeist 1992; Polednak 1996; Collins and Williams 1999), or on social policies that lead to progressive disinvestments in human capital—education, jobs, health care, and so on (Kaplan et al. 1996, Kaplan and Lynch 1997). It is possible, of course, that all of these explanatory pathways are involved to some extent, analogous to the health-enhancing effects of high levels of social integration at the individual level (House et al. 1988).

Fourth, it is not clear at what level of community social capital processes exert their influence on health: is it the country as a whole, the state, the city, or the neighborhood? The available evidence suggests that important effects may occur at each of these levels. But even if this is so, how one intervenes in these processes to promote health in communities depends on the level of community that is under discussion. Public health policy interventions target social capital processes (specifically, structural inequalities) that function primarily at the state or national level. On the other hand, interventions designed to strengthen social networks or increase the frequency of positive contact among different social networks target social capital processes that operate primarily at the level of the neighborhood or the city. Each type of intervention has an important contribution to make, and the contribution of each is undoubtedly strengthened, or weakened, depending on how well it interfaces with other social processes operating at different levels of the overall social system.

In concluding this section, we return to the question raised by Edwards and Foley (1997) concerning the extent to which the concept of social capital yields a distinct analytic payoff in public health above and beyond analogous, pre-existing constructs. Based on our review of the emerging evidence, we conclude that the explanatory potential of the social capital construct for public health research and policymaking resides less in its theoretical uniqueness than in its potential to reveal hidden linkages among the various domains of public health research that focus on the origins of social and economic inequality in America and the multiple pathways through which that inequality undermines the public's health. We believe this to be a potentially important theoretical contribution. In the following section, we present a conceptual model that specifies some of these potential linkages and pathways.

SOCIAL CAPITAL AND COMMUNITY HEALTH: A CONCEPTUAL MODEL

Our conceptual model (figure 7.1) elaborates on recent conceptualizations of social capital within the field of public health and attempts to address some of the shortcomings noted earlier in this chapter. First, it distinguishes conceptually between

FIGURE 7.1 / Social Capital and Community Health: A Conceptual Model

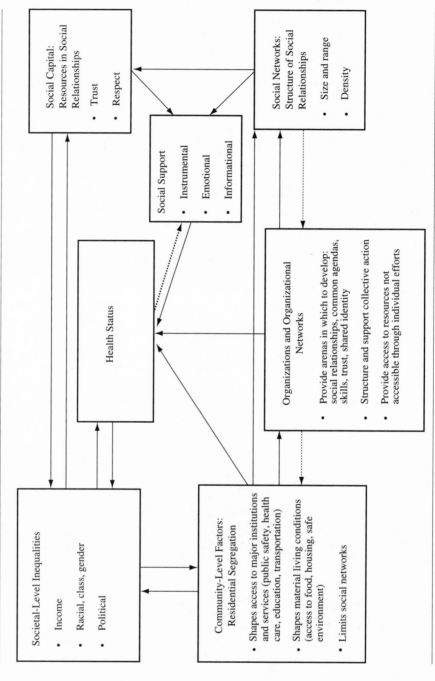

Source: Authors' configuration.

the structure of group relationships and the resources that might be mobilized within those relationships. Second, it specifies pathways through which the social, economic, and political context may influence social capital and health. Third, the model suggests the importance of including the sociocultural as well as structural factors that influence social relationships and the resources that can be mobilized within them. Fourth, the model specifies multiple pathways through which social relationships may influence health status and emphasizes the synergistic effects of these multiple pathways and their cumulative effects on health. And finally, the model represents social capital as both a dependent and an independent variable; that is, it delineates factors that presumably contribute to the building of social capital as well as the putative effects of social capital on health.

Beginning in the upper left corner of the model, societal-level inequalities such as income inequalities both reflect and exacerbate the social distance between population subgroups. These distances have direct effects on social networks and the resources within them, shown on the right side of the model. Furthermore, we suggest that societal-level inequalities also operate through class- or race-based residential segregation (lower left corner of the model), which influences social networks by physically separating groups and limiting the resources available to them. The effects of race-based residential segregation on social relationships are also mediated through community organizations, as shown in the lower center of the model. Importantly, each component of the model has a direct link to health status.

We have suggested that the construct of social capital would benefit by distinguishing conceptually between the group relationships within which social capital inheres and the resources that can be mobilized within these relationships. The model thus distinguishes between three characteristics of social relationships: social networks as the *structure* of social relationships; social support as one *resource* that can be mobilized through these networks; and *interactional characteristics* of social relationships, such as reciprocity, trust, and stability (see Israel 1982). Until now, research on social capital and health has emphasized measures such as reciprocity and trust, giving little or no attention to the ways in which these dimensions are shaped by network structure.

We envision these three aspects of social relationships as an interrelated system with, for example, the structure of social relationships influencing the mobilization of resources within and across those networks, and influenced by the interactional characteristics of those relationships.

Disentangling these dimensions would permit us to examine the interplay between them as well as their distinct contributions to health. For example, some evidence suggests that dense social networks (groups whose members are in close geographic proximity) may be effective in maintaining health when emotional support is needed. Under conditions of social change or transformation, however, social networks that are larger, more diffuse, and characterized by less intensive ties may be more adaptive, since they facilitate outreach and the exchange of a wider range of information (Heaney and Israel 1997; Heying 1997; Wilson 1998). Thus, different kinds of network structures may be more or less effective in mobilizing different kinds of resources within various social contexts.

Our model also suggests that societal-level factors, such as political and economic systems, influence the shape of social networks and the resources that can be mobilized within them. In addition to the direct effects illustrated by the arrow at the top of the model, the lower left of the model depicts effects on social networks mediated through race-based residential segregation. For example, the combined forces of income inequalities and racism result in race-based residential segregation and concentrated poverty (Massey and Fisher 2000), circumscribing the range of resources that can be mobilized within social networks and decreasing their flexibility in responding to the social environment.

The model locates organizations as mediating structures between broad social and community characteristics and social networks. In addition to structuring relationships through the organization of work and civic participation, they play a central role in the mobilization of resources (Berger and Neuhaus 1977; Israel et al. 1994; Goodman et al. 1998; McCarthy and Zald 1977; Schwartz and Paul 1992; Minkoff 1995). Organizations provide opportunities to develop and strengthen social ties, develop a sense of shared identity, define common goals, pool resources, and develop skills and a sense of shared power as they work toward collective goals (Berger and Neuhaus 1977; Israel et al. 1994). Economic, political, and social inequality, combined with the concentration of poverty tied to race-based residential segregation, contributes to the exodus of businesses and health and social service providers from economically marginalized communities. These processes have clear and substantial impacts on community life (Wilson 1987). Nevertheless, economically impoverished communities retain other associations and assets that provide arenas for the development and mobilization of social networks toward common goals (Kretzman and McKnight 1993; Israel et al. 1994; Parker et al. 1998).

In addition to the pathways through which societal inequalities influence social networks and the resources available within them, these inequalities compound each other. For example, communities experiencing concentrated poverty also tend to experience political marginalization (Cohen and Dawson 1993), which effectively reduces their ability to influence local, state, and national policies related to the distribution of social and economic resources.

Collectives (social movements, communities, identity groups) are founded on relationships defined as meaningful by the individuals who are part of them. These relationships form the foundation for the mobilization of resources within and between groups (Steuart 1978; Friedman and McAdam 1992; Morris 1984; Snow, Zurcher, and Ekland-Olson 1980; McMillan and Chavis 1986; Heaney and Israel 1997; Eng and Parker 1994; Israel et al. 1994, 1998). Group boundaries and the meanings of group membership are associated with relationships between groups and the distribution of resources within and between groups. Thus, the symbolic meanings associated with race and ethnicity in the United States influence, and are influenced by, social policies that in turn contribute to political, economic, and social inequalities. These sociocultural processes influence the resources available to create or resist social change processes, with profound implications for the health of group members (Israel et al. 1994; Goodman et al. 1998). Finally, the model suggests reciprocal pathways through which health status may influence the size and resilience of social networks. For example, as the health and stamina of individuals in poor communities deteriorate owing to sustained high-effort coping with social or economic adversity (Geronimus 1992; James 1994), the social resources that can be mobilized to address community problems are correspondingly reduced (House et al. 1988; Heaney and Israel 1997).

The multiple pathways described in our conceptual model suggest many potential avenues to influence the structure of social relationships, the resources that inhere within them, and their impact on community health. In the next section, we describe a public health intervention case study illustrating some of the key dimensions of our conceptual model.

BUILDING COMMUNITY CAPACITY AND SOCIAL CAPITAL TO PROMOTE HEALTH: A CASE STUDY

In this section, we present a case study of an ongoing, community-based, public health intervention on the East Side of Detroit, one of the most economically distressed areas in the city. Although improving the general health status of the community is the ultimate goal, increasing community empowerment and capacity by strengthening and expanding existing social networks is considered a prerequisite for attaining this goal (Israel et al. 1998; Parker et al. 1998; Schulz et al. 2000).

Background

In 1990, Detroit reported a population of 1,027,974 (U.S. Bureau of the Census 1990), 76 percent of which was African American. This makes Detroit the largest African American–majority city in the United States. Many of the African Americans who migrated to Detroit from the 1940s through the 1960s in search of jobs settled on the East Side, which historically had been known as the gateway to the city for successive groups of immigrants (Parker et al. 1998). Following World War II, the city began to experience a steady outflow of whites to the suburbs, a trend that was greatly accelerated after the 1967 civil unrest (Babson 1986). By 1990, Detroit was one of the most racially segregated cities in the country (Sugrue 1996; Massey and Denton 1993), and also one of the most impoverished: 29 percent of all families with children lived below the poverty line (U.S. Bureau of the Census 1990).

In keeping with its high percentage of families in poverty, Detroit's infant mortality rate in 1990 was 20.45 per 1,000, more than double the rate for the country as a whole (U.S. Bureau of the Census 1990). Moreover, a recent study contrasting all-cause mortality rates in selected low-income urban and rural areas of the United States found that death rates for young adults in Detroit (especially African Americans) were among the very highest in the country (Geronimus et al. 1996).

These statistics do not, however, provide a complete portrait of the city of Detroit. Many neighborhoods in the city, including the East Side, have assets that bode well for public health interventions designed to build community capacity and social capital. For example, Detroit has a strong history of union and neighborhood organizing, and African Americans have made strong contributions to both. Block clubs have been an important feature of neighborhood life in Detroit since the 1950s. Moreover, unlike many other large metropolitan areas, close to 75 percent of Detroit's population lives in single-family dwellings, 53 percent of which are owner-occupied (Parker et al. 1998). Others (for example, Saegert and Winkel 1998) have noted that higher rates of resident homeownership are associated with improved property maintenance and less residential mobility, environmental attributes that strengthen a sense of community. Collectively, these varied community assets provide a solid basis on which to launch "capacity-building" public health interventions in neighborhoods on the East Side.

The Intervention

The intervention builds on epidemiological studies linking poor health among residents of impoverished communities to structured racial, economic, and political inequalities (Williams and Collins 1995; LaVeist 1992). As highlighted in our conceptual model, the cumulative effects of these various forms of social inequality on individuals are presumed to be mediated by the layers of social networks in which those individuals are embedded (Bronfenbrenner 1979; Israel 1982; Gottlieb and McLeroy 1994; Parker et al. 1998; Schulz et al. 1998). If collective action at the community level is a precondition for reducing these various forms of structured inequality, then building community capacity for social change logically must become a major focus of public health interventions (Steuart 1993; Israel et al. 1994; Fisher 1995; Parker et al. 1998).

The East Side Detroit Village Health Worker Partnership involves about forty community residents acting as village health workers (VHWs) and a steering committee made up of representatives from ten institutions: the Detroit Health Department, Friends of Parkside, the Henry Ford Health System, the Butzel Family Center, the Warren-Conner Development Coalition, Mack Alive!, the Island View Development Coalition, the Kettering Butzel Health Initiative, the East Side Parish Nurse Network, and the School of Public Health at the University of Michigan. Two VHWs also serve on the steering committee as voting members. The steering committee is thus a forum for building and extending social networks among representatives from the constituent organizations and for identifying and mobilizing resources that can be used to address the problems identified by community residents.

The first substantive undertaking of the steering committee was to build a sense of common purpose and mutual trust (Parker et al. 1998). In-depth interviews with key community informants and focused discussion among members of the steering committee contributed to an improved understanding of both the challenges and the resources available to families on the East Side. Themes identified through these processes were incorporated into a household survey instrument. The instrument was used to assess the prevalence of selected problems and their baseline association with self-perceived health among a random sample of East Side women with child-rearing responsibility (Schulz et al. 1998). Consistent with the literature on social integration and health (House et al. 1988; Heaney and Israel 1997), results from this baseline survey indicated that women who had limited contact with neighbors, or who were not involved in block clubs, reported higher levels of stress and symptoms of depression than more socially integrated women (James et al. 1998).

The VHWs involved with the project are residents of the East Side. Most were asked to participate in the partnership on the basis of their identification by community members or organizations as people who were considered trustworthy and competent problem solvers. Many have histories in local organizing, while others are firmly embedded in social networks in which they play key roles in providing instrumental and emotional support to other members. The partnership is grounded in the lay health adviser models that have been used successfully in developing countries and in rural areas of the United States (Steuart 1993; Eng, Hatch, and Callan 1985; Eng and Young 1992). The East Side intervention is one of relatively few efforts to implement this model in a large urban area (Parker et al. 1998).

Owing to their leadership roles within existing local social networks, lay health advisers can intervene (or alternatively, help to organize interventions) at multiple levels (Eng and Young 1992). These levels are analogous to those described in our conceptual model of social capital. Specifically, these advisers may strengthen and extend social networks as well as mobilize resources within networks for the benefit of individuals or groups (for example, by relaying information to individuals or providing instrumental support for network members). Collectively, they may act at the organizational level (for example, on the steering committee) to mobilize the acquisition of new resources, or the transfer of existing ones from participating institutions to community residents. Finally, they may work toward broad-scale community change by mobilizing community residents and community-based organizations to promote positive change in the surrounding community or in the broader social system, in ways that promote community health and well-being.

In addition to the overall structure of the intervention and its links to aspects of our conceptual model, there are important conceptual issues related to the process of enhancing community capacity for change. The Village Health Worker Partnership is grounded in a theoretical model that emphasizes the development of partnerships between multiple actors, each bringing unique perspectives and resources to the table (Israel et al. 1998). This model emphasizes the power differentials among all participants in the process: it recognizes that community capacity involves effective management of both internal social power processes and differential power relationships with external organizations and communities. Today there is considerable dialogue within public health and related fields regarding power differentials between researchers and community members, but less attention has been given to differentials in power and resources within communities, as conditioned, for example, by gender, social class, or race. If they do not explicitly pay attention to the social power differentials among their members, partnerships—including public health partnerships—may simply reproduce existing social inequalities.

These power differentials may be addressed at multiple levels. The active participation and influence of community members in the process of establishing the goals, framing the specific agenda and assessing the results of the intervention, is essential if the goal of community capacity building is to be realized (Hatch et al.

1993; Israel et al. 1998). In the East Side Village Health Worker Partnership, attention to these processes is guided by principles arrived at through discussion and consensus among community members, organizational representatives, and academic partners (Schulz et al. 1998). Corollary changes in the relationships between funding agencies in the health arena, both public and private, and the communities that will be affected by the funding are also urgently needed.

None of the goals of the East Side Village Health Worker Partnership will be easy to achieve. There are major challenges at every level, from the time constraints on VHWs to the need to avoid reproducing unequal power relationships within decisionmaking structures of the partnership, to the search for effective pathways to engage the structural inequalities that lie at the root of the social, economic, and health problems in the community. These are formidable challenges, but the participants are fully committed to the principle that building sustainable community capacity (and increasing social capital) must incorporate a partnership approach that engages community members, community-based organizations, and other institutions in the process of addressing the institutional structures that reinforce racial and economic inequalities.

POLICY IMPLICATIONS AND RECOMMENDATIONS

Enlightened public policy plays a critical role in addressing the societal-level factors and institutional structures that reinforce racial and economic inequalities. In this section, we discuss two levels at which public policy can foster the development of social capital in poor communities. First, governmental agencies and foundations can support social capital development through funding initiatives that build community capacity to promote health. Second, progressive legislation that counters the cumulative impact of poverty and racism on the health of communities should be developed and enforced.

Funding agencies and organizations can facilitate the production and development of social capital in communities by addressing the pathways of influence reflected in our conceptual model. Economic development within communities should undergird all promising community-based initiatives in order to address the societal-level factors that impede the development of social capital. In addition, activities supported by funding agencies could increase community capacity if forums were convened in which the skills and leadership of local residents were strengthened, as well as the relationships and commitment of local residents and others to the community. Community-based health initiatives should also recognize the critical role of mediating organizations, as noted earlier, in building social capital and fostering connections between residents and organizations, both inside and outside the community. Initiatives that actively incorporate community-based organizations as crucibles for the development and mobilization of social capital should be encouraged. Finally, funding decisions should be made only after a realistic appraisal of the length of time the community development process takes and the resources it requires.

Social policies that address the disproportionate burden of health-compromising factors in economically impoverished communities would complement these efforts. Specific attention should be directed to the excessive burden of health problems borne by low-income women, many of whom are raising children as single heads of households. Since they are overrepresented in the low-wage labor force, policies related to child care, parental leave, and the general conditions under which women labor are needed in order to improve their overall health (Geronimus 1992).

Finally, a number of our policy recommendations would directly address the broad societal-level risk factors that influence both social capital and the health of community residents. Along with others (for example, Link and Phelan 1995), we argue that health disparities between subgroups of the population cannot be reduced without addressing the fundamental social processes that accelerate the deterioration of community health. Policies that would moderate the wide disparities in income and wealth (for example, ensuring a living wage, capping wage differentials within organizations, or attending to corporate taxation loopholes) and facilitate the political participation of groups with modest economic resources are worthy of special consideration. Finally, policies that curtail residential segregation by race would facilitate wealth accumulation by working-class families while increasing the potential for social networks to become more racially diverse. All of these recommendations would make a substantial contribution to building social capital and improving the public's health within and across U.S. communities.

The authors thank Barbara Wieman and Mollie Williams for their assistance in preparing this manuscript, and Barbara A. Israel, Edith A. Parker, David R. Williams, and Arline Geronimus for their comments on an earlier draft.

NOTE

1. We read this use of the word "community" as referring to a social and political system that fails to invest equitably in the well-being of all of its members. This interpretation is in contrast to a specific, identifiable community that runs the risk of "community-blaming," analogous to "victim-blaming" in reference to individuals.

REFERENCES

Aday, LuAnne. 1994. "Health Status of Vulnerable Populations." *Annual Review of Public Health* 15: 487–509.

Almaguer, Tomas. 1994. *Racial Fault Lines: The Historical Origins of White Supremacy in California*. Berkeley: University of California Press.

Babson, Steve. 1986. *Working Detroit: The Making of a Union Town*. Detroit: Wayne State University Press.

Berger, Peter, and Richard Neuhaus. 1977. *To Empower People: The Role of Mediating Structures in Public Policy*. Washington, D.C.: American Enterprise Institute for Public Policy Research.

Bourdieu, Pierre. 1987. "What Makes a Social Class?: On the Theoretical and Practical Existence of Groups." *Berkeley Journal of Sociology* 32: 1–8 (3–4).

Bronfenbrenner, Urie. 1979. *The Ecology of Human Development*. Cambridge, Mass.: Harvard University Press.

Cassel, John. 1976. "The Contribution of the Social Environment to Host Resistance." American Journal of Epidemiology 104(2): 107–23.

Clark, Noreen M., and Kenneth R. McLeroy. 1995. "Creating Capacity Through Health Education: What We Know and What We Don't." *Health Education Quarterly* 22(3): 273–89.

Cohen, Anthony P. 1985. *The Symbolic Construction of Community*. London: Routledge.

Cohen, Cathy. 1996. "Contested Membership: Black Gay Identities and the Politics of AIDS." In *Queer Theory: Sociology*, edited by Steven Seidman. Oxford: Blackwell.

Cohen, Cathy, and Michael Dawson. 1993. "Neighborhood Poverty and African-American Politics." *American Political Science Review* 87: 286–302.

Cohen, Sheldon, William J. Doyle, David P. Skoner, Bruce S. Rabin, and Jack M. Gwaltney. 1997. "Social Ties and Susceptibility to the Common Cold." *Journal of the American Medical Association* 277(24): 1940–44.

Cohen, Sheldon, and S. Leonard Syme, eds. 1985. *Social Support and Health*. Orlando: Academic Press.

Coleman, James. 1988. "Social Capital in the Creation of Human Capital." *American Journal of Sociology* 94: S95–120.

———. 1990. *The Foundations of Social Theory*. Cambridge, Mass.: Harvard University Press.

Collins, Chiquita A., and David R. Williams. 1999. "Segregation and Mortality: The Deadly Effects of Racism?" *Sociological Forum* 14: 495–523.

Cottrell, Leonard. 1976. "The Competent Community." In *Further Explorations in Social Psychiatry*, edited by Berton H. Kaplan, Robert N. Wilson, and Alexander H. Leighton. New York: Basic Books.

Edwards, Bob, and Michael W. Foley. 1997. "Social Capital and the Political Economy of Our Discontent." *American Behavioral Scientist* 40(5): 669–78.

Eng, Eugenia, John Hatch, and Anne Callan. 1985. "Institutionalizing Social Support Through the Church and into the Community." *Health Education Quarterly* 12: 81–92.

Eng, Eugenia, and Edith Parker. 1994. "Measuring Community Competence in the Mississippi Delta: The Interface Between Program Evaluation and Empowerment." *Health Education Quarterly* 21: 199–219.

Eng, Eugenia, and R. Young. 1992. "Lay Health Advisors as Community Change Agents." *Family and Community Health* 15: 24–40.

Ferber, Abby. 1998. *White Man Falling: Race, Gender, and White Supremacy*. New York: Rowman and Littlefield.

Fisher, Edwin B., Jr. 1995. "The Results of the COMMIT Trial." American Journal of Public Health 85: 159–60.

Foley, Michael W., and Bob Edwards. 1997. "Escape from Politics?: Social Theory and the Social Capital Debate." *American Behavioral Scientist* 40(5): 550–61.

Frankenberg, Ruth. 1993. *White Women, Race Matters: The Social Construction of Whiteness*. Minneapolis: University of Minnesota Press.

Friedman, Debra, and Doug McAdam. 1992. "Collective Identity and Activism: Networks, Choices, and the Life of a Social Movement." In *Frontiers in Social Movement Theory*, edited by Aldon D. Morris and Carol M. Mueller. New Haven, Conn.: Yale University Press.

Fullilove, Mindy T. 1998. "Injury and Anomie: Effect of Violence on an Inner-City Community." *American Journal of Public Health* 88(6): 924–27.

Geronimus, Arline T. 1992. "The Weathering Hypothesis and the Health of African-American Women and Infants: Evidence and Speculations." *Ethnicity and Disease* 2: 207–21.

Geronimus, Arline T., John Bound, Timothy A. Waidmann, Marianne M. Hillemeier, and Patricia B. Burns. 1996. "Excess Mortality Among Blacks and Whites in the United States." *New England Journal of Medicine* 335: 1552–58.

Goodman, Robert M., Marjorie Speers, Kenneth McLeroy, Stephen Fawcett, Michelle Kegler, Edith Parker, Steven Smith, Terri Sterling, and Nina Wallerstein. 1998. "Identifying and Defining the Dimensions of Community Capacity to Provide a Basis for Measurement." *Health Education and Behavior* 25(3): 258–78.

Gottlieb, Neil H., and Kenneth R. McLeroy. 1994. "Social Health." In *Health Promotion in the Workplace*, 2nd ed., edited by Michael P. O'Donnell and Jeffrey S. Harris. Albany, N.Y.: Delmar.

Hatch, John, Nancy Moss, Ama Saran, Letitia Pressley-Cantrell, and Carol Mallory. 1993. "Community Research: Partnership in Black Communities." *American Journal of Preventive Medicine* 9: 27–31.

Heaney, Catherine A., and Barbara A. Israel. 1997. "Social Networks and Social Support in Health Education." In *Health Behavior and Health Education: Theory, Research, and Practice*, 2nd ed., edited by Karen Glanz, Frances M. Lewis, and Barbara K. Rimer. San Francisco: Jossey-Bass.

Heying, Charles H. 1997. "Civic Elites and Corporate Delocalization." *American Behavioral Scientist* 40(5): 657–68.

House, James S., Debra Umberson, and Karl Landis. 1988. "Structures and Processes of Social Support." *Annual Review of Sociology* 14: 293–318.

Iscoe, Ira. 1974. "Community Psychology and the Competent Community." *American Psychologist* 29: 607–13.

Israel, Barbara A. 1982. "Social Networks and Health Status: Linking Theory, Research, and Practice." *Patient Education and Counseling* 4(2): 65–79.

Israel, Barbara A., Barry Checkoway, Amy Schulz, and Marc Zimmerman. 1994. "Health Education and Community Empowerment: Conceptualizing and Measuring Perceptions of Individual, Organizational, and Community Control." *Health Education Quarterly* 21(2): 149–70.

Israel, Barbara A., Amy J. Schulz, Edith A. Parker, and Adam B. Becker. 1998. "Review of Community-Based Research: Assessing Partnership Approaches to Improve Public Health." *Annual Review of Public Health* 19: 173–202.

James, Sherman A. 1993. "Racial and Ethnic Differences in Infant Mortality and Low Birthweight: A Psychosocial Critique." *Annals of Epidemiology* 3: 130–36.

———. 1994. "John Henryism and the Health of African-Americans." *Culture, Medicine, and Psychiatry* 18: 163–82.

James, Sherman A., Edith A. Parker, Amy J. Schulz, and Barbara A. Israel. 1998. "Community-Based Research on Detroit's East Side: Baseline Correlates of Depression Symptomatology in African-American Women." Paper presented at Conference on Public Health in the Twenty-first Century: Behavioral and Social Science Contributions, Atlanta (May 9).

Kaplan, George K., and John W. Lynch. 1997. "Editorial: Whither Studies on the Socioeconomic Foundations of Population Health." *American Journal of Public Health* 87(9): 1409–11.

Kaplan, George K., Elsie R. Pamuk, John W. Lynch, Richard D. Cohen, and Jennifer L. Balfour. 1996. "Inequality in Income and Mortality in the United States: Analysis of Mortality and Potential Pathways." *British Medical Journal* 312: 999–1003.

Kawachi, Ichiro, Bruce P. Kennedy, Kimberly Lochner, and Deborah Prothrow-Stith. 1997. "Social Capital, Income Inequality, and Mortality." *American Journal of Public Health* 87: 1491–98.

Kennedy, Bruce P., Ichiro Kawachi, Kimberly Lochner, Camara Jones, and Deborah Prothrow-Stith. 1997. "(Dis)respect and Black Mortality." *Ethnicity and Disease* 7(3): 207–14.

Kennedy, Bruce P., Ichiro Kawachi, and Deborah Prothrow-Stith. 1996. "Income Distribution and Mortality: Cross-sectional Ecological Study of the Robin Hood Index in the United States." *British Medical Journal* 312: 1004–7.

Kennedy, Bruce P., Ichiro Kawachi, Deborah Prothrow-Stith, Kimberly Lochner, and Vanita Gupta. 1998. "Social Capital, Income Inequality, and Firearm Violent Crime." *Social Science and Medicine* 47(1): 7–17.

Kretzman, John, and John McKnight. 1993. *Building Communities from the Inside Out: A Path Toward Finding and Mobilizing a Community's Assets.* Chicago: ACTA Publications.

Kreuter, Marshall. 1998. "Is Social Capital a Mediating Structure for Effective Community-Based Health Promotion?" Working Paper. Atlanta: Health 2000.

LaVeist, Thomas A. 1989. "Linking Residential Segregation to the Infant-Mortality Disparity in U.S. Cities." *Sociology and Social Research* 73(2): 90–94.

———. 1992. "The Political Empowerment and Health Status of African-Americans: Mapping a New Territory." *American Journal of Sociology* 97(4): 1080–95.

Link, Bruce G., and Jo Phelan. 1995. "Social Conditions as Fundamental Causes of Disease." *Journal of Health and Social Behavior* (extra issue): 80–94.

Lomas, Jonathan. 1998. "Social Capital and Health: Implications for Public Health and Epidemiology." *Social Science and Medicine* 47(9): 1181–88.

Lynch, John W., George A. Kaplan, Elsie R. Pamuk, Richard D. Cohen, Katherine E. Heck, Jennifer L. Balfour, and Irene H. Yen. 1998. "Income Inequality and Mortality in Metropolitan Areas of the United States." *American Journal of Public Health* 88(7): 1974–80.

Massey, Douglas, and Nancy Denton. 1993. *American Apartheid: Segregation and the Making of the Underclass.* Cambridge, Mass.: Harvard University Press.

Massey, Douglas S., and M. J. Fischer. 2000. "How Segregation Concentrates Poverty." *Ethnic and Racial Studies* 23(4): 670–91.

McCarthy, John D., and Mayer Zald. 1977. "Resource Mobilization and Social Movements: A Partial Theory." *American Journal of Sociology* 82: 1212–41.

McMillan, John W., and David M. Chavis. 1986. "Sense of Community: Definitions and Theory." *Journal of Community Psychology* 14: 6–23.

Minkoff, Debra C. 1995. *Organizing for Equality: The Evolution of Women's and Racial-Ethnic Organizations in America, 1955–1985.* New Brunswick, N.J.: Rutgers University Press.

Morris, Aldon. 1984. *The Origins of the Civil Rights Movement.* New York: Free Press.

Parker, Edith A., and Eugenia Eng. 1995. "Conceptualizing Community Problem-solving Capacity: Results of a Grounded Theory Study." Ann Arbor: University of Michigan. Unpublished paper.

Parker, Edith A., Amy J. Schulz, Barbara A. Israel, and Rose Hollis. 1998. "Detroit's East Side Village Health Worker Partnership: Community-Based Lay Health Advisor Intervention in an Urban Area." *Health Education and Behavior* 25(1): 24–45.

Patrick, Donald L., and Thomas M. Wickizer. 1995. "Community and Health." In *Society and Health,* edited by Benjamin C. Amick, Sol Levine, Alvin R. Tarlov, and Diana C. Walsh. New York: Oxford University Press.

Pearce, Neil. 1996. "Traditional Epidemiology, Modern Epidemiology, and Public Health." *American Journal of Public Health* 86: 678–83.

Polednak, Anthony P. 1991. "Black-White Differences in Infant Mortality in Thirty-eight Standard Metropolitan Areas." *American Journal of Public Health* 81(11): 1, 480–82.

———. 1993. "Poverty, Residential Segregation, and Black/White Mortality Ratios in Urban Areas." *Journal of Health Care for the Poor and Underserved* 4(4): 363–73.

———. 1996. "Segregation, Discrimination, and Mortality in U.S. Blacks." *Ethnicity and Disease* 6(1–2): 99–108.

Portes, Alejandro, and Patricia Landolt. 1996. "The Downside of Social Capital." *The American Prospect* 26: 18–22.

Putnam, Robert D. 1993. *Making Democracy Work: Civic Traditions in Modern Italy*. Princeton, N.J.: Princeton University Press.

———. 1995. "Bowling Alone: America's Declining Social Capital." *Journal of Democracy* 6: 65–78.

Saegert, Susan, and Gary Winkel. 1998. "Social Capital and the Revitalization of New York City's Distressed Inner-City Housing." *Housing Policy Debate* 9(1): 17–60.

Schulz, Amy J., Barbara A. Israel, Edith A. Parker, and Adam B. Becker. 2000. "I Started Knocking on Doors in the Community: Women's Participation and Influence in the East Side Village Health Worker Partnership." In *Empowerment of Women and Mothers for Health Promotion*, edited by Snehendu Kar. Thousand Oaks, Calif.: Sage.

Schulz, Amy J., Barbara A. Israel, Susan Selig, and Irene Bayer. 1998. "Development and Implementation of Guidelines for Community-Based Research." In *Research Strategies for Community Practice*, edited by R. H. MacNair. New York: Haworth Press.

Schulz, Amy J., Barbara A. Israel, Marc A. Zimmerman, and Barry N. Checkoway. 1995. "Empowerment as a Multi-level Construct: Perceived Control at the Individual, Organizational, and Community Levels." *Health Education Research* 10(3): 309–27.

Schulz, Amy J., Edith A. Parker, Barbara A. Israel, Adam B. Becker, Barbara J. Maciak, and Rose Hollis. 1998. "Conducting a Participatory Community-Based Survey for a Community Health Intervention on Detroit's East Side." *Journal of Public Health Management and Practice* 4(2): 10–24.

Schwartz, Michael, and Paul Schuva. 1992. "Resource Mobilization Versus the Mobilization of the People." In *Frontiers in Social Movement Theory*, edited by Aldon D. Morris and Carol McClung Mueller. New Haven, Conn.: Yale University Press.

Shaw, Clifford, and Henry McKay. 1942. *Juvenile Delinquency and Urban Areas*. Chicago: University of Chicago Press.

Snow, David A., Louis A. Zurcher, and Steven Ekland-Olson. 1980. "Social Networks and Social Movements: A Microstructural Approach to Differential Recruitment." *American Sociological Review* 45(5): 787–801.

Snow, John. 1936. *Snow on Cholera*. New York: Commonwealth Fund; London: Oxford University Press.

Stack, Carol. 1974. *All Our Kin: Strategies for Survival in a Black Community*. New York: Harper and Row.

———. 1996. *Call to Home: African-Americans Reclaim the Rural South*. New York: Basic Books.

Steuart, Guy W. 1978. "Social and Cultural Perspectives: Community Intervention and Mental Health." Paper presented at the Fourteenth Annual John W. Umstead Series of Distinguished Lectures, Raleigh, N.C.

———. 1993. "Social and Behavioral Change Strategies." *Health Education Quarterly* Supplement 1: S113–35.

Sugrue, Thomas J. 1996. *The Origins of the Urban Crisis: Race and Inequality in Postwar Detroit*. Princeton, N.J.: Princeton University Press.

Thomas, Rosalind P., Barbara A. Israel, and Guy W. Steuart. 1985. "Cooperative Problem Solving: The Neighborhood Self Help Project." In *Advancing Health Through Education*, edited by Helen P. Cleary, Jefferey M. Kichen, and Phyllis G. Ensor. Palo Alto, Calif.: Mayfield.

U.S. Bureau of the Census. 1990. *Subcommunity Profiles for the City of Detroit, October 1993: United Community Services of Metropolitan Detroit*. Washington: U.S. Government Printing Office.

Wacquant, Loic J. D., and William Julius Wilson. 1989. "The Cost of Racial and Class Exclusion in the Inner City." *Annals of the American Academy of Political and Social Sciences.* 501: 8–25.

Wallace, Robert. 1990. "Urban Desertification, Public Health, and Public Order: Planned Shrinkage, Violent Death, Substance Abuse, and AIDS in the Bronx." *Social Science and Medicine* 31: 801–13.

Wallerstein, Nina. 1992. "Powerlessness, Empowerment, and Health: Implications for Health Promotion Programs." *American Journal of Health Promotion* 6: 197–205.

Wallerstein, Nina M., and Edward Bernstein, eds. 1994. "Community Empowerment, Participatory Education, and Health: Part II." *Health Education Quarterly* 21: 279–419.

Wandersman, Abraham, Paul Florin, Robert Friedmann, and Richard Meier. 1987. "Who Participates, Who Does Not, and Why?: An Analysis of Voluntary Neighborhood Organizations in the United States and Israel." *Sociological Forum* 2(3): 534–55.

Wilkinson, Richard G. 1996. *Unhealthy Societies: The Afflictions of Inequality.* London: Routledge.

———. 1997. "Comment: Income, Inequality, and Social Cohesion." *American Journal of Public Health* 87: 1504–6.

Williams, David R., and Chiquita Collins. 1995. "U.S. Socioeconomic and Racial Differences in Health: Patterns and Explanations." *Annual Review of Sociology* 21: 349–86.

Wilson, T. D. 1998. "Weak Ties, Strong Ties: Network Principles in Mexican Migration." *Human Organization* 57 (4): 394–403.

Wilson, William J. 1987. *The Truly Disadvantaged: The Inner City, the Underclass, and Public Policy.* Chicago: University of Chicago Press.

Wolf, Stewart, and J. G. Bruhn. 1993. *The Power of Clan: The Influence of Human Relationships on Heart Disease.* New Brunswick, N.J.: Transaction Publishers.

Yen, Irene, and S. Leonard Syme. 1999. "The Social Environment and Health: A Discussion of the Epidemiologic Literature." *Annual Review of Public Health* 20: 287–308.

Zimmerman, Marc A., and Julian Rappaport. 1988. "Citizen Participation, Perceived Control, and Psychological Empowerment." *American Journal of Community Psychology* 16: 725–50.

Chapter 8

Transforming Urban Schools Through Investments in the Social Capital of Parents

Pedro A. Noguera

This chapter explores some of the ways in which parental involvement at local school sites can generate social capital that can be used to improve inner-city schools and the communities they serve. The form of involvement examined goes beyond traditional calls for parents to be more interested in the education of their children and more supportive of teachers (Epstein 1991). I make the case for schools to become more responsive to and supportive of the children, families, and communities they serve by consciously developing partnerships based on mutual accountability and responsibility.

Given the poor state of most inner-city public schools, social capital—which can be viewed as the by-product of and the collective benefits derived through participation in social organizations and networks (Putnam 1995; Sampson 1998)—is most likely to become manifest in efforts to improve student achievement and through various forms of parental empowerment. Efforts to raise academic performance, though not the subject of this analysis, are likely to serve as a focal point for the development of social capital because research shows that high levels of achievement among poor children are generally made possible through organized cooperation between teachers and parents (Ladson-Billings 1994; Fischer et al. 1996). Similarly, efforts to organize the parents of disadvantaged children and to empower them as decision-makers and advocates for their children have been shown to contribute to the improvement of schools and the betterment of the communities they serve (Hess 1995; Bryk et al. 1998).

Despite the importance of schools as social institutions, there has been little recognition of the need to incorporate strategies for their improvement into development efforts in low-income communities (Fantini et al. 1970; Noguera 1996). Moreover, strategies for organizing and involving parents are typically not incorporated into most school reform plans, particularly since the advent of high-stakes testing (Ayers and Klonsky 2000). Such omissions undoubtedly contribute to the consistent failure of most poverty alleviation and school reform efforts in economically depressed urban areas.

This chapter focuses on how efforts to organize and empower low-income parents so that they are able to exert influence over the education of their children can contribute to the improvement of inner-city schools. A central theme of the analysis presented in these pages is that such organizing efforts transform relations between school personnel and the parents they serve. Specifically, we examine how strategies aimed at increasing parental participation in school site decisionmaking can either compel schools to become more responsive toward the needs of students and parents or, put more positively, open up possibilities for constructive partnerships between the two parties. Using the role and treatment of parents as the central feature of this discussion, I will show that the primary benefit derived from social capital in this context is greater power and control by poor parents over the institutions that serve them.

To illustrate this point, I begin by recounting two experiences that provide insight into my thinking on the central problem that I believe investments in social capital can help to address. As a researcher and educator, I am frequently called on to speak to students and teachers, to organize workshops for parents, and to assist in addressing some of the many problems facing urban schools. I often work on projects with parents, teachers, and students designed to improve conditions in schools through the use of action-oriented research. In some cases, I develop working relationships with schools based on a collaborative project that is carried out over an extended period of time, sometimes over the course of several years. Despite the intractability of the problems and issues we take on—student achievement, teacher effectiveness, discipline and safety, support services for children and families, race relations, bilingual education—I derive a great deal of satisfaction from the work because it provides me with a sense that I am doing something concrete about issues that affect people's lives in important ways.

Because I spend a lot of time in urban schools, I've become fairly adept at discerning how the aesthetic aspects of the physical environment and the subtleties of the interactions between adults and children relate to the character of a particular school and the cultural norms that operate within it. The lighting of hallways, the cleanliness of restrooms, the positioning and demeanor of secretaries in the front office, the absence or prevalence of greenery on the playground—these are just some of the signs I take note of to obtain insights into the culture and atmosphere of a particular school. Certainly, I learn even more about a school from talking with teachers, administrators, and students, examining school records, and observing students in classrooms, on the playground, or the school cafeteria, but the initial observations are often the most telling and informative.

Two of my recent visits to urban schools—one a large high school, the other a small elementary school—provide examples of how significant first impressions can be. In his own work, Pierre Bourdieu has referred to such examples or vignettes as "structural anecdotes," which he describes as "incidents in which the key structural elements are revealed."[1] In his own use of this concept, Troy Duster (1989) suggests that structural anecdotes can "reveal how institutional and organizational forces converge around what on the surface may appear to be an individual, personal or idiosyncratic matter." In the next section, I employ two structural anecdotes to demonstrate the role of social capital in relationships between parents and school personnel, and between urban schools and the communities they serve.

WHO COUNTS, WHO DOESN'T: SOCIAL CAPITAL AND THE UNEVEN RELATIONSHIP BETWEEN PARENT AND PRINCIPAL AT URBAN SCHOOLS

I had been approached by the principal of a large urban high school in the San Francisco Bay Area who wanted to discuss her strategic plan for reforming the school; she planned to submit it to the school board for review that evening. I arrived at the high school in the late afternoon just as school was letting out. As I parked and walked toward the front office, I noticed groups of students casually milling around the front of the building. It was one of the few sunny and warm days we had in the month of January, and it felt good to be outdoors. Some kids dressed in athletic gear moved across the parking lot quickly, with a clear sense of direction, and appeared to be on their way to practice. Most of the students were hanging out casually in small groups throughout the campus. Most were engaged in light conversation, and the occasional burst of laughter suggested to me that, for the moment at least, things were calm on this Thursday afternoon.

About five minutes into my conversation with the school principal—an African American woman in her early forties—we were interrupted by one of her assistant principals, a Caucasian man in his mid to late fifties. His furrowed brow conveyed a look of deep concern. Interrupting our conversation, he informed the principal that a large group was in his office demanding to see her immediately. They were there to protest the decision she had made earlier in the day to suspend a student who had been fighting with another student. He explained that the group, which included the suspended student's mother, sought an audience with the principal to explain her daughter's side of the conflict.

The principal responded by saying, "Tell them I can't see them now, but that if the girl hit the other student, she's out for three days. Period." By the troubled look on the assistant principal's face, it was evident that the principal's response was of little help to him. He informed her that the student claimed she had been attacked and only struck back at her assailants in self-defense. Again, the principal was dismissive. "It doesn't matter. If you hit another person, you're outta here. If they need to talk to me about it, tell them they can wait, but it's gonna be at least an hour."

As she turned to me to resume our conversation about her plan, I asked her what students were expected to do if they felt compelled to defend themselves. I confessed to her that as a parent I instructed my own children to defend themselves if they were attacked and no adults were present to intervene. With the assistant principal gone, she smiled and confided, "I met with these folks earlier today, and let me tell you, the momma is worse than the daughter. She probably wants to beat them girls up herself. If I see her, she'll just get in my face and start to hollering. I really don't need that. Sure, I think that self-defense is legitimate at times, but I know when I'm dealing with problem people, and this girl and her momma have serious problems."

The second incident occurred at an urban elementary school where I had been invited by the principal to speak to her teachers about expectations for African American children. The principal, a white woman in her mid-fifties, contacted me because she was under pressure from central administration in the school district to raise reading test scores. She wanted me to speak to the faculty about their expectations toward African American children because she believed "these teachers don't think these kids can learn."

I arrived at the school about 8:30 A.M., parked in the lot out front, and walked to the main office. As I entered the building, I was greeted by the principal, who was standing with a broad smile on her face in the main entrance. She extended her hand and told me how glad she was that I had taken the time to visit her school. Just as she was about to launch into the issues that had prompted my visit, three girls—Latinas who appeared to be ten or eleven years of age—entered the building laughing playfully with each other. At the moment of their arrival, the principal stopped in midsentence to confront the girls. "Young ladies! Is that the way we carry ourselves in the halls when class is in session? I do believe you're tardy, aren't you?" The girls nodded sheepishly, and as one attempted to speak to explain her tardiness to the principal, she was immediately cut off. "I don't want to hear why you are late. I want to see you walk quietly into the office to get a late pass. Your parents can send me a note explaining why you are late."

Just as she finished her sentence, a well-dressed woman in her mid-forties entered the front door. From the look on her face, it was evident that she was accompanying the three girls. It was also immediately clear that she was not at all happy about the scolding that was in progress as she entered, and her face revealed her displeasure toward the principal. Upon noticing the woman and immediately recognizing her as a parent of one of the girls, the principal abruptly changed her tone of voice and facial expression. Her frown melted into a forced smile, and the stern manner in her voice transformed into a warm, though insincere, greeting. "Good morning. I was just telling the girls that they have to use their inside voices when they enter the school building because classes are in session." Then, turning to the girls with the same warm and friendly tone of voice, the principal continued, "Girls, since your mother is here, you won't need a late pass. So hurry off to class, you don't want to be too late." The parent did not return the smile. Instead, she nodded her head with disgust that seemed to convey her displeasure and spoke directly to the girls. "Come on, I don't want you to be late for your class either, and I've got to get to work." The parent then shot a quick glance of disdain at the principal, shaking her head as if the very sight of her was distasteful. As the group left, the principal turned to me, and said, "That's just some of what I deal with all day, every day, around here. I'm the authority figure, and not everyone's comfortable with the rules, but we have to have 'em." She then led me to the teachers' lounge for our first meeting of the day.

These two vignettes provide profound insights into the ways in which what Bourdieu (1985) has termed cultural capital influences the character of interactions between school officials and the parents they serve, a phenomenon that has been well documented by scholars such as Annette Lareau (1989), Ann Ferguson (1995), and Michelle Fine (1993). However, the two incidents also reflect more than just the peculiarities of the individuals involved. To the extent that interactions like these follow broader patterns of interaction between school officials and parents, and to the extent that these interactions are influenced by racial and class-based norms and social conventions, they also tell us a great deal about the role of social capital.

Several scholars have suggested that urban public schools have the potential to serve as sources of either negative or positive social capital (Wacquant 1998; Gargiulo and Benassi 1997; Bourdieu and Wacquant 1992). Schools where academic failure is high and low achievement is accepted as the norm and schools that isolate themselves from the neighborhoods they serve because they perceive the residents as "threatening" tend to undermine the social capital of the community. Often the presence of such schools contributes to the exodus of families with resources, both financial and social, from poor communities and the lowering of property values. To the extent that such schools are perceived as ineffective and incapable of serving the needs of children, they operate as a source of negative social capital because they further the marginalization of the community; eventually such schools serve only those who are unable to escape them.

In contrast, effective urban public schools—and though their numbers are small, some do exist (Hilliard 1991; Edmonds 1979)—can further the development of social capital within poor communities because they are perceived as sources of opportunity and support, primarily because they provide students with the means to improve their lives. Schools that achieve positive academic outcomes from the majority of the students they serve tend to rely heavily on the support and cooperation of parents. As will be seen from the two case studies presented here, such cooperation can lead to the formation of social networks that promote the broader interests of the families residing in inner-city neighborhoods.

A key factor determining which form of social capital will be produced is the nature of the relationship between the school—and the individuals who work there—and the community, including the parents of the children enrolled. Where connections between school and community are weak or characterized by fear and distrust, it is more likely that the school will serve as a source of negative social capital. However, when school and a community have formed a genuine partnership based on respect and a shared sense of responsibility, positive forms of social capital can be generated.

In the first vignette, a school rule—the prohibition against assaulting another student—is applied rigidly and with no regard for mitigating circumstances. How the matter is handled is based on the principal's belief that the student and her mother have "serious problems." The vague reference to problems in this instance seems to mean that their behavior is perceived as hostile, aggressive, and irrational. According to the principal, who has the power to determine how this situation will be handled, such people have serious problems, and consequently, both child and parent are in need of discipline by the rules.

Closer examination of this interaction also reveals the degree of social distance between the school official and the parent—a separation that may be based on differences in class and social status as well as differences in their roles and positions.

As an outsider in this situation who had not met the girl, her mother, or the family, I immediately assumed that the principal would behave in such a callous manner only if the parent and child were poor and black. I drew this conclusion because in my many visits to urban schools I have often witnessed parents, especially African Americans and recent immigrants, being treated with disregard and disrespect by school officials. This pattern of treatment is also well documented in research on relations between parents and staff at urban schools (Comer 1981; Epstein 1991; Fine 1993). Sometimes the affront is blatant: a dismissive explanation of a rule or policy, or even a direct insult. More often the disrespect is less obvious and more nuanced, taking the form of a condescending bit of advice, or a less than prompt response to a request for help.

My assumption about the parent was confirmed when I encountered the group (parent, child, and relatives) as I left the principal's office. Agitated by the long wait and the sense that they had been wronged by the school rules, the family sat impatiently waiting for the principal in the adjoining office until our meeting was over. As I prepared to depart, the principal passed the group without acknowledging their presence and walked me to the door, an action I took as further evidence that in her eyes these people didn't "count." Because the principal believed they had "problems," she saw no need to discuss their side of the issues and felt completely justified in her resolve to deal sternly with the matter.

Given that both the principal and the parent were African American, it was not immediately clear how race or class may have influenced the nature of this interaction. However, what was clear was that the principal had all of the power in this situation, and that she could determine how it would be handled. It is typically the case that the personnel at most urban public schools do not reside within the communities they serve, and that social barriers related to differences in race, culture, and class contribute to tremendous barriers between school and community (Noguera 1996; Haymes 1995). Such separations tend to reinforce or contribute to the development of biases among the outsider professionals, who come to see poor children, their families, and the communities in which they live as deficient, dysfunctional, and even hopeless (Lipman 1998). When school personnel have all of the power to determine how the students and families they work with will be served (Anyon 1997; Payne 1984; Maeroff 1988), such an imbalance reinforces their tendency to reproduce forms of inequality and undermine the interests of the communities they serve.

In the second vignette, a different balance of power is on display. The sudden change in the attitude and behavior of the principal that I observed was triggered by the arrival of the middle-class parent. In her presence, the students were no longer treated as mere wards of the school who could be scolded without retort and dispatched quickly to their classrooms. In the presence of the mother, the principal treated the girls as welcomed members of the school community, and the possibility that they had a legitimate reason for being late to school was suddenly taken into consideration. She spoke to the girls with kindness and accorded their middle-class mother the respect and deference typically extended to clients whose patronage is valued and whose approval is sought.

In this case, the status of the parent elicited treatment premised on respect. As an observer of the interaction, I sensed that the principal's change in tone and behavior was based on her understanding that a white, middle-class parent has a keen sense of her individual rights and a powerful sense of entitlement with regard to how she expects to be treated by teachers and administrators in a public school (Nocera 1990). Unlike the parent in the first scenario, the middle-class parent also possessed a powerful weapon that is typically inaccessible to the poor—the power to withdraw her children from the school if she was not satisfied with how she was served. This is an essential difference between the two parents in these examples, and between poor and middle-class parents generally: middle-class parents have the resources and wherewithal to assert their rights if they do not like how they or their children are treated. In contrast, a poor parent is more likely to feel that the school her child attends is the only one available to her, and thus, the principal holds all of the power when the two meet. In any conflict, the principal has the ability to exercise power unilaterally over the student and the parent. Social capital is the only means available to counter this power imbalance and to bring about a respectful and supportive relationship.

PROBLEMATIZING FAILURE: THE ROLE OF URBAN SCHOOLS IN THE REPRODUCTION OF SOCIAL INEQUALITY

Examples such as these reveal some of the ways in which the structure of the interactions between school administrators and parents is based on the distribution of power and social capital. The ability of parents to influence the actions and decisions of school personnel is often directly related to their level of education, class, and status. Poor parents generally exercise less influence over school decisions, even decisions that may directly affect the education of their children, than middle-class parents (Fine 1993), and relations between poor parents and teachers and administrators are more likely to be characterized by distrust and hostility (Moore 1992). The power of school personnel is rooted in their institutional authority, while the relative powerlessness of poor parents is based on their lack of social and cultural capital. Lacking the traits and personal attributes that are more likely to lead to an automatic measure of respect and fair treatment, poor parents are constrained in their ability to serve as effective advocates for their children. Parents who feel unfairly treated are more likely to become hostile, but irate individuals generally cannot succeed in altering unequal social relationships, at least not by themselves.

Beyond the power imbalances at the micro level, it is also important to understand how broader patterns of interaction operative at the community level influence the formation of social capital. As has been demonstrated in numerous studies, public schools in the United States serve as great sorting machines through which inequality and privilege are reproduced (Bowles and Gintis 1976; Carnoy and Levin 1985; Katznelson and Weir 1985). Schools are not alone in carrying out this function, but they more than any other social institution reproduce existing social and economic inequities with an air of legitimacy that makes the process seem fair and almost natural (Apple 1982; Giroux 1988). This is because the production of workers and professionals, future leaders and future criminals, conforms to prevailing ideological conceptions of merit and mobility. That is, those we expect to succeed, such as children from affluent families, tend to be more likely to succeed, while those we expect to fail—namely, poor children, especially black and Latino children from the inner city—tend to be more likely to fail. The conventional wisdom is that the winners and losers earn what they receive in the end, and that the process of sorting is fair and based largely on achievement (Bowles and Gintis 1976, 52). It is also assumed that school failure is the by-product of individual actions—a failure to study and do homework, to behave in class, to attend school regularly—while the collective and cultural dimensions of school failure are ignored (Apple 1982, 91–102).

The fact that the production of winners and losers corresponds so closely to larger societal patterns of race and class privilege has not generated much public concern in recent years, at least not beyond those most directly affected. This lack of concern is due in large part to hegemonic forces that condition popular attitudes and expectations such that the persistence of these patterns is expected and perceived as "normal" (MacLeod 1987). For this reason, even during a period when more public attention and resources are being directed toward education than at any other time in this nation's history (Tyack and Cuban 1995), little if any of the public discourse focuses on the issues and questions related to the role that schools play in reproducing inequality.

Amid all the outpouring of concern about the state of public education, the factors seen by those most directly involved in the educational process as most relevant—access to resources and materials, the state of facilities, the availability of trained professionals—often receive little attention. There is little debate over the need to promote greater equity in funding between schools (Anyon 1996; Henig et al. 1999), to significantly raise teacher salaries, or to renew and further desegregation efforts (Orfield and Eaton 1996). Furthermore, there is no urgent effort afoot to address the acute lack of resources in personnel, materials, and services for schools in the most economically and socially marginal communities (Kozol 1991).

If there is a crisis in public education, few commentators would disagree that it is most acute in America's urban areas. The inner city, especially those areas now referred to by some urban planners as "no-zones"—no banks, no grocery stores, no community services, no hospitals (Greenberg and Schneider 1994)—possess more than their share of failing schools. Nationally, dropout rates at inner-city schools hover at around 50 percent, test scores are generally well below national averages, and metal detectors are increasingly as ubiquitous as swings and slides on the playground (Maeroff 1988).

Urban schools in the United States are the backwater of public education, and their continued failure blends in easily with the panorama of pathologies afflicting the inner city and its residents. This fact is so well known and so taken for granted that, like inner-city crime, the issue is often not even deemed newsworthy. Hence, the failure of urban schools and of the children they serve is not problematized; rather, it is expected. New programs and policies are adopted with some regularity, but there is little willingness to address the fact that urban schools are inextricably linked to and affected by the economic and social forces present within the urban environment. However, it would be going too far to suggest that schools are merely products of their environment. Given that there is some variation among similar schools in student achievement indicators, it is possible to argue that urban schools could either contribute to the further decline of the quality of life in urban areas or serve as viable social assets that could promote the development of positive social capital. The degree to which poor parents are organized to exert influence and control over schools can be a decisive variable that determines whether schools serve as a source of positive or negative social capital.

My own experience working with urban schools leads me to believe that any serious policy for improving urban public schools must address the educational issues in concert with a broad array of social issues, such as poverty, joblessness, and the lack of public services. Such an approach has not been attempted on a mass scale since the Great Society programs of the 1960s (Pinkney 1984; Wilson 1980), and under the present paradigm of neoliberalism, there is little likelihood that such a comprehensive effort will be launched again in the near future.

Absent the political will to support the re-creation of social welfare programs and social investments that would spur development in economically depressed urban areas, it may still be possible to initiate social reforms that bring gradual and concrete improvement to conditions in the inner city. Such an approach must focus centrally on the development of social capital through the improvement of urban public schools. Specifically, the goal must be to transform urban schools into sources of social stability and support for families and children by developing their potential to serve as sources of intracommunity integration and to provide resources for extracommunity linkages. These forms of social capital have been identified by James Coleman (1988), Michael Woolcock (1998), Robert Putnam (1993), and others as key elements of strategies designed to address the needs of poor communities. I believe the urban public schools are uniquely and strategically situated to contribute significantly in both of these areas, and that the benefits of such developments would extend beyond the confines of school to the broader community.

Before explicating the elements of such a strategy, two points must be made regarding why it is needed. First, urban schools are increasingly the most reliable source of stability and social support for poor children. This is largely because, unlike other public and private institutions, public schools are required to provide access to all children regardless of their status (Noguera 1996; Comer 1981). Children who are homeless, undocumented, sick or disabled, hungry or abused, all have a right to public education. Given the harsh realities confronting the poorest people in this country, schools are often the only place where children can be guaranteed at least one meal, a warm building, and relative safety under adult supervision. Public schools are, in effect, the most significant remnant of the social safety net available to poor people in the United States (Fischer et al. 1996). Because schools generally have stable funding and therefore follow fairly predictable operating procedures, they are the most consistent and stable aspect of the lives of many poor children.

Second, at an ideological level the notion of equal opportunity through education continues to have broad appeal in American society.[2] The first public schools were created in part because of broad popular support for the ideal that public schools were needed to ensure some degree of equal opportunity (Katznelson and Weir 1985). Legal precedent continues to favor universal access to public education even though the right to an education is not guaranteed in the U.S. Constitution (Kirp 1982). Though there is little evidence of public support for radically equalizing funding among schools, there is considerable public support for utilizing education to extend opportunities to the lower class for social mobility through education. (For an analysis of public support for Head Start and Title I programs, see Orfield and DeBray 2001.)

The implication of both of these points is that while a return to the Great Society policies is unlikely, it may be possible to generate significant investments in urban public schools (and charter schools) as a strategy for addressing poverty, social isolation, and economic marginalization in the inner city. If such investments are to contribute to broader community development, they must be directed toward the development of social capital among inner-city residents. Specifically, strategies that encourage the development of organizations and networks that can exert influence over local schools and other neighborhood institutions are needed. As shown later in the chapter, the cultivation of these forms of social capital can facilitate a greater degree of empowerment, accountability, and control by parents and community residents over the schools that serve them. I argue that such outcomes can enable urban schools to become a powerful resource for community development and can facilitate other forms of political and economic empowerment that will ultimately transform the character and quality of life of urban areas, through bottom-up, grassroots initiatives.

EMPOWERING A CAPTURED POPULATION

Structural factors related to the political economy of urban areas, and more specifically to deindustrialization, globalization of the world economy, suburbanization, and middle-class flight, have contributed to the isolation of the poor and had a profound effect on the character of urban areas (Wilson 1980; Massey and Denton 1993). Other factors, however, such as social disorganization and the ineffective or unresponsive operation of public institutions such as schools, hospitals, and police departments, exacerbate and further the decline of inner-city communities. Robert Sampson (1998, 24) argues that when public institutions fail to serve the needs of neighborhoods, as is often the case with urban public schools (Payne 1984; Maeroff 1988), they actually contribute to the deterioration of social capital, because "when people shun local facilities fewer opportunities exist for local networks and organizations to take hold."

As I pointed out in the two vignettes, a major difference between the middle-class parent and the lower-class parent is the power of choice. By virtue of their human capital (education and information) and economic capital, middle-class parents can leave a school if they do not like the way their children are treated or if they perceive the quality of education as inadequate. They may enroll their child in another public school or opt out of the system altogether by sending their child to a private school. Moreover, leaving is not the only option available: middle-class parents also have other resources at their disposal with which to fight for what they want. Politically savvy middle-class parents can petition higher authorities such as the superintendent or school board; they can utilize organizations such as the PTA (parent-teacher association), churches, or the NAACP (National Association for the Advancement of Colored People) to exert influence on school officials; and they can draw on external resources, such as lawyers or the media, to press for what they want.

In contrast, lower-class parents typically lack the ability to choose the school their children attend, both because the cost of private school is prohibitive and because they lack transportation that would give them access to better schools in more affluent neighborhoods (Fuller 1996). Furthermore, unlike middle-class parents, poor parents are often limited in their ability to fight for what they want because they tend not to receive the same kind of respect and responsiveness from school authorities. Like the parent in the first vignette, lower-class parents, even when angry or passionate about their concerns, are more likely to be disregarded and not taken seriously by school officials (Lareau 1988; Henig et al. 1999; Kozol 1991; Comer 1981; Fine 1993).

For this reason, we should consider how social capital—that which is derived from organization and association—can offset the relative powerlessness of low-income parents. Robert Putnam (1995, 76) suggests that we ask ourselves: "What types of organizations and networks most effectively embody—or generate—social capital, in the sense of mutual reciprocity, the resolution of dilemmas of collective action, and the broadening of social identities?" To the extent that parents and concerned community allies are able to marshal resources, both organizational and legal, and expand their social networks in ways that enable them to increase the support they receive from churches, businesses, nonprofit organizations, and established civic groups, I believe that urban schools in economically depressed areas can be transformed into community assets that more effectively respond to the needs of those they serve. Organization can serve as a source of power for low-income parents and counter the powerlessness they typically experience when interacting with public agencies as isolated individuals.

TRANSFORMING URBAN SCHOOLS BY INCREASING COMMUNITY CONTROL

The notion that schools can be improved by increasing parental and community control over them is not new, though the idea has recently gained interest and popularity. The first and most famous effort of this kind was launched in New York City in 1968, when an experiment referred to as "community control" was launched in the Oceanhill-Brownsville section of Brooklyn (Fantini et al. 1970). Under the plan, governance of the district was turned over to a locally elected board made up of parents, church leaders, and community residents. The board was empowered to make decisions related to the governance of the schools (three elementary, one intermediate, and one middle school) in the district. This included the hiring and firing of administrators, the allocation of resources, and general oversight of educational performance. The experiment began in the fall of 1968 with the hope that increased local involvement in school governance would improve the quality of schools in this low-income neighborhood (Fantini et al. 1970, 163).

Shortly after the experiment commenced, conflict between the United Federation of Teachers (UFT) and the board erupted when the board, acting on the recommendation of Superintendent Rhody McCoy, called for the involuntary transfer of eighteen teachers. These teachers were accused of undermining the goals of the experiment in community control, and the board used their dismissal as a signal to the union that they were indeed in control. The UFT responded by calling for a city-wide strike, which brought public education in New York City to a halt for more than one million children.

More than just an issue of who had power and who could exercise control, the conflict between the community board and the union also exposed profound differences related to the racial implications of the experiment. To a large degree, the concept of community control was embraced because it satisfied two distinct needs: a desire to improve schools in a low-income neighborhood that had long been perceived as dysfunctional and of low quality, and a desire for a concrete, local manifestation of black and Puerto Rican nationalism, which at the time was interpreted as exercising greater control over neighborhood institutions. Through community control, parents and activists, religious leaders and politicians, united in wresting control of neighborhood schools out of the hands of educators, who were perceived as indifferent and unsympathetic to the needs of the community and its children. In their place, educators who shared the racial and cultural background of residents, as well as the ideological aspirations of the board, were invited to help implement this larger agenda of political empowerment.

Despite the controversy associated with initiatives such as the one in Oceanhill-Brownsville, the call for greater community control of schools and other public services was a strategy that had been growing in popularity in antipoverty programs for some time. Beginning in 1964 with the passage of the Equal Opportunity Act, community action programs serving low-income communities were encouraged to "develop, conduct and administer programs with the maximum feasible participation of residents of the area and members of the groups served" (quoted in Fantini et al. 1970, 10). Similar proposals for greater community control over public services had been made with regard to the management of public housing and police departments: citizens' review boards had been called for as a way of improving relations between community and police and reducing charges or police brutality (Skolnick and Currie 1994). Although such proposals in housing and law enforcement represented a significant departure from past practice, community control at an urban public school in New York City was not unlike the kind of relationship between schools and the communities they served in many other parts of the country. In fact, the logic of the idea was completely consistent with the principle of local control—an idea central to the character of American public schools since their creation in the mid-nineteenth century (Cremin 1988; Katznelson and Weir 1985; Tyack 1974). Kenneth Clark, the psychologist who championed the racial integration of schools, articulated the fundamental logic of the proposal:

If an epidemic of low academic achievement swept over suburban schools drastic measures would be imposed. Administrators and school boards would topple, and teachers would be trained or dismissed. If students were regularly demeaned or dehumanized in those schools, cries of outrage in the PTAs would be heard—and listened to—and action would be taken immediately. Accountability at schools in small towns and suburbs is so implicitly a given that the term "community control" never is used by those who have it. (quoted in Fantini et al. 1970, 8)

Although a certain degree of control might be taken for granted in middle-class suburban schools, in the economically and socially marginal communities of the inner city the notion that community residents had the ability to elect representatives to govern local schools was seen as a radical and risky experiment. Critics of the idea, such as the sociologist Daniel P. Moynihan (1969, 57), argued that placing poor people in control of neighborhood schools "simply weighs them down with yet another burden with which they are not competent to deal." Similar arguments were made by UFT President Albert Shanker, who argued that community control would turn the schools over to vigilantes and racists, and by others who condemned the Oceanhill-Brownsville experiment as "too political" (Schrag 1969) and "overly ambitious" (Fantini 1970).

Ultimately, it was the UFT strike and the capitulation of Mayor John Lindsay (who initially supported the plan) to the teachers' union that brought an end to community control in Oceanhill-Brownsville. Yet despite the fact that the community control experiment was aborted long before its impact on the educational performance of children could be assessed—as has often been true with other policy innovations—the idea of improving urban schools through various forms of decentralized management and parental empowerment has resurfaced in recent years and gained new credibility. "Community control" is no longer the label affixed to these initiatives, but throughout the country reforms aimed at increasing parents' influence on school decisionmaking bodies have become popular. The Comer (1981) model is one of the better-known reform strategies that advocates such an approach. Site-based management is another, though typically it leads to greater power for school personnel than for parents in the decisionmaking process (Fine 1993). Many charter schools have also been designed with the intent of providing parents with a greater voice in school governance (Wells 1998), and many public schools have granted decisionmaking authority to locally elected boards (Wong et al. 1999).

The most widely heralded of these initiatives is the Chicago Local School Council initiative—which was approved by the Illinois State Legislature in 1989—and the community-parent organizing efforts led by the Industrial Areas Foundation (IAF) in Texas (Shirley 1997). Ironically, both models are similar to the older Oceanhill-

Brownsville experiment of 1968, though the similarity has never been acknowledged by the policymakers who supported it. The same underlying principle—that schools serving poor people can be improved by providing parents with the organizational capacity to exert control and hold them accountable—is still operative. Interestingly, in both places where these reforms have been instituted, significant gains in student achievement have been recorded. Although it is nearly impossible to prove that changes in governance have served as the catalyst for improvements in student performance, there is evidence that many parents in Chicago and the Texas public schools have expressed greater satisfaction with the quality of their schools since these reforms have gone into effect (Wong et al. 1999; Shirley 1997).

LESSONS FROM EXISTING MODELS OF PARENTAL EMPOWERMENT

Before describing how parental empowerment can transform urban schools, it may be helpful to return briefly to the theory underlying such an approach. Building on the arguments made by Michael Woolcock (1998) and others (Sampson 1998; Putnam 1993), poor communities are typically characterized by what William Julius Wilson (1980) describes as social isolation caused by concentrations of poverty and a lack of extracommunity linkages. Some poor urban areas may also have weak intracommunity ties owing to the physical and economic deterioration of the community (Greenberg and Schneider 1994), high levels of distrust among residents, a lack of formal and informal civic associations, and what Edward Banfield (1968) has termed "amoral familism." However, even when such ties do exist at either a neighborhood (Jacobs 1961; Whyte 1981) or a kinship level (Stack 1974), lack of access to resource-rich social networks can prevent a community from prospering.

Efforts to enhance the control of parents over the schools that serve them can undergird the development of both of these aspects of social capital. Because families are required by law to send their children to school, schools exert a centripetal force on neighborhoods, bringing together residents who might otherwise have no reason to interact (Noguera 1996). It is true that the interaction required is often limited to making sure that children attend school, and that most of the interaction happens among children. However, through connections created by children, parents are frequently brought into contact with one another, and thus the potential arises for other forms of association. Of course, not all contacts between children of different racial and cultural backgrounds are harmonious, and in neighborhoods experiencing rapid demographic transition, schools may in fact become sites of racial conflict (Metz 1978; Noguera 1995). However, it is also often the case that schools serve as social spaces where interaction across race and culture is possible, and moreover, schools are often sites where new identities and connections between groups are forged (Darder 1991). The main point is that urban schools can create or enhance a key aspect of social capital—intracommunity ties.

Schools can also serve as a medium through which low-income parents develop extracommunity linkages to actors who can provide access to resources. Local schools are typically connected to larger districts and political institutions. By gaining control over local schools, parents can begin to exert political influence at a broader level and tap into other resources. In cities across the country, a number of active parents, particularly women of color, have used the experience and connections developed from school-based organizing to run for local elected office (Valle and Torres 1998). Finally, politicians are more likely to notice and take interest in parents who are organized, and foundations and public organizations that have an interest in supporting poor people generally find it easier to work with established organizations rather than random individuals.

In the final pages, I describe how efforts aimed at empowering parents can lead to the development of social capital and facilitate school improvement in urban areas. These examples are drawn from two schools with which I have worked closely: Berkeley High School (BHS) and the San Francisco Unified School District (SFUSD). There are undoubtedly other schools and school districts in other cities that have employed similar strategies. However, I have chosen to present these two cases because my intimate involvement with the process of parental involvement provides me with greater insight into how such policies have contributed to change. In my own experience, on matters pertaining to the empowerment of poor people, firsthand knowledge derived from direct observation and participation is more valuable, and perhaps even more reliable, than evaluative reports written by detached outsiders. I have found that it is too easy for researchers to exaggerate, distort, or fail to comprehend whether participation is genuine and authentic, or whether those said to be empowered actually feel that way (Fine 1993).

Putnam (1995, 35–36) has argued that the most important forms of social capital consist of "features of social organizations, such as networks, norms and trust, that facilitate action and cooperation for mutual benefit." Coleman (1988, 107) applies the concept of closure to his analysis of social capital to argue that norms and sanctions on behavior that support group goals and aspirations develop only when "the trustworthiness of social structures allows for the proliferation of obligations and expectations." Coleman argues that congruity in values leads to a reinforcement of social norms that promote regular school attendance, conformity to school rules, and concern for academic achievement. In contrast, Coleman contends, public schools tend to have relatively low social closure with the families they serve, and consequently, children often get lost in the discontinuity between the values and norms promoted at school (which may be nebulous and difficult to discern) and those supported by families.

Building on Coleman's point, I argue that public schools can more effectively serve the needs of the children who attend them when efforts aimed at producing greater closure are pursued. Such an approach has been actively pursued in the San Francisco Unified School District, where a concerted effort to invest in parents has been in place for the last six years (Noguera 1996). As part of Superintendent Waldemar Rojas's strategy for raising student achievement, the following policies and actions have been taken. An office of parent relations has been established for the purpose of coordinating communication between the district and parents. Parent centers, located in poor neighborhoods and aimed specifically at Latino, Asian, and African American parents, have been funded and developed. Several kinds of community-based mobilizations, including marches, conferences, and rallies, have been organized for the purpose of generating active parental participation in school and districtwide affairs. Finally, parents have been delegated a greater role in the governance of the district and particular schools.

In addition to these steps, a representative of the districtwide PTA sits on the superintendent's cabinet and on the committee that negotiates with the various collective bargaining units in the district. Parents also have decisionmaking authority at schools that have been reconstituted, particularly in the selection of new teachers and administrators.[3]

Documenting the impact of these strategies is difficult. Test scores and other key indicators of student performance (grades, graduation rates, admission to college, and so on) for all ethnic groups have risen steadily for each of the six years that the plan has been in place. There is no way of knowing, however, how much credit should be assigned to the district's strategy of investing in parents for this change in student outcomes.

As a consultant to the district over the last five years, I have witnessed firsthand how the district's emphasis on parental empowerment has influenced the character of discussion of educational issues at both the site and district levels.[4] Though the ability of low-income parents to participate in schools is frequently limited by time, language, and lack of access to transportation, in San Francisco there has been a concerted effort to overcome these constraints, and the evidence shows that it has been successful.

For the last three years, the district has organized a citywide parent empowerment conference that has attracted more than eight hundred parents each year. Most significant for me was the fact that the district provided transportation, translation, and child care to make it possible for parents from the poorest parts of the city to participate. Beyond providing workshops on what is commonly referred to as parent education (for example, how to help your child with homework, how to be an advocate for your child, what a parent should know about college), the sessions also addressed some of the controversial policy issues facing the district. Sessions on the impact of propositions 187, 209, and 227 have been held, as well as policy-oriented discussions on issues such as social promotion.[5] All three of the parent centers were created as a result of the conferences, and each of the centers currently reports active involvement at the workshops and other events for parents that they sponsor at schools in the community.[6]

Finally, and perhaps most significantly, in the raucous and bitter hearings over reconstitution, which pitted angry members of the teachers' union against an adamant district administration, parents have played an unpredictable role. Both sides have courted parents heavily to support their dichotomous positions on the issue: for the union, reconstitution is too heavy-handed and disruptive, but the administration feels that drastic measures are needed to improve conditions in schools. However, instead of being manipulated by one side or the other, parents have frequently staked out independent positions, favoring reconstitution in some cases, opposing it in others. Their presence at meetings has influenced board decisions because, unlike members of the two combatant groups, the union and the administration, the parents live in San Francisco and vote in elections.

The other sign that the district's emphasis on parental empowerment is having an impact on schools comes from visiting the schools themselves. I have had firsthand experiences at only a handful of schools, so I do not claim that my impressions are at all generalizable, but at those I have visited I have been struck by the extent to which parents work with faculty and feel a sense of ownership toward their school.

For example, in March 1998 I was asked to speak at E. R. Taylor Elementary School at a meeting of parents and teachers that was set up to determine how funds from a newly won Healthy Start grant would be used. The school was located in a predominantly black, low-income neighborhood known as Bayview, and most of the parents attending the meeting came from housing projects in the area. Before my speech, I met with a small group of parents and teachers who explained how much work they had put into writing the grant. One of the parents, a Samoan woman in her mid-forties who appeared to be a leader in the group, explained to me how the use of the funds would be prioritized:

> We have a lot of children at this school who don't eat breakfast in the mornings. Some of them haven't seen an eye doctor or dentist. The people from the State Department said that this grant is a Healthy Start grant, which means it should be for the health of the children. Nothing else can come before that. We believe that healthy children will do better in school.

As the woman spoke, the rest of the group looked on, smiling and nodding with approval. It was clear to me that this woman, regardless of her lack of education or income, was the recognized leader in the group, not merely a token representative. After my speech, the same parent, not the principal who had originally contacted me, took it upon herself to invite me back to the school in three months to see the progress they had made toward achieving their goals.

What is most striking to me about this experience is how significantly it contrasts with my visits to most other urban schools. More often than not, in my conversations with teachers and administrators at urban public schools, parents are described as uncaring, dysfunctional, unsupportive, and part of the problem. Rather than being seen as partners capable of making meaningful contributions to the education of their children, they are more likely to be seen as obstacles in the way of progress, and as problems to be overcome.

This was the case at Berkeley High School, where for the longest time the poor academic performance of black and Latino students was explained as a by-product of parent disinterest in education. BHS is a relatively large school with approximately 3,000 students and more than 180 teachers, counselors, and administrators. According to the school district's data, approximately 40 percent of the students are white, 40 percent are African American, 10 percent are Latino, and 10 percent are

Asian American. Racial differences generally correspond to class differences in that the vast majority of white students are from middle-class and affluent backgrounds, while the majority of African American and Latino students come from low-income families.

To an outsider, the school seems amazingly diverse, but from within, racial fragmentation is apparent in almost every aspect of the school. On the basis of almost every significant indicator, BHS is a school that does not serve its black and Latino students well. Nearly 50 percent of black and Latino students who enter BHS in the ninth grade fail to graduate from the school, and among those who do graduate, few complete the course requirements necessary for admission to the University of California or the state college system (WASC Report 1996). These students also make up the overwhelming majority of students who are suspended or expelled for disciplinary reasons. Moreover, the adjunct continuation high school, which was established to serve students with poor attendance and behavioral problems, is almost entirely attended by African American and Latino students.

As might be expected, not only are African American students disadvantaged and marginal within the school community, but so are their parents. At most school activities that call for parental involvement and participation, African American and Latino parents are vastly underrepresented. This is also true on decisionmaking bodies where parents have a say in how resources are allocated, and it is most dramatically evident on the "back to school" nights, when parents are invited to meet their children's teachers. Historically, the auditorium where several hundred parents gather prior to visiting the classrooms is nearly entirely filled with white parents, with little more than a handful of black and Latino parents sprinkled throughout the crowd.

In 1996 a group that I helped to establish known as the Diversity Project began searching for ways to increase the involvement of parents who previously had been most marginal to the school.[7] We did this because we believed that if we were going to be successful in our efforts to address disparities in academic achievement within the school, we would have to find ways to empower those who were most disenfranchised. We recognized that those who benefited under the present circumstances might perceive themselves as having a vested interest in preserving the status quo and resist efforts to support change that would produce greater equity. As we carried out our work, we positioned ourselves as facilitators of discussion rather than as advocates for a particular agenda, because we wanted to avoid becoming trapped in a polarized conflict over change at the school. It was our hope that organizing African American and Latino parents would provide us with a means to ensure that the change effort would not depend on our advocacy alone, and that once organized, the parents could also counterbalance the influence that would be exerted by the opponents of change.

Research in the form of a series of focus group discussions with parents served as our entrée into organizing. Focus group discussions were set up for Latino and African American parents to elicit their views on the state of the school. Specifically, we wanted to know what concerns they had about the education their children were receiving, what kinds of obstacles they encountered when interacting with school officials on behalf of their children, and what kinds of changes they felt would help make BHS more receptive to their concerns.

Over the course of six months, more than seventy-five focus groups were conducted with more than four hundred parents. To ensure that maximum opportunity was provided for open communication, all of the sessions with Spanish-speaking parents were conducted in Spanish. Food and child care were also provided as an added incentive to attract high levels of participation. Finally, the focus groups were tape-recorded, the sessions were transcribed, and a report summarizing the issues raised was presented to a newly formed strategic planning committee for inclusion in its report to the school.

The parent outreach committee of the Diversity Project also recruited parents to join it in conducting the focus groups and carrying out the research. This was an important step, because the active core group of the committee is now taking leadership at the school in devising strategies aimed at institutionalizing parental involvement. The group has already persuaded the BHS administration to designate a surplus classroom to serve as a parent center, and they have written grants to foundations for the purpose of hiring two part-time parent organizers.

Aside from these accomplishments, there is other evidence that the organization of black and Latino parents is already beginning to have an impact on the school. At a community forum in May 1998 that was held for the purpose of soliciting responses to the plan as it was being drafted, nearly half of the parents present were African American or Latino. Most were parents who had become active in the leadership of the parent outreach group. During the meeting, several spoke openly about their criticisms of the plan and freely offered suggestions on what they would like to see included in it. After the meeting, several teachers commented that it was the first meeting they had attended in which the composition of the parents present matched that of the student body. The Diversity Project hopes to build on this accomplishment so that the ongoing effort to undermine racial inequality within the school is led and actively supported by the parents of the children who have the most to gain.

CONCLUSION

When parents are respected as partners in the education of their children, and when they are provided with organizational support that enables them to channel their interests to the benefit of the school, the entire culture of the organization can be transformed. Parents have a knowledge of their children's lives outside of school that teachers typically do not have, and that knowledge can prove helpful in developing effective pedagogical strategies (Ladson-Billings 1994). More important, the familiarity between school and parent that develops as a result of such partnerships can also begin to generate social closure and transform urban schools from alien and hostile organizations into genuine community assets.

There is evidence that in Chicago and San Francisco, two cities where efforts to empower parents have been most extensive, the academic performance of students is also improving (Hess 1995; Shirley 1997). There is also anecdotal evidence in these communities that parents perceive themselves as exerting a greater degree of ownership and control over the schools their children attend. Realistically, such developments do not mean that urban schools that serve large numbers of poor children will suddenly be transformed into well-functioning organizations where children receive high-quality education. The obstacles present in low-income areas—joblessness, environmental degradation, crime, lack of access to social services, and so on—will not disappear because parents exercise leadership at local schools, and these external constraints will continue to have an impact on children, families, and schools. However, if we adopt the approach advocated by the Brazilian educator Paulo Freire (1969, 154) and treat conditions of oppression as "limit situations" in which both the constraints and the possibilities for action are analyzed in relation to each other, then new ways of imagining change can be considered. This is not the same as exhortations to the powerless to pick themselves up by their boot straps or naive calls for volunteerism as strategies for alleviating poverty. Rather, it is a recognition that those victimized by poverty and marginalization have the capacity to act against it and, if supported with resources and allies, can do more to change social reality than any government program or philanthropic gesture. Such a recognition is premised on adopting a view of social conditions as something that can be acted upon rather than accepting them fatalistically as fixed and unchangeable.

I close with the words of Paulo Freire (1969, 155), who makes this point in clear and compelling terms:

> To present this human world as a problem for human beings is to propose that they "enter into" it critically, taking the operation as a whole, their action, and that of others on it. . . . The more they review critically their past and present experiences in and with the world, the more they realize that the world is not a cul-de-sac for men and women, an unalterable state which crushes them.

NOTES

1. Bourdieu used the term "structural anecdote" in a seminar presented at the Institute for the Study of Social Change at the University of California at Berkeley in March 1986.

2. This finding is supported by a poll conducted in 1994 by Public Agenda (1994–1995) on behalf of the American Federation of Teachers and in California by a poll conducted by PACE (Policy Analysis for California Education, Berkeley, Calif.: The University of California) in March 1996.

3. Reconstitution is a strategy that was made available to the SFUSD as a result of the consent decree on school desegregation. The policy allows the district to reconstitute a school—remove all or part of the personnel from a school deemed low-performing—as a way to improve achievement for minority students. Since 1993, fourteen schools in the SFUSD have been completely or partially reconstituted.

4. My consulting work with the SFUSD has focused on an evaluation of the impact of the new admissions policy at Lowell High School on students admitted under the plan. For additional information on the work, see Noguera (1998).

5. Proposition 187, approved by voters in 1996, was intended to restrict undocumented aliens and their children from having access to public services. Proposition 209 was approved by voters in 1997 and eliminated the use of race and gender as factors that could be considered in admissions for higher education, employment, and contracting in publicly funded organizations. Passed in 1998, proposition 227 banned the use of bilingual education in public schools.

6. I have attended parent education workshops, honor roll marches, and issue-oriented events sponsored by all three centers. Each event drew a significant number of parents from constituencies not typically involved in school activities.

7. The Diversity Project is a research and reform collaboration that was created to find ways to reduce academic disparities among students at BHS. The project was established in 1996 and will continue its work through June 2000.

REFERENCES

American Federation of Teachers. 1994–1995. "What Americans Expect from the Public Schools." *American Educator* (Winter): 16–18.

Anderson, James. 1988. *The Education of Blacks in the South, 1860–1935*. Chapel Hill: University of North Carolina Press.

Anyon, Jean. 1997. *Ghetto Schooling: A Political Economy of Urban Educational Reform*. New York: Teachers College Press.

Apple, Michael. 1982. *Education and Power*. Boston: ARK Publications.

Ayers, William, Michael Klonsky, and Gabrielle Lyon, eds. 2000. *A Simple Justice: The Challenge of Small Schools*. New York: Teachers College Press.

Banfield, Edward. 1968. *The Unheavenly City: The Nature and Future of Our Urban Crisis*. Boston: Little, Brown.

Bourdieu, Pierre. 1985. "Social Space and the Genesis of Social Groups." In *Theory and Society* 14(6): 36.

Bourdieu, Pierre, and Loic Wacquant. 1992. *An Invitation to Reflexive Sociology*. Chicago: University of Chicago Press.

Bowles, Samuel, and Herbert Gintis. 1976. *Schooling in Capitalist America*. New York: Basic Books.

Bryk, Anthony S., Penny Bender Sebring, David Kerbow, Sharon Rollow, and John Q. Easton. 1998. *Charting Chicago School Reform: Democratic Localism as a Lever for Change*. Boulder, Colo.: Westview Press.

Carnoy, Martin, and Henry Levin. 1985. *Schooling and Work in a Democratic State*. Stanford, Calif.: Stanford University Press.

Coleman, James. 1988. "Social Capital in the Creation of Human Capital." *American Journal of Sociology* 94(supp.): S95–120.

Comer, James. 1981. "New Haven's School-Community Connection." *Educational Leadership* (March): 42–48.

Cremin, L. 1988. *American Education*. New York: Harper & Row.

Darder, Antonia. 1991. *Culture and Power in the Classroom*. New York: Bergin and Garvey.

Delpit, Lisa. 1988. "The Silenced Dialogue: Power and Pedagogy in Educating Other People's Children." *Harvard Educational Review* 58(3): 280–98.

Duster, Troy. 1989. "The Structured Anecdote in Social Analysis." Paper presented at the meeting of the American Sociological Association, San Francisco (August 9).

Edmonds, Ron. 1979. "Effective Schools for the Urban Poor." *Educational Leadership* 37(1): 15–27.

Epstein, Joyce. 1991. "School and Family Connections: Theory, Research, and Implications for Integrating Societies of Education and Family." In *Families in Community Settings: Interdisciplinary Perspectives*, edited by D. G. Unger and M. B. Sussman. New York: Hayworth Press.

Fantini, Mario, Marilyn Gittell, and Richard Magat. 1970. *Community Control and the Urban School*. New York: Praeger.

Ferguson, Ann. 1995. "Boys Will Be Boys: Defiant Acts and the Social Construction of Black Masculinity." Ph.D. diss., University of California at Berkeley.

Ferretti, Frank. 1968. "Who's to Blame in the School Strike?" *New York Magazine* 1(November 18): 22–35.

Fine, Michelle. 1993. "(Ap)parent Involvement: Reflections on Parents, Power, and Urban Schools." *Teachers College Record* 94(4): 26–43.

Fischer, Claude, Michael Hout, Martin S. Jankowski, Sam Lucas, Anne Swidler, and Kim Voss. 1996. *Inequality by Design: Cracking the Bell Curve Myth*. Princeton, N.J.: Princeton University Press.

Frazier, Edward F. 1957. *Black Bourgeoisie*. New York: Free Press.

Fredrickson, George. 1981. *White Supremacy: A Comparative Study of American and South African History*. Oxford: Oxford University Press.

Freire, Paulo. 1969. *The Pedagogy of the Oppressed*. New York: Continuum Press.

Fuller, Bruce, and Richard Elmore. 1996. *Who Chooses, Who Loses?* New York: Teachers College Press.

Gargiulo, Michelle, and Michael Benassi. 1997. "The Dark Side of Social Capital." Special report. New York: Paul H. Lazerfeld Center for the Social Sciences.

Giroux, Henry. 1988. *Teachers as Intellectuals: Toward a Critical Pedagogy of Learning*. New York: Bergin and Garvey.

Greenberg, Mark, and Debborah Schneider. 1994. "Violence in American Cities: Young Black Males Is the Answer, but What Was the Question?" *Social Science and Medicine* 39(2): 179–87.

Hall, Stuart. 1992. "What Is This 'Black' in Black Popular Culture." In *Black Popular Culture*, edited by Gina Dent. Seattle: Bay Press.

Haymes, Stephen. 1995. *Race, Culture, and the City*. Albany: State University of New York Press.

Henig, Jeff, Richard Hula, Marion Orr, Desiree Pedescleax. 1999. *The Color of School Reform*. Princeton, N.J.: Princeton University Press.

Hess, G. Alfred, Jr. 1995. *Restructuring Urban Schools: A Chicago Perspective*. New York: Teachers College Press.

Hilliard, A. 1991. "Do We Have the Will to Educate All Children?" *Educational Leadership* 49(1): 31–6.

Jacobs, Jane. 1961. *The Death and Life of Great American Cities*. New York: Vintage.

Katznelson, Ira, and Margaret Weir. 1985. *Schooling for All*. Berkeley: University of California Press.

Kirp, David. 1982. *Just Schools*. Berkeley: University of California Press.

Kochman, Thomas. 1969. "Rapping in the Black Ghetto." In *Trans-Action*, reprinted in *Rapping and Stylin' Out: Communication in Urban Black America*. Chicago: University of Illinois Press.

Kozol, Jonathan. 1991. *Savage Inequalities*. New York: Crown Books.

Ladson-Billings, Gloria. 1994. *The Dreamkeepers: Successful Teachers of African American Children*. San Francisco: Jossey-Bass.

Lareau, Annette. 1989. *Home Advantage: Social Class and Parental Intervention in Elementary Education*. New York: Falmer Press.

Lipman, Pauline. 1998. *Race, Class, and Power in School Restructuring*. Albany: State University of New York Press.

MacLeod, Jay. 1987. *Ain't No Makin' It*. Boulder, Colo.: Westview Press.

Maeroff, Gene. 1988. "Withered Hopes, Stillborn Dreams: The Dismal Panorama of Urban Schools." *Phi Delta Kappan* 69: 632–38.

Massey, Douglas, and Nancy Denton. 1993. *American Apartheid: Segregation and the Making of the Underclass*. Cambridge, Mass.: Harvard University Press.

Metz, Mary. 1978. *Classrooms and Corridors: The Crisis of Authority in Desegregated Secondary Schools*. Berkeley: University of California Press.

Moore, Donald R. 1992. "The Case for Parent and Community Involvement." In *Empowering Teachers and Parents: School Restructuring Through the Eyes of Anthropologists*, edited by G. Alfred Hess Jr. Westport, Conn.: Bergin and Garvey.

Moynihan, Daniel P. 1969. *Maximum Feasible Misunderstanding: Community Action in the War on Poverty*. New York: Free Press.

Nocera, James. 1990. "How the Middle Class Helped Ruin the Public Schools." *Utne Reader* (September–October): 16–29.

Noguera, Pedro. 1995. "Ties That Bind, Forces That Divide: Berkeley High School and the Challenge of Integration." *University of San Francisco Law Review* 29(3): 46–73.

———. 1996. "Confronting the Urban in Urban School Reform." *Urban Review* 28(1): 1–27.

———. 1998. *An Evaluation Report on the Lowell High School Admissions Policy*. San Francisco: San Francisco Unified School District.

Ogbu, John. 1978. *Minority Education and Caste: The American System in Cross-cultural Perspective*. New York: Academic Press.

———. 1987. "Variability in Minority Student Performance: A Problem in Search of an Explanation." *Anthropology and Education Quarterly* 18: 312–34.

Olsen, Laurie. 1997. *Made in America: Immigrant Students in Our Public Schools*. New York: New Press.

Orfield, Gary, and Elizabeth DeBray, eds. 2001. *Hard Work for Good Schools*. Cambridge, Mass.: Civil Rights Project of Harvard University.

Orfield, Gary, and Susan Eaton. 1996. *Dismantling Desegregation*. New York: New Press.

Payne, Charles M. 1984. *Getting What We Ask For: The Ambiguity of Success and Failure of Urban Education*. Westport, Conn.: Greenwood Press.

Pinkney, Alphonse. 1984. *The Myth of Black Progress*. Cambridge: Cambridge University Press.

Putnam, Robert. 1993. "The Prosperous Community: Social Capital and Public Life." *The American Prospect* 13(Spring): 35–42.

———. 1995. "Bowling Alone: America's Declining Social Capital." *Journal of Democracy* 6(1): 65–78.

Sampson, Robert. 1998. "What Community Supplies." In *Urban Problems and Community Development*, edited by Ronald F. Ferguson and William T. Dickens. Washington, D.C.: Brookings Institution Press.

Schrag, Peter. 1969. "The New Black Myths." *Harper's* 238(May): 37–42.

Shirley, Dennis. 1997. *Community Organizing for Urban School Reform*. Austin: University of Texas Press.

Skolnick, Jerome, and Elliott Currie. 1994. *Crisis in American Institutions.* New York: HarperCollins.

Stack, Carol. 1974. *All Our Kin.* New York: Harper and Row.

Steele, Claude. 1997. "A Threat in the Air: How Stereotypes Shape Intellectual Identity and Performance." *American Psychologist* (June): 12–37.

Tyack, David. 1974. *The One Best System.* Cambridge, Mass.: Harvard University Press.

Tyack, David, and Larry Cuban. 1995. *Tinkering Toward Utopia.* Cambridge, Mass.: Harvard University Press.

Valle, Victor, and Rudolfo Torres. 1998. "Latinos in a Post-industrial Disorder." In *The Latino Studies Reader,* edited by Antonia Darder and R. Torres. Malden, Mass.: Blackwell.

Wacquant, Loic. 1998. "Negative Social Capital: State Breakdown and Social Destitution in America's Urban Core." *Netherlands Journal of Housing and the Built Environment* 13(1):118–42.

Wells, Amy S. 1998. *Beyond the Rhetoric of Charter School Reform: A Study of Ten California School Districts.* Baltimore: Annie E. Casey Foundation.

Wells, Amy S., and Robert Crain. 1997. *Stepping Over the Color Line.* New Haven, Conn.: Yale University Press.

Western Association of School Creditation (WASC). 1996. Report on Berkeley High School. Unpublished Manuscript.

Whyte, William. 1981. *Street Corner Society.* Chicago: University of Chicago Press.

Wilson, William Julius. 1980. *The Declining Significance of Race.* Chicago: University of Chicago Press.

Wong, K., D. Anagnstopoulos, S. Rutledge, L. Lynn, and R. Dreeben. 1999. *Implementation of an Educational Accountability Agenda: Integrated Governance in the Chicago Public Schools Enters Its Fourth Year.* Chicago: Department of Education.

Woolcock, Michael. 1998. "Social Capital and Economic Development: Toward a Theoretical Synthesis and Policy Framework." *Theory and Society* 27: 151–208.

Part III

Institutional Settings

Chapter 9

Social Capital, Religious Institutions, and Poor Communities

Michael W. Foley, John D. McCarthy, and Mark Chaves

R eligious institutions play a significant, if little understood, role in poor com-munities in the United States. Among the institutions of civil society, churches are often the last to leave deteriorating neighborhoods and dwindling com-munities and the first to return. Religiously based social service efforts carry an important part of the burden of providing for the needs of poor communities. Congregations and local denominational bodies frequently build broad community coalitions on behalf of policy change and to strengthen both private and public social services for the poor. Congregation-based community-organizing programs have been among the most successful efforts to mobilize residents of poor neighbor-hoods for political action on behalf of local needs. What some call "para-church" organizations—religious-based outreach and community action groups like Habitat for Humanity, Bread for the World, and Teen Challenge[1]—devote themselves to addressing the needs of individuals and groups in poor communities in diverse and sometimes controversial ways.

To what degree these diverse religious-based organizations have proven effective agents for generating and mobilizing social capital within and for poor communities remains an open question. In this chapter, we review recent research on the social capital profile of religious institutions and their significance for poor communities with the aim of laying out a research agenda and sketching concrete policy propos-als for assessing and strengthening the social capital of these institutions. In doing so, we call attention to three particularly powerful foci of activity: congregations them-selves, congregation-based organizing, and the relatively unknown para-church organizations and interfaith coalitions.

The role of religion in social life continues to be viewed with great ambivalence by many social scientists. Strongly held expectations that modern life would erode the importance of religious belief through secularization have been resistant to the accu-mulated evidence of its ongoing centrality to the lives of most Americans (Casanova 1994; Warner 1993). Recent manifestations of religiously inspired collective action have been met with great consternation. For instance, the mobilization of evangeli-cal Christians during the last several decades has led many scholars to anticipate threats to "democratic civility, and . . . social and political tolerance . . . [leading to] . . .

a group of self-assured, uncompromising political activists whose self-righteousness might lead to dangerous political conflict" (Wilcox 1992, xv). These concerns have only been reinforced by the recent resurgence of the Christian Patriot movement, whose adherents are described as extreme in both thought and action (Aho 1991, 1996). In contrast, other scholars have positively evaluated the disruptive potential of religiously inspired collective action, stressing its potential for empowering disadvantaged groups, such as the U.S. civil rights and peace movements, the Solidarity movement in Poland, and the anti-apartheid movement in South Africa (see, for example, Smith 1996). Such analyses agree that intense solidarity can be generated within religious groups. They disagree, however, in their valuation of the uses that are made of that solidarity. That ambivalence toward what the editors of this volume call "bonding social capital" (chapter 1) is particularly acute for religious groups precisely because of their great potential for creating intense in-group solidarity. We remain alert to this dilemma of religious solidarity in what follows. And we are particularly concerned with how religious groups, at the same time, create bridges to diverse groups beyond their own boundaries, a theme that is far more characteristic of analysts of the details of religious life in American communities (see, for example, Ammerman 1997; Green 1996).

In the first section, we sketch the reasons why we must take religion seriously as an actor in poor communities. The next section discusses the notion of social capital and how it might be applied to the activities of religious institutions. Here we map the religious terrain, distinguishing between a number of forms of religious organizations and their significance for poor communities from a social capital perspective. In the ensuing discussion in the following section of social capital at the congregational level, we consider data from an innovative recent survey of congregations to provide a sketch of the evidence on religiously based social capital in poor communities. In the following sections, we take up the relatively unknown work of denominations, interfaith coalitions, and para-church organizations and congregation-based organizing efforts. The closing sections draw out implications of our review for future research and policymaking.

RELIGION AND POVERTY IN THE UNITED STATES

The United States is a religiously active nation where the vast majority of citizens profess a belief in God and identify with an organized religion. Rates of religious involvement are quite high compared with other nations: somewhere between 25 and 40 percent of adults regularly attend worship services.[2] Religiously active citizens give substantial amounts of money and time to their churches, a proportion of which supports the activities of denominational bodies. And although the religious sector of the U.S. economy is only about the size of the motion picture industry, as Robert Wuthnow (1996) has remarked, *Giving USA* estimates that in 1995 Americans gave more than $60 billion to religious congregations and related institutions.[3] A 1992 Independent Sector study (Hodgkinson and Weitzman 1993) suggests that about 20 percent of congregational income is devoted to purposes beyond organizational maintenance (for example, paying clergy, maintaining buildings, supporting congregation-related activities), including substantial support for health and housing programs, community development, and advocacy. And the volunteer labor potential of congregational members is enormous (Hoge et al. 1998).

Many religious groups take various forms of action that either are explicitly aimed at combating poverty in poor communities or indirectly may affect it. These reflect classic positions in long-standing debates about the role of religion in economic justice (Hart 1996). First, religious groups may provide resources to poor individuals and poor community institutions from their own stock or through linkages with governmental and nongovernmental sources. Second, religious groups may proselytize in poor communities in an effort to absorb poor individuals and families into religious groups already endowed with social capital. Third, they may attempt to empower poor communities by employing their own social capital in ways that benefit not only their own members but also individuals and families who are not members.

In practice, of course, the programs of many religious organizations combine some part of each of the three elements. For example, the many Catholic Worker hospitality houses inspired by Dorothy Day feed hungry people in poor communities; they also serve to empower their communities and, incidentally, have brought many into religious activism (Rader 1986). And the urban ministries of many mainline Protestant denominations in the early post–World War II period explicitly combined all three elements in their efforts to act out their understanding of "what the Lord requires" Christian communities to do for the less fortunate (Green 1996). Our presentation focuses on efforts to provide resources and empowerment; we give little attention to the extent and consequences of proselytism for the social capital of poor communities.

SOCIAL CAPITAL IN THE ACTIVITIES OF RELIGIOUS INSTITUTIONS

The understanding of social capital adopted in this volume asks us to take social organization seriously and to nest individuals and their possibilities for individual and collective advancement within their social context. Individual human capital (education, training, language ability, and so on) is independently important to individual success, but the social networks in which individuals are embedded have an important impact on the degree to which such potential is realized (Burt 1997). Thus, the social capital argument insists that we will see higher yields from the same human capital in communities that have more social capital. And those effects are commonly supposed to redound to the good of the community as a whole to one degree or another. Any institution that creates and builds on social networks builds social capital, and to the degree that such an institution also links the group to others in the same community and beyond the community, it has a multiplier effect, at once creating and making available resources to a widening array of actors.

Both the kinds of resources available to individuals and groups and the character of this availability are important from the social capital perspective (Foley and Edwards 1999). Social ties may give individuals access to dead-end jobs or opportunities for criminal gain and encourage the formation of antisocial groups like gangs. Dense but closed social networks may effectively isolate individuals and groups or polarize communities. In the analysis that follows, we pay attention to both the kinds of resources provided to poor communities by religious institutions and the character of the ties they encourage, including within groups ("bonding" social capital) and across groups, communities, and institutions ("linkages," or "bridging" social capital).

Mapping the Religious Terrain

Congregations and other religious institutions, simply by virtue of being social organizations, embody social capital. Although congregations are the most numerous of religious institutions, there are also a great many religiously inspired organizations that bring together large numbers of individual congregations, provide services to congregations, or carry on activities alongside congregations at both the local and national levels. The landscape includes everything from a welter of religious professional and trade organizations to specialized national-level education and advocacy groups, to local interfaith coalitions.

We can distinguish four categories of organizations that might provide significant social capital for poor communities:

1. *Denominations and other large-scale associations of congregations that provide representation and support for congregations:* At the local level, these may be represented as dioceses or other local judicatory bodies, federations of congregations of the same religious tradition, or councils of churches; some, but not all, provide direct financial assistance to congregations, support religious schools and training centers, and engage in or support communitywide advocacy and social service activities.

2. *Local coalitions of religious bodies designed to carry out community services and local advocacy across denominational lines:* These are sometimes congregation-based, generally through the voluntary participation of local clergypeople with special interests in interfaith dialogue or community service; in other cases, they rest on local representatives of national-level structures, such as denominations, federations, and councils of churches.

3. *Community development and social service organizations, both denominationally based and freestanding, that provide specialized social services or community development activities at the local level, with or without direct connection to congregations:* These range from such denominationally supported entities as Catholic Charities USA to freestanding organizations like Habitat for Humanity, to congregation-based organizing efforts.

4. *Congregations, or groups of believers (from a handful to several thousand) who meet together on a regular basis at a fixed place or places for worship and other activities:* Congregations typically claim a regular membership that may or may not be formally registered, as well as occasional or even regular participants who are not formally counted as members. (The variation in ways of counting members among religious groups makes most congregation-based censuses of membership highly unreliable.)[4]

CONGREGATIONS AS SOURCES OF SOCIAL CAPITAL

Congregations build both human and social capital, providing access to resources in a wide variety of ways.[5] Of all religious institutions, they are the most intimately involved in the life of their community, though the degree and character of that involvement varies considerably. We distinguish characteristics of the social structures that congregations generate and in which they are enmeshed from the resources available to poor communities through religious bodies and their activities. Inevitably, the discussion of each side of social capital invokes the other. Here we can only sketch the main categories of each.

At key points in our discussion, we draw on new data from the National Congregations Study (NCS) that allow us to profile the comparative social capital position of two sorts of congregations: those heavily composed of low-income participants, and congregations located in communities with heavy concentrations of low-income people.[6]

We are interested in understanding the social capital potential of both poorer congregations and those congregations located in poor communities, many of which may not be made up primarily of members from poor households. To define "poor community" congregations, we used the 1990 census designation of the percentage of persons below the poverty line in a given census tract. Recent analysis of poor neighborhoods using census tract boundaries to circumscribe neighborhoods (Jargowsky 1997) suggests that neighborhoods in which more than 40 percent of the residents are poor are substantially different from those with lower concentrations of the poor. Very few census tracts (5.7 percent, according to Jargowsky) qualify as poor by the 40 percent criterion, and almost 85 percent of them are located in urban areas. The results indicate that 5.4 percent of the congregations in the sample are located in these areas, and that 11 percent of the congregants worship in congregations located in census tracts of 40 percent or more poor.[7] (The equivalent figures for a 30 percent and 20 percent cutoff are 21 percent and 39 percent, respectively.) This evidence suggests that congregations are as well represented in the poorest neighborhoods as in better-off ones, and that whatever the truth to claims that there has been an institutional flight from the poorest neighborhoods over the last twenty or thirty years (Wilson 1996), many congregations remain as sources of social capital within those communities.

Social Capital as Structured Access to Resources

EXTENDED SOCIAL NETWORKS   Congregations provide both adults and youth with extended social networks that offer informal support, an environment of trust and acceptance (reinforcing such networks), and access to educational and job opportunities. A study by Christopher Ellison and Linda George (1994, 47) based on three thousand household interviews, for instance, demonstrates that church attendees "enjoy larger, denser, and more satisfying social networks, and greater access to social support than do their unchurched counterparts." These effects were relatively modest in size,[8] but robust across both income and denomination, suggesting that the enhancing social network consequences of religious involvement do not appear to be greater in conservative Protestant congregations, which are well known for their high rates of internal social solidarity, nor are they weaker in poorer, typically smaller congregations.

Such effects are not necessarily positive for the community at large (though we have to remember that churchgoers are a significant proportion of most poor communities), as frequent warnings about the "downside of social capital" make clear (Portes and Landolt 1996). Some social network theorists pose arguments that call into question the degree of efficacy of the sort of tight social ties encountered in some congregations from a social capital perspective (see, for example, Knoke 1990; Olson 1989).

In general, we have very little systematic evidence about the structure of social networks within congregations, the processes that produce them, the variation in the structure of social ties that link congregations to wider social networks, or the social and demographic features of congregations (for example, racial-ethnic and class composition) that might shape those structures. We would expect that congregations that enjoy more mixed membership, whether racially or socioeconomically, would provide greater social capital to their poorer members.

Results from the National Congregations Study survey point to somewhat surprising conclusions in this regard. Table 9.1 shows the socioeconomic composition of congregations by the varying poverty concentrations of the neighborhoods in which they are located, based on the NCS data. The pattern of results is quite striking, indicating that the vast majority of members of congregations located in even the poorest neighborhoods are not themselves poor. Fully 82 percent of the households in congregations located in census tracts with 40 percent or more of the residents below the poverty line earn more than $25,000 per year. And 83 percent of the households in tracts with 30 percent of the residents below the poverty line do as well. These results suggest that churches in very poor communities remain socioeconomically heterogeneous, with all the advantages in terms of greater and more diverse social capital that status entails.

The results presented in table 9.2 also suggest that most churchgoers in poor communities participate in relatively stable congregations. In contrast to the figures already cited, the figures reported in tables 9.2 through 9.5 refer to the percentage of parishioners in congregations with the specified characteristic, not the percentage of congregations.[9] We see in table 9.2 that congregations in poor neighborhoods

TABLE 9.1 / The Socioeconomic Composition of Congregations by Neighborhood Poverty Concentration

Congregational Membership Composition	Community Poverty Threshold		
	Equal to or Greater than 20 Percent	Equal to or Greater than 30 Percent	Equal to or Greater than 40 Percent
Low-income	22%	21%	19%
Middle- and upper-income	78%	79%	81%
N	251	111	59

Source: Chaves 1998, *National Congregations Study.*
Note: A low-income congregation is defined as one in which at least 60 percent of the adult members live in households with incomes below $25,000. Community poverty threshold is determined by the percentage of people in the congregation's resident census tract who lived below the poverty line in 1990.

are older. They appear to be stable organizations: 95 percent of congregants in these neighborhoods belong to congregations that own their own buildings. Poorer congregations, by contrast, are on average smaller and close to the national mean in average age (table 9.4). Not surprisingly, both congregations in poorer neighborhoods and poorer congregations are more likely than average to be African American; more than one-third of congregants in poor neighborhoods worship in predominantly African American churches.

BROADER SOCIAL LINKAGES   Congregations are rarely isolated social organizations. More commonly, they enjoy relations with other community institutions and congregations, larger religious bodies, and specialized, parallel religious organizations or private and public institutions. Interfaith coalitions specialize in such linkages, as do many of the specialized para-church organizations.

The National Congregations Study data can give us some insights into the extent and kind of linkages that congregations in poor neighborhoods provide. As table 9.2 shows, like their counterparts elsewhere, roughly half the congregants in these neighborhoods belong to congregations that maintain linkages with sources of outside consultant aid, and most belong to a national denomination, dispelling the image of the predominance of disconnected, storefront churches in neighborhoods like these. When we turn to poor congregations per se, however, the picture changes. Tables 9.4 and 9.5 report findings on poor congregations, referring to the percentage of parishioners in poor as opposed to better-off congregations. In contrast to our findings for congregations in poor neighborhoods, those that are heavily composed of low-income participants (which may or may not be located in poor neighborhoods) appear to be less well endowed with social capital and less able, accordingly, to reach out to their communities. As can be seen in table 9.4, poor congregations are smaller than more affluent congregations. They are less likely to be linked to their community through use of their facilities, less likely to belong to a national denomination, and less likely to draw on outside assistance in managing their affairs.

TABLE 9.2 / Resources and Community Linkages for Congregations Located in
Low-Income Neighborhoods Versus Congregations Located in
All Other Neighborhoods

Congregational Characteristic	Characteristics of Congregations in Low-Income Neighborhoods[a]	Characteristics of Congregations in Middle- and High-Income Neighborhoods	Statistical Significance
Human, material and ecological resources			
Mean year founded	1904	1921	**
Mean number of adult regular participants	709	783	n.s.
Median number of adult regular participants	300	275	N/A
Owns own building	95%	95%	n.s.
More than 50 percent of members walk to church	18%	16%	n.s.
More than 80 percent of the congregation is African American	37%	10%	**
More than 80 percent of the congregation is Hispanic	5%	1%	**
Has a school	22%	24%	n.s.
Receives government funding	7%	3%	n.s.
Linkages			
Any use of building by outsiders	67%	67%	n.s.
Receives consultant aid	45%	44%	n.s.
Mean number of outside groups using facilities	8	5	n.s.
Does not belong to a national denomination	10%	12%	n.s.
Minimum N[b]	125	1060	

Source: Chaves 1998, *National Congregations Study.*
[a]The figures in the column refer to the percentage of religious service attenders in congregations located in low-income neighborhoods with the specified feature, not the percentage of congregations with the feature. Low-income neighborhoods are defined as those with 30 percent or more persons below the poverty line in 1990.
[b]N's may differ slightly from cell to cell due to missing data.
* = $p \leq .05$. ** = $p \leq .01$.
n.s. No significance.

TABLE 9.3 / Programs and Leadership-Mobilization for Congregations Located in Low-Income Neighborhoods Versus Congregations Located in All Other Neighborhoods

Congregational Characteristic	Characteristics of Congregations in Low-Income Neighborhoods[a]	Characteristics of Congregations in Middle- and High-Income Neighborhoods	Statistical Significance
Programs			
Has a religious education program	95%	97%	n.s.
Has a food for the poor program	49	47	n.s.
Has a homeless program	19	14	n.s.
Has a housing assistance program	36	28	*
Leadership and Mobilization			
Regular congregation group meetings	82	89	*
Organized efforts to discuss politics	22	11	**
Organized efforts to encourage volunteering	59	59	n.s.
Organized efforts to lobby officials	21	11	**
Percentage of participants in some leadership position	25	27	n.s.
Minimum N[b]	123	1060	

Source: Chaves 1998, *National Congregations Study.*
[a]The percentages in the columns refer to the percentage of religious service attenders in congregations located in low-income neighborhoods with the specified feature, not the percentage of congregations with the feature. Low-income neighborhoods are defined as those with 30 percent or more persons below the poverty line in 1990.
[b]N's may differ slightly from cell to cell due to missing data.
* = $p \leq .05$. ** = $p \leq .01$.
n.s. No significance.

TABLE 9.4 / Resources and Community Linkages for Congregations with High Concentrations of Low-Income Members Versus All Other Congregations

Congregational Characteristic	Characteristics of Low-Income Congregations[a]	Characteristics of Middle- and High-Income Congregations	Statistical Significance
Human, material and ecological resources			
Mean year founded	1921	1919	n.s.
Mean number of adult regular participants	395	822	**
Median number of regular adult participants	103	300	N/A
Owns own building	91%	95%	n.s.
More than 50 percent of members walk to church	26%	14%	**
More than 80 percent of the congregation is African American	25%	10%	**
More than 80 percent of the congregation is Hispanic	6%	0.5%	**
Has a school	18%	23%	n.s.
Receives government funding	2%	4%	n.s.
Linkages			
Any use of building by outsiders	50%	72%	**
Receives consultant aid	28%	48%	**
Mean number of outside groups using facilities	3	6	**
Does not belong to a national denomination	17%	10%	*
Minimum N[b]	124	882	

Source: Chaves 1998, *National Congregations Study.*
[a]The percentages in the columns refer to the percentage of religious service attenders in congregations with the specified feature, not the percentage of congregations with the feature.
[b]N's may differ slightly from cell to cell due to missing data.
* = p ≤ .05. ** = p ≤ .01.
n.s. No significance.

TABLE 9.5 / Programs and Leadership-Mobilization for Congregations with High
Concentrations of Low-Income Members Versus All Other Congregations

Congregational Characteristic	Percentage of Members in Low-Income Congregations[a]	Percentage of Members in Middle- and High-Income Congregations	Statistical Significance
Programs			
Has a religious education program	90%	98%	**
Has a food for the poor program	36	50	**
Has a homeless program	2	15	**
Has a housing assistance program	14	32	**
Leadership and mobilization			
Regular congregation group meetings	82	91	**
Organized efforts to discuss politics	9	13	n.s.
Organized efforts to encourage volunteering	48	62	**
Organized efforts to lobby officials	11	13	n.s.
Percentage of participants in some leadership position	28	26	n.s.
Minimum N[b]	127	894	

Source: Chaves 1998, *National Congregations Study.*
[a]The figures in these columns refer to the percentage of religious service attenders in congregations with the specified feature, not the percentage of congregations with the feature.
[b]N's may differ slightly from cell to cell due to missing data.
* = $p \leq .05$. ** = $p \leq .01$.
n.s. No significance.

These findings are suggestive. Nevertheless, we know very little about the character of such ties across religious groups, their importance for local congregations, particularly in poor communities, and their significance for religious-based social capital generation in and for poor communities. Such questions await further research.

Resources and Outcomes

Social capital provides access to resources—financial, human, cultural, and social. The following discussion focuses on those resources enjoyed or provided by congregations that are most relevant to addressing poverty, including resources that might contribute to building, expanding, or sharing social capital.

INFORMATION FLOWS   Congregations provide conduits of information on community problems, available resources (for both individual and community advancement), and the state of the world. They may also provide language classes or job training, early childhood education, and regular schooling.

One specialized form of information flow has to do with referrals of individuals to social service agencies. Local congregations often enter into cooperative arrangements with other organizations, such as denominational offices, affiliated social service agencies, and sometimes government agencies, or they may maintain lists of suitable contacts for individuals requiring social services. Such ties, which are prime examples of "bridging social capital," also provide church officials and members with information, training, contacts, and occasionally funding to further their own social service delivery efforts.

FREE SPACES   Congregations often provide "free space" for social and political organizations within their community (Evans and Boyte 1986). A number of studies have indicated that the use of congregations' facilities by other religious groups, social service agencies, and community and political organizations of many sorts is widespread. Church halls and meeting rooms host everything from crafts fairs to Alcoholics Anonymous chapters, to candidates' forums for local and national elections, sometimes as a part of congregation-sponsored activities, sometimes for a fee, sometimes gratis. Some congregations open their doors to candidates, allowing them to speak at regularly scheduled services; others avoid any hint of political involvement. Still others accommodate campaigners for special issues of public concern, such as abortion, gay rights, or school prayer, while eschewing direct involvement with electoral politics. Congregations and their denominations range from liberal to ultraconservative in their political preferences. The more important question, however, from the point of view of providing such "bridging" opportunities, has to do with their willingness to host outsiders or actively support broader civic events within the purview of their work. NCS data show that most congregants belong to congregations that make their facilities available to outsiders (67 percent). Congregations in poor neighborhoods are as likely to do so as others, but poor congregations are much less likely to provide such a service to the community (tables 9.2 and 9.4).

SOCIALIZATION, COMMUNITY SERVICE, AND POLITICAL PARTICIPATION   Many religious organizations specialize in the education, indoctrination, and training of young people, through religious schools, catechetical instruction, Bible study, workshops, and summer camps. NCS data show that 22 percent of congregants in poor neighborhoods attend churches that maintain a school, while 18 percent of those in poor congregations have one (see tables 9.2 and 9.4). Ninety percent of the membership of poor congregations and 95 percent of those who attend churches in poor neighborhoods have a religious education program in their congregation (tables 9.3 and 9.5). Although the content of such efforts is often controversial from the point of view of secular institutions and values, it may include significant components of secular education and training, leadership development, and community service orientation. Church-run schools, for example, often not only provide essential academic preparation but also incorporate notions of community service into the curriculum (Youniss, McLellan, and Yates 1997).

James Coleman's own notion of social capital was shaped by his analysis of the impact of Catholic schooling on students from poor communities. Coleman and others have argued that such schools provide superior social capital for their students, owing to the combination of distinctive values, close supervision by teachers, and greater parental involvement than is true of public schools (Coleman and Hoffer 1987; Teachman, Paasch, and Carver 1997). In such a setting, values of community service and civic engagement are reinforced on a daily basis through interaction with committed adults and other students undergoing the same experience. James Youniss and Miranda Yates (1997), in a comparative and longitudinal study of Washington, D.C., black high school students who participated in a yearlong course devoted to community service and issues of civic responsibility, have shown that the impact of "values-based" education on adult levels of civic engagement is long-term and significant.

Congregations also provide volunteer opportunities and occasionally political information to their members. NCS data show that 59 percent of those involved in congregations in poor neighborhoods (and an equal percentage in other neighborhoods) belong to churches that sponsor organized efforts to encourage volunteering; 22 percent (as opposed to 11 percent elsewhere) are exposed to organized efforts to discuss politics; and 21 percent (versus 11 percent in more affluent neighborhoods) are part of efforts to lobby public officials (table 9.3). By contrast, just 9 percent of the membership of poor congregations belong to churches that have organized efforts to discuss politics, 48 percent are exposed to volunteering programs, and 11 percent belong to churches that lobby public officials. In each category, poorer congregations are at or below the means for more affluent congregations (table 9.5).

Thus, congregations—particularly those in poor neighborhoods—can be important arenas for building and nurturing community leadership as well as serving as platforms for civic participation and collective mobilization. They can be places, in Nancy Ammerman's phrase (1997, 363), "where otherwise voiceless people have a voice, where those denied leadership learn to lead." Recent research on civic participation in the United States backs up these claims. In *Voice and Equality* (1995), Sidney Verba, Kay Lehman Schlozman, and Henry Brady have shown that membership in a local congregation provides citizens with opportunities to develop civic skills through involvement in the everyday activities of their church. Thus, 32 percent of church members reported attending a meeting where decisions were made; 17 percent said they had planned such a meeting; and 18 percent said they had made a speech or a presentation (1995, 312). The authors also show that a large proportion of political activity follows from personal contacts and direct solicitation, and that, while the workplace and other voluntary organizations are important loci of such activities, churches play the biggest role in that regard (147). They argue that religious participation is especially important for poor and minority citizens since they are as likely to be church members as their better-off counterparts but substantially less likely to learn civic skills through higher education, on the job, or in other voluntary associational settings (317).[10]

Finally, we know that weekly church attenders devote more than twice as much time a week to volunteer work as citizens who do not attend—3.4 hours versus 1.6 hours (Hodgkinson and Weitzman 1992, 162). Andrew Greeley (1997) has re-analyzed several Independent Sector national surveys to show the important role that churches play in encouraging people to volunteer and providing them with information about opportunities to do so. He summarizes his results for adults: "52 percent of Americans had volunteered, and 28 percent of the volunteers, by far the largest proportion, volunteered for religious projects. Moreover, of the volunteers, 34 percent said that religious structures (either organizational or interpersonal) were responsible for their volunteering" (Greeley 1997, 591). These volunteers accounted for 33 percent of the political volunteers, 29 percent of the human service volunteers, and 26 percent of the health volunteers. As we have seen, NCS data confirm these findings, showing that 59 percent of all congregation members belong to religious bodies that actively encourage volunteering (table 9.3). Although the extent of religious participation is related to more extensive volunteering for all denominations, the sacred-secular mix varies by religious affiliation: liberal Protestants and Catholics are more likely to direct their volunteering toward the secular realm, and conservative Protestants are more oriented toward the religious realm (Wilson and Janoski 1995).

AUTHORITY AND LEGITIMACY   Harder to measure or assess, religious bodies may lend their authority and legitimacy to a wide range of community activities and initiatives. Congregations and their religious and lay leaders often enjoy a prima facie legitimacy that allows them to carry out activities and engage the moral energies of citizens where others might face a more uphill battle. At the same time, of course, the identification of a religious body with a cause or project may diminish its appeal for some citizens and groups.

In practice, the presumed authority and legitimacy conferred on religious bodies by their members enhances the ability of pastors, religious publishers, and denominational spokespeople to transmit their version of the received truth for a given religious tradition. The shared understandings that result contribute to the solidarity experienced among members of a tradition (bonding social capital), a solidarity that in the best of cases transcends racial, ethnic, linguistic, or national boundaries. Messages about the state of the world, the role of believers in the community, and appropriate forms of behavior can also partake of this legitimacy (though with varying degrees of persuasive power), at times lending strength to religious and community organizations, but in other instances weakening their ability to build bridges and sustain action.[11]

Clergy are highly likely to speak out on social issues, and many church members receive encouragement in church to engage in political action as well as volunteer work of many kinds. A recent national study reports that regular worshipers say that clergy at their place of worship regularly speak out on public issues, including 87 percent on hunger and poverty, 60 percent on abortion, 56 percent on prayer in public schools, 27 percent on the death penalty, 26 percent on health care reform, and 21 percent on candidates and elections (Kohut et al. 2000). The findings of the *Voice and Equality* study are consistent with these results: 16 percent of that sample reported that clergy frequently or sometimes discuss political issues from the pulpit, and 35 percent of Protestants and 33 percent of Catholics reported having been asked in church to take political action of some kind, including voting and contacting officials (Verba, Schlozman, and Brady 1995, 373–78). As we saw earlier, NCS data confirm these findings, showing that political discussion and even lobbying activities are common in a significant percentage of congregations, and still more common among congregations in poor neighborhoods.

The southern civil rights movement illustrated how congregations could be mobilized to become the building blocks of both local and national efforts aimed at achieving justice for oppressed people, providing early and determinative leadership to the movement (Morris 1984; McAdam 1982). Mark Chaves and Lynn Higgens (1992), in an analysis of a national survey of congregations, show that congregations made up of mostly African Americans remain quite a bit more likely to participate in civil rights and social justice efforts than all-white congregations, and that they are substantially more likely to engage in community development activities (73 percent to 44 percent reported having done so). Although many community development activities among African Americans are the work of individual churches, coalitions of local congregations devoted to empowering poor communities are the main vehicle in congregation-based organizing (Day 1996). Leaders of such coalitions can build on the social networks provided at the congregational and denominational levels to mobilize people and resources for community action.

DENOMINATIONS, INTERFAITH COALITIONS, AND SPECIALIZED SERVICE ORGANIZATIONS

Congregations are the most numerous of religious organizations and the closest to their communities in many respects. But congregations generally originated in the efforts of supra- or extracongregational organizations to meet local needs. In this sense, they are an example of the process that Theda Skocpol (1999) has described for the development of American civil society in general—not the spontaneous emergence of local organizations, but the spreading, through the institution-building efforts of national networks, of local affiliates throughout the country. These origins, as well as later efforts to draw together or support local congregations, have left their mark in the often multiple ties that congregations maintain to congregations of the same religious tradition, supracongregational organizations like denominations, interfaith coalitions, and extracongregational religious agencies and organizations of all sorts. These are rich sources of social capital for local religious groups and their communities. Though our knowledge is limited, we explore in this section what we do know about the ways in which these sources of social capital affect poor communities.

Supracongregational Organizations

Denominations and associations of nondenominational congregations such as the American Council of Christian Churches often focus their energies at the national level, in public education and advocacy on behalf of religious interests. Many such associations have little direct control over the activities of local congregations, and the divisions between local pastors and national organizations on such issues as "charitable choice" are often significant.[12] Nevertheless, most such organizations provide educational resources to local congregations; their national and regional meetings enable local religious leaders to acquire a wider circle of contacts; and some associations provide significant levels of financial and other support to poorer local congregations. They thus represent an important layer of social capital for both pastors and their congregations.

The nationally sponsored educational and advocacy campaigns of these associations of congregations, moreover, can have a significant impact at the local level in encouraging or discouraging certain types of political activities on the part of congregation members, highlighting some aspects of the "social gospel" at the expense of others, and encouraging community service of one type or another within congregations, as well as providing information about national policy issues. Any evaluation of the impact of these activities on communities, however, has to take into consideration the large degree of "slack" between positions advocated at the national level and those acceptable to local pastors and their constituents.

More important perhaps from a social capital perspective, national associations of congregations provide local religious leaders with ties that can be crucial to mobilizing resources for local initiatives and the maintenance or strengthening of local congregations. In this respect, such associations help extend the reach and effectiveness of local social capital, overcoming the narrowing effects of homophilous association at the congregational level (Olson 1989) as well as providing access to extracongregational resources. Such resources, moreover, can include training (building human capital) and financial support.

Any evaluation of the impact of the ties and opportunities represented by associational membership must take into account the considerable variability between and within religious traditions. Catholic dioceses have varied considerably in their willingness to subsidize urban schools and parishes from the center or through sister parish arrangements with affluent suburban parishes, or to shut them down in response to white out-migration. Declining personnel has led many denominations, including the Catholic Church, to decide more often to move with the membership rather than try to serve (and attract) a new black or immigrant membership in the old neighborhoods. Many denominations simply lack the organizational structure required to tax richer congregations in support of poorer ones. Some, however, manage to supplement their own resources through "cooperative ministry" with other denominations.

The "weak ties" (Granovetter 1973) fostered through associational membership at the local, regional, and national levels thus vary considerably in both level and significance from one religious tradition to another and from congregation to congregation. Evidence from the NCS is mixed in this regard. Poorer congregations are much less likely than others to receive consultant help, and less likely to be affiliated with a denomination. On the other hand, roughly half of both poor congregations and those located in poor neighborhoods belong to one or another local association (see tables 9.2 and 9.4).

Interfaith Coalitions

Especially among poorer congregations without strong denominational or other national-level ties, resource scarcity and social isolation may be overcome by participation in local interfaith coalitions, united ministries, and other associations of congregations. Most communities of any size appear to have at least one such body. Of the 223 interfaith coalitions listed in the 1997 *Yearbook of American and Canadian Churches,* an admittedly partial listing, most feature advocacy, social service, and community development activities, from sponsoring the UNICEF Children's Fund Drive to operating community food banks or homeless shelters, to holding workshops on racism and cultural diversity (Bedell 1997). Many coalitions house local chapters of larger movements with a social agenda, such as Church Women United, CROP, or Habitat for Humanity. A small minority of such coalitions focus exclusively on religious concerns and interfaith dialogue. Though some appear to lean to the more conservative side of the political spectrum on social issues, most can be categorized as distinctly liberal. In their ability to link congregations and parachurch organizations in programs and projects of benefit to the larger community, they are an important instance of social capital mobilized for both congregations and communities.

There has been almost no research on such organizations, despite their evident importance in many communities. The limited literature that does exist suggests that most pastors would be reluctant to support such efforts, particularly when they involve a possibly controversial religious or social agenda (Tamney and Johnson 1990), and that these organizations might do best when supported, not by local congregations, but by overarching judicatory bodies, such as dioceses, federations of religious bodies of the same faith tradition, or councils of churches (Takayama and Darnell 1979; for one such example of this sort of structure, see Wiseman 1997). The research is thus in the position of Mancur Olson's (1965) "dilemma of collective action" in suggesting that there should be far fewer of this sort of organization than actually exist. In this respect, this work underlines just how little is known about how these organizations function and what they contribute to their communities. The Tamney and Johnson study suggests that conservative evangelical pastors are less likely to support such efforts than others, but the existence of "shared" or "united" ministries among nondenominational churches should alert us to the dangers of overgeneralizing on the basis of this research.

From the point of view of the sorts of social capital available to poor communities, in fact, interfaith coalitions appear to provide one of the most important vehicles through which local religious bodies and affiliated organizations attempt to address problems of poverty, social isolation, and personal and family distress in poor communities. Such organizations play a number of roles: they serve as collective advocates on such issues as gun control and local spending for community problems; they provide social services of all kinds, in many cases recruiting volunteers from local churches and the larger community; they engage in community education on social issues, through workshops, training programs, work in the schools, and publicity; and they provide "free spaces" and resources for other, specialized organizations devoted to volunteerism in service to the community, community development, or social service delivery.

CONGREGATION-BASED ORGANIZING AND POOR COMMUNITIES

It has been estimated that six thousand community organizations are working to organize and empower people in poor communities in the United States (Delgado 1994). These groups take a number of distinct forms, including: those whose primary membership and constituency is poor community residents, like those groups that make up the ACORN network and the groups loosely affiliated with the Third World Organizing Center (TWOC);[13] issue-based coalitions of local organizations; and congregation- or church-based organizations. Although certain individual membership groups and issue-based coalitions may receive support from and even include local religious groups in their coalitions, church-based groups are defined by their use of local congregations as building blocks for creating organizational structures.

The congregation-based organizational template was developed by Industrial Areas Foundation (IAF) leaders after the death of the organization's longtime leader, the notorious community organizer Saul Alinsky. There are now at least sixty IAF groups in U.S. communities, with a number more in formation (Warren 1998). Some of the IAF's best-known and most successful groups include COPS in San Antonio, Texas (Rogers 1990), BUILD in Baltimore, Maryland (Greider 1992), and South Bronx Churches in the South Bronx of New York (Rooney 1995). We are most knowledgeable about the groups that make up the IAF network, and hence about the details of the IAF model, since so much effort has been devoted to describing it. In addition, there are several other networks of local groups that mirror the IAF model, including the Gamaliel Foundation, based in Chicago; the Pacific Institute for Community Organization (PICO), based in Oakland, California; and Direct Action and Research Training (DART), based in Florida. Each of these networks includes organizations in states beyond their home base, and together with the IAF-affiliated organizations, they include at least 133 congregation-based organizations (Warren and Wood 2001). Although we have more limited secondary accounts of them compared with the IAF groups, it appears that the basic outlines of organization building, organizational structure, financing, leadership training, and relational organizing are quite similar across the groups (see Hart, 2001; Wood 1999).[14]

The CBO Formula for Organization Building

The several congregation-based organizing (CBO) networks enter communities in a pretty similar fashion, looking for ecumenical support from a number of congregational leaders before they commit an organizer to a community.[15] The support includes enough financial resources, from dues assessed from member congregations, to hire a lead organizer and provide the rudiments of an umbrella organization linking the participating congregations. An organizing committee is formed, and the lead organizer meets with pastors and lay leaders from participating congregations, typically in "one-on-ones"—short meetings aimed at sizing up their leadership potential and creating bonds with them. In this way, a cadre of leaders is formed out of the congregations to take part in leadership training. These leaders, in turn, carry on one-on-ones aimed at identifying additional leaders who can also receive leadership training. Thus, the premise of the organizing strategy is to build on the preexisting relationships between congregational members. It is driven by the desire to identify and train local leaders in relational skills and to have them build ever-widening circles of relationships. Eventually, leaders work to build relationships with outside allies, community leaders, power brokers, and ordinary citizens outside of their own group. Jim Rooney (1995, 226), summarizing what he learned studying the creation of South Bronx Churches, calls this process "organizing relationally" and observes that a CBO "is built piece by piece, person by person. Therein lies its strength." This process is tremendously labor-intensive and time-consuming, and it is not unusual for these organizations to spend years creating the thick relations of trust and respect between members from the constituent congregations that ultimately allow them to act collectively.

How CBOs Create Social Capital in Poor Communities

Other community-organizing strategies, such as ACORNs, may also create social capital in poor communities. But the CBO is the one strategy that does so primarily by exploiting the preexisting social capital of religious congregations in organizing efforts that may expand community social capital. The question that needs to be asked is whether the CBO adds social capital value to poor communities beyond that which we have previously argued already exists as a result of the special characteristics of religious congregations. We believe that it does in a variety of ways.

HUMAN DEVELOPMENT   Each of several CBO networks concentrates significant resources on what they call leadership development. Beyond the ongoing systematic training in one-on-ones already described, each network fields longer-term training sessions for leaders that include elements of what used to be called civic education, led by experienced trainers and shaped by systematic curricula. These training sessions range from the standard IAF ten-day sessions to weekend retreats. And while the network leaders would almost universally eschew the terminology and its associated imagery, these training regimens appear to dramatically increase the self-confidence of leaders. One study found that CBO groups were one and a half times as likely (71 percent versus 49 percent) to devote resources to leadership development as were non-CBO community organizations (McCarthy and Castelli 1994). If the widespread efforts of CBOs are at all successful in motivating and encouraging their local leaders through such training to build denser social relations, they have, by definition, added to the stock of community social capital.[16] As far as we can determine, there have been no systematic efforts to assess the consequences of these experiences for the behavior, self-confidence, and individual situation of the community leaders who have been exposed to them.

SOCIAL NETWORKS   A key to relational organizing is the ongoing development of new relationships between leaders and ever-expanding circles of community members. Each of the networks has its own variation on how to cultivate new social relations. The IAF's method has been described in some detail (see, for example, Rooney 1995; Rogers 1990) and includes the one-on-one described earlier. These are not just idle conversations, however, but instrumental interactions designed to find out what is most important to the persons being approached in order to determine whether those priorities are a likely basis for group leadership. The IAF's ten-day training for leaders includes an entire day of practice in carrying out one-on-ones. Such a mechanism seems ideally suited for developing expanded "weak" social ties between leaders and other community members. Leaders, through these efforts, become acquainted with large numbers of their fellow citizens. If we were to compare the network density of social ties in a neighborhood before such relational organizing was launched with that same density after several years of organizing, we would expect that the density would increase dramatically. In this way, then, relational organizing by CBOs by definition creates social capital by expanding social ties among community residents.

ORGANIZATIONAL LINKS   CBOs also work to create linkages among organizations. Their organizational template explicitly links numerous congregations together into a coherent structure, and as a result, the pastors and members of each congregation are tied to one another. One consequence of the thickening of ties across congregations is access to one another's organizational networks. So, for instance, a Methodist congregation attached to a CBO might thereby be linked to the local Catholic diocesan structure through ties to constituent Catholic parishes. Each of the networks links its constituent local affiliates to the others through a central structure, so that local congregations and leaders can develop ties to individuals and organizations in distant communities. In each of the networks there is a steady flow of information between communities as a result of these ties. Moreover, several of the CBO networks have created statewide organizations more tightly linking all of their affiliates as a basis for statewide mobilization. The IAF has done so effectively with its Texas Network (Texas IAF Network 1990; Warren 2001), as has PICO with its California Project. Structures like these inevitably link local CBOs to a wider array of individuals and organizations outside of their own communities, both drawing on the social capital of the constituent organizations and building social capital in the process.

SOCIALLY HETEROGENEOUS SOCIAL TIES   Congregation-based organizations aim to build organizations to empower poor communities. By building on congregations, they inevitably build class-heterogeneous groups, first, because most congregations in poor communities include many families who are not poor, and second, because many CBOs include among their affiliate congregations some that are more middle-class. Finally, relational organizing induces leaders to develop social ties broadly and offers training in accomplishing this goal. As a result, the social capital built through the CBO strategy is highly likely to build socially heterogeneous social capital.

The CBO networks work hard to build social capital in order to mobilize people in poor communities to bring about social change. The strategy draws criticism, however, from other advocates of change on several grounds. First is the claim that CBOs do not organize the poorest of the poor, thereby neglecting to empower the neediest community members (Delgado 1994). Second, there is concern about the narrowness as well as localized focus of the issues on which CBOs can achieve consensus (Miller 1987). And third, some argue that building CBOs on a congregational base merely reinforces the traditional hierarchical structures of religious organizations (Robinson and Hanna 1994).

RESEARCH IMPLICATIONS

Various levels of social relations form the core of the social capital concept. Research approaches that embody these relations and linkages, then, seem most appropriate. In general, our inclination is to encourage research that gathers evidence at a variety of levels of structure in such a way that social networks, organizations, and individuals may be linked to one another for purposes of analysis. Many variants on network sampling, as a consequence, seem to recommend themselves.

Congregations

We can approach research on congregational social capital by gathering samples of congregations, either at the national or community level. The hyper-network sampling approach of the NCS, employed at the national level, can and should also be applied to congregational studies in communities, the level at which many congregational surveys have been conducted (see, for example, Wineburg 1990–91; Cnaan 1998). We know that it is quite difficult to enumerate all congregations in a community. For instance, a 1989 resurvey of the National Council of Churches' annual survey of congregations found that the NCC count, the most serious data collection effort of its kind, failed to include the many independent congregations of Baptist, Holiness, and Pentecostal churches. The resurvey analyzed tax assessors' records for 30 counties in middle Tennessee. Where the NCC data listed only 2,391 congregations in this area in 1980, the study identified 4,039 church buildings (Ethridge 1989). In addition, samples of members of such national samples of congregations would be capable of addressing a variety of questions about the interaction of the social network and organizational structure of congregations.

Interfaith Coalitions

One particular form of religious institution, we have suggested, may be an important creator of religious social capital: the interfaith coalition. Such institutions are among those noncongregational structures that are also not denominational structures. One way to enumerate these local networks of congregations is to go through Internal Revenue Service records of nonprofit organizations. Our preliminary survey of tax records for such organizations in the state of Maryland turned up some fifty-six organizations that appear to fit the profile of an interfaith coalition sketched earlier; average assets and incomes for those that reported such figures were $953,000 and $1,962,000, respectively.[17] Although tax records may help considerably in tracking the larger coalitions, it is likely that many of them do not incorporate or register with the IRS. Again, community surveys of congregations could be used to enumerate these coalitions at the community level.

Congregation-based community organizations are one type of interfaith coalition and could be studied fruitfully, we believe, in contrast to other kinds of interfaith coalitions of local congregations. Many of the ways in which CBOs create social capital in poor communities may stem from their unique approach, as we have suggested, but others may create social capital simply as the result of knitting together local congregations for common community purposes.

SOCIAL POLICY IMPLICATIONS

How might the social capital resources of religious groups in poor communities be expanded? Let us address this question in the context of the two foci of activity we have discussed: congregation-based organizing, and para-church organizations and interfaith alliances.

Congregation-Based Organizing

We have suggested that the CBO formula effectively expands the stock of many dimensions of social capital in communities where it has nurtured strong congregation-based organizations, overcoming some of the limits of the "bonding" social capital encountered in congregations. If this is the case, then mechanisms to expand the CBO effort can be expected to improve the social capital position of poor communities where it happens. Congregation-based organizations depend in large part on their constituent congregations for resources, but the mature organizations we have mentioned have shown the ability to absorb significant grant resources from outside funders for furthering their work, and there has been a steady flow of grant resources to many CBOs (McCarthy and Castelli 1994; Warren and Wood 2001). The Catholic Campaign for Human Development (CCHD) has been a strong supporter of CBOs through such grants, and the Neighborhood Funders Group, a coalition of foundations, has been encouraging the expansion of such support among a broader range of foundations. These groups have extensive experience working with CBOs, and their experiences would serve as useful templates for any effort to expand funding support to this sector aimed at increasing the social capital in poor communities.

Para-Church Organizations and Congregational Alliances

Though we know very little about para-church organizations and they are extremely varied in their compositions, structures, and programs, it should be apparent that they represent an enormous resource for poor communities. Although some, such as Habitat for Humanity, are largely self-supporting, others depend on grants from various sources, as well as individual donations and volunteer labor, to support their efforts. The most visible of such organizations at the local level are the congregational alliances, or interfaith coalitions, which typically provide a range of social and community services, drawing on the resources of local congregations as well as local, state, and federal government. The charitable choice provisions of the new welfare reform law apparently have opened the door to greater use of public funds by these organizations, many of which boast a broad "ecumenical" approach and, in some cases, a professional staff. It is likely that they could absorb greater funding in ways that would be responsive to community needs. At the same time, it is apparent that many of these organizations, like some congregations, have already found ways to accommodate state and federal standards and make use of public funds.

CONCLUSION

The various forms of social capital and social resources enumerated here collectively contribute significantly to community well-being in poor communities, particularly through the ability of congregations to mobilize their members around local needs. The networks, social solidarity, and broader linkages enjoyed by many religious institutions can provide the basis for community building, community organizing and political action, and individual advancement. They provide access to resources such as education, community service, and leadership opportunities; information about social service agencies, community organizations, and political events; leadership, foot soldiers, and "free space" for social and political initiatives; and formal and informal social services of all kinds.

The varied resources embedded in religious congregations have not escaped the notice of social service providers and planners. Targeting churches as sites for public health intervention, for example, has become a widespread practice recently (see, for example, Altman 1997). Community health program professionals have for some time capitalized on the legitimacy of church educational programs in designing church-based health education programs and community health outreach efforts, particularly among African American churches (Eng, Hatch, and Callan 1985; Hatch and Lovelace 1980; Hatch 1981; Hatch et al. 1984; Thomas et al. 1994; Wiist and Flack 1990).

These same social networks and reserves of legitimacy explain the ability of local congregations to mobilize citizens, whether directly, through religiously sponsored social and political activities, or indirectly through the skills and leadership training that they provide and through activities that use the physical plant and resources of congregations for social and political action on behalf of the community. The congregation-based organizing program of the Industrial Areas Foundation is the best known of such efforts, but ACORN and other organizing initiatives have turned to congregations for the social capital they provide (and to supracongregational organizations, such as the Catholic bishops' Campaign for Human Development, for seed money). And social service agencies of all sorts depend on the support and volunteer labor of congregations or their members in virtually every community in the United States.

Religious participation is less affected by socioeconomic position than almost any other form of social behavior, so that church membership is relatively stable across the economic spectrum. To the degree that churches provide training in civic skills, opportunities and motivation for participation in civic affairs and politics, and networks for upward mobility, they are among the great equalizers in American society as Verba, Schlozman, and Brady (1995) have argued. The evidence presented here, however, points strongly to significant differences on almost all measures of social capital between poor congregations (those whose membership is predominantly poor people) and congregations in poor neighborhoods, where we find many multi-class congregations. The latter are richer in social capital and in the resources that make social capital especially important in poor communities. They are also more likely to have strong linkages to the larger society and to be more deeply involved in community affairs and political life than either congregations in more affluent neighborhoods or those made up mostly of poor members.

The social capital that religious congregations represent, however, is not without its limitations. Sometimes the relative homogeneity of congregations and the close interpersonal ties among members may lead to isolation. More frequently perhaps, religiously defined social boundaries limit the participation of the broader community in programs and constrain the sort of work congregations undertake (Schneider 1999). Religious bodies can also be potent vehicles for the perpetuation of inequalities, through some of the same mechanisms by which they train members in citizenship and provide leadership to the larger community. Most of the more hierarchical institutions, and even many of the more egalitarian ones, restrict the degree to which women may play leadership roles, though the degree and extent to which this is true has shifted back and forth over time. These limitations are not exclusive to religious organizations, but they tend to stand out and be reinforced by the power of religious symbols and teachings to create distinctive identities that are sometimes at variance with secular norms. We know far too little about these processes to make sweeping judgments.

The important role that many religious organizations can and do play in poor communities, however, should prompt greater attention among social scientists and policymakers alike to the ways in which such social capital is developed and deployed by institutions. Even poor congregations may be rich in social capital, but congregations of all sorts are apt to be relatively poor in precisely those resources necessary to address the problems of joblessness, poverty, crime, ill health, and low levels of educational achievement in poor communities. The efforts of religious bodies can be strengthened through local coalition building and support from denominations, other supracongregational bodies, and specialized, religious-inspired agencies (though poor congregations often lack such linkages as well). But even the multi-class congregations often found in poor neighborhoods, rich as they are in social capital, have so far proven unable to reverse larger trends of capital flight, labor market change, urban and rural deterioration, and government neglect. The entrepreneurial skills of a few pastors and the community mobilization efforts of the congregation-based organizing movement have proven the most able contenders against poverty in poor neighborhoods. Even these efforts, however, have depended on responsive and generous government action. What congregations and other religious bodies can do in poor communities is to build the human bases for community renewal and individual advancement. Any lasting impact, however, will depend on the larger environment, including first of all governments with the resources and the will to reverse long-term trends toward wage deflation and shrinking government services.

NOTES

1. Habitat for Humanity was founded in 1976 to provide decent housing to the poor through a program that includes significant donations of "sweat equity" on the part of beneficiaries, no-interest loans, and donated volunteer labor and materials. Describing itself as a "nonprofit, ecumenical Christian housing ministry," it has attracted the support of former President Jimmy Carter and claims to have provided some 350,000 people around the world with decent, affordable homes of their own (Habitat for Humanity 1999). Bread for the World is an ecumenical anti-hunger lobby, founded in 1974, with headquarters in Washington, D.C., and a membership of both individuals and congregations. Teen Challenge was created by the evangelist David Wilkerson in connection with his work with New York City teenage gangs. It runs drug rehabilitation centers for young people at 120 locations throughout the United States and another 130 around the world. Strongly evangelical in tone and methods, it has attracted the support of mainstream evangelicals such as Pat Boone (Teen Challenge 1999).

2. Although there is some dispute about religious attendance rates (see Hadaway, Marler, and Chaves 1993; ASR 1998), revolving around whether self-report is an adequate indicator, there is no dispute about the extraordinarily high rate of involvement of Americans compared with citizens of other nations.

3. There is substantial variation in levels of giving between denominations, as well as in the proportion of contributions that are given by congregations to denominational bodies (Hoge and Fenggang Yang 1994).

4. There are other specialized bodies that might be relevant to our concerns but are omitted here, including a large number of organizations that provide support to congregations in the form of religious publications (Bible societies and nonprofit educational publishing organizations), theological training of laypeople and religious personnel, consulting services, and "mission" or evangelization organizations and coalitions (for example, the Billy Graham crusades). Some of these are undoubtedly important for strengthening congregations, and thus their capacity to serve their communities. But the four types listed here arguably are the most important for building social capital expressly oriented toward community service and development. Because of their importance and the relative lack of research on certain of them, we take up each separately.

5. See Ammerman (1997, 362–67) and Cnaan et al. (1999) for parallel discussions of the ways in which congregations create and embody social capital. Cnaan and his associates make the claim that "local religious congregations are among the key producers of social capital and human capital at the local level" (1).

6. The NCS results reported here are drawn from Chaves (1999). The NCS yields data on congregations as the unit of analysis, though it makes it possible for us to report characteristics of both congregants and their congregations. The sampling frame for the NCS survey starts with the 1998 General Social Survey (GSS). If respondents indicated attendance at religious services, they were asked to provide a link to their congregation. Telephone or face-to-face interviews were then conducted with key informants from each designated congregation, in most cases the pastor. This "hyper-network sample" of congregations makes this survey of congregations the most comprehensive and accurate one to date. Where earlier congregational surveys depended on telephone books to locate congregations and thereby missed many small congregations, the NCS sample is able to include just such groups. The zip code and street address of each congregation were used to locate it in a census tract, allowing us to characterize each congregation by features of its surrounding community. The response rate was 80 percent, and the total number of congregations was 1,236. Greater detail about the sampling method and the data set can be found in Chaves (1998).

Respondents (pastors or other informed individuals) were asked a wide variety of questions about their congregation including, for example: the number of members and their demographic makeup; the physical facilities and their use; the congregation's religious, social, and political activities; its programs; and its formal and informal linkages to the broader community. Respondents were asked: "Of the regular adult participants, what percent would you say live in households with incomes under $25,000 a year?" As a result, we could isolate those congregations with larger concentrations of lower-income households. We used a cutoff of 60 percent of adult congregation members in households with income of under $25,000 a year to define low-income congregations. (We ran analyses comparing congregations with a number of different cutoff points, including 40 percent and 20 percent of members in households earning under $25,000. The results were consistent across the analyses using different cutoff points.)

Twenty-six percent of the congregations in the sample qualify as low-income by this criterion, but this figure includes only 12 percent of the individuals who make up the membership of the congregations in the sample. This is the case because the poorer congregations tend to be smaller than the others, as will be seen later in the chapter.

7. In subsequent analyses of this data, we employ a cutoff of 30 percent in order to define poor neighborhoods. The logic of this choice was based on the small number of congrega-

tions and congregants in those neighborhoods. Use of the 30 percent cutoff allows for more stable statistical comparisons.

8. For instance, "*the average person who attends church several times a week* enjoys roughly 2.25 more nonkin ties than the person who *never* attends. This relationship persists net of the potentially confounding effects of a wide range of covariates" (Ellison and George (1994, 54). The same pattern holds for telephone contacts: the difference between "never" and "several times a week" attendance is one contact per week.

9. We use these figures rather than the percentage of congregations with the feature since it reflects the actual number of parishioners in the congregations with the feature. Since congregations vary dramatically in size, relying on the percentage of congregations with the feature has less intuitive appeal.

10. Though Verba and his associates (1995) found no significant gender differences in the practice of civic skills in churches, their evidence does point to substantial differences between Catholics and Protestants in the extent to which religious involvement leads to civic skills. Involvement in Catholic parishes is less likely to provide the opportunity for exercising those skills, and this explains, in part, why Latino respondents reported practicing fewer civic skills (320–33).

11. See Wood (1999) for a subtle analysis of the ways in which different religious cultures can contribute to or detract from the work of churches involved in congregation-based organizing efforts.

12. The so-called charitable choice provision of the Personal Responsibility and Work Opportunity Reconciliation Act of 1996—the "welfare reform" bill currently in effect— requires states, in contracting with nonprofit organizations for social service delivery, to count religious organizations among the eligible contractees and loosens regulations governing their participation. In the debate surrounding the charitable choice provision of the bill, representatives of conservative Protestant groups, notably the Christian Coalition, the Family Research Council, and the Christian Legal Society, actively supported expansion of government funding for religious organizations. Catholic, Jewish, and mainline Protestant groups by and large opposed such funding, alongside proponents of the separation of church and state such as the American Civil Liberties Union and Americans United for the Separation of Church and State. Drawing on NCS data, Chaves (1998) shows that those congregations most likely to take advantage of the new law are associated with the mainline denominations.

13. The National Organizers Alliance, based in Washington, D.C., works to knit organizations of this type together into a national force.

14. PICO converted its existing groups during the 1980s from membership-based to congregation-based, under the inspiration of an organizer who had worked previously with the IAF (Bauman 1995).

15. We provide only a brief sketch of the CBO organizing template here before we discuss how the actions of these groups can be thought of as increasing the stock of social capital in the communities in which they work. More extensive treatments can be found in Rogers (1990), Warren (2001), Robinson and Hanna (1994), Rooney (1995), Speer (1995), Reitzes and Reitzes (1987), and McCarthy and Castelli (1994), among others.

16. Community-organizing models are increasingly used as the templates for public health interventions. One large intervention aimed at mobilizing anti-tobacco forces at the

community level concluded that one of the most important components of success was leadership training efforts (Blaine et al. 1997).

17. We searched the IRS database for Maryland nonprofits using a handful of keywords that regularly appear in the names of such organizations ("interfaith," "ecumenical," "united ministries," "cooperative ministries," and so on). Undoubtedly, some of the organizations identified in this way do not fit the profile developed here; other organizations that may fit the profile but have not used any of these terms in their name remained uncounted.

REFERENCES

Aho, James. 1991. *The Politics of Righteousness: Idaho Christian Patriotism*. Seattle: University of Washington Press.

———. 1996. "Popular Christianity and Political Extremism in America." In *Disruptive Religion: The Force of Faith in Social Movement Activism*, edited by Christian Smith. New York: Routledge.

Altman, David G. 1997. "Church-Based Trial in North Carolina Targeting Youth Tobacco Use." Proposal submitted to Public Health Service, Department of Health and Human Services. Winston-Salem, N.C.: Bowman Gray School of Medicine.

American Sociological Review. 1998. "A Symposium on Church Attendance in the United States." *American Sociological Review* 63(1): 111–37.

Ammerman, Nancy T. 1997. *Congregation and Community*. New Brunswick, N.J.: Rutgers University Press.

Bauman, John. 1995. Interview by John D. McCarthy, October 19. Oakland, California.

Bedell, Kenneth B. 1997. *Yearbook of American and Canadian Churches, 1997*. Nashville, Tenn.: Abingdon Press/National Council of Churches.

Blaine, Therese M., Jean L. Forster, Deborah Hennrikus, Stephen O'Neil, Mark Wolfson, and Huy Pham. 1997. "Creating Tobacco Control Policy at the Local Level: Implementation of a Direct Action Organizing Approach." *Health Education and Behavior* 24: 640–51.

Burt, Ronald S. 1997. "The Contingent Value of Social Capital." *Administrative Science Quarterly* 42: 339–65.

Casanova, José. 1994. *Public Religions in the Modern World*. Chicago: University of Chicago Press.

Chaves, Mark. 1998. "Religious Congregations and Welfare Reform: Who Will Take Advantage of 'Charitable Choice.'" Tucson: Department of Sociology, University of Arizona. Unpublished paper.

———. 1998. *National Congregations Study*. Data file and codebook. Department of Sociology, University of Arizona, Tucson.

———. 1999. "Congregations' Social Service Activities." No. 6 in *Charting Civil Society*, a series of policy briefs by Center on Nonprofits and Philanthropy, The Urban Institute, Washington, D.C.

Chaves, Mark, and Lynn Higgins. 1992. "Comparing the Community Involvement of Black and White Congregations." *Journal for the Scientific Study of Religion* 31: 425–40.

Cnaan, Ram A. 1998. *Social and Community Involvement of Religious Congregations Housed in Historic Religious Properties: Findings from a Six-City Study*. Philadelphia: University of Pennsylvania School of Social Work.

Cnaan, Ram A., Mona Basta, Stephanie C. Boddie, Ayala Cnaan, Lina Hartocollis, Karin Prochezka, and Gaynor Yancey. 1999. "Bowling Alone but Serving Together: The Congregational Norm of Community Involvement." Philadelphia: University of Pennsylvania School of Social Work. Unpublished paper.

Coleman, James S., and Thomas Hoffer. 1987. *Public and Private High Schools: The Impact of Communities*. New York: Basic Books.

Day, Donna C. 1996. "Prelude to Struggle: African American Clergy and Community Organizing for Economic Development in the 1990s." Ph.D. diss., Temple University.

Delgado, Gary. 1994. *Beyond the Politics of Place: New Directions in Community Organizing in the 1990s*. Oakland, Calif.: Applied Research Center.

Ellison, Christopher G., and Linda K. George. 1994. "Religious Involvement, Social Ties, and Social Support in a Southeastern Community." *Journal for the Scientific Study of Religion* 33: 46–61.

Eng, Eugenia, John Hatch, and Anne Callan. 1985. "Institutionalizing Social Support Through the Church and into the Community." *Health Education Quarterly* 12: 81–92.

Ethridge, F. Maurice. 1989. "Underreported Churches in Middle Tennessee: A Research Note." *Journal for the Scientific Study of Religion* 28(4): 518–29.

Evans, Sara M. and Harry C. Boyte. 1986. *Free Spaces: The Sources of Democratic Change in America*. New York: Harper and Row.

Foley, Michael W., and Bob Edwards. 1999. "Is It Time to Disinvest in Social Capital?" *Journal of Public Policy* 19(2): 199–231.

Granovetter, Mark S. 1973. "The Strength of Weak Ties." *American Journal of Sociology* 78: 1360–80.

Greeley, Andrew. 1997. "Coleman Revisited: Religious Structures as Sources of Social Capital." *American Behavioral Scientist* 40: 587–94.

Green, Clifford J., ed. 1996. *Churches, Cities, and Human Community: Urban Ministry in the United States 1845–1985*. Grand Rapids, Mich.: Eerdmans.

Greider, William. 1992. *Who Will Tell the People: The Betrayal of American Democracy*. New York: Simon & Schuster.

Habitat for Humanity. 1999. "Habitat for Humanity Fact Sheet." Available at: *www.habitat.org/how/factsheet.html*.

Hadaway, C. Kirk, Penny Long Marler, and Mark Chaves. 1993. "What the Polls Don't Show: A Closer Look at U.S. Church Attendance." *American Sociological Review* 58: 741–52.

Hart, Stephen. 1996. *What Does the Lord Require?: How Christians Think About Economic Justice*. New Brunswick, N.J.: Rutgers University Press.

———. 2001. *Cultural Dilemmas of Progressive Politics: Styles of Engagement Among Grassroots Activists*. Chicago: University of Chicago Press.

Hatch, John W. 1981. "North Carolina Baptist Church Program." *Urban Health* (May): 70–71.

Hatch, John W., Anne E. Callan, Eugenia Eng, and Curtis Jackson. 1984. "Rediscovering Traditional Community Health Resources: The Experience of the Black Churches in the USA." *Contact* 77: 1–7.

Hatch, John W., and Kay A. Lovelace. 1980. "Involving the Southern Rural Church and Students of the Health Professions in Health Education." *Public Health Reports* 95: 23–28.

Hodgkinson, Virginia A., and Murray S. Weitzman. 1992. *Giving and Volunteering in the United States*. Washington: Independent Sector.

———. 1993. *From Belief to Commitment: The Community Service Activities and Finances of Religious Congregations in the United States*. Washington, D.C.: Independent Sector.

Hoge, Dean R., and Fenggang Yang. 1994. "Determinants of Religious Giving in American Denominations: Data from Two Nationwide Surveys." *Review of Religious Research* 36: 123–48.

Hoge, Dean R., Charles Zech, Patrick McNamara, and Michael J. Donahue. 1998. "The Value of Volunteers as Resources for Congregations." *Journal for the Scientific Study of Religion* 37: 470–80.

Jargowsky, Paul A. 1997. *Poverty and Place: Ghettos, Barrios, and the American City.* New York: Russell Sage Foundation.

Knoke, David. 1990. *Political Networks: The Structural Perspective.* New York: Cambridge University Press.

Kohut, Andrew, John C. Green, Scott Keeter and Robert C. Toth, eds. 2000. *The Diminishing Divide: Religion's Changing Role in American Politics.* Washington, D.C.: Brookings Institute.

McAdam, Doug. 1982. *Political Process and the Development of Black Insurgency, 1930–1970.* Chicago: University of Chicago Press.

McCarthy, John D., and Jim Castelli. 1994. *Working for Justice: The Campaign for Human Development and Poor Empowerment Groups.* Washington, D.C.: Life Cycle Institute, Catholic University.

Miller, Mike. 1987. "Organizing: A Map for Explorers." *Christianity and Crisis* 47(2): 1.

Morris, Aldon. 1984. *The Origins of the Civil Rights Movement: Black Communities Organizing for Change.* New York: Free Press; London: Collier Macmillan.

Olson, Daniel V. A. 1989. "Church Friendships: Boon or Barrier to Church Growth?" *Journal for the Scientific Study of Religion* 28: 432–47.

Olson, Mancur, Jr. 1965. *The Logic of Collective Action : Public Goods and the Theory of Groups.* Cambridge, Mass.: Harvard University Press.

Portes, Alejandro, and Patricia Landolt. 1996. "The Downside of Social Capital." *The American Prospect* 26(May–June): 18–22.

Rader, Victoria. 1986. *Signal Through the Flames: CCNV, Mitch Snyder, and America's Homeless.* Kansas City, Mo.: Sheed and Ward.

Reitzes, Donald C., and Dietrich C. Reitzes. 1987. *The Alinsky Legacy: Alive and Kicking.* Greenwich, Conn.: JAI Press.

Robinson, Buddy, and Mark G. Hanna. 1994. "Lessons for Academics from Grassroots Community Organizing: A Case Study—The Industrial Areas Foundation." *Journal of Community Practice* 1: 63–94.

Rogers, Mary Beth. 1990. *Cold Anger: A Story of Faith and Power Politics.* Denton: University of North Texas Press.

Rooney, Jim. 1995. *Organizing the South Bronx.* Albany: State University of New York Press.

Schneider, Jo Anne. 1999. "Trusting That of God in Everyone: Three Examples of Quaker Based Social Service in Disadvantaged Communities." *Nonprofit and Voluntary Sector Quarterly* 28(3): 269–95.

Skocpol, Theda. 1999. "How Americans Became Civic." In *Civic Engagement in American Democracy,* edited by Theda Skocpol and Morris P. Fiorina. Washington, D.C.: Brookings Institution/Russell Sage Foundation.

Smith, Christian, ed. 1996. *Disruptive Religion: The Force of Faith in Social Movement Activism.* New York: Routledge.

Speer, Paul W. 1995. "Community Organizing: An Ecological Route to Empowerment and Power." *American Journal of Community Psychology* 23(October): 729–48.

Takayama, K. Peter, and Susanne B. Darnell. 1979. "The Aggressive Organization and the Reluctant Environment: The Vulnerability of an Interfaith Coordinating Agency." *Review of Religious Research* 20(summer): 315–34.

Tamney, Joseph B., and Stephen D. Johnson. 1990. "Religious Diversity and Ecumenical Social Action." *Review of Religious Research* 32(summer): 16–26.

Teachman, Jay D., Kathleen Paasch, and Karen Carver. 1997. "Social Capital and the Generation of Human Capital." *Social Forces* 75: 1343–59.

Teen Challenge. 1999. "About Teen Challenge." Available at: *www.teenchallenge.com/main/tc/abouttci.htm*.

Texas IAF Network. 1990. *Texas IAF Network: Vision, Values, Action*. Austin: Texas Industrial Areas Foundation.

Thomas, Stephen B., Sandra Crouse Quinn, Andrew Billingsley, and Cleopatra Caldwell. 1994. "The Characteristics of Northern Black Churches with Community Health Outreach Programs." *American Journal of Public Health* 84: 575–79.

Verba, Sidney, Kay Lehman Schlozman, and Henry E. Brady. 1995. *Voice and Equality: Civic Voluntarism in American Politics*. Cambridge, Mass.: Harvard University Press.

Warner, R. Stephen. 1993. "Work in Progress Toward a New Paradigm for the Sociology of Religion in the United States." *American Journal of Sociology* 98: 1044–93.

Warren, Mark R. 1998. "Community Building and Political Power." *American Behavioral Scientist* 42(September): 78–92.

———. 2001. *Dry Bones Rattling: Community Building to Revitalize American Democracy*. Princeton, N.J.: Princeton University Press.

Warren, Mark R., and Richard L. Wood. 2001. "Building Bridges in the Public Sphere: Findings from a National Survey of Faith-Based Organizing." Paper presented to the Religion and Culture Workshop, Princeton University, April 27.

Wiist, William H., and John M. Flack. 1990. "A Church-Based Cholesterol Education Program." *Public Health Reports* 105: 381–88.

Wilcox, Clyde. 1992. *God's Warriors: The Christian Right in Twentieth-Century America*. Baltimore: Johns Hopkins University Press.

Wilson, John, and Thomas Janoski. 1995. "The Contribution of Religion to Volunteer Work." *Sociology of Religion* 56: 137–52.

Wilson, William Julius. 1996. *When Work Disappears: The World of the New Urban Poor*. New York: Random House.

Wineburg, Robert J. 1990–91. "A Community Study on the Ways Religious Congregations Support Individuals and Human Service Networks." *Journal of Applied Social Sciences* 15: 51–74.

Wiseman, James. 1997. "The Interfaith Conference of Metropolitan Washington." *Journal of Ecumenical Studies* 34: 223–38.

Wood, Richard L. 1999. "Religious Culture and Political Action." *Sociological Theory* 17(3): 307–32.

Wuthnow, Robert. 1996. "The Religion Industry: Further Thoughts on Producing the Sacred." Paper presented at the annual meeting of the Society for the Scientific Study of Religion, Nashville, Tenn. (November 9).

Youniss, James, Jeffrey A. McLellan, and Miranda Yates. 1997. "What We Know About Engendering Civic Identity." *American Behavioral Scientist* 40(5): 620–31.

Youniss, James, and Miranda Yates. 1997. *Community Service and Social Responsibility in Youth*. Chicago: University of Chicago Press.

Chapter 10

Capitalizing on Labor's Capital

Margaret Levi

The recent history of labor organizations in attacking poverty and building the social capital of poor communities is a complex one. Unions have been a major force in improving the salaries, working and living conditions, and health of workers in the United States. Nonetheless, racism, sexism, and xenophobia continue to mark segments of the labor movement, and many unions have been more concerned with servicing their dues-paying members than with building movement organizations or using their political and economic resources to combat persistent social and economic inequality. Even so, as this chapter attempts to demonstrate, there have been important efforts by unionists to build coalitions with community groups.

The "new leadership" of the AFL-CIO has pledged to correct past shortcomings of the American labor movement and to revitalize the role of unions in political and economic development. Unions have the resources in money and votes to influence policy as well as to actually assist communities and community groups. There have been success stories in the past and present, but there are also serious obstacles to building coalitions between unions and communities of poor people, particularly poor people of color.

The major obstacle is the long history of distrust grounded in the experiences of unions and community-based groups with each other. Even when unions proffer alliance or direct support to community groups, they may be rebuffed. The behaviors that make community groups distrustful of unions have institutional bases that rest, first, in the emphasis by many unions on member service and business unionism, and second, on the laws, regulations, and policies that have intensified employer hostility and focused union attention on survival. However, the ideological and resource shifts being undertaken by the AFL-CIO national office and many central labor councils, international unions, and locals may have the effect of changing the rules and practices of unions, and the long-term secular decline in union density may refocus union attention on the need for allies.

Overcoming distrust, building coalitions, and even using resources are only part of the process by which unions can provide social capital of the sort that bridges diverse groups and builds political alliances (Warren, Thompson, and Saegert this volume; Putnam 2000, 22–24), in this instance between unions and communities of the unemployed and working poor. Equally important are the actual development of sustained organizational capacity, successful campaigns for policy change, and real improvements in the standards of living in the communities. If the union efforts make no positive difference to the quality of community life and politics, then there is less incentive for those they are trying to attract and assist to engage in future coalition partnerships.

In this chapter, I analyze the extent to which recent organizational and institutional changes by unions might enable them to assist communities of the economically disadvantaged to develop social capital. The emphasis here is on initiatives and other behavior by unions. In no way do I wish to suggest that the community organizations are passive partners; it is sometimes the community organizations that initiate an action, as with most living wage campaigns. Moreover, community groups must find the coalition beneficial, or they will not join.

For unions to contribute to the growth of social capital among the poor, the first and necessary step is overcoming the distrust among groups that have long been divided and often hostile toward each other. Only then will it be possible to forge coalitions and alliances or to make profitable use of the material resources that unions can provide. The next step may be the actual building of trust, growing out of regular interactions and becoming the basis for future partnerships over a greater range of issues. Trust may arise as union and community activists get to know each other as people and, ultimately, friends. Building trust is quite a different proposition from overcoming distrust, however, and its study requires evidence outside the scope of this chapter's investigations. After explicating the theoretical arguments for overcoming distrust, I consider the plausibility of the theory in light of four union strategies for reaching out to communities of poor people: coalition campaigns; project-labor agreements as a means to ensure employment opportunities to the underrepresented in the labor force; the actual use of union resources, such as pension funds, to create jobs, infrastructure, housing, and other services; and unionizing among low-income workers.

DISTRUST AND UNSOCIAL CAPITAL

James Coleman (1990), Robert Putnam (1993, 1995), and Francis Fukuyama (1995) conceptualize trust as one component of social capital (see also Edwards and Foley 1997). Whether trust is really an essential ingredient for widespread cooperation and exchange is not so clear, but what is clear is that distrust undermines coalitions and other forms of coordination (Levi 2000; see also Kenworthy 1997). Distrust breeds distrust, and it can widen the social and economic distance between those groups that would benefit from trust but have reasons to be mistrustful (Hardin 1993).

The primary bases for distrust are beliefs that the potential coalition partner either has competing and possibly hostile interests or is not competent to carry out the pledged action. A potential coalition partner perceived as antagonistic, incompetent, or both will be considered untrustworthy. This is especially the case when there is evidence that the potential partner does not care sufficiently about the potential trustor to take her concerns into account or otherwise lacks the incentive or capacity to fulfill a trust.[1]

The traditional relationship between unions and community groups tends to have these characteristics (see, for example, Chen and Wong 1998). Too many unions in the past have demonstrated their lack of concern for the poor, whose occupations or lack of employment either made them threats to union jobs or put them outside the union framework. Unions in the United States have often been ethnic or racial enclaves; many have restricted membership or fought immigration as a means of protecting the labor market power of those who are already union members. Certainly since the urban renewal programs of the 1960s, the experiences of both community-based groups and unions have tended to confirm that their interests in issues of economic and community development are often competing. Urban renewal projects and, more recently, stadium building, transportation programs, and downtown redevelopment may create jobs, but often at the expense of the residents and businesses of a neighborhood. Those in community-based organizations (CBOs) have often found themselves in opposition to union positions on urban development while being denied jobs in union-supported building projects that raze their homes and neighborhoods.

Unions, on the other hand, find that projects for which they have won hard-fought battles to ensure employer neutrality and jobs for union members are put at risk by the protests and lobbying of community groups. They find themselves put on the defensive by political and legal attacks on union apprentice programs and exclusive practices, and at least some of these attacks appear to have sources and support in community groups.

Distrust also has roots in lack of confidence in the political and economic competence of potential coalition partners. Unions fear that community groups lack the numbers and discipline necessary to mobilize all the people they promise to bring to the picket line, hearing, or ballot box. Community groups perceive unions as part of the establishment in the way they practice politics and economics.

Overcoming Distrust

Unions have some old and some new incentives for overcoming the mutual distrust between their members and community residents and groups. The advance of the labor social agenda would benefit from the active political support of community-based organizations. But the more pressing incentive is union survival. The labor movement needs to increase union density, or at least slow its decline, and this concern has led AFL-CIO strategists to encourage organizing drives among service and low-wage workers, who are often people of color or recent immigrants. Success in organizing such groups often requires community support.

These reasons are the basis for the union interest and demand in overcoming mutual distrust, but what would motivate community groups to ally with labor? Sometimes they share common interests around a particular campaign, sometimes there are overlapping memberships or other bases for social networks that encourage reciprocity, and generally unions have resources that CBOs need in money and people who can protest and vote. The argument of this chapter is that it is not enough for unions to identify and build on common interests, nor even to develop social networks based on interdependency and reciprocity. What is most important is that unions provide credible commitments that demonstrate their concern for the poor and their willingness and capacity to carry out promises.

Some of the problems in building a coalition are the result of real differences in interests, at least short-term interests. Many union officers and rank and file believe that the only concern of the union should be membership service, and even those committed to organizing will make alliances only when they are certain that the result will be new members in a fairly short time span. Sometimes a misperception or contested interpretation of interests undermines recognition of shared interests. Unions do not count the poor as part of the working-class coalition unless they work or are temporarily laid off from a union kind of industry, and community groups are not always aware of the extent to which union members are working poor. In fact, both groups have a similar stake in winning affordable housing, health care and social insurance, and a living wage. They also can make their interests more compatible around major transportation and construction projects.

Common interests are insufficient, however, to overcome distrust. In fact, free-rider problems are an effect of the disjunction between common and individual interests. All parties may prefer the provision of the collective good to its non-provision, yet would prefer even more the benefits of the collective good without bearing its costs. Someone who mistakenly expects others to cooperate will suffer a welfare loss, whether or not that loss is the noncooperator's gain and intention.

It is much easier for individuals to both recognize and act on their common interests when they work and live together, a point Marx and Engels made more than a century ago (1978[1848]). The overlap between work and community life creates crosscutting networks that can heighten solidarity and the capacity for collective action; such networks and social relations are exactly what many contemporary political scientists and sociologists mean by social capital.[2] However, these kinds of connections seem to be rare, and in fact the effect of the physical divide between neighborhood and work may be to pit interests based in community against interests based in work.[3] The development of social networks requires bringing people together in associations in which they get to know each other sufficiently to make them willing to help each other. One of the most effective means may be collective action organizations engaged in contentious politics (Tarrow 2000). Such organizations are very likely to enhance trust and reciprocity among activists if they are in fact able to build and sustain a coalition. However, coalitions are difficult to achieve even among unions, let alone between unions and non-union organizations (see, for example, Levi and Olson 2000).

There is some chance that social networks will develop as a result of the AFL-CIO's renewed emphasis on geographic, not just workplace, organizing. This may help union and community activists to discover shared causes. Historically, the central labor councils (CLCs) played a crucial role in coordinating political, social, and economic action by the working class within an urban area.[4] Union Cities, initiated in 1997, aims to create a regional strategy that fits with the current structure of labor unions and labor laws and provides the institutional preconditions for coalition building.

Arguably, the most effective way to overcome distrust is by a credible commitment, that is, procedures, rules, and institutional arrangements ensuring that the incentives of those asking to be trusted are compatible with those being asked to give their trust. Credible commitments involve not only the commitment by the trusted to serve the interests of the trustor, but automatic sanctions against the trusted if the trust is violated. Thus, the parliament was willing to vote public funds to the Crown in the eighteenth century only after the creation of institutions that assured the populace that the Crown would and could be punished for misuse of funds and would be prohibited from securing future funds (North and Weingast 1989). The Crown recognized that only by ceding its traditional prerogatives to parliament could it secure funds and ensure the continuation of the monarchy.

In the cases under consideration here, credible commitments by unions require going further than rhetorical recognition of the poor as part of the working class. They require more than dedication to minimum-wage campaigns and social insurance schemes that aid the working poor and unemployed, be they union members or not. In these cases, unions must commit resources—in money, people, and reputation—to specific community groups. The aim is to overcome distrust among specific groups of people in order to achieve particular goals in particular places.

One way to make commitments credible is by making something of value to the trusted "hostage"—to use Oliver Williamson's term (1993)—to the trustor. For unions, this means, at the minimum, giving community groups an effective veto over how the union's organizational resources and capital will be used and, at the limit, putting those resources and capital at the actual disposal of the community groups with which they are seeking an alliance. Those resources and capital will be lost to the union unless it actually delivers on its promise to stay in a campaign until the community's goals are met as well as those of the union. It also balances out inequality among alliance partners when a strong and well-organized union seeks a coalition with an emerging or weaker community organization; such inequities can contribute to resentment and be a source of distrust. In a period of union decline, the potential loss of valuable union assets sends a strong signal to community-based groups that the unions are eager to overcome traditional barriers, build trust, and develop the social networks and cooperative exchanges essential for a real and vital coalition.

STRATEGIES FOR OVERCOMING DISTRUST AND BUILDING SOCIAL CAPITAL

Coalitions

The most obvious way for unions to help build their own social capital as well as that of poor communities is by supporting campaigns that community groups have instigated. This strategy fits with the "iron rule" of the Industrial Areas Foundation (IAF): "Never do for others what they can do for themselves" (Saul Alinsky, as quoted in Cortes 1993). There are some cases in which a union campaign also serves the interests of poor people and in which it behooves unions to elicit community support. Whether labor or community organizations inaugurate the campaign, however, both must be partners in decisionmaking, and each must be able to deliver people when needed. Failure to meet these conditions will engender greater distrust, not reduce it.

The most prevalent coalitions are around living-wage campaigns and around union-organizing efforts that affect minority and immigrant communities. There are also joint efforts to ensure that large-scale development projects are union (or at least union-neutral) and provide jobs and, when appropriate, housing, to the poor as well as to the union membership; to fight poorly conceived and discriminatory welfare reforms; and to protect and extend the right to organize.

LIVING-WAGE CAMPAIGNS Numerous cities and counties around the country[5] have passed living-wage ordinances that require service contractors in projects using public money to provide a "living wage," often a wage above the federally mandated minimum wage (Kusnet 1998, 175; Medina, McBride, and Windham 1998, 51; Pollin and Luce 1998). The ordinances, at least so far, do not apply to employees of companies without government contracts (Fine 1998, 129). Living-wage legislation can be instigated by either community-based organizations, such as the IAF or ACORN (Association of Community Organizations for Reform Now), or by unions, either particular unions or CLCs. As Janice Fine notes,[6] successful campaigns require the involvement of both types of organizations from the very beginning; it is hard to bring a missing partner aboard once the action has begun. Moreover, these campaigns must be bottom-up if they are actually to produce meaningful legislation that will be enforced by demands from those to be affected and if they are to contribute to the long-term building of social networks that can be mobilized for future actions.[7] If those involved in the labor movement and those in community-based organizations begin to work together, they begin to recognize common interests and to build social networks and solidarity. If the campaign succeeds owing to their efforts, they develop greater confidence in their capacity to influence policy and make change (Lipsky and Levi 1972).

The history of the Baltimore living-wage campaign provides a case in point.[8] The catalyst to a coalition around community development and workplace organizing was the Inner Harbor development. This large-scale urban project required public subsidy, which in turn depended on support—or at least the absence of protest and resistance—from the city's predominantly black population. An alliance was formed between BUILD (Baltimoreans United in Leadership Development), an IAF organization, and the international AFSCME (American Federation of State, County, and Municipal Employees), the largest union representing government employees. The immediate result was an intensive joint organizing campaign, especially among building service workers such as janitors.

The first step was to encourage the mayor to pass a "right to organize" ordinance, which he helped to do in the summer of 1994. The legislation protects the worker by voiding the contract of a contractor who fires someone for organizing and by hiring the fired person onto the city payroll. The next step was a campaign for a living wage pegged to the inflation rate and applicable to city contractors. The Baltimore City Council passed a living-wage ordinance in 1995. The organizers believed that these two ordinances would ensure some job stability, but they failed to inhibit the firing of activists and organizers.

ACORN has also been involved in several living-wage campaigns that represent alliances between community groups and labor unions (ACORN 2001). Some of these campaigns, such as the one in Detroit, were initiated by the national AFL-CIO, some (San Jose, for instance) by the CLC, and some (as in Cook County, Illinois) by union locals and ACORN together, but all required a joint partnership and commitment of resources. There are campaigns currently under way in St. Louis, Little Rock, Dallas, and Denver.

Because the living-wage campaigns are most likely to be successful and sustained when linked with organizing drives, even failures in passing legislation, from the labor movement's point of view, can represent labor movement gains. In Houston the ordinance lost citywide but won in low-wage neighborhoods. Moreover, the joint campaign with SEIU (Service Employees International Union) Local 100 helped the union succeed in its efforts to organize Head Start workers. In New Orleans the community-labor coalition targeted hotel workers, who then became the focus of an organizing drive by HERE (Hotel and Restaurant Employees). In Oakland, where the ordinance passed, the effect was to frighten the Port Authority, which was initially excluded from the ordinance and which then commenced conversations about how to get covered by its terms.[9]

Despite these and other successes, there are inherent tensions in coalition building. Many unions do not see enough for themselves in the living-wage campaigns to justify serious or long-term involvement unless the campaigns are directly tied to organizing drives. Nor are the community groups always convinced of the benefits to them. For example, in Los Angeles the CLC started living-wage campaigns around two large-scale projects that were receiving public subsidies: the extension of the Los Angeles airport and the development of Dreamworks.[10] The aim of the labor movement was to ensure living wages not only for the construction workers but also for those involved in the janitorial services, concessions, and other occupations that would result from the projects, and they wanted to ensure job retention for those who joined the unions. Forming a coalition with community groups and churches, the CLC took the campaign to city hall, where they succeeded in winning a living-wage ordinance and worker retention. However, they still have to ensure that contractors and vendors meet the terms. Moreover, the community groups involved often disagreed among themselves and with the unions about the protections their members would receive in regard to jobs and housing from these large-scale projects. While the unions, especially those in the building trades, won protections under project labor agreements (discussed in more detail later), the poor people affected by the projects received no such binding contractual coverage. Nor were the members of the community organizations confident that labor had formed an alliance with them for the long haul. Anthony Thigpenn of AGENDA, a community organization based in South Los Angeles, argues that the labor movement has to demonstrate not only the tactical advantages but the strategic advantages of coalitions; such a demonstration requires a comprehensive and long-term regional development plan that serves the interests of both unions and communities (Levi 1998).

Unions also have their share of concerns about the community organizations and their share of internal conflicts. When the IAF or ACORN are involved from the outset, unions have assurances that there will be allies able to plan and mobilize as full partners. When no such group is involved, the unions become more wary. Moreover, there are real differences of opinion among labor activists about the value of coalition politics. The internationals and the locals are not always in agreement about strategy. Sometimes the impetus comes from one, and sometimes from the other; only occasionally are both in agreement. The AFL-CIO national, regional, and metropolitan offices add yet more layers in negotiating strategy. Even among some of the staff of CLCs committed to Union Cities, with its emphasis on regional development and organizing, there is disagreement about the value of living-wage campaigns. Unions have limited resources and must consider trade-offs. Should energy and resources be put into mobilizing for living-wage campaigns or put straight into workplace organizing? When a first contract is under negotiation, should low-wage workers hold out for the higher living wage or settle for salaries lower than those mandated by a living-wage ordinance but still representative of a victory for that local?

ANTI-SWEATSHOP CAMPAIGNS The campaigns to eliminate sweatshops in the United States often originate among community groups, and the campaigns against sweatshops internationally begin among students. These campaigns generally become coalitional campaigns with organized labor and sometimes are linked to organizing drives.

An exemplary anti-sweatshop campaign is the boycott in San Francisco of Jessica McClintock as a response by the Asian Immigrant Women Advocates (AIWA) to the complaints of Chinese immigrant women about the horrible working conditions and employer abuses they were having to bear. With the help of UNITE (Union of Needletrades, Industrial, and Textile Employees), APALA (Asian Pacific American Labor Alliance), and other labor groups, AIWA was able to help the women run a campaign and win back wages. The workers achieved concrete gains, and the unions and other advocacy groups received new coalition partners and ideas in their efforts to improve sweatshop and child labor (Needleman 1998, 74–77).

The student-inspired campaigns are quite different. Based on campuses and on using the purchasing power of the students themselves as well as the university, they are initially directed at issues of social and economic justice for workers of developing countries. What is interesting from the unionist perspective is that as students learn more about corporate and university practices, many become involved in support of living-wage and organizing campaigns on their campuses. The student occupation of the administration building at Johns Hopkins in February 2000 was intended to raise the wages of university laundry workers. In April, students at Wesleyan occupied a building and won improvements in wages and benefits for the school's janitors, and an occupation at SUNY-Albany that same month joined issues of university complicity in international sweatshops and in the practices of a union-busting food vendor, which the university subcontracted.

At first glance, such campaigns do not seem to provide evidence of union and community-based coalitions. It is students who are demonstrating, and on behalf of workers who may or may not be unionized. A closer look reveals a different picture. These campaigns are increasingly multi-racial and multi-class (Featherstone 2000). The students may initiate them, but local unions often become active partners, committing their own resources in support of the students and the affected workers. This was the case at both Hopkins and the University of Washington, where local unions provided daily meals and other forms of aid to students sleeping out in front of the administration building as part of the anti-sweatshop campaign. By joining a coalition originating with others, unions demonstrate their solidarity with a larger social movement and their willingness to act in ways not always immediately beneficial to them.

GETTING SUPPORT FOR ORGANIZING   The labor movement, recognizing its need for increased public support of union efforts, has been directly involved in the initiation of several associations whose role is to link organizations based in poor and minority communities with organizing drives and other efforts to protect the rights of workers and their standard of living.

The constituency groups of the AFL-CIO provide one example of such associations. The constituency groups are composed of trade unionists who share characteristics, such as race, national origin, or gender, that have often made them misfits within the labor movement or even subjects of discrimination. By forming an advocacy group within the larger labor movement, they help to change traditional union practices. And by providing a link between the labor movement and the specific communities of which they are members, they help create new social networks and overcome distrust. These constituency groups include the Coalition of Black Trade Unionists (CBTU), the Coalition of Labor Union Women (CLUW), and, of more recent origin, the Asian Pacific American Labor Alliance (APALA), the Labor Council for Latin American Advancement (LCLAA), and Pride at Work.

Another important development has been the creation of the Jobs with Justice (JwJ) coalitions. Inaugurated in 1987 in Miami, Jobs with Justice now has more than thirty such coalitions in twenty-one states, bringing together union, community, and religious activists and organizations on behalf of issues that affect the rights and welfare of workers and their families. JwJ encourages widespread signing of pledge cards to attend at least five actions a year on behalf of someone else's fight, and it then follows up with leaflets, mailers, and phone banks. It is thus hardly surprising that Jobs with Justice plays a key role in many locales in mobilizing people to join picket lines and demonstrations. In 1993 the Vermont Jobs with Justice started the first of the workers' rights boards (WRBs), which can now be found in more than a dozen localities. These are committees of prominent citizens drawn from the community, religious and educational institutions, legislatures, and influential organizations. The WRBs investigate violations of the rights of workers, both organized and unorganized, hold public hearings, and promote campaigns to correct abuses they have identified.

Where JwJ mobilizes support for civil rights and community actions as well as for strikes and other labor actions, it builds a network of activists who begin to recognize the overlap in the interests of unions and community-based groups. Where WRBs focus on problems that are important to poor and minority peoples, whether or not they are members of unions, they overcome distrust of unions as narrowly self-interested. For the most part, however, Jobs with Justice has support from only a limited number of unions in a growing but still small number of locales. It stands outside and apart from the mainstream labor movement. JwJ and its workers' rights boards probably have a positive effect on labor-community relations where they exist, but the actual extent of their impact remains a matter for future empirical investigation.

Project Labor Agreements

One of the domains in which unions and community-based organizations have been most hostile is over construction projects. The labor organizations representing the building trades are too often emblematic of white, racist, sexist unions. They are noted for insensitivity and outright resistance to the concerns of the poor people whose homes, jobs, and services they are displacing with the developments they are constructing, and to the women who walk by the construction site. More important, they have a history of exclusion of people of color and women from their ranks, apprenticeship programs, and the highly skilled and highly paid crafts jobs they control. Since the 1960s and 1970s, they have often found themselves under attack for discriminatory practices.

Originally motivated to protect only their own jobs and members, some building trade unions have been trying to change their reputation among people of color and women. In several locales, they have negotiated project labor agreements (PLAs) as a means to provide union security, on the one hand, and to provide job opportunities for women and minorities, on the other. These are special collective bargaining agreements unique to the building trades, establishing basic terms and conditions for all contractors on a specific construction project. In return for union assurances of high quality, on-time performance, and agreement to strict enforcement of prohibitions against work stoppages, employers agree to the use of union labor, no lockouts, job safety, and other union-favorable conditions. According to Rich Feldman, director of the Worker Center, King County Labor Council of the AFL-CIO (1999), non-union contractors may bid—and without prejudice—on a job, but "the unique characteristics of a PLA are that it requires all contractors and subcontractors to hire first out of union halls. . . . Under a PLA, all workers are required to be members of the union or to join after hiring on to the project."

In the years since the Supreme Court's ruling in the Boston Harbor case legalizing their use in government construction, PLAs have become a more common tool of the labor movement. Their major purpose is to protect the jobs and wages of traditional union members. However, in cities with construction trade and CLC leadership dedicated to using PLAs to open up opportunities for women and minorities in the construction trades, these agreements increasingly include provisions for apprenticeships. In these cities, PLAs have become not only an important basis for giving workers access to the potential of middle-class incomes but also a basis for increased coalitions between labor and community-based groups. The question remains, of course, about how widespread such progressive practices really are.

In Atlanta, for example, an alliance of organized labor and the African American community threatened to block construction if the developers for the Olympic building projects refused to agree to a PLA with minority access provisions (Feldman 1999). In Milwaukee, the PLA ensured that 25 percent of jobs went to minority group members and that minority communities also had significant control over the training opportunities (Levi 1998, 6).

In Seattle, the King County Labor Council, the metropolitan area's CLC, focused initially on the major construction being undertaken by the Port of Seattle, won a PLA, and then demonstrated that the unions would bring the project in on time and under budget.[11] That success gave the PLA credibility, and the unions went from that one to many others. In the process, the CLC, in collaboration with the building trades, took advantage of the state-approved apprenticeship programs. Working with community people, churches, and other organizations, they made sure that, from the very first PLA, 15 percent of all hours went to apprenticeship opportunities targeted at traditionally deprived groups, including people of color and women. They hope that this will have the effect of not only increasing better-paying jobs for disadvantaged individuals but also changing the view of—and actual nature of—the building trades as bastions of white male privilege (Levi 1998).

There are, of course, limits to what PLAs can achieve. First of all, they are unique to the building trades. As with the Westin Hotel project at the Seattle-Tacoma airport and the Los Angeles airport extensions, some agreements may ensure employer neutrality toward the service workers to be employed in the hotels and concessions, but these are the exception, not the rule. Second, the provision of apprenticeship positions to minorities and women of color is only a beginning and unlikely to be particularly successful unless the programs also address transportation, child care, and the particular learning problems these new workers may have (Levi 1998, 6). Third, these projects often need special taxing arrangements. Fourth, in recent years they have been more successful in public than in private construction projects, and the unions are only just beginning to consider how to extend them to a sphere where public pressure has less impact.

Project labor agreements, despite these limitations, do overcome some of the distrust of unions often most symbolic of racism and sexism. They succeed by creating credible commitments and providing access to actual jobs, at least for the term of the project the agreement covers. The commitment of the building trades to building alliances would be even more credible, however, if they made more of their resources hostage to these new workers by giving them actual union cards and ongoing access to jobs and training.[12]

Capital Investments

Unions have several major financial resources they can put to use in assisting poor people. Most significant are their pension funds, but there are also other forms of deferred workers' savings. If community groups suspect that unions are using them for tactical advantage but lack a long-term commitment to the interests of poor people, the investment of workers' money—money on which they will rely for their retirements—is a way to put their funds hostage. Investments in housing and long-term economic redevelopment plans that benefit poor people as well as higher-paid union members can represent a credible commitment.

BUILDING HOUSING   Unions have been involved in helping to develop workers' housing since the nineteenth century, but the more recent efforts date from the years following World War II. Although such housing does not always reach the poorest sectors of the population, it has often been an important source of housing for low-income workers and has ensured that the cities, even in the midst of the 1960s redevelopment projects, retained affordable housing for working families. The financing for these housing developments usually comes from the pension funds of particular unions, but it can come from a coalition of unions, spearheaded by a CLC.

The first cooperative housing project on the West Coast, St. Francis Square, was a project of the ILWU (International Longshore and Warehouse Union) in San Francisco in 1960. The aim was to provide decent, affordable housing within the city for working families, regardless of race, color, creed, or national origin. The trustees of the Longshore pension fund, jointly administered by the ILWU and the Pacific Maritime Association (PMA), bought land full price in the Western Addition after unsuccessfully appealing to the mayor and the Redevelopment Authority to ensure the minimum land price set by the authority. With an FHA loan, the ILWU-PMA built 299 middle-income garden apartments and provided low-interest loans through the FHA. The terms of sale prevent purchase for speculation and provide for an ownership share in the project and for self-government. Although the pension fund could get a higher return for its money in other kinds of investment, this is an instance of a union making a commitment to social goals at a cost to itself.[13]

St. Francis Square catered to moderate-income working families, but more recent projects have focused on households with even lower incomes whose members may indeed be working but at wages that do not permit home purchase or even payment of rent for decent housing in major metropolitan areas. In 1964 the AFL-CIO started the Housing Investment Trust (HIT), in which pension funds, whose beneficiaries are union members, are invested in loans for housing construction by union contractors and mortgage loans. The investor participants include 394 public-sector and Taft-Hartley pension plans, whose total gross rate of return from HIT is a competitive 11.22 percent. By the end of 1997, the trust's net assets were $1.67 billion, an all-time high and one that represents a 3 percent increase in reinvestment by participants (AFL-CIO 1998, 3).

In St. Louis, Boston, and elsewhere, at least some of the new construction in housing has been for low-income households (AFL-CIO 1998, 5–6). In 1997 the trust began developing a partnership with the Department of Housing and Urban Development (HUD) to revitalize public housing, but its major new venture was the Homeownership Opportunity Initiative, a $250 million three-year partnership between HIT and Fannie Mae. The aim is to construct and make available homes for low-, moderate-, and middle-income households in thirteen pilot cities (AFL-CIO 1998, 7). The initiative provides an extremely flexible and affordable mortgage program and a lower-than-market-rate contribution from the borrower. Each selected municipality had to develop a suitable set of partnerships with local governments and banks. Seattle, for example, received an allocation of $30 million as a result of a partnership that includes the city of Seattle, King County, and Continental Savings Bank as well as the King County Labor Council, HIT, and Fannie Mae (AFL-CIO Housing Investment Trust 1998).

The major beneficiaries of these projects are union members, however, or those willing to join unions. The jobs created, the best financing, and other such advantages disproportionately accrue to union members. Of course, low-wage workers, be they union or not, can belong to the working poor or to traditionally disadvantaged groups. Moreover, the creation of affordable housing in the inner cities ensures that these metropolitan areas will continue to be diverse and that their neighborhoods will not become bastions of only the rich or only the poor.[14]

VENTURE CAPITAL   Workers' money can also have an important impact in revitalizing depressed communities. By providing venture capital for firms that would be unable to continue or start up, labor-sponsored investment funds can help sustain and create jobs (Hebb 1996; Moburg 1998; Schlesinger and Markey 1996; and Fung et al. 2001).

The models for this kind of investment are four Canadian funds (Kreiner 1996). The first labor-sponsored venture capital corporation, the Quebec Solidarity Fund, was a response in 1984 by the Quebec Federation of Labour (FTQ) to persistent high unemployment. The Working Opportunity Fund in British Columbia, the Crocus Fund in Manitoba, and the First Ontario Fund in Ontario were built on the model created by the FTQ. All provide equity interest in small and medium-size businesses that pass a "social audit" of their labor relations and employment, health, safety, and environmental practices and that agree to high-road workplaces. The criteria for investment include the probability of a positive effect on job retention and economic regional development as well as competitive returns for the funds.

The Canadian funds draw on workers' savings and call on federal and provincial governments to provide tax credits for investing in these union-created funds, which in turn go to support small and medium-size Canadian businesses. Regional labor investment funds have been undertaken in Pittsburgh with the involvement of the United Steelworkers of America and are currently being organized in Seattle (Croft, Bute, and Feldman 1996).

Unionizing Low-Income Workers

The commitment of union resources to organizing low-income workers can be mutually beneficial to both the labor movement and community groups. These drives can result in a significant increase in union membership while also giving the labor movement new allies and support groups among minority, immigrant, and working poor. At the same time, they indicate organized labor's commitment to overcoming the usual definitions of who is "union." The newly organized may gain considerable improvements in wages, working conditions, and job security while also gaining the confidence to act collectively on behalf of economic and social issues of consequence to them.

Four of the most successful organizing drives of this kind have been among janitorial staff in New York, Washington, D.C., and Los Angeles, sweatshop workers in New York and San Francisco, hotel and restaurant employees in Las Vegas, and home-care workers in California. The targets of these drives are disproportionately people of color, immigrants, and women, groups with backgrounds different from those of the bulk of the union membership. Most union locals have developed a system of representation based in another language or languages and another gender or racial group, and they are not well prepared to represent another. If the unions are to organize these workers, they must form alliances with the organizations involved with the relevant groups; these are the organizations to whom the workers are most likely to turn first before turning to the union. At the same time, the community-based organizations lack the skills to organize or affect the workplace. Together, however, the labor movement and the community associations can build effective organizations to secure economic justice for these workers.

Both the SEIU's Justice for Janitors (JfJ) (see, for example, Waldinger et al. 1998) and HERE's wall-to-wall organizing of the employees of the Las Vegas casinos and hotels provide excellent cases of the new kind of community-based union organizing. Reminiscent in some ways of the nineteenth-century social movements, these union drives won members and political allies in unexpected numbers and among unexpected groups. However, such successes sometimes come at the cost of local rebellion against campaigns that are so much more the program of the international than of the local. This was what happened with JfJ in Los Angeles, and that reaction may undermine the long-term achievement there (Waldinger et al. 1998, 118–19). Also worrying are the renewed and increased instances of employer hostility and mobilization in many regions of the country.

Sometimes organizing drives have also led to coalitions grounded in providing services for workers. For example, the campaign by SEIU 616 to organize home-care workers in the San Francisco Bay Area led to a recognition that the largely minority and female population of home-care workers needed a variety of services and supports that unions did not often—if ever—provide (Needleman 1998, 78–82). SEIU consequently turned to organizations such as the Labor Project for Working Families to provide a service center for the African American, Mexican, Central American, and Filipino women whom SEIU 616 was trying to reach. The partnership between SEIU and the Labor Project facilitated access to funding, produced a real team effort—and a real team—among the union and community organizers, and offered the kinds of services and networks that the workers needed to maintain their commitment to the union. This strategy bore fruit in Los Angeles in February 1999 when seventy-five thousand home-care workers, in the largest election ever won by the AFL-CIO, voted to affiliate with the SEIU. This victory appears to have provoked serious gubernatorial proposals to significantly improve the wages and benefits of home-care workers in the state.

UNITE has also recognized the need for service centers for minority and immigrant garment workers toiling in the sweatshops, and the union has created its own garment workers justice centers (GWJCs) in New York City, Miami, Los Angeles, and San Francisco (Ness 1998). The long-term goal of the centers is to use a neighborhood base to unionize workers in a dispersed and highly competitive industry, but their immediate goals are to provide ideological and material support to workers and to create the capacity for collective action. The GWJCs are open to nonmembers as well as the members of UNITE and offer skills training, language education, and education about immigrants' rights in the country and in the workplace. Clearly, UNITE hopes the GWJCs will be not merely settlement houses but the base for industrial organizing. In a survey of individuals coming to the GWJC in New York's fashion district, Immanual Ness (1998, 95–100) found that the centers do engender support for unionization and collective action. Nonetheless, there are three major problems with this strategy from UNITE's perspective. First, the GWJCs may accomplish the important goal of assisting the workers, but they do little to insulate manufacturers from contractors who are able to move to where there is less organizing and workers are more willing to accept lower pay and worse conditions. Second, the nature of contract unionism makes it difficult for UNITE to protect non-unionized workers. Finally, however much the GWJCs may contribute to increasing union density, it will be a long process; in the meantime, the unions may lose patience with using their limited resources to support service centers rather than direct, workplace organizing.

UNITE's experience with service centers is in fact emblematic of the problem that unions face in promoting social capital in poor communities. Where unions focus their skills is on negotiating collective bargaining contracts and obtaining union coverage of the previously organized or unorganized. In a period of union decline, unions are willing to try new strategies (and in some cases, revive old ones) and to reach out to new partners and allies, but they also need results sooner rather than later. For most local leaders, even international leaders, it is not enough simply to have a long-term vision; being subject to periodic reelection, they must also demonstrate success in attracting members and winning contracts.

Most workers' centers are not affiliated with unions. One example is the Workplace Project on Long Island (Fine 1998, 133–36). This center has the relative advantage of being organized and owned by the immigrants it is meant to serve. However, it also reveals the continuing problems that bedevil the relationship between unions and immigrants: the lack of bilingual organizers and business agents, the bureaucratic approach of the union staff, and most important, the continuing demonstration of indifference, or at least lack of enthusiasm, for the immigrants' complaints, concerns, and needs. It appears evident that unions will have to invest in their own social capital if they are to be effective in promoting the social capital of the poor and unorganized.

How Real Is the Promise?

As this new millennium dawns, organized labor in the United States is forging major new alliances and committing its own resources to do so. Nowhere was this illustrated more dramatically than in Seattle during the week of the WTO ministerial meetings, November 29 to December 3, 1999 (see, for example, Levi and Olson 2000). The AFL-CIO and its member internationals mobilized money and people for the demonstration by more than thirty thousand protesters on November 30, and its leadership was actively involved in coordinating efforts with the full spectrum of protesters. "Teamsters and Turtles" symbolizes the emerging link between unionists and environmentalists, but there are also important links being forged with groups representing immigrants, people of color, students, and others who have felt marginalized or ignored by organized labor. There are important stirrings of a truly internationalist and culturally pluralistic union movement.

Yet most of these new allies remain skeptical about their long-term relationship with organized labor—and with good reason. The AFL-CIO and the internationals still tend to be highly hierarchical and bureaucratic—certainly more so than the new social movement and community-based organizations. Although they have engaged in major efforts to rid the unions of racism, labor leaders are still disproportionately white men—as could be attested by anyone who attended the rally preceding the AFL-CIO march. Homophobia is still prevalent in the unions, although there have been heroic efforts within the labor movement to change itself (Hollibaugh and Singh 1999).

The greatest change has been among the ranks of organizers and local leadership, where the proportion of people of color, women, and immigrants has increased; more and more of these unionists are engaged in transforming traditional union culture to make it more open to those who do not fit the stereotypes of the rank and file. The stories captured by Ruth Milkman and Kent Wong (2000) reveal both how much the labor movement has changed and how far it still has to go to be credible among a truly diverse population and to fundamentally refurbish its organizing and governance structures (see also Fletcher and Hurd 2000).

CONCLUSION

Both unions and community organizations can benefit from working together. The community organizations provide access to low-wage workers and help the unions overcome the distrust or fear with which their efforts might otherwise be greeted. The unions offer resources in money and people and real experience in improving conditions and wages in the workplace. The union can provide a fixed point in an economy in which there is considerable job turnover and labor mobility (Fine 1998, 126). Finally, the unions can be sources of capital, job-creating programs, and housing.

The advantages may be clear to the outside observer, but they are not always so apparent to the on-site participants. The major goal of the labor movement in the United States right now is to increase union density by attracting new members and retaining old ones. Without membership, it is impossible for the labor movement to carry out other important goals: winning contracts, raising the living standard of Americans, securing economic and social justice, pursuing regional development. Moreover, unions are diverse: the differences among various locals, internationals, and CLCs are vast. Not all see organizing as primary, and many believe that their only function is to serve the bread-and-butter needs of their membership.

Although the labor movement and community-based organizations both benefit from unionizing low-wage workers and providing them with higher salaries, better working conditions, benefits, and enhanced political efficacy, this shared interest is not enough for a sustained and joint war on poverty and discrimination. The kinds of campaigns, coalitions, and investments described in this chapter can go a long way toward overcoming distrust, creating credible commitments, and building the social networks essential for a significant labor role in facilitating the development of social capital among the poor and minorities. Bringing workplace and neighborhood together produces friendships, trust, better understanding of the needs and concerns of the other, and thus the groundwork for further collective action and more equal partnerships.

Perhaps the most important factor in overcoming the well-grounded distrust of community groups toward coalitions with unions is the union's willingness to make its organizers, investment funds, and other resources hostage to the community groups it is seeking as partners. Making resources hostage provides a credible commitment—evidence, that is, that the union means what it says when it claims to be contributing to the development of social capital in a poor community.

There is little question that the labor movement capitalizes on the social capital of poor communities as it tries to extend its organizing among low-wage workers, immigrants, and people of color. It may even be the case that labor gains more from the community than it gives. The fact that labor has a stake in these communities can also, however, work to the advantage of the communities. That stake gives the community group a bargaining chip in negotiating decisionmaking power in joint campaigns, a veto over strategy and goals, and greater resources.

The alliance between labor and community organizations can also benefit community-based organizations. There will continue to be small and significant success stories as long as there are unionists—and there are many of them—pledged to organizing low-income workers and overcoming poverty and discrimination as part of their core mission. Nevertheless, potential community group partners will remain wary—and should remain so—as long as the labor movement is perceived as using its partners for its own immediate goals or is perceived as so split that its credibility as an effective and long-term partner is in doubt. Capitalizing on the labor movement's political resources, social networks, and actual capital nonetheless can be a means to enhance the social capital of poor people attempting to build the organizational infrastructure necessary to transform their neighborhoods and circumstances.

This research is based partially on work done in the Trust Project, funded by the Russell Sage Foundation. I wish to thank Theresa Buckley for her extraordinary research assistance. I also wish to thank Victoria Hattam, Janice Fine, Sid Tarrow, Jess Walsh, the students in my undergraduate research seminar, and the editors of this volume for their thoughtful and useful comments.

NOTES

1. I am generally following Russell Hardin's definition of trust (1998, 12), but with some modifications (Levi 2000).

2. It is social networks that Putnam claims he now means by social capital, as he argued in his remarks to the conference at which drafts of this volume's papers were presented and to one at Duke in October 1998 (see Putnam 2000, 19).

3. And as Ira Katznelson (1981) has shown, in the United States the split between the political and economic lives of workers often undermines political militancy or allows ethnicity to be the more crucial determinant in politics than class. In her work, Janice Fine (1998) argues that racialization today tends to reinforce class identity among the low-wage workers in African American, Latino, immigrant, and other ethnic communities. See also the discussion in Putnam (2000, passim) about the effects of suburbanization and commuting.

4. Colin Gordon (1999) documents this strategy and offers an explanation of its demise that makes him skeptical that it could be resuscitated.

5. For the most recent counts, see ACORN (2001), which enumerates fifty-eight as of March 2001 but recently reported several more, and Employment Policies Institute (2001), which maintains an alternative current list by state.

6. Fine's statements are drawn from notes taken for Levi (1998).

7. Ron Judd, executive secretary of the King County Labor Council, AFL-CIO, describes how he has had to resist the efforts of Seattle and King County council persons to initiate such legislation before the community and union base were ready. Steve Kest, executive director of ACORN, has had similar experiences and also argues that it is essential that it be a grassroots movement if it is to build the kind of power base necessary to sustain the change (see Levi 1998).

8. This description of the campaign is drawn from that provided by Arnie Graff of the Industrial Areas Foundation and recorded by Levi (1998), Fine (1998), and Walsh (1999).

9. These examples are drawn from the verbal description offered by ACORN Executive Director Steve Kest (Levi 1998).

10. This paragraph draws largely on the remarks of Miguel Contreras of the Los Angeles County Federation of Labor and Anthony Thigpenn of AGENDA (Levi 1998).

11. This paragraph draws largely on the remarks of Ron Judd, executive secretary of the KCLC (Levi 1998).

12. Janice Fine made this point to me.

13. The information on St. Francis Square comes from material in the ILWU archives in San Francisco. This includes a press release (June 10, 1960) and an article in *The Dispatcher* (1963).

14. Janice Fine told me in an e-mail (May 15, 1999) that the best contemporary example is in Stamford, Connecticut, where a multi-union organizing project is working in coalition with black ministers. The AFL-CIO is helping to staff and fund a campaign for affordable housing as well as putting money into the actual development of housing.

REFERENCES

ACORN (Association of Community Organizations for Reform Now). 2001. "Living Wage Campaigns." Available at: *www.livingwagecampaign.org/index.html.*

AFL-CIO. 1998. "Housing Investment Trust Annual Report 1997." Washington, D.C.: AFL-CIO.

AFL-CIO Housing Investment Trust. 1998. "AFL-CIO Housing Investment Trust and Fannie Mae Bring National $250 Million Homeownership Opportunity Initiative to Seattle: Mayor Paul Schell, County Executive Ron Sims, and King County Labor Council (AFL-CIO) Executive Secretary Ron Judd Announce Partnership to Benefit Area's Homeowners." News release, March 19. Washington, D.C.: AFL-CIO.

AFL-CIO Investment Program. 1997. *Investor* (Winter).

Chen, May, and Kent Wong. 1998. "The Challenge of Diversity and Inclusion in the AFL-CIO." In *A New Labor Movement for a New Century,* edited by Gregory Mantsios. New York: Monthly Review Press.

Coleman, James S. 1990. *Foundations of Social Theory.* Cambridge, Mass.: Harvard University Press.

Cortes, Ernesto. 1993. "Reweaving the Fabric: The Iron Rule and IAF Strategy for Power and Politics." In *Interwoven Destinies: Cities and the Nation,* edited by Henry G. Cisneros. New York: Norton.

Croft, Thomas, Joseph Bute Jr., and Rich Feldman. 1996. "The Regional Labor Investment Fund: The Critical Nexus for a National Investment Strategy." Paper presented at the Industrial Heartland Labor Investment Forum, sponsored by the United Steelworkers of America, the AFL-CIO Industrial Union Department, the AFL-CIO Public Employee Department, and the Steel Valley Authority, Pittsburgh (June 14–16).

The Dispatcher. 1963. "Pioneer ILWU Project Near Completion." (January 25): 4–5.

Edwards, Bob, and Michael W. Foley, eds. 1997. *Social Capital, Civil Society, and Contemporary Democracy.* Special issue of *American Behavioral Scientist* 40(5). Thousand Oaks, Calif.: Sage Periodicals Press.

Employment Policies Institute. 2001. "LivingWage.org." Available at: *www.epionline.org/livingwageframe.htm.*

Featherstone, Liz. 2000. "The New Student Movement." *The Nation* 270(19): 11–18.

Feldman, Rich. 1999. Telephone interview with the author, 15 May 1999.

Fine, Janice. 1998. "Moving Innovation from the Margin to the Center." In *A New Labor Movement for a New Century,* edited by Gregory Mantsios. New York: Monthly Review Press.

Fletcher, Bill, Jr., and Richard W. Hurd. 2000. "Is Organizing Enough?: Race, Gender, and Union Culture." *New Labor Forum* 6(Spring-Summer): 58–69.

Fukuyama, Francis. 1995. *Trust.* New York: Basic Books.

Fung, Archon, Tessa Hebb, Joel Rogers, and Leo Gerard, eds. 2001. *Working Capital: The Power of Labor's Pensions.* Ithaca, N.Y.: Cornell University Press.

Gordon, Colin. 1999. "The Lost City of Solidarity: Metropolitan Unionism in Historical Perspective." *Politics and Society* 27(4): 561–85.

Hardin, Russell. 1993. "The Street Level Epistemology of Trust." *Politics and Society* 21(4): 505–29.

———. 1998. "Trust in Government." In *Trust and Governance,* edited by Valerie Braithwaite and Margaret Levi. New York: Russell Sage Foundation.

Hebb, Tessa. 1996. "U.S. Private Placement Debt Markets in the 1990s." Paper presented at the Industrial Heartland Labor Investment Forum, sponsored by the United Steelworkers of America, the AFL-CIO Industrial Union Department, the AFL-CIO Public Employee Department, and the Steel Valley Authority, Pittsburgh (June 14–16).

Hollibaugh, Amber, and Nikhil Pal Singh. 1999. "Sexuality, Labor, and the New Trade Unionism." *Social Text* 61(Winter): 73–88.

Katznelson, Ira. 1981. *City Trenches.* New York: Pantheon Books.

Kenworthy, Lane. 1997. "Civic Engagement, Social Capital, and Economic Cooperation." *American Behavioral Scientist* 40(5): 645–56.

Kreiner, Sherman. 1996. "Labor-Sponsored Investment Funds in Canada." Paper presented at the Industrial Heartland Labor Investment Forum, sponsored by the United Steelworkers of America, the AFL-CIO Industrial Union Department, the AFL-CIO Public Employee Department, and the Steel Valley Authority, Pittsburgh (June 14–16).

Kusnet, David. 1998. "The 'America Needs a Raise' Campaign: The New Labor Movement and the Politics of Living Standards." In *Not Your Father's Union Movement,* edited by JoAnn Mort. London: Verso.

Levi, Margaret, ed. 1998. "Notes on the Metro Unionism Conference." Seattle: University of Washington (June 12–14).

————. 2000. "When Good Defenses Make Good Neighbors." In *Institutions, Contracts, and Organizations: Perspectives from New Institutional Economics,* edited by Claude Menard. Colchester, Eng.: Edward Elgar.

Levi, Margaret, and David Olson. 2000. "The Battles in Seattle." *Politics and Society* 28(3): 217–37.

Lipsky, Michael, and Margaret Levi. 1972. "Community Organization as a Political Resource." In *People and Politics in Urban Society,* edited by Harlan Hahn. Beverly Hills, Calif.: Sage Publications.

Marx, Karl, and Friedrich Engels. 1978[1848]. *Manifesto of the Communist Party.* In *The Marx-Engels Reader,* edited by Robert C. Tucker, 2nd ed. New York: W.W. Norton.

Medina, Kim, Elissa McBride, and Lane Windham, eds. 1998. *Faculty@Work.* Washington, D.C.: AFL-CIO Organizing Institute.

Milkman, Ruth, and Kent Wong, eds. 2000. *Voices from the Front Lines.* Los Angeles: Center for Labor Education and Research, University of California at Los Angeles.

Moburg, David. 1998. "Labor's Capital Strategies." In *Not Your Father's Union Movement,* edited by Jo-Ann Mort. London: Verso.

Needleman, Ruth. 1998. "Building Relationships for the Long Haul: Unions and Community-Based Groups Working Together to Organize Low-Wage Workers." In *Organizing to Win,* edited by Kate Bronfenbrenner, Sheldon Friedman, Richard W. Hurd, Rudolph Oswald, and Ronald L. Seeber. Ithaca, N.Y.: ILR Press.

Ness, Immanual. 1998. "Organizing Immigrant Communities: UNITE's Workers Center Strategy." In *Organizing to Win,* edited by Kate Bronfenbrenner, Sheldon Friedman, Richard W. Hurd, Rudolph Oswald, and Ronald L. Seeber. Ithaca, N.Y.: ILR Press.

North, Douglass C., and Barry R. Weingast. 1989. "Constitutions and Commitment: The Evolution of Institutions Governing Public Choice in Seventeenth Century England." *Journal of Economic History* 49(4): 803–32.

Pollin, Robert, and Stephanie Luce. 1998. *The Living Wage: Building a Fair Economy.* New York: The New York Press.

Putnam, Robert D. 1993. *Making Democracy Work: Civic Traditions in Modern Italy.* Princeton, N.J.: Princeton University Press.

————. 1995. "Bowling Alone, Revisited." *The Responsive Community* (Spring): 18–33.

————. 2000. *Bowling Alone.* New York: Simon & Schuster.

Schlesinger, Tom, and Regina Markey. 1996. "America's Restructured Financial System: The Role of Workers' Savings and Impediments to Long-term Investing in Jobs." Paper presented at the Industrial Heartland Labor Investment Forum, sponsored by the United Steelworkers of America, the AFL-CIO Industrial Union Department, the AFL-CIO Public Employee Department, and the Steel Valley Authority, Pittsburgh (June 14–16).

Tarrow, Sidney. 2000. "Mad Cows and Activists: Contentious Politics in the Trilateral Democracies." In *Disaffected Democracies: What's Troubling the Trilateral Democracies,* edited by Susan J. Pharr and Robert D. Putnam. Princeton, N.J.: Princeton University Press.

Waldinger, Roger, Chris Erickson, Ruth Milkman, Daniel J. B. Mitchell, Abel Valenzuela, Kent Wong, and Maurice Zeitlin. 1998. "Helots No More: A Case Study of the Justice for Janitors Campaign in Los Angeles." In *Organizing to Win,* edited by Kate Bronfenbrenner, Sheldon Friedman, Richard W. Hurd, Rudolph Oswald, and Ronald L. Seeber. Ithaca, N.Y.: ILR Press.

Walsh, Jess. 1999. "Organizing the Scale of Labor Regulation in the United States Service Sector: Activism in the City." Adelaide, Australia: Faculty of Architecture, Building, and Planning, University of Adelaide. Unpublished paper.

Williamson, Oliver E. 1993. "Calculativeness, Trust, and Economic Organization." *Journal of Law and Economics* 34: 453–500.

Chapter 11

Social Capital, Intervening Institutions, and Political Power

Cathy J. Cohen

As we enter the new millennium, we find ourselves grappling once again with the question of social capital. This time the social capital of which we speak (or at least the social capital that will be central in this discussion) consists of the networks, trust, norms, and interactions in which people engage daily to both survive and to become enriched. For many political scientists, social capital, especially in the form of associations and informal affiliations, is the building block of civil society. Through such formal and informal activity, residents learn lessons of reciprocity and trust, build networks that can be used to tackle local problems, and develop skills and resources that can be deployed in formal political institutions. It is therefore not surprising that, in a time when the promise of universal citizenship seems available to most, scholars would turn to organizations, trust, networks, and associations to explain what appears to be the waning of participatory democracy in the United States.

In this chapter, I briefly explore how the concept of social capital is deployed and how it might be used to enhance the lived conditions of poor communities. I argue that, before we celebrate the divine nature of social capital, it seems important that we interrogate what we mean by social capital. For example, does it benefit most communities, and how can it be used with other institutions and processes to improve the lives of our most vulnerable citizens? To that end, this chapter uses a case study of the city of New Haven, Connecticut, to explore the complexities of social capital in poor communities. Receiving special attention are the avenues through which community-based social capital can be infused with outside resources, in particular those that I call *intervening institutions,* to consolidate and institutionalize political power in the hands of neighborhood residents.[1]

In the New Haven case, community activists were instrumental in electing the first black mayor of New Haven, John Daniels, in 1989. Upon his election, the mayor then facilitated the creation of community management teams to help with the implementation and regulation of community policing. From this concretized community-based political structure, participants were integrated into the governing structure of New Haven's enterprise community (EC). This involvement, especially through newly created institutions and governing processes, would prove instrumental in converting the social capital of these poor communities into political power that they could deploy in more formal governing institutions.

However, before I turn my attention to the New Haven case, I first want to explore social capital as it is conceptualized today. Specifically, I begin with a discussion of the importance of associations and voluntary activity to scholars such as Tocqueville and Putnam. I then highlight some of the problems associated with the conceptualization and use of social capital as *the* concept that can explain recent declines in participation. Most important, this section explores how feminist scholars and those who study marginalized groups attempt to provide what might be considered a more comprehensive explanation of the status and political activity of poor communities. However, before totally discarding the concept of social capital, I introduce the idea of intervening institutions as a way to leverage social capital into democratic political power.

FROM ASSOCIATIONS TO SOCIAL CAPITAL— MAKING DEMOCRACY WORK

The idea that civil society, as facilitated through social trust and participation in associations, is central to the working of democracy has a long tradition in American political thought. The fascination with the voluntary associations and social activity of Americans evident in the writings of contemporary scholars such as Benjamin Barber (1984), Michael Sandel (1984), and Robert Putnam (1995a, 2000) similarly shaped Alexis de Tocqueville's writing on American democracy more than one hundred years earlier in his classic *Democracy in America* (1969 [1835]). Tocqueville describes an American society defined most prominently by its equal condition, resulting in a civic culture distinct in its proliferation of associations and voluntary groups. He writes: "Americans of all ages, all stations in life, and all types of dispositions are forever forming associations. There are not only commercial and industrial associations in which *all* take part, but others of a thousand different types—religious, moral, serious, futile, very general and very limited, immensely large and very minute" (1969, 513, emphasis added).

For Tocqueville, these associations were no less important to American democracy than equality: "If men are to remain civilized or to become civilized, the art of association must develop and improve among them at the same speed as equality of condition spreads" (517). Through associations and associating, Tocqueville believed, citizens would learn not only the skills required for effective political participation but also the social control he perceived as necessary if democracy was to function under citizen control. Thus, for Tocqueville, associations signaled and sustained a vibrant civic and political life through which citizens learned social responsibility and became "orderly, temperate, moderate, and self-controlled citizens. . . . They thus learn to submit their own will to that of all the rest and to make their own exertions subordinate to the common action" (522). Civic engagement, he thought, benefited the populace not only by bringing able participants into the public arena but also by generating stability among citizens who knew what their appropriate role was in the collective unit. For example, it was exactly this concept of complementary roles that allowed Tocqueville to view women's absence from formal decisionmaking not as problematic but as emblematic of a system in which everyone had a role, along with varying degrees of status and power.

I invoke Tocqueville to remind us that for quite some time voluntary associations and small informal gatherings of Americans have been seen as central to American democracy. And while Tocqueville may be the most cited author on the topic of civic engagement, Robert Putnam is now undoubtedly running a close second. In the last ten years, the importance of civic involvement, as it is mapped onto the concept of social capital, has once again received heightened attention. This time the view of civic engagement in American society is not as glorious or magnanimous as in years gone by. Scholars now lament the disappearance of social capital—that is, the social trust, norms, networks, and resulting civic engagement that presumably make democracy work in the United States. They are particularly concerned about the relationship between depleted levels of social capital and an assumed decline in political activity. Fewer people are going to the polls, fewer are working on campaigns, and some are even "bowling alone," reports Putnam (1995a) and other scholars. Thus, in the nation's post-isolationist period, it is argued that Americans (or at least residents of the United States) have become more isolated, autonomous, and private entities who shy away in both disgust and disinterest from the state and civic arenas.

Although the new wave of concern over social capital has many of its roots in the work of James Coleman (1988, 1990), it has been Robert Putnam's (1993a, 1993b, 1995a, 1995b, 2000) formulation of social capital—one that began with his study of Italy and now has been applied to contemporary American politics—that has become both the focus and the target of political scientists like myself. Putnam has described social capital as those "features of social life—networks, norms, and trust—that enable participants to act together more effectively to pursue shared objectives" (1995b, 664–65). Putnam professes to be concerned with two issues. The first is the general decline in civic engagement and the underlying social capital that drives such activity. From Putnam's view, we are no longer a nation of joiners, in large part because of our eroding trust, interactions, and norms. His second concern is the effect of a decline in social capital on the political activity of the country. For Putnam, our participation in the civic arena is closely tied to our participation in the political arena. He urges us therefore to consider how trends marking the decline of political participation are connected to the "disappearance of social capital."

As we might expect, a small cottage industry has emerged around Putnam's claims of the importance of social capital. And though many adhere to and support Putnam's view of the decline in social capital and its tie to civic participation, there are those who dispute his findings and formulation. For example, some of the discussion of Putnam's work has centered on the data he presents to support his arguments (Ladd 1996). Other critiques have taken issue with the conceptual map that informs Putnam's investigation (Minkoff 1997). Whatever the point in question, these debates have been lively and often informative.

Luckily, because others have already pointed out the apparent flaws in Putnam's work, and because fully engaging in such an effort would be beyond the scope of this chapter, I have chosen to focus on forms of community-based activism that Putnam and others concerned with participation may be ignoring. Here I am referring to the community-based struggles that do not often show up in our national databases, in part because of the questions that researchers ask as well as the people who are surveyed. For example, David Wagner and Marcia Cohen (1991, 543) describe the activities of homeless activists as "hidden movements of poor people." They contend that while researchers and federal bureaucrats try to estimate the homeless population in the United States, few if any scholars have recognized and analyzed the activism among homeless people and their advocates. Wagner and Cohen note that, "despite growing protest and political consciousness among groups of homeless people (the pitched battles in New York City's Tompkins Square Park, years of confrontation in Washington, D.C., led by the Coalition for Creative Non-violence, and dozens of localized tent cities and sit-ins), neither social scientists studying the homeless nor social movement theorists have investigated the impact of protest on the lives of the very poor" (543). In their own research, Wagner and Cohen have found "strong social ties and social networks among the homeless and formerly homeless" (547).

Lisa Sullivan (1997) makes a similar argument, but from a different perspective. Specifically, Sullivan contends that, though social capital in poor communities is underdeveloped—in particular, the social capital among young black residents—there still exists, she finds (unlike Putnam), ample activity illustrating the social organization and community affiliations of this maligned generation. She writes:

> Although academics like Harvard political scientist Robert Putnam have warned that our current civic crisis has much to do with a decline in formal associational life, my activism and organizing experience in central cities suggests that informal associational life is alive and well—especially among the poor and young. While Putnam may have observed a general decline in citizen participation in traditional social and civic associations, a significant number of citizens from the inner city are creating and participating in vibrant informal networks of twenty-first century associational life. (235)

Sullivan astutely argues that, far from there being an absence of social capital in poor black communities, black politicians and traditional leaders consumed with the process of formal incorporation have largely ignored the trust and social networks at work in these communities and among this generation. "Alienated from mainstream American politics and public life, the young and poor have also increasingly found themselves estranged from the black civil rights establishment. Disengaged from traditional black liberal organizations, their social capital has gone under utilized, underdeveloped, and ignored in the late twentieth century" (237). Therefore, in the absence of traditional participatory avenues, young and poor community members may be creating new political and social formations that are invisible to social scientists looking for social capital in all the old places (national data sets) and in all the traditional forms.

STRUCTURE, EXCLUSION, AND SOCIAL CAPITAL

In addition to those scholars and activists who are concerned with the numbers that people use to talk about social capital, another group of scholars and activists make a more fundamental critique, focusing exclusively or disproportionately on concepts such as social capital. Specifically, these researchers worry that by offering social capital as *the* explanation for our participation woes, we are missing an important part of the picture, namely, formal and informal structural constraints. Scholars and activists, concerned about the empowerment of vulnerable and marginalized groups, have written extensively, and with great insight, about our often piecemeal approach to fostering political participation. These researchers do not totally discount the importance of such factors as social capital, but they seek to provide what they view as a more comprehensive understanding of the multiple sites of power that work to repress not only political activity but also political standing among the least empowered. Thus, included and often highlighted in their formulations of political activity are the structural constraints that poor people face daily.

One could, for example, read much of the recent literature bemoaning the downturn in participation, marked most significantly by a decline in voter turnout, as devoid of any attention to the structural constraints that people encounter when trying to exercise their franchise. Seemingly missing from such stories are the laws and regulations that disqualify more than one-fourth of African American men from voting because of their status as current or former felons. No amount of social capital is going to allow an individual to vote when state law says that he cannot.[2] By focusing only on the social capital that individuals control and using aggregated, individual-level data to assess the existence and work of social capital, we miss the impact of institutions and politics on patterns of participation.

Jean Cohen (1998) is more specific in her demand that the state play an active role if we are to witness the successful and effective use of social capital to enhance democracy. She argues, for example, that "far too many political theorists and actors pretend that we can have a vital, well-integrated, and just civil society without states constitutionally guaranteeing that universalistic egalitarian principles (open of course to critique and revision) inform social policy regardless of which social institution or level of government carries it out" (6–7). We must never forget that there are numerous examples of communities having social capital without corresponding political power. Without some contextual elaboration of the dominant structures and institutions that regulate, guarantee, and produce participation and political power, our understanding of the importance of social capital becomes inflated. In turn, our expectations about its ability to cure all that ails our "failing democracy" are raised, and we may view any contribution of a structural analysis as inadequate or unimportant.

Going one step beyond a focus on institutions, Michael Dawson (1994) has written and talked persuasively of a racial ordering in which the hierarchical cleavages surrounding race, gender, and class, among other social identities, intersect and situate citizens both individually and as a group differently. Dawson questions the degree to which increased formal political participation, motivated through social capital or some other mechanism, can significantly challenge the racial order—as is evident in the current allocation of power, resources, and status in society. Instead, he believes, if we are really concerned, as researchers, with fostering a reordering or transformation of political power and access, we must work with a more comprehensive understanding of political actors, political participation, and political power. Specifically, he concludes that heightened attention to social capital might be helpful in altering patterns of political participation at the margins, but that it is only when such local activity is matched with organized extrasystemic political action and the opening and reconstitution of formal political institutions that we find real progress being made.

Feminist scholars have similarly argued that a more comprehensive understanding of political power—one that rejects the patriarchal distinction between the public and private realms—is needed to revitalize participatory democracy. This argument sounds similar to Putnam's social capital focus, but these scholars center their analysis on the question of power. Specifically, they suggest that power relationships and their resulting inequality, even those that originate and exist in what has been labeled the private realm, are critical in constituting the political subject with which "social capitalists" are so concerned (Mansbridge 1980; Young 1989). In this formulation, political standing or power in formal democratic institutions is understood to be directly connected to and to flow from economic, social, and cultural standing in the informal relationships and market economy designated as separate from the state. These researchers therefore contend that any strict attempt to dichotomize the two will prove fruitless. For example, Nancy Fraser (1989), in her discussion of Habermas's conception of the public sphere, highlights the ways in which gendered patterns of talk or deliberation work to privilege male voices even though the formal institutions and the civil society appear to be open to all:

> Feminist research has documented a syndrome that many of us have observed in faculty meetings and other mixed-sex deliberative bodies: men tend to interrupt women more than women interrupt men; men also tend to speak more than women, taking more turns and longer turns; and women's interventions are more often ignored or not responded to than men's. In response to the sorts of experiences documented in this research, an important strand of feminist political theory has claimed that deliberation can serve as a mask for domination. Mansbridge rightly notes that many of these feminist insights into ways in which deliberation can serve as a mask for domination extend beyond gender to other kinds of unequal relations, like those based on class or ethnicity. They alert us to the ways in which social inequalities can infect deliberation, even in the absence of any formal exclusion. (119)

From such seemingly subtle observations it becomes clear that any analysis of political participation that does not attend to both the inequality among citizens and its corresponding effect on formal patterns of political participation will never generate "political parity" among citizens. In the quote, Fraser directs our attention to the gendered nature of the deliberative process, but we can only imagine the impact of, for instance, economic inequalities on the deliberative process and the distribution of political power more generally. So while promoters of social capital push us to expand our political analysis to include and make central the important "private" domain of voluntary associations, networks, and neighborhood groups that exist outside of formal political institutions, often left unexplored in these investigations are the gender, race, class, and sexual hierarchies that condition and limit the effectiveness of such activity on the part of poor people and people of color.

Finally, there is the issue of the negative consequences associated with social capital, in particular, the power to regulate and exclude. I want to be fair and acknowledge that early in his *PS: Political Science and Politics* article (1995b), Putnam discusses examples of what he considers negative social capital: "Groups like the Michigan militia or youth gangs also embody a kind of social capital, for these networks and norms, too, enable members to cooperate more effectively, albeit to the detriment of the wider community" (665). This is an important acknowledgment of the possible problematic uses of social capital, but Putnam does not go far enough. I too worry about the deployment of social capital in ways that are unquestionably dangerous to "the wider community." However, I am just as concerned about the subtle deployment of social capital in ways that threaten and police more vulnerable segments of marginalized communities.

We must remember that at all times community residents have multiple identities. Moreover, in the absence of structures, there is nothing to preclude a majority or even a vocal minority of community residents from either excluding "outsiders" (nonresidents) or marginalizing other "insiders" (residents). For example, how do we evaluate the operation and effectiveness of social capital when residents in poor communities bond together to have the homeless removed from their neighborhoods? Or to have sex workers arrested? Or to ban AIDS education from their schools? Or to prevent the home language of newly arrived immigrants from being taught in the schools? Thus, in our march to empower communities politically, in this case poor communities, it seems irresponsible if we avoid discussion—especially among members of those communities—of what Alejandro Portes and Patricia Landolt (1996) call "the downside of social capital."

MAKING SOCIAL CAPITAL WORK: POOR COMMUNITIES, SOCIAL CAPITAL, AND INTERVENING INSTITUTIONS

In spite of all the difficulties I have noted with current conceptualizations of social capital, I do not advocate abandoning the project of building social capital. Anyone familiar with poor and marginalized communities knows that social capital has been integral to their survival and progress. Numerous scholars, especially those engaged in ethnographic research on poor communities, have documented the existence of social capital—at least the reciprocity, trust, and networks highlighted by Putnam (Saegert et al. 1998; Edin and Lein 1997; Hagedorn 1991; Stack 1974). However, distinct from Putnam's limited use for such properties—namely, to facilitate political participation—many poor residents use such assets to guarantee adequate food for their children, safe housing for their families, and disposable income that might make life a bit more manageable and possibly enjoyable.[3] And though every neighborhood and community could benefit from more social capital, there is no evidence to suggest that poor communities are more deficient in social capital than other, more affluent communities. Instead, it seems that what poor communities are missing is the political power to force a reallocation of needed resources.

Susan Saegert and her colleagues (1998), for example, argue that the problem is not the absence of social capital in poor communities, but the fact that social capital is being asked to compensate for a lack of other resources in so many areas that it cannot work effectively. Therefore, what we need is a more textured understanding of the complexities that poor people face as political actors. With such information, we can begin to assess how existing social capital in poor communities might work in conjunction with other institutions and resources to empower residents. To that end, this section explores the question: How do we build on or leverage the social capital that exists in poor communities to generate greater political power? More specifically, what is the role of intervening institutions in providing both needed resources and the infrastructure necessary to convert social capital into political power?

Institutions Making Things Worse?

The point has been made repeatedly that poor communities are increasingly isolated—economically, politically, and socially (Wilson 1987; Cohen and Dawson 1993; Alex-Assensoh 1997). One school of thought sees structural changes in the economy, particularly the depletion of low-skilled, living-wage jobs, as the engine driving the isolation increasingly experienced by people in poor communities (Wilson 1987, 1996). Another framework focuses on past and present residential segregation as it concentrates poor blacks in particular in urban areas (Massey and Denton 1993). In both accounts, the isolation of poor residents from working- and middle-class city residents is thought to have been precipitated not only by structural changes in the economy or continued residential segregation but also by other factors such as federal policies on urban renewal and highway construction that destroyed buildings, leveled neighborhoods, and ravaged any social capital that existed.

Clearly, for a multitude of reasons, poor communities find themselves increasingly removed from the working heart of cities and what Douglas Glasgow (1981) has called "feeder institutions" such as unions, banks, civic organizations, social agencies, even large chain grocery stores that link residents in a proactive manner to the labor market, and, more generally, the public sphere. In the absence of such feeder institutions, we should not be surprised to find that concentrated in severely impoverished areas are high levels of outcome variables that signal community stress: crime, HIV-AIDS, drug addiction, teenage pregnancy, and state assistance. In correspondence with their high stress indicators, many poor communities have been inundated with "helper institutions." Specifically, as the geographic space of poor communities transforms from markedly poor to intensely blighted areas in need of social services, these neighborhoods are often hit with an influx of government programs—including many that no other community will allow in its environs. The anthropologist Ira Susser (1996, 415) writes: "Such invisible and relatively powerless communities concomitantly become sites of last resort for methadone clinics, housing for the mentally ill, and—partially as a consequence of the well-known phenomenon of Not in My Backyard (NIMBY)—industrial waste disposal plants." This pattern suggests that those of us who believe that poor neighborhoods have social capital but lack the intervening institutions to convert their trust, networks, and norms of reciprocity into political power must be more specific in our broad demands for infrastructure in those communities. As we call for more resources and intervening institutions in poor communities, we should be clear, as the ensuing discussion delineates, that not all institutions facilitate democratic participation and empowerment, in particular among poor residents. Specifically, the mere presence of federal, state, or city services does not mean that adequate intervening institutions and resources are available to poor communities. Instead, government policies and programs meant to service poor communities sometimes, possibly unintentionally, destroy social capital.

What Intervening Institutions Must Do

The examples noted here clearly indicate that not all outside resources are successful in empowering resource-poor communities. Instead, more often than not they have done unexpected harm. In light of this pattern, I offer three conditions that I believe provide the best opportunity, when met, to use outside resources or intervening institutions to empower marginal communities. First, third-party resources must be put under the democratic control of local residents and be structured to build on existing infrastructure and assets within the community. Far too often, federal resources and social service agencies are present in poor communities, but without any connection to or respect for the existing institutional and social networks of community residents. Moreover, the decisionmaking process enmeshed in these outpost agencies is usually off-limits to the residents they are supposed to serve. Again, the intervening institutions I am promoting would build on, not dismiss, the social capital, stability, and infrastructure that already exist in poor communities. For example, John Hagedorn (1991), writing about poor, gang-ridden neighborhoods in Milwaukee, argues that, "rather than proposing specific new model gang programs or narrowly calling for a federal office of gang control, our data suggest a focus on strengthening neighborhood social institutions [would be more effective]." He continues: "While very poor neighborhoods have been devastated by economic and demographic changes, they also have important strengths to build on. The residents who live in poor neighborhoods need stable, well-funded agencies and institutions in which to participate" (536).

Second, in addition to encouraging the participation of local residents in their decisionmaking process, intervening institutions must also be able to address demographic changes and the complex social groupings, beyond those delineated by geography, that are used to generate and control social capital in poor communities. For example, while poor communities have been experiencing increasing isolation, the demographics of these neighborhoods have also changed significantly over the years. Specifically, poor communities have experienced the increasing feminization of poverty, along with a growing population of immigrants. The increasing number of women and children living below the poverty line has been commented on for some time. A statistical brief on poverty areas recently published by the U.S. Bureau of the Census (1995, 3) reported that "families in poverty areas [where at least 20 percent of the residents were classified as poor] were nearly twice as likely as those elsewhere to have a female householder." Along with the continued feminization of poor communities, researchers have also begun to examine the growing number of recent immigrants living in poverty and in impoverished neighborhoods. The *Current Population Report* entitled "The Foreign-Born Population: 1996" (U.S. Bureau of the Census 1997, 1) notes that "recent arrivals among the foreign-born are more likely to be in poverty, to have lower incomes, and to have higher unemployment rates that the native born."

So as we think about social capital in poor communities and the characteristics of the neighborhoods in which intervening institutions will be rooted, we have to explore the degree to which social capital in these communities is not only bounded geographically but also associated with social identities like race, ethnicity, gender, and sexuality. Although residents of poor communities are typically tied together through the lack of resources and services in their neighborhoods, there is nothing in our explorations to suggest that the use of social capital to alleviate such deficits crosses the boundaries of race, ethnicity, language, and class. In fact, in city after city we can point to poor census tracts that are segregated—for example, into poor Latino neighborhoods and poor black neighborhoods. It is therefore inaccurate and dangerous to assume that the existence of social capital among, for example, Latinos in poor neighborhoods is related to or benefits other racial and ethnic groups in the same geographic area. As we build institutions and mount interventions meant to spur social and political capital in poor communities, we must be attuned to the social identities that not only give these norms and behaviors meaning for local residents but limit their usefulness to certain communities or groupings.

Similarly, our efforts to leverage social capital in poor communities must be designed to coincide with the gendered nature of social capital in these neighborhoods. It is clear from the demographics and scholarly case studies that women disproportionately populate and sustain poor communities. It is therefore necessary to develop a model of community empowerment different from those that point to the election of local, usually male leaders as signifying community empowerment (Bobo and Gilliam 1990; Gilliam and Kaufmann 1998). Instead, we must support a framework of community empowerment that focuses not only on the election of political leaders from poor communities but on grassroots systems of participatory decisionmaking in which significant segments of the community can feel ownership over and involvement in the development of their neighborhoods and cities. In the absence of such a grassroots structure, community residents may find it difficult to hold elected leadership accountable while simultaneously making invisible the *political* activity of women in these neighborhoods.

Third, and finally, when thinking about the deployment of intervening institutions that will allow poor communities to leverage the social capital they control into political power and economic development, we must use a model that does not begin and end with the federal government. As Jean Cohen (1998) argues, the state has a significant role to play in the social capital process, but other institutions, such as labor unions, political parties, private foundations, and banks, are also integral to the conversion of social capital in poor communities. For instance, almost every current study of political participation points to the importance of mobilization, primarily from political parties, as a significant factor influencing participation (Wolfinger and Rosenstone 1980; Rosenstone and Hansen 1993; Verba, Schlozman, and Brady 1995).

Historically, political parties have been important institutions, facilitating the political incorporation of immigrants, women, and racial minorities.[4] Whether in forms like the Democratic machines of urban cities early in this century or the Union Leagues in the South after Reconstruction, political parties and political clubs have provided needed resources in mobilizing resource-poor groups. Political mobilization by intervening institutions is even more important in poor communities, as Michael Dawson and I (Cohen and Dawson 1993) argue in our study on the political behavior of people in severely impoverished areas. Specifically, we found that while living in an impoverished neighborhood had a negative impact, over and above individual characteristics, on almost every measure of political behavior we explored, mobilization was "one effective way to increase the probability of individuals engaging in political acts" (298). Correspondingly, it has also been argued that mobilization from outside sources is most effective when run through legitimizing indigenous institutions, elites, and infrastructure. For example, institutions such as political parties, civil rights organizations, and labor unions have all experienced the greatest success when working in tandem with local neighborhood groups and leaders.

The unique importance of mobilization in guaranteeing democracy should not be lost on the reader. Without massive mobilization, power and decisionmaking end up consolidated in the hands of the few. I do understand that concentrating power, albeit the modest power available in poor communities, in the hands of what often turn out to be the few and relatively familiar can be both beneficial and potentially problematic. For instance, individuals who both know each other and are known to others—because they are longtime residents of the neighborhood, because they have worked on different projects together, or because they are recognized by outside officials as leaders in their community—often come together to guide and participate in struggles around community empowerment. This is in fact what anyone focused on social capital hopes to see happen. However, even as we search for ways to leverage social capital into community power, we must always keep our eyes on the means or the participatory nature of that movement. That is, we do not want to build power in poor communities at the expense of an inclusive participatory process. Instead, our goal as researchers and activists must be to facilitate the use of social capital for political empowerment built on open democratic participation that generates greater political activity among all the residents of these communities.

A TALE OF ONE CITY: NEW HAVEN, CONNECTICUT

Many suggest that no other city, except possibly Chicago, has been studied as much as New Haven, Connecticut. Known most notably for the community studies that emerged during the 1960s, with Robert Alan Dahl's classic *Who Governs?* (1961) leading this school of thought, political scientists, sociologists, historians, and an army of graduate students from Yale University (not to mention other local campuses) have mapped the development, the depression, and the reemergence of New Haven as a classic East Coast city. It is therefore not surprising that I turn my attention to the city of New Haven in an attempt to explore both the constraints on and the benefits to political participation gained from social capital in poor communities, especially as new intervening institutions emerge.[5] More specifically, I want to address a different component of political participation, namely, the ability of community residents to participate in political decisions regarding the development and future of their neighborhoods.

To that end, this section briefly examines New Haven's experience as a federally designated enterprise community (EC). Specifically, I explore the ways in which some of New Haven's poorest communities used third-party resources, in particular intervening institutions, to continue their march toward greater political access. Central to this discussion is a brief exploration of the conflicts that emerged within the EC governing structures between, for example, different neighborhoods vying for the same resources, as well as the conflicts that emerged outside the governing structure between EC neighborhoods and other entities claiming to represent poor people in New Haven. What emerges from this discussion is a picture of both the difficulties and the benefits that develop as social capital in poor communities is institutionalized and newly created political power is exercised.

I should note that others, in particular, Marilyn Gittell and her colleagues (1998), have also explored the opportunities for civic engagement generated through urban development projects such as empowerment zones. Furthermore, there is a developing literature on the margins of the social capital "field" that looks broadly at the role of institutions and policies, usually those associated with the government, in facilitating both the development of social capital and the conversion of social capital into observable political power (Gittell and Vidal 1998; Schneider et al. 1997; Vidal 1996). This very brief case study, however, tries to add another dimension to that literature by examining the ways in which poor communities can use third-party resources to develop intervening institutions and political power built on principles of democratic participation and inclusion. This, of course, is not an easy task. As the case study demonstrates, outside resources usually gravitate toward established neighborhood leaders, reinforcing a hierarchy of access and input even in poor communities. In part this happens because outside parties are usually interested only in superficial participation—activity that legitimizes but does not threaten the stable working of the project. Thus, it takes an active commitment to democratic inclusion on the part of community leaders to break such a pattern of appropriation and legitimization.

Institutionalizing Social Capital

In 1989 John Daniels, New Haven's first black mayor, was elected to office on a platform emphasizing concerns relevant to black and poor communities. It was in large part the informal networks and mobilization among poor, black, Latino, and white liberal residents of New Haven that delivered city hall to Daniels. One of the prominent topics of the campaign was his critique of conventional police tactics (Summers and Klinkner 1996). In an attempt to follow through on the promises he made during his campaign, Daniels began restructuring the police department as soon as he assumed office. Driving this restructuring was the idea of moving from a police force that provided traditional police services to one centered on the idea of community policing—where officers would get out of their cars to walk the beat and build relationships with community members. Eventually, Mayor Daniels, New Haven, and the newly appointed police chief, Nicholas Pastore, would all become poster children for community policing, appearing in story after story as the successful embodiment of a community-based policing strategy.

New Haven's community policing plan was structured around the establishment of thirteen community-based policing substations. In neighborhoods across the city, new physical structures were erected to house the police. These substations not only included the essential material and equipment needed for any policing operation but also housed extra amenities such as community meeting rooms. The physical markers of policing were not the only parts of the system to undergo scrutiny and change; also under reconstruction was the hierarchy between the police and community residents. Thus, in each neighborhood where community policing was implemented there developed an accompanying community (policing) management team (CMT or CPMT).

Initially, these teams, which included both neighborhood activists and longtime residents, focused their attention on developing a strategy for community policing in their neighborhood. They had to tackle such questions as: How will police be deployed? How will residents exert (some) control over their neighborhoods while supporting the cops on the beat? Questions detailing the relationship between community residents and this historically brutal institution in minority and poor communities all had to be addressed during this early period in the program. Although this initial planning would later be heralded as having laid the groundwork for an eventual drop in violent crimes in New Haven, what often goes unnoticed is the role of such work in beginning the transformation of social capital in these neighborhoods.

In each community, longtime residents, recognized community leaders, and stable forces within neighborhoods were brought together under the auspices of the CMT. The institutionalization of CMTs brought with it neighborhood resources and infrastructure, including: a regular meeting place and time for community leaders to come together to strategize about how to improve their neighborhoods; an opportunity for community members and leaders to work together to build a sense of trust and unified vision; an open meeting process in which anyone in the neighborhood could come and talk face to face with other residents about important issues; and the ear of local officials who recognized the CMTs as legitimate sources of power in poor communities. This work simultaneously changed the neighborhood's interaction with the city's most visible presence, the police, and provided an intervening institution, the CMTs, that helped to institutionalize the existing social capital in some of New Haven's poorest neighborhoods. As one resident explained it to me, "For the first time in a long time folks in the neighborhoods felt like someone in city hall was listening to what we said."

Social capital had long been used in New Haven's poor communities as a buffer between the brutality of dominant institutions like the police and the resource-poor condition of many residents in these neighborhoods. However, the emergence of CMTs laid the groundwork for what would become the infrastructure of power and influence in these communities. Quickly, the community management teams moved from an agenda focused strictly on the police to one that was more civic in nature. No longer content to be a regulatory or oversight committee, CMTs in some neighborhoods planned community festivals, sponsored fairs, and engaged in other activities meant to service and mobilize community residents.

In 1993 the work of the management teams in some of the poorest neighborhoods in New Haven would take an even greater step toward formal power. It was in this year that President Clinton put forth his funding initiative for cities: the Empowerment Zones and Enterprise Communities Program. This program was meant to revitalize some of the country's poorest neighborhoods and cities by focusing on their economic development. New Haven submitted a funding application that included input from the major stakeholders in the city, including representatives from the CMTs. In the initial round, only six cities, Atlanta, Baltimore, Chicago, Detroit, New York, and Philadelphia-Camden, New Jersey, were awarded an empowerment zone designation that carried with it a prize of $100 million in federal grants and $250 million in tax incentives over ten years. Sixty-six cities, however, of which New Haven was one, were awarded the enterprise community designation. Although accorded fewer benefits than empowerment areas, ECs were allotted $3 million in federal aid, eligibility for certain tax breaks, and preferred status in the federal grant process (Gittell and Vidal 1998).

New Haven's application was built around seven census tracts in which severe poverty and unemployment were present: Dwight, Hill North, Hill South, Dixwell, Newhallville, West Rock, and Fairhaven. Central to the awarding of this designation was the expectation that administrative bodies would be established at both the city and neighborhood levels to facilitate strategic planning around economic development issues in these areas. The Department of Housing and Urban Development also required award winners to ensure that community participation would be integrated into both the administrative structure and the planning and implementation processes. In accordance with this requirement, New Haven established neighborhood implementation committees (NICs), or enterprise community management teams (ECMT), in each census tract included in the application. Initially, each NIC-ECMT had its own set of working committees and advisory groups and was structurally distinct from existing community (policing) management teams in over-lapping neighborhoods. However, over time the ECMTs and CPMTs would merge in many communities, since many of the same individuals served on both teams.

At the citywide level, coordination occurred through the Enterprise Community Council (ECC). This body was composed of twenty-nine representatives: seventeen from the seven neighborhoods, six institutional reps, two elected aldermen, and four mayoral appointees. Supporting the work of the ECC were three standing committees and three staff members. The governing structure of the ECC also included two co-chairs and an executive committee. The ECC was responsible for such tasks as distributing funding and tax incentives, overseeing and coordinating the strategic planning at the neighborhood level, and providing letters of support for local grant proposals to the federal government. Such letters were necessary if groups and organizations were to receive priority in the federal granting included with an enterprise community designation.

Questions of Power and Infrastructure

Enterprise communities were established, first and foremost, to promote economic development in the form of jobs in poor communities. However, the internal struc-ture of many ECs, in particular that found in New Haven, illustrates the possible unintentional benefits of such government intervention. Specifically, through the cre-ation of the intervening institutions necessary for the EC governing process, we can see one route through which poor communities can begin to institutionalize and con-solidate the power of their neighborhoods. In New Haven, for example, although the ECC has been what one alderperson referred to as peripheral to the development process up to this point, the management team structure associated with community policing and the enterprise effort, he suggested, could also politically empower res-idents who generally have little voice in city affairs.

One visible benefit from the management team structure has been its use as an alternative route into public office. For example, in the last New Haven election four of the six newly elected alderpeople came out of the management team struc-ture. Not surprisingly, considering the feminization of poor communities, this neighborhood-based structure has recognized and promoted the leadership of women in these communities. In fact, of the four candidates with management team experience elected to office, three were women. This outcome is a bit more complicated than it appears at first glance, however, considering that all three newly elected female alderpeople replaced other women. So while the manage-ment team structure may work to promote women's leadership—not an unimpor-tant characteristic—their route into elected office may still be narrowly construed such that the only offices for which they are viewed as credible competitors are those currently held by other women.[6]

In addition to the movement of community members into formal office, management teams may also be instrumental in mobilizing community members around important neighborhood issues. In New Haven, we have already witnessed the use of management teams to mobilize community members in the Fairhaven and Dixwell areas around environmental justice issues. As noted by one neighborhood resident who occasionally goes to management team meetings, "Management teams turn out fifty to sixty people in a meeting, on a good day. It would be ridiculous not to think that they didn't have the power to make a difference politically. The problem is that they don't see that as that important. Folks are so busy tying to create jobs and CDCs, they don't care about a lot of other things."

Although this person does not think that individuals participating in the management teams have an eye on participation, others do. For example, one local stakeholder argued that the politicization of ECMTs would be a slow process—first planning festivals for youth, then trying to get jobs for local residents, then using their resources to get people to the polls—but that it would happen eventually. Again, the resources and infrastructure that accompany ECMTs—money for mailings, community space for meetings, briefings from city officials—can be used both to increase the participation of individual residents in poor communities and to leverage the social capital of the community into formal and informal political power. One question remains: Can the dominant agenda pursued by these bodies, jobs for poor residents, be expanded to include political participation and community empowerment as outcome goals?

Conflicts of Interest Within

It would be disingenuous to suggest that there are not serious limitations related to the management structure detailed in this section. For example, echoing Marilyn Gittell and her colleagues (1998, 532), who note that "competition among potential participants for approval of their own project diverted attention from the general need to expand citizen participation," one management team member confirmed the difficulty in getting anything through the ECC because of narrow neighborhood interests. He suggested that almost everything that developed out of the neighborhoods was stalled at the citywide level because the other neighborhoods would vote against the allocation of resources to other communities if they thought their neighborhood had similar needs. Almost all of the stakeholders I interviewed complained about the narrow construction of interests that developed within neighborhood management teams. One alderman stated that the neighborhood ECMTs were limited in their ability to mobilize poor people across the city because they were "always thinking parochially about my block, my block, my block! That type of thinking doesn't allow for big coalitional activism. The problem is that management team discourse puts their block at the center of the universe. They also can't see past development issues." He went on to explain why management team leaders were so consumed with jobs and why political officials might encourage such a narrow agenda. "Jobs are something you can quantify, and participation is something you can't. Also, there is a trade-off, if all of a sudden too many people have their hand in decisionmaking. Most of the aldermen worry about having too many people think they run the ward, because then they can't get anything done." So while most alderpeople publicly support community participation in the decisionmaking process, privately some are reluctant to endorse extensive community involvement, arguing that such involvement would make it difficult to run the government efficiently.

Conflicts of Interest Outside

Competition between neighborhood management teams was not the only tension to develop from the EC process. Neighborhood management teams also found themselves matched against local civil rights and, in some cases, labor unions for control of limited resources. The struggle over a job training program at a newly opened Omni Hotel in New Haven is probably the clearest example of how the newly institutionalized interests of the ECMTs were attempting to redefine the political landscape, this time in direct opposition to local civil rights groups that professed to be representing the interests of the poor. In the months before the hotel opened, Omni management found itself in numerous battles with community groups and labor unions. The focus of these battles ranged from a struggle over Omni management's request that buses be rerouted away from the hotel, to one centered on the hotel's unwillingness to agree to a neutrality agreement with the union, to questions over Omni's commitment to training and hiring New Haven residents, particularly people of color (Warren and Cohen 2000). In fact, it would be the struggle over what type of training program the Omni would offer potential workers that pitted the Enterprise Community Council against a coalition of unions, civil rights organizations, and community activists.

Specifically, a coalition of community activists, led by both union officials and the head of the local NAACP chapter, argued that the Omni planned to implement a job training program that would focus on "soft" skills, or attitude training, and neglect the "hard" or job-specific skills that participants needed for long-term employment. Community activists further contended that the planned training program would relegate participants in the program (largely minority) to "back-of-the-house" jobs—low-skilled, low-pay, service employment—reserving the higher-paid "front-of-the-house," skill-specific jobs for whites and commuters. Roger Vann, chair of the New Haven NAACP, succinctly delineated the boundaries of this battle: "They're interested in having people who don't necessarily have any skills training but have 'good attitudes.' . . . We're asking them to buy into a process that will ensure that people of color will be able to get jobs, not just in the back of the house, but in the front of the house as well" (Zaretsky 1997).

Ironically, the city and the Enterprise Community Council would end up defending the Omni's proposed job training program against the protests of this coalition, since, unbeknownst to many players, the ECC had helped to develop the program proposed by the Omni as a way of guaranteeing that jobs made available through the program would be funneled into *their* poor communities. ECC Chairman Bill

Battle of Newhallville, one of the few powerful black conservatives in New Haven, was reported to be a staunch supporter of the project, arguing that the program should have been strictly limited to EC residents, excluding poor residents from other neighborhoods. The conflict was never formally settled, but the final program resembled the soft-skills design promoted by the ECC and endorsed by the Omni. On February 24, 1998, the Omni "graduated" eighty-five New Haven residents from its newly titled Career TEAM training program. Not surprisingly, a substantial number of the new employees came from EC neighborhoods.

The Omni Hotel struggle in New Haven is clearly one example of how interests can be narrowly constructed and organizations thought to represent the poor and poor communities can be pitted against each other. This example also illustrates the dangers of concentrating power in the hands of a few individuals. People stated rather consistently, but out of earshot of anyone with power (thus they were happy to say it to me), that part of the reason the Omni struggle took the direction it did was the inability of more liberal ECC members to challenge the leadership of a black male conservative from one of the poorest neighborhoods in New Haven. I cannot comment on the extent to which power has been concentrated on the ECC. However, the centralization of power in the hands of a small minority in any body responsible for decisionmaking should concern us. This scenario only underscores the importance of developing a community infrastructure that encourages and mandates extensive community involvement in decisionmaking as well as rotating terms in the leadership of the organization.

CONCLUSION

Again, this very brief discussion of the neighborhood structure of ECMTs in New Haven is not meant to serve as a perfect example of the conversion of social capital into political power. As we have just seen, there are significant liabilities attached to the current structure of New Haven's ECs. Instead, I hope this example can help illustrate the type of interventions, with regard to resources and infrastructure, that are possible and necessary if poor communities are to expand their participation, access, and power. Repeatedly, as I talked informally with people to figure out the working of the EC project in New Haven, it became clear that many believed that the ECMTs could become an important political institution. However, it was also evident from their comments that this transformation would not occur unless some outside force, possibly the federal government or a private funder, mandated attention to the political empowerment of poor communities.

Notwithstanding the urgent need for such an intervention, there seem to be a few research agendas that must be pursued first if social capital, intervening institutions, and outside resources are to have the impact we desire. First, we need to know more about poor communities. How does social capital operate within neighborhoods, across racial and ethnic groups, and in relation to formal political institutions? Addressing this question requires more case studies, surveys, and general mapping of the structure, interactions, and needs of poor communities.

Second, we need to make an in-depth assessment of the resources, institutions, and infrastructure required to leverage existing social capital in poor communities into political power. Beyond the three characteristics I outlined earlier in the chapter, what attributes of intervening institutions increase their probability of success?

Third, we need to detail closely the relationship between community empowerment and individual participation by residents in poor communities. Does expanding power at the community level spill over into individual acts of participation? To put it differently, do individuals living in enterprise communities and empowerment zones, for example, participate at higher rates than others living in poor communities that have not been awarded an EZ or EC designation?

Fourth, how can we promote and ensure accountability and participation within the governing structures instituted in poor communities? More specifically, how do we minimize the process of exclusion?

Fifth, what is the goal of this work? It is important here to distinguish between the goal of limited community input in a program and the goal of politically empowering communities so that they might develop their own agendas. Are we interested in facilitating a form of community involvement that legitimizes and possibly minimally influences the development of policies and strategic plans, while securing stability and protection from the growing inequality between the poor and the affluent? Or are we prepared to develop policies and programs that facilitate and support community empowerment without any guarantee that this newly formed power will not turn against us?

Answering these questions will give us a clearer focus on the types of policies and interventions that poor communities can pursue regarding social capital, intervening institutions, and political power.

Let me end by posing one final question: What role can social capital per se play in tackling the racial order discussed by Dawson (1994) or the cumulative inequality and multiple hierarchies of power explored by feminist scholars highlighted earlier in the chapter? Although participation in decisionmaking is clearly an important step in the process of political empowerment, social capital and its resulting increased participation will not by themselves transform the social and economic ordering that dictates the differential standing of political subjects. Moreover, little of the scholarship on social capital seems attuned to exploring how such relationships can be used to challenge the structures of power that sustain poverty, reinforce traditional and discriminatory gender and racial dynamics, or maintain the dominance of heterosexism, guaranteeing the subordinate political status of most citizens and residents. Without a more comprehensive approach to altering the lived condition and its resulting influence on the political power of poor people, social capital will never have the effect imagined in current studies of this concept.

Thus, I wonder sometimes whether some are turning to social capital as a way to instill, oh so subtly, the social control of earlier times, when everyone knew or at least was forced into their complementary place. As the earlier quote from Tocqueville suggests, through the process of civic inclusion "citizens" are thought to be transformed, by submitting their individual will to the desires of the collective body, a kind of civic republicanism. However, we must ask: What does it mean for those most vulnerable in society to submit their individual will to the collective whole? Specifically, though such a transformation may be good for the stability of the state and those who benefit from the current distribution of resources, what does such stability mean for the poor, the disempowered, the marginalized? We live, for example, in a time when those who seek to impose greater armed control over our cities are now armed with a burgeoning literature on the "underclass" and their threatening pathologies. Moreover, confronted with real evidence, in the form of the 1992 Los Angeles revolt-riot-rebellion, that poor people of color will burn things down in the face of blatant disregard and increasing systemic inequality, scholars, policymakers, and ordinary folk may be willing to support the expansion of social capital in poor communities if it promises to settle down "those people."

Social capital, as a kinder, gentler means of social control, looks much less menacing enmeshed in a political environment where the policies of a "liberal" president send increasing numbers of poor people and people of color to prison; force poor women, disproportionately women of color, to work in jobs that pay less than the minimum wage with little training; and put one hundred thousand more cops into neighborhoods, increasing the risk of brutality at the hands of the police. In such a political atmosphere, it is not a far stretch for someone less cynical than myself to wonder whether our new focus on social capital has as much to do with social control as with community empowerment. This concern should not be read as a wholesale indictment of an effort to build or leverage social capital in poor communities, but instead as a caution that, before we proceed to anointing social capital the missing link in the puzzle of participation, we understand the complexity of this effort, which can have both positive and negative consequences.

NOTES

1. By intervening institutions I mean state agencies and programs, labor unions, political parties, private foundations, and other sources of resources outside of neighborhoods that can be used to leverage community social capital—what Xavier de Souza Briggs (1997) calls "resources to get by"—into community political power (significant involvement in decisionmaking regarding the distribution of resources).

2. Here I'm referring to social capital in its current state, not the preventative social capital that might have worked to keep the individual from being arrested in the first place.

3. Xavier de Souza Briggs (1997) discusses two uses for social capital. One is "to get by"(for social support). The other is to "get ahead." He details what he means by getting ahead: "Social capital is used for social leverage, that is to change or improve our life circumstances or 'our opportunity set'" (112).

4. In conversations with the author (22 January, 1998), Jocelyn Sargent has argued astutely that what may have been lost in poor communities is not social capital based on informal neighborhood associations, but the institutionalized forms of social capital (that is, political machines) that were instrumental in mobilizing voters and facilitating other forms of participation.

5. Although my topic in this section is political participation, my analysis is not structured around individual measures of political activity. Instead, I focus on the political activity, representation, and agency of poor communities. Of course, I am interested in whether those who reside in communities with high levels of social capital (however we might measure this) participate at higher levels. Do these individuals go to the polls more often? Do they work for campaigns or participate in boycotts? Possibly a more appropriate question for our interest in social capital is, do such residents talk to their neighbors and friends more often about politics? However, this level of analysis, which concentrates on individual acts of participation, will have to be pursued in future research.

6. Notwithstanding this somewhat conflictual result, researchers in the future will need to explore whether the governing styles of these newly elected women are different from those of the women who previously held their positions. Are the newly elected officials more neighborhood-based in their policy agenda? Is there a greater level of activism among community members in their wards? Are they, for example, more sensitive to the plight of women in poor communities, fashioning legislation to address their needs?

REFERENCES

Alex-Assensoh, Yvette. 1997. "Race, Concentrated Poverty, Social Isolation, and Political Behavior." *Urban Affairs Review* 33(2): 209–27.

Barber, Benjamin R. 1984. *Strong Democracy: Participatory Politics for a New Age.* Berkeley: University of California Press.

Bobo, Lawrence, and Franklin D. Gilliam Jr. 1990. "Race, Sociopolitical Participation, and Black Empowerment." *American Political Science Review* 84: 377–93.

Briggs, Xavier de Souza. 1997. "Social Capital and the Cities: Advice to Change Agents." *National Civic Review* 86(Summer): 111–17.

Cohen, Cathy J., and Michael C. Dawson. 1993. "Neighborhood Poverty and African American Politics." *American Political Science Review* 87(2): 286–302.

Cohen, Jean L. 1998. "Does Voluntary Association Make Democracy Work? The Contemporary American Discourse of Civil Society and Its Dilemmas." Unpublished manuscript.

Coleman, James. 1988. "Social Capital in the Creation of Human Capital." *American Journal of Sociology* 94(summer supp.): S95–120.

———. 1990. *Foundations of Social Theory.* Cambridge, Mass.: Harvard University Press.

Dahl, Robert Alan. 1961. *Who Governs?: Democracy and Power in an American City.* New Haven, Conn.: Yale University Press.

Dawson, Michael C. 1994. "A Black Counterpublic?: Economic Earthquakes, Racial Agenda(s), and Black Politics." *Public Culture* 7: 195–223.

Edin, Kathryn, and Laura Lein. 1997. *Making Ends Meet.* New York: Russell Sage Foundation.

Fraser, Nancy. 1989. "Rethinking the Public Sphere: A Contribution to the Critique of Actually Existing Democracy." In *Habermas and the Public Sphere,* edited by Craig Calhoun and Graig Calhoun. Cambridge, Mass.: MIT Press.

Gilliam, Franklin D., Jr., and Karen M. Kaufmann. 1998. "Is There an Empowerment Life Cycle?: Long-term Black Empowerment and Its Influence on Voter Participation." *Urban Affairs Review* 33(6): 741–66.

Gittell, Marilyn, Kathe Newman, Janice Bockmeyer, and Robert Lindsay. 1998. "Expanding Civic Opportunity: Urban Empowerment Zones." *Urban Affairs Review* 33(4): 530–58.

Gittell, Ross, and Avis Vidal. 1998. *Community Organizing: Building Social Capital as a Development Strategy.* Thousand Oaks, Calif.: Sage Publications.

Glasgow, Douglas G. 1981. *The Black Underclass: Poverty, Unemployment and Entrapment of Ghetto Youth.* New York: Vintage Books.

Hagedorn, John M. 1991. "Gangs, Neighborhoods, and Public Policy." *Social Problems* 38(4): 529–42.

Ladd, Everett C. 1996. "The Data Just Don't Show Erosion of America's 'Social Capital.'" *The Public Perspective* (June–July): 1, 5–6.

Mansbridge, Jane. 1980. *Beyond Adversarial Democracy.* New York: Basic Books.

Massey, Douglas S., and Nancy A. Denton. 1993. *American Apartheid: Segregation and the Making of the Underclass.* Cambridge, Mass.: Harvard University Press.

Minkoff, Debra C. 1997. "Producing Social Capital: National Social Movements and Civil Society." *American Behavioral Scientist* 40(5): 606–19.

Portes, Alejandro, and Patricia Landolt. 1996. "The Downside of Social Capital." *The American Prospect* 26(May–June): 18–21.

Putnam, Robert D. 1993a. *Making Democracy Work: Civic Traditions in Modern Italy.* Princeton, N.J.: Princeton University Press.

———. 1993b. "The Prosperous Community: Social Capital and Public Life." *The American Prospect* (Spring): 65–78.

———. 1995a. "Bowling Alone: America's Declining Social Capital." *Journal of Democracy* 6(1): 65–78.

———. 1995b. "Tuning in, Tuning out: The Strange Disappearance of Social Capital in America." *PS: Political Science and Politics* 28(December): 664–83.

———. 2000. *Bowling Alone: The Collapse and Revival of American Community.* New York: Simon & Schuster.

Rosenstone, Steven J., and John Mark Hansen. 1993. *Mobilization, Participation, and Democracy in America.* New York: Macmillan.

Saegert, Susan, Phillip Thompson, Robert Engle, and Jocelyn Sargent. 1998. "Stretched Thin: Employment, Parenting, and Social Capital Among Mothers in Public Housing." Unpublished paper.

Sandel, Michael J. 1984. *Liberalism and Its Critics.* Oxford: Blackwell.

———. 1996. *Democracy's Discontent: America in Search of a Public Philosophy.* Cambridge, Mass.: Belknap Press of Harvard University Press.

Schneider, Mark, Paul Teske, Melissa Marschall, Michael Mintrom, and Christine Roch. 1997. "Institutional Arrangements and the Creation of Social Capital: The Effects of Public School Choice." *American Political Science Review* 91(1): 82–93.

Stack, Carol B. 1974. *All Our Kin: Strategies for Survival in a Black Community.* New York: Harper and Row.

Stevens, Jacqueline. 1995. "Beyond Tocqueville, Please!" *American Political Science Review* 89(4): 987–90.

Sullivan, Lisa Y. 1997. "Hip-Hop Nation: The Underdeveloped Social Capital of Black Urban America." *National Civic Review* 86(Fall): 235–43.

Summers, Mary, and Philip A. Klinkner. 1996. "The Election and Governance of John Daniels as Mayor of New Haven." In *Race, Politics, and Governance in the United States,* edited by H. L. Perry. Gainesville: University of Florida Press.

Susser, Ira. 1996. "The Construction of Poverty and Homelessness in U.S. Cities." *Annual Review of Anthropology* 25: 411–35.

Tocqueville, Alexis de. 1969 [1835]. *Democracy in America,* edited by J. P. Mayer. Translated by George Lawrence. New York: Anchor Books.

U.S. Bureau of the Census. 1995. *Statistical Brief—Poverty Areas.* Washington: U.S. Government Printing Office (June).

———. 1997. *The Foreign-Born Population: 1996.* Report by Kristen A. Hansen and Carol S. Faber. P20–494. Washington: U.S. Government Printing Office (March).

Verba, Sidney, Kay Lehman Schlozman, and Henry Brady. 1995. *Voice and Equality: Civic Voluntarism in American Politics.* Cambridge, Mass.: Harvard University Press.

Vidal, Avis C. 1996. "CDCs as Agents of Neighborhood Change: The State of the Art." In *Revitalizing Urban Neighborhoods,* edited by W. Dennis Keating, Norman Krumholz, and Philip Star. Lawrence: University of Kansas Press.

Wagner, David, and Marcia B. Cohen. 1991. "The Power of the People: Homeless Protesters in the Aftermath of Social Movement Participation," *Social Problems* 38(4, November): 543–61.

Warren, Dorian, and Cathy J. Cohen. 2000. "Organizing at the Intersection of Labor and Civil Rights: A Case Study of New Haven." *University of Pennsylvania Journal of Labor and Employment Law* 2(4): 629–55.

Wilson, William Julius. 1987. *The Truly Disadvantaged: The Inner City, the Underclass, and Public Policy.* Chicago: University of Chicago Press.

———. 1996. *Why Work Disappears: The World of the New Urban Poor.* New York: Knopf.

Wolfinger, Raymond E., and Steven J. Rosenstone. 1980. *Who Votes?* New Haven: Yale University Press.

Young, Iris Marion. 1989. "Polity and Group Difference: A Critique of the Ideal of Universal Citizenship." *Ethics* 99(2): 250–74.

Zaretsky, Mark. 1997. "Job Issue Next for Omni Hotel." *New Haven Register,* September 16.

Chapter 12

Social Capital, Political Participation, and the Urban Community

Ester R. Fuchs, Robert Y. Shapiro, and Lorraine C. Minnite

The decline of political participation in the United States is most serious in its central cities, where the lowest levels of political engagement can be found among new immigrants, poor African Americans and Latinos, and Asian Americans. In recent years, U.S. citizenship applications have been increasing, although citizenship among new immigrants remains extraordinarily low, and those immigrants who become citizens are generally less likely to vote than native-born Americans. Latinos and Asian Americans, even those born in this country, have demonstrated a persistent pattern of low voter turnout. Voter turnout in the African American community has also been low relative to voter turnout for white ethnics, and especially so in the absence of mobilizing factors such as black candidates on the ballot.

The subject of the decline of political participation in poor communities has been part of a far-reaching discussion on social capital and civic engagement. Social capital is viewed as both a collective asset (Coleman 1988; Putnam 2000) and an individual asset (Putnam 2000) derived from membership in voluntary associations or informal social networks (Putnam 1995a, 1995b, 2000) or from being part of a community where neighbors talk to one another (Berry, Portney, and Thomson 1993) and foster norms of reciprocity, trustworthiness, and collective capacity beyond the association (Putnam 2000; Stolle and Rochon 1998). The decline of social capital has become an important part of the explanation for the decline in political participation in poor urban communities, as well as in middle-class suburbs.

Much of the debate over the social capital thesis has focused on the fundamental character of its decline (Skocpol 1996), whether current empirical measures of it are accurate (Schudson 1996; Skocpol 1996; Goldberg 1996), and the nature of its relations to democracy (Levi 1996; Tarrow 1996; Booth and Richard 1998). Robert Putnam's (1993) earlier work on government devolution in Italy found that the presence of social capital was a powerful determinant of government responsiveness in Italy's new regional governments. He has focused his work on social capital in America on what he sees as a massive erosion of social capital since the 1970s (Putnam 1995a, 1995b, 2000) and its implications for "making democracy work" (Putnam 1993, 185). In *Bowling Alone* (2000), Putnam states his theory in the broadest terms. "We shall review hard evidence that our schools and neighborhoods don't work so well when community bonds slacken, that our economy, our *democracy* and even our health and happiness depend on adequate stocks of social capital" (27–28, emphasis added). The decline in communal forms of political participation as well as voting are documented by Putnam in his articles (1995a, 1995b) as well as in his book (2000, 32–47) in support of this thesis. He clearly distinguishes between formal political participation, including voting, and other forms of civic and religious participation:

> For present purposes, I am concerned with the forms of social capital that, generally speaking, serve civic ends. Social capital in this sense is closely related to political participation in the conventional sense, but these terms are *not* synonymous. Political participation refers to our relations with political institutions. Social capital refers to our relations with one another. (1995b, 665, emphasis added)

The second chapter of Putnam's book is devoted to documenting the decline in political participation, beginning with voting and other "partisan activities" and ending with communal forms of political participation ranging from attendance at public meetings on town affairs to membership in good government groups. The next two chapters demonstrate the decline in civic and religious participation as reflected in association memberships, church memberships, and church attendance.

If we are to take Putnam's claims seriously that the decline in social capital has contributed to the decline in American democracy, then we must also assume that Putnam is arguing that the decline in social capital in America is a fundamental explanation for the much observed decline in communal forms of political participation, as well as voting. Voting, Putnam (2000, 35) states, "is by a substantial margin the most common form of political activity, and it embodies the most fundamental *democratic* principle of equality. Not to vote is to withdraw from the political community." The problem of causation becomes more confusing later in Putnam's book when he uses political participation as both an indicator of social capital and an outcome: Putnam's Social Capital Index includes "turnout in presidential elections" and "attended public meetings on town or school affairs" measures (2000, 291).

While the debate continues over the causes of social capital's decline and ways to measure it, we think it is important to disentangle the implications of the debate for democratic theory. Particularly confusing is the role of social capital for prescriptions of how to stem, if not reverse, the decline in political participation, especially among the inner-city, poor African Americans and immigrants.

Before social capital was developed as a theoretical construct, Sydney Verba and Norman Nie (1972) examined the relationship between participation in voluntary associations and political participation. They argue, like the social capital theorists, that participation in voluntary associations engenders norms of cooperation among their members and that these norms are precisely those required for political participation. Recent work by Sydney Verba, Kay Schlozman, and Henry Brady (1995) also finds an important relationship between organizational activity and political participation. For Verba and his colleagues, the social capital that derives from membership in voluntary associations includes learning the civic skills and acquiring the resources needed for political participation.

If political participation requires social capital, then what does this mean for America's inner-city communities? It is, after all, in the large urban centers with diverse ethnic communities and high concentrations of poverty that social capital has become scarce. William Julius Wilson (1987) finds that Chicago neighborhoods with high concentrations of poverty also have weak social networks and that residents are more likely to be politically isolated. Cathy Cohen and Michael Dawson (1993) find that African American residents of Detroit census tracts with more than 30 percent of residents living in poverty are less likely to engage in civic and social activities compared to African Americans living in neighborhoods that are less poor. The study by Jeffrey Berry and his colleagues (1993) of fifteen cities finds that both low- and middle-income residents of neighborhoods with strong organizations participate more in face-to-face political activity than do those of similar income levels living in neighborhoods with weaker organizations. Put another way, civic engagement is declining in America's cities because the social institutions best capable of promoting the norms of cooperation are also declining. The argument is simple: in communities where social capital has become scarce, political participation is invariably low. The practical implications of this argument are clear: increase social capital in poor African American and immigrant city neighborhoods and political participation will increase as well.

Yet a series of difficult questions emerge from this simple proposition. First, there is an empirical question that must be resolved. Has social capital really declined in poor and immigrant communities, or have researchers simply been looking for the wrong kind of activities? The empirical evidence on the decline of social capital remains inconclusive. Everett Ladd (1996) argues that Putnam is simply wrong about the general decline in social capital, particularly Americans' rate of participation in voluntary associations. Recent studies have also suggested that there has not been a massive erosion of social capital in poor communities, but that different types of social networks exist in black and Hispanic urban neighborhoods (see, for example, Sullivan 1997). Our recent work in New York City's Russian-Jewish community indicates a strong network of communal, social service, and economic organizations in Brooklyn, including the Brighton Beach YMHA, the Church Avenue Merchant Block Association (CAMBA), and the American Association for Jews from the Former Soviet Union. The community also has about seven Russian-language media outlets, newspapers, radio programs, and cable TV stations. According to the Jewish Community Relations Council (JCRC), until the passage of the welfare reform act in 1996 this community of nearly two hundred thousand had little interest in political participation, or even in becoming citizens. There have also been many ethnographic studies, which have found elaborate socioeconomic networks in poor immigrant enclaves (see, for example, Zhou 1992; Haslip-Viera and Baver 1996; and Waldinger 1996). Yet these communities of Asian Americans, Latinos, and Caribbean Americans have very low levels of traditional political participation. Although the problems faced by poor new immigrants and poor native-born African Americans are not the same, it is important to consider both these groups in discussions of poor inner-city communities and the decline of political participation.

Why would involvement in purely social organizations necessarily produce involvement in the political process? To what extent does participation in neighborhood-based social organizations further isolate the poor from engagement in activity that might require cross-class or interracial coalition formation? Moreover, is social capital as a collective asset limited to a geographic community? Can individuals living in poor inner-city communities gain social capital from being part of an ethnic or religious organization that may not be located in their neighborhood? For these same poor individuals, do social organization memberships based on race or ethnicity produce the social capital that might be required to engage in politics in a multi-ethnic or multi-racial neighborhood? According to work by Dietlind Stolle and Thomas Rochon (1998), homogeneous associations in the United States, Germany, and Sweden are less likely to have memberships with high levels of generalized trust and community reciprocity.

Although the decline in social capital may be part of the explanation for the decline in political participation, it is our contention that the decline in political participation in poor urban communities requires a more careful examination of the purpose of the organization and its explicit agenda as it relates to promoting political activity. This argument is suggested by the recent work of Bob Edwards and Michael Foley (1997) and Mark Warren (1998) and in the earlier work of Verba and Nie (1972) and Verba, Schlozman, and Brady (1995). Moreover, if social capital is viewed as a collective asset—a tool in community building that ultimately leads to solving the problems that face poor urban communities (Putnam 1993, 39; Putnam 2000, 297–335)—then it is critical to understand how social capital links individuals and communities directly to the political process, through which they can engage in coalitions with other communities. Specifically, to what extent can bridges be constructed out of the neighborhood to create the citywide alliances needed for winning elections? If elections are considered an important democratic tool for changing public policy, then voting must be a central part of the discussion of how social capital can promote political participation in urban communities. Finally, is it enough simply to belong to organizations that promote norms of cooperation without considering the substantive agenda of the organization? Using the Michigan militia and youth gangs as examples, Putnam (1995b, 2000) acknowledges that not all forms of social capital promote positive societal norms. Alejandro Portes (1998) further argues that some forms of social capital created from belonging to gangs or exclusionary neighborhood associations can be antithetical to the values of a democratic society.

There is another problem with social capital when it is considered a significant resource for solving the problems of poor urban communities. These communities cannot solve their problems simply by relying on their own social capital, no matter how weak or strong their networks may be. Certainly, the life chances of individuals can change when the building blocks of community are reinforced, whether through churches, tenant associations, or neighborhood improvement organizations. Yet poor communities, by definition, have too few resources to change the economic conditions of most of the individuals living in them. In chapter 1, Mark

Warren, Phillip Thompson, and Susan Saegert recognize the need for "bonding" and "bridging" social capital. Yet we would argue that the bridges required for systemic political change in America's poor urban communities require political organizations that emphasize the value of traditional forms of political engagement, especially voting. If the benefits of social capital are to affect large numbers of residents in poor urban communities, there must be, at a minimum, access to the same basic services that other income groups receive in their neighborhoods. Even in today's world of public-private partnerships, the policies needed to improve local public schools, transportation services, libraries, and sanitation services, as well as to provide access to job training and affordable housing, require some formal relationship to the citywide political process. Social capital may be useful for promoting community-based voluntary activity, but it does not necessarily promote traditional forms of political participation: seeking citizenship, registering to vote, and voting in elections.

To this end, it is our view that the conventional social capital thesis falls short as a fully satisfying explanation of the decline of political participation, applied especially to urban democracy. It falls short because it is premised on an inadequate conceptualization of the urban tradition of political participation, which is rooted more in conflict than in consensus building. The social capital argument generally assumes a model of democracy based primarily on America's ideal of a small community engaged in direct or participatory self-government, involving face-to-face relationships (see Mansbridge 1980; Morone 1990; and Berry et al. 1993).[1] These conceptualizations fail to take into account historical differences in urban political participation.

Cities, by virtue of their size, complexity, diversity, and concentrations of low-income people, are unlikely places for communal forms of democratic practice. Communitarian activity in churches and voluntary associations may be typical of poor African American and immigrant urban communities, but communitarian values have hardly dominated their political life, whether local party activities, boycotts, protests, strikes, or voter mobilization efforts. Communitarian forms of political participation imply that individuals engage in political activity to pursue a common interest with their neighbors or to build consensus to achieve shared political values. The other form of democratic political engagement is adversarial or oppositional, usually motivated by self-interest, distrust, or exclusion by the dominant culture. Motivation for political involvement might be getting a job through political contacts, organizing to ensure that the sewage treatment plant or drug treatment facility is not built in one's neighborhood, or getting better or fairer treatment from government authorities.

Unions, traditional African American civil rights organizations, and political machines are institutions that have successfully used an adversarial model of democratic mobilization. Until the 1960s, traditional political involvement in most major American cities was mediated by strong local party organizations. In the highly contentious battles over urban turf, new immigrants had material incentives to become citizens, involve themselves in political campaigns, and vote for the candidates who best represented their interests (Banfield and Wilson 1963; Allswang 1977; Erie 1988). The situation was complicated for African Americans who confronted racism and legal barriers to political incorporation even when they were part of a machine's majority electoral coalition. Steven Erie (1988) criticizes political machines for selectively incorporating and mobilizing city residents, yet that is simply one of the hallmarks of adversarial democratic institutions. Political machines, after all, were party organizations in the business of maintaining a majority coalition to win elections.

Frederick Harris (1998) and Richard Shingles (1981) argue that African Americans' distrust in government and political cynicism provide a "paradoxical" link to their civic engagement. Harris explains that the norm of the African American community has been to mix system-oriented participation and protest, which has been sustained historically by what he calls an "oppositional civic culture." Phillip Thompson (personal communication, 2000) argues that the strongest adversarial civil rights organizations, like the Southern Christian Leadership Conference (SCLC), were also the ones with the strongest internal bonds of friendship and loyalty. Frances Fox Piven and Richard Cloward's (1979) seminal work on poor people's movements shows that civil rights organizations, unions, and welfare rights organizations have a history of promoting adversarial democracy. In a recent study of the Industrial Areas Foundation (IAF) in San Antonio, Warren (1998) points out that the IAF recognized that conflict might be an important part of a mobilization strategy. Indeed, the relational organizing strategy, considered the hallmark of the IAF, engages poor people who are already connected through their churches. Clearly, the concept of social capital as currently formulated fails to recognize that urban political participation and the political activism of disenfranchised groups have their roots in political conflict and exclusion rather than in consensus-building experiences.

There is no question that there has been a decline in political incorporation and general political participation in the historical period that coincides with the decline of the local party organization, the decline of union membership, and the decline of the civil rights organizations. By paying little attention to the rich history of urban party politics, union activism, civil rights protests, and issue-based mobilization in American cities, social capital theory offers a curiously apolitical model of urban democracy, missing a significant part of the explanation for the decline in political participation: the decline of institutions that mobilize and promote political involvement (Rosenstone and Hansen 1993).

To better understand the relationship between social capital and urban democracy, we have developed a related concept we call "political capital" (Fuchs, Minnite, and Shapiro 1999). Political capital, like social capital, adheres in the relations between people (Coleman 1988). Like social capital, it is acquired through participation in voluntary associations, including social and church organizations, but only when these organizations also engage in political activity. Verba and Nie (1972) and Verba, Schlozman, and Brady (1995) made a similar distinction when they considered the impact of nonpolitical organizations on political participation.

It is quite possible, and very likely, that political capital may be acquired apart from social capital. In a sense, the IAF's strategy, as outlined by Warren (1998), and that of other church-based organizing efforts, like the Pacific Institute for Community Organization (PICO) (Wood 1997), is to use the existing social capital in the community to create political capital. Interestingly, the collaboration of these community-based organizations with political partners developed from a confrontational or conflict strategy.

Implicit in this study is the notion that government ("the state") has an impact on the life chances of poor and immigrant city residents. We argue that government responsiveness to the needs of a poor community is influenced by the level of political participation in that community, including traditional forms of participation like voting, contacting local officials, and issue mobilization. The strongest proponents of this thesis are Rufus Browning, Dale Rogers Marshall, and David Tabb (1997a, 1997b). Their volume presents compelling evidence that minorities have gained important benefits from political incorporation and from participating in biracial coalitions. Certainly, traditional forms of political participation are not the only ones available to these communities; protest and movement organizing and single-issue mobilization are also important in building political capital. It is our contention that poor groups can best promote systemic change by becoming partners in a majority electoral coalition, and ultimately part of a governing coalition with the power to change public policy.

Thus, the long-term benefits of improving social capital in a poor urban community, we argue, depend on its capacity to build political capital as well. Poor communities can construct self-contained networks and achieve important improvements in their condition, but alone they can never produce sufficient social capital to bring about systemic change. Poor communities need political capital as well as social capital to engage successfully in the adversarial political process that is characteristic of most major American cities.

In this chapter, we examine the relationship between social capital, political capital, and the decline of political participation, especially voting, among native-born African Americans and immigrants in New York City. We address the theoretical problem of distinguishing between social and political capital and examine more carefully the empirical data on socioeconomic and political networks in poor urban communities. This study is intended to refocus the discussion of social capital from primarily social institutions to the declining institutions of political incorporation in poor communities, especially the local political party, civil rights organizations, and labor unions. First, we present data on the ethnic, racial, and income distribution of big-city populations. We then briefly consider the economic and fiscal conditions of America's largest immigrant cities. Second, we consider trends in political participation in order to determine the extent to which the poor and immigrant communities are being left out of traditional forms of political participation. Third, we present a new model that explains traditional political participation, separating the effects of political and social capital. Finally, we propose a research agenda to consider the types of organizations that would work best to build political capital in immigrant and poor urban communities.

URBAN POPULATION TRENDS AND THE QUESTION OF POLITICAL PARTICIPATION

In this section, we present data on the racial and ethnic distribution of the population, on trends in electoral participation and citizenship, and on the fiscal and economic conditions of five American cities—New York, Los Angeles, Chicago, Houston, and Miami-Dade County.[2] All are considered the ports of entry for the majority of America's new immigrants, and they also have large concentrations of poor native-born African Americans and Latinos. According to the census, about one-half of new immigrants entering the United States in the 1980s live in one of eight metropolitan areas: Los Angeles, New York, Miami, Anaheim, Chicago, Washington, D.C., Houston, and San Francisco (Smith and Edmonston 1997, 61).

Racial and Ethnic Distribution of Populations

The racial and ethnic distribution of the populations of these five cities has changed dramatically since 1980.[3] According to the census, the white (non-Hispanic) population in New York City dropped from 51.9 percent in 1980 to 35.6 percent in 1997. At the same time, the most significant growth was in the Hispanic population, which grew to 25.6 percent of the population. Blacks have remained fairly constant, with a 29.7 percent share of the city's population in 1997. The number of Asians has also grown dramatically since 1980 but still remains only 8.7 percent of the population. In Los Angeles, the growth in the number of Hispanics is even greater than in New York. In 1990 Hispanics became the largest group in the Los Angeles population, at 39.3 percent. Significantly, the black population declined to only 13.2 percent of the population in 1990. Los Angeles has the largest proportion of Asians among these cities. In 1990 Asians were 9.4 percent of the city's population, and they experienced the greatest growth rate during the 1980s.

Chicago experienced a greater decline in its white population before 1980, as compared to the other cities. By 1990 Chicago's white population constituted 38.2 percent of its total population, similar to the proportion in Houston and Los Angeles. Chicago's black population declined slightly, while its Hispanic population grew to 19.2 percent of the total. Significantly, in 1990 blacks (38.7 percent) and white non-Hispanic (38.2 percent) constituted virtually the same proportion of the population in Chicago. By 1990 Houston's white population had dropped to 40.8 percent, while its Hispanic population grew to 27.2 percent. Interestingly, its black population remained relatively unchanged between 1980 and 1990.

Miami-Dade County's population showed the most significant change between 1980 and 1990. The white population declined to 30.4 percent, the black population grew slightly to 19.2 percent, and the Hispanic population increased to 40 percent. By 1997 Hispanics constituted a majority of the county's population at 54.2 percent.

The demographic trends show a continuing decline in the white proportion of these cities' populations, a leveling-off or a decline in their black populations, and the greatest growth rates among the Hispanic and Asian populations. Although the changes are more dramatic in these cities, the direction of the change mirrors national trends. In 1997 the nation's white population declined to 71.9 percent, its black population grew slowly to 12.5 percent, and its Hispanic (11.1 percent) and Asian (3.8 percent) populations showed the most significant growth rates. The difference between national trends and city trends is in the proportional distribution. Nationally, whites remain 71.9 percent of the population, but they no longer constitute a majority of the population in any of the nation's largest cities.

Although the white population in our central cities has declined, those who remain tend to be better off than their black, Hispanic, and Asian neighbors. Whites are the group least likely to fall below the poverty line in all of these cities except Miami. Blacks fall below the poverty line in extraordinarily high numbers in all of these cities; 46 percent of Miami's black population lived below the poverty line in 1990. Hispanics are even more likely than blacks to fall below the poverty line, except in Miami, where there is a large middle-class Cuban population. Even in the city of Miami, 28.5 percent of Hispanics fall below the poverty line. Asians are less likely than blacks and Hispanics to be poor but still have greater poverty levels than the white population in these cities.

Economic and Fiscal Indicators

As part of our justification for focusing on local political participation, there should be some real evidence that these cities have the capacity to provide opportunity for their new immigrants and native-born poor. In this section, we present data on the fiscal and economic conditions for New York, Los Angeles, Chicago, Houston, and Miami-Dade County. Although the distribution of resources is politically determined, cities with extremely weak economies and unstable fiscal conditions have a limited capacity to assist their poverty populations (see Fuchs 1992). The particular cities we are considering do have sufficient local resources to affect economic opportunities for their poor communities, but whether or not those opportunities become available is ultimately determined by each city's policy priorities.

Growing populations and growth in local revenue are two important indicators that a city has a strong economy and a tax base capable of supporting the city's budget. The total population grew in Houston, Los Angeles, Miami-Dade County, and New York between 1980 and 1997. Only Chicago's population declined in this period, by 9.4 percent. Although the rates vary, all of these cities showed continued growth during the 1990s, and even Chicago's rate of population loss slowed. The most significant growth was in Miami-Dade County, which showed a 29.2 percent increase in its population between 1980 and 1997. Los Angeles is a close second, with a 23.9 percent increase in its population.

The revenue a city raises from its own tax base, not including state and federal intergovernmental transfers, is a useful measure of the strength of the local economy. According to the census, all four cities and Miami-Dade County showed significant growth in revenues derived from their own tax base between fiscal years

1990 and 1994.[4] Per capita growth in own-source New York City revenue was highest for this period, at 20.5 percent, and Los Angeles was the lowest at 4.2 percent. Miami-Dade County per capita revenues from own sources grew 122 percent between 1987 and 1994.

The life chances of residents in poor urban communities will not change unless their social and political capital is ultimately linked to economic opportunity. Although it is an important goal to bring private capital into poor communities, most of the economic resources and institutions that affect individual life chances in poor immigrant and African American communities are either controlled or partly funded by the state. These institutions include schools, public or supported housing, libraries, health care institutions, recreation centers, criminal justice facilities, job training programs, and church-based social service activities. Government may not be the primary employer in most poor communities, but government is usually subsidizing or completely funding the activities in the private and not-for-profit institutions. We are not suggesting that cities should begin engaging in massive redistributive programs funded from their own revenues. Rather, it is partly a question of redirecting existing resources; the funds already available in a city's budget for existing services could be used more effectively in poor communities. Moreover, in periods of record city budget surpluses, funds could also be earmarked for capacity-building programs in poor communities. New York City ended fiscal year 1998 with a record $2 billion surplus, and fiscal year 1997's surplus was $1.4 billion (Onishi 1998). Chicago proposed a 3.7 percent increase in its 1998 budget because of higher-than-expected revenues and a "robust local economy" (Spielman 1997). In Los Angeles, budgeted revenue in fiscal year 1999 represented a 4 percent increase over the last fiscal year, "reflecting continued economic growth" (City of Los Angeles 1998).

Electoral Participation and Citizenship

In this section, we present data on the political participation of ethnic and racial and immigrant groups for the cities, when available, and for the nation.[5] These data provide evidence of the differences in political behavior between racial and ethnic groups and between immigrants and native-born Americans. The significant differences among these groups speak to the seriousness of the problem. The decline in political participation among Americans has been well documented (see, for example, Wolfinger and Rosenstone 1980; Piven and Cloward 1988; and Rosenstone and Hansen 1993). The extent to which we have failed to incorporate immigrants into the mainstream of American politics is just starting to surface. Moreover, because new immigrants tend to live in cities with high concentrations of African Americans and Latinos in poverty, we are compounding the alienation of both these populations.

The nationwide trend in citizenship for the foreign-born voting-age population shows a dramatic decline over the past fifty years. In 1950 only 25.8 percent of the foreign-born population had not become citizens. By 1997 this proportion had increased to an extraordinary 62.4 percent. Census data also show that there is a significant disparity in citizenship rates across racial and ethnic groups. In 1997 Hispanics were the least likely to become citizens. Only 23 percent of foreign-born Hispanics of voting age had become citizens, compared with 39 percent of blacks and 47 percent of whites. The national data also show that there was only an 8 percent difference in voter registration rates and a 7 percent difference in turnout rates between immigrants and native-born in the 1996 presidential election.

The biggest hurdle to political participation for immigrant groups appears to be citizenship. According to the census, the differences between whites and blacks are not that significant when it comes to registering and turning out to vote in the most recent presidential elections (1992 and 1996). However, whites and blacks were almost twice as likely as Hispanics to register or turn out to vote in these presidential elections.

What accounts for the serious change in immigrant political incorporation since 1950? It is possible that the 1950s immigrant cohort had simply been in the United States longer than the 1990s cohort. We know that the longer immigrants stay in this country, the more likely it is that they will become citizens. Yet the steep decline in citizenship rates among immigrants between 1970 and 1990 and the magnitude of the difference between 1950 and 1997 make that an unlikely explanation. It is possible that today's immigrants are simply less interested than earlier immigrants in becoming citizens because of their transnational status. Michael Jones-Correa (1998) argues that attachments to their home country make Hispanic immigrants less likely to become citizens. Transnationalism seems like an insufficient explanation, however, for the lack of interest in and alienation from American politics that many immigrants experience. Perhaps today's immigrants are less interested than earlier immigrant groups in becoming citizens simply because the institutions responsible for incorporating them into American politics worked a lot better fifty years ago than they do today.

Finally, table 12.1 offers some longitudinal data for local political participation in New York City over the last thirty-six years. The New York City voting-age population has increased by 5.7 percent, and the number of people registered to vote has increased by 6.5 percent, but the number of registered voters who actually vote in mayoral elections *decreased by 44 percent* between 1961 and 1997. This is even more dramatic when we consider that only 24.7 percent of the voting-age population actually voted in the last mayoral race.

How do these data inform our discussion of urban democracy? The transformation in the racial and ethnic composition of these cities should have had enormous political consequences, if earlier patterns of political incorporation and "ethnic succession" had continued after 1960. If electing representatives from your own racial or ethnic group is a measure of political succession, all of these cities have experienced some measure of real political change. All of these cities have elected black or Hispanic mayors and increased their black and Hispanic representation in their city councils. In 1993 even Miami-Dade County, after being forced by the federal courts to create a nondiscriminatory government, elected a majority of blacks and

TABLE 12.1 / Selected Measures of Voter Participation in New York City, 1961 to 1997

Year	Voting-Age Population (VAP)	Registered Voters	Mayoral Vote	Percentage VAP Registered	Percentage VAP Voting	Percentage Registered Voters Voting
1961	5,341,080	3,239,879	2,424,990	60.7	45.5	74.8
1965	5,320,903	3,281,689	2,554,210	61.7	48	77.8
1969	5,300,726	3,026,745	2,378,240	57.1	44.9	78.6
1973	5,599,343	3,565,147	1,705,660	63.7	30.5	47.8
1977	5,480,526	2,778,506	1,435,154	50.7	26.2	51.7
1981	5,302,472	2,585,464	1,222,648	48.8	23.1	47.3
1985	5,400,000	3,014,459	1,170,904	55.8	21.7	38.8
1989	5,475,000	3,183,741	1,899,845	58.2	34.7	59.7
1993	5,632,374	3,280,918	1,783,936	58.3	31.7	54.4
1997	5,646,605	3,452,023	1,357,403	61.1	24.7	39.3

Sources: 1961–1989: New York City Board of Elections and U.S. Census Bureau estimates, as cited in Charles Brecher and Raymond D. Horton, *Power Failure: New York Politics and Policy Since 1960*, Oxford University Press, 1993.

1993: New York City Board of Elections and U.S. Census Bureau estimates, as cited in George E. Hall and Courtenay M. Slater, *1994 County and City Extra: Annual Metro, City, and County Guidebook*, Bernan Press, 1994.

1997: New York City Voter Assistance Commission; and U.S. Census Bureau estimates are for 1996, as reported in George E. Hall and Courtenay M. Slater, *1997 County and City Extra: Annual Metro, City and County Data Book*, Bernan Press, 1997.

Hispanics to its county commission. Yet many would argue that Tom Bradley in Los Angeles, Harold Washington in Chicago, David Dinkins in New York City, and Lee Brown in Houston did not (in Brown's case, will not) significantly change the life chances of poor inner-city residents. The experience of these black mayors should simply reinforce notions that political disengagement is not really a problem for inner-city minority communities, since elections cannot change their economic opportunities. In fact, Adolph Reed (1988) argues, electing black mayors with a biracial coalition produces even fewer benefits for poor blacks, because their votes are taken for granted in elections. Clearly, the failure of prominent black mayors to change the policy priorities and significantly improve basic services in their poor communities has exacerbated the political alienation of poor, minority, inner-city residents.

These cases speak to the problem that Clarence Stone (1989) describes in his study of Atlanta—namely, for systemic change to occur, a city must transform its governing coalition or "regime." Stone is pessimistic that new electoral coalitions can change governing coalitions. Yet in each instance, we could argue, these mayors did make a difference in their cities. Rufus Browning and his colleagues (1997b) present convincing evidence that electoral incorporation can change governing coalitions in time, and that this produces significant change in the construction of urban policy. The data we present also have clear implications for the efficacy of future electoral coalitions. Except for Miami, no one racial-ethnic group has a majority of the voting-age population in any of these cities. Winning citywide elections requires the formation of a coalition. Although the African American and Hispanic poor (both native-born and new immigrants) are a significant part of the adult voting-age population, their citizenship, voter registration, and voter turnout rates are notably lower than those of their middle-class, native-born, white counterparts, reducing their political influence. In reality, we could hardly identify them as important partners in the majority electoral coalitions in any of the cities we consider. As a consequence, it should not be surprising that governing coalitions have not paid serious attention to the needs of these communities. We have yet to test the real power of voting as an instrument for transforming poor communities in America's largest cities.

It is not simply the experience of black mayors that has made poor and minority communities question the value of elections. The widespread agreement with the "city limits" argument (Peterson 1981) has also had a perverse impact on local political participation, especially voting. Acceptance of the position that the federal government is the appropriate arena for funding policies that target the poor has been used by elected officials to relieve city governments of responsibility for the problems in their poor neighborhoods. It has also made many think that there is little value gained by engaging in traditional electoral politics that focuses on city government. We are arguing that our major cities have the capacity to change the conditions in their poor communities by improving basic services, beginning with neighborhood schools. This does not require cities to fund large-scale, redistributive programs, but it does require the political will to make service delivery in poor communities a city priority.

URBAN DEMOCRACY AND LOCAL POLITICAL PARTICIPATION: A NEW MODEL

If traditional political participation is necessary to change the opportunities for most individuals in poor and immigrant urban communities, as we have argued, then how do we explain both the low levels and the decline in political participation in these communities? Are low levels of social capital the critical explanation for low levels of political participation? To answer these questions, we analyze data collected in a 1997 telephone survey of a sample of 1,123 adult New Yorkers age eighteen and over, supplemented by additional samples of blacks and Latinos.[6] Many researchers who have not studied New York City are quick to dismiss it as an anomaly among America's cities. In this instance, New York's racial, religious, and ethnic diversity, its geographically concentrated poverty populations, its neighborhood enclaves, and its continuing attraction to new immigrants make it an ideal case for considering the relationship between social capital, community building, and political participation. Furthermore, the decline in political participation in New York—in voter turnout in particular—no doubt reflects a national trend.

As government, foundations, and not-for-profits begin to focus resources on building social capital in poor and immigrant communities as part of a strategy to increase political participation in these communities, it is useful to consider the empirical evidence concerning the relationship between social capital and political participation. If social capital, as it is conventionally defined, is not the answer to increasing political participation, can we consider other forms of social capital that might produce engagement in the political process? The data presented in this chapter allow us to consider the different opportunities available to those who choose to engage in politics as compared to those who do not participate. We argue that political capital is a distinctive variant of social capital that must be considered separately to best explain political participation. The basic model in studying the influences of social and political capital on local political participation can be depicted as follows:

FIGURE 12.1 / Influences on Political Participation

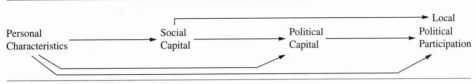

Personal Characteristics → Social Capital → Political Capital → Local Political Participation

Source: Authors' configuration.

The variables that explain political participation are what we have called *social* and *political capital*. The causal sequencing in the model allows for social capital to affect or lead to political capital or to otherwise be correlated with it. Theorists who have emphasized social capital do so by conflating social capital and political capital. We take issue with this conceptualization, since it is quite possible—and we think likely—that political capital can be acquired quite apart from social capital. We would at minimum want to treat this as an empirical question and allow both political and social capital to have separate as well as overlapping effects. The *personal characteristics* refer to the important differences between individuals, including most notably race, gender, age, income, education, and employment status. These are demographic variables that we analyze as control variables to avoid finding spurious relationships in estimating the effects of social and political capital on political participation (see, for example, Verba and Nie 1972; Verba, Schlozman, and Brady 1995). The appendix provides further information about how the demographic variables were measured.

Measuring Local Political Participation

Our first task in the data analysis was to measure the dependent variable, *local political participation*. We developed a simple 0–4-point local participation scale in which each respondent was given a score equal to how many of the following acts he or she had engaged in: voted in the 1993 mayoral election; voted in a school board election;

contacted a local official in the last year; took a political action during the recent battle at the time over rent control. The appendix reports the specific question wordings for the four participation questions. These questions were the most appropriate since they asked specifically about participation in explicitly *local* politics.

A factor analysis was done to ensure that all four variables loaded as a single dimension, with loading of .5 or better; they all did so. This factor accounted for 40 percent of the variance in the items, and the Cronbach's alpha for the reliability of the resulting scale was .51.

DISTINGUISHING MEASURES OF SOCIAL CAPITAL FROM POLITICAL CAPITAL

The notion that individuals who participate in social organizations are also more likely to participate in politics is not particularly novel (Verba and Nie 1972). One could argue, however, that these early studies were framing a participatory personality. The contribution of this more recent construction of social capital comes from recognition that involvement in social institutions, such as the church, teaches participatory norms and promotes democratic values. The concept of social capital is to a large extent institutionally based. Another form of social capital comes simply from attachments to a community. Individuals or families who have these attachments are more likely to engage in political activity.

In our study, we consider all three dimensions of social capital. We construct measures for social organizational membership and church attendance to get at the role of individual involvement in social institutions. Length of time at present address, whether the individual planned to leave the city, and homeownership were considered measures of community attachment. We also added Internet access, hypothesizing that Internet activity is conceivably another form of community building. Internet utopians have argued that virtual community may someday take the place of the more traditional forms of social organization in which we currently involve ourselves. Alternatively, it may be the case that those who are more active socially and politically are thereby led to use the Internet. By including it in our statistical analysis, we may be giving this too much credit as a source of social capital.

As compelling as the concept of social capital has become, we contend that it is insufficient for explaining patterns of local political participation. We have chosen to develop the concept of political capital for the simple reason that politics matters for political mobilization and participation. Political capital may be particularly important in determining levels of participation in poor, urban ethnic communities. Many ethnographic studies have found immigrant enclaves with elaborate socioeconomic networks (see, for example, Zhou 1992; Haslip-Viera and Baver 1996; Waldinger 1996). Yet these communities of Asian Americans, Latinos, and Caribbean Americans have much lower levels of political involvement compared to whites, as we showed earlier in the chapter. Asian Americans have the lowest voter turnout rate among ethnic and racial groups in New York City, but they have highly successful networks of social and economic organizations.

We define political capital as those organizational memberships, networks, structural positions, and attitudes that explicitly build opportunities and capacities to participate in *politics*, especially elections. It is our position that individuals who join social organizations are not particularly interested in engaging in politics, and that the norms they are learning do not particularly relate to the adversarial forms of political participation that are characteristic of large cities. If organizational involvement is to lead to political participation, the organization must have an explicitly political agenda that allows its members to move beyond participation in the ordinary functions of the organization expressly to confront contentious and interest-based political issues.

Measuring Social Capital and Political Capital

The appendix reports the question wordings and categories of our measures of social capital and political capital. Our measures of social capital include memberships in strictly social organizations, residence length, whether the respondent planned to leave New York City, homeownership, frequency of attendance at church or religious services, and Internet access at home. The measure of memberships in social organizations is the number of organizations in which the respondent is a member, but it includes only memberships that are social and not at all related to politics. That is, we did not include organizations that the respondents reported were involved in politics—*as perceived by our respondents.* We considered memberships in organizations involved in politics as sources of *political* capital. Specifically, we created a separate measure of the number of memberships in organizations involved in politics, so that we had two organization membership scales, one social and one explicitly political.

Table 12.2 shows that type of organization is insufficient information for understanding how the organization relates to politics. Interestingly, the same type of organization could be strictly social or involved in political activity. For example, religious institutions had the highest level of membership (37.3 percent), but only 26.5 percent of their members said that their religious institution engaged in political activity. Sports organizations, charitable or social service organizations, and hobby clubs are generally not viewed as political by their members. Civic groups and ethnic, professional, and veterans' associations are most likely to engage in political activity.

Our other measures of political capital had other explicitly institutional bases. To assess the importance of political parties as institutions fostering participation, we constructed a dummy variable that took on a value of 1 (and 0 otherwise) if a person was both registered to vote in a political party and reported that he or she was a strong Democrat or Republican. We also examined the effect of direct mobilization by responses to a survey question asking whether the respondent had recently been contacted to register or to vote; we treat this item as a rough measure of whether the respondent is in a position to be reached for mobilization efforts (Rosenstone and Hansen 1993). We also examined the importance of citizenship as

TABLE 12.2 / New York City Political Participation Survey (1997)
Organizational Membership

Type of Organization	Percentage of Total Sample With Membership*	Percentage of Membership in Organizations Engaged in Political Activity**
Religious	37.3	26.5
	(1022)	(362)
Labor union	24.1	83.0
	(1021)	(223)
Professional	17.1	56.8
	(1021)	(206)
Neighborhood association	17.1	47.0
	(1021)	(168)
Sports	16.8	10.9
	(1020)	(156)
Parent-teacher association	15.9	42.8
	(1020)	(152)
Literary-arts group	11.6	25.9
	(1017)	(108)
Ethnic association	10.1	60.8
	(1014)	(97)
Hobby club	8.9	22.4
	(1018)	(85)
Charitable or social service	8.3	38.0
	(1018)	(79)
Civic group	6.4	56.3
	(1017)	(64)
Veterans' association	4.7	63.4
	(1020)	(41)

Source: Authors' compilation.

*Numbers in parentheses in column 1 represent the valid number of responses for questions about organizational affiliation.

**Numbers in parentheses in column 2 represent the valid number of respondents with organizational affiliations for each type of organization.

political capital. On the one hand, it may be so obvious that we should have limited our analysis only to citizens, since only citizens are eligible to vote. On the other hand, noncitizens are permitted to vote in school board elections in New York, and they may also contact local officials and take action, other than voting, on issues such as rent control. In any case, we need to control for citizenship, regardless of how we interpret its effect on participation.

Another measure of political capital is union membership, which we distinguish fully from memberships in other social or political organizations. In New York City, if not nationally, unions are distinctive organizations that are actively involved in politics. Indeed, 83 percent of the union members in our sample reported that their unions were involved in politics (see table 12.2). The importance of unions as distinctive political institutions that cultivate political capital cannot be ignored. In fact, the way we would interpret Putnam's lament about the decline of league bowling is that this is a metaphor for the decline of unions, which, in some places, helped organize, or at least facilitate, workers' bowling leagues.

We also hypothesized that in urban areas people might be motivated to take political action to voice disapproval of neighborhood services. But this is clearly an empirical question, since those who are satisfied with such services may acquire political capital by having confidence in local government. Similarly, we included in our analysis a measure of explicitly *local* political efficacy, as described in the appendix. Our last measures of political capital concern the influences of respondents' personal networks of family, friends, and coworkers with whom they interact and have the opportunity to discuss politics. One measure included is a scale of frequency of political discussion with friends, family, and coworkers combined. The other measures are whether the respondent's family, friends, and coworkers usually vote. Our expectation is that one acquires political capital by being situated among others who are interested and active in politics (see the appendix for further details).

ANALYSIS

Table 12.3 reports the bivariate correlations between and among measures of political capital, social capital, and local political participation. The causal processes that we are examining involve the effects of social capital and political capital on participation, pitting one against the other as dominant causal explanations. But another way in which social capital can influence political participation is by leading to political capital. So that once we control statistically for political capital, we might expect no direct effect of social capital on political participation. For this to be an important mechanism for social capital to affect participation, we should find two things in our data. First, our measures of social capital should be significantly correlated with our measure of local political participation. Second, our measures of social capital should be more strongly correlated with political capital than they are with political participation, which would produce a substantial *indirect effect* of social capital on participation through processes involving political capital. This assumes too, as we would also expect, that political capital is significantly related to political participation. All of this, of course, would have to be sorted out further through our multivariate analysis.

To start, table 12.3 reveals what we would expect: our measures of both political capital and social capital are significantly correlated with local political participation. Among the social capital measures, the strongest correlates with participation are social organization memberships ($r = .22$), residence length ($r = .27$), home-ownership ($r = .17$), and church attendance ($r = .14$), while Internet access at home is insignificant. These results bear out what we would expect from social capital. But

TABLE 12.3 / Pearson's Correlations for Social and Political Capital Variables

	Local Participation Scale	Efficacy Scale	Organizational Memberships—Social	Plan to Leave NYC in Future	Length of Time at Present Address	Homeowner	Church Attendance	Internet
Local participation scale	1.000*** (983)	.109*** (924)	.220*** (890)	-.055 (856)	.272*** (898)	.166*** (925)	.144*** (901)	.038 (904)
Efficacy scale	.106*** (924)	1.000*** (988)	.100*** (874)	-.107*** (849)	.056 (882)	.073** (905)	-.041 (886)	.116*** (886)
Organizational memberships—political	.367*** (890)	.006 (874)	.019 (931)	-.022 (817)	-.012 (858)	.064 (883)	.218*** (859)	.182*** (860)
Union membership and union is political	.195*** (957)	.032 (936)	.013 (928)	.010 (892)	.039 (936)	.086*** (963)	.070** (938)	-.031 (940)
Family members vote	.275*** (981)	.141*** (987)	.086*** (930)	-.048 (894)	.145*** (937)	.108*** (965)	.102*** (940)	.001*** (942)
Friends vote	.178*** (982)	.121*** (988)	.044 (930)	-.104*** (894)	.128*** (938)	.055 (966)	.111*** (941)	.027 (943)
Co-workers vote	.106*** (981)	.140*** (987)	.067** (929)	.007 (893)	-.068** (937)	.050 (965)	.072** (940)	.159*** (942)
Discuss politics scale	.234*** (969)	.155*** (960)	.150*** (919)	.008 (883)	-.066** (926)	.064** (952)	.009 (927)	.215*** (929)
Citizenship	.368*** (918)	.068** (901)	.023 (875)	-.002 (876)	.282*** (928)	.156*** (954)	-.044 (937)	.073** (941)
Strong party ID	.386*** (817)	.042 (815)	.064 (778)	-.079** (773)	.227*** (807)	.075** (828)	.121*** (810)	.045 (694)
Recently contacted to register or vote	.088*** (973)	-.017 (977)	.081** (922)	.016 (885)	-.046 (931)	.049 (958)	.028 (932)	.055 (935)
Local services satisfaction scale	-.072** (963)	.134*** (971)	-.017 (910)	-.154*** (878)	-.012 (921)	.013 (947)	.057 (922)	-.060 (925)

Source: Authors' compilation.
** significant at the .05 level.
*** significant at the .01 level.

the bivariate correlations for the political capital measures are somewhat more impressive. First and foremost, the correlation between local participation and memberships in organizations involved in politics is particularly striking (r = .37) compared with the moderate but noticeably weaker correlation between participation and more strictly social memberships. Memberships in unions also matter (r = .20). Discussing politics and interacting with people who participate in politics is pertinent too, although these variables may be endogenous to participation itself. Citizenship is especially important (r = .37), and we also find that mobilization—being contacted about voting (r = .09)—and discontent with local services (r = −.07 for satisfaction with services) are at least weakly correlated with local political activity. In addition to these correlates, the single largest is for strong political partisanship, which we have also emphasized as a crucial influence on participation in city politics. In particular, it is highly correlated with local political participation as membership in organizations engaged in politics (r = .39).

We also find some very telling relationships—or rather, the lack of some expected relationships—bearing on the influences of social capital on participation. Although both social and political capital are clearly correlated with local political participation, what we consider one of our most striking findings is that there is no statistically significant correlation between memberships in purely social organizations and memberships in organizations involved in politics (r = .02). The same applies for its insignificant correlation with strong political partisanship (r = .06). This is a very important result, since nonpolitical social memberships are the centerpiece of theories that emphasize the importance of social capital for political engagement. We do find, however, that a few of the other measures of social capital are noticeably correlated with important measures of political capital. Residence length and church attendance are related to strong political partisanship (r's of .23 and .12, respectively), and that church attendance is also correlated moderately with memberships in social organizations involved in politics (r = .22). Last, in terms of correlates of social capital with political capital, Internet access is, at least bivariately, moderately to strongly correlated with politically oriented organizational memberships (r = .18) and discussing politics (r = .22).

Based on this simple bivariate analysis, the evidence suggests that political capital matters more than social capital when it comes to political participation, and that social capital overall seems to contribute neither persistently nor substantially to political capital, since only a few of our measures of social capital are appreciably correlated with our measures of political capital, and these do not include memberships in strictly social organizations. These preliminary evaluations need to be compared further with the results of the critical multivariate analysis.

The results of our multivariate regression analysis are presented in table 12.4. The coefficients reported are our best estimates of likely causal effects of social capital and political capital on political participation. Overall, they substantially strengthen our main arguments and inferences thus far.

Some caveats, however, are in order. Although we are confident that our measures are adequate, as we have discussed, the measure of the dependent variable, local participation, is not quite as reliable a measure as we would have preferred (Cronbach's

TABLE 12.4 / Influences on Local Political Participation[a]

| | Unstandardized Coefficients | | |
	Demographics	Social Capital	Political Capital
Demographic measures			
Currently working	.167**	.178**	−.048
Age	.002**	.019**	.014**
Female gender	.128*	.078	.043
Black	.151*	.160*	−.029
Latino	−.077	−.066	.016
Other race	−.343**	−.276**	.017
Social capital measures			
Organizational memberships—social		.130**	.121**
Plan to leave NYC in future		.107	.085
Length of time at present address		.078**	.021
Homeowner		.158*	.082
Church attendance		.047*	.020
Internet access		.086	−.088
Political capital measures			
Organizational memberships—political			.248**
Union member and union is political			.159**
Family members vote			.132*
Friends vote			−.010
Co-workers vote			.049
Discuss politics scale			.037**
Citizenship			.619**
Strong party identification			.469**
Recently contacted to register or vote			.181**
Local services satisfaction scale			−.012**
Local political efficacy scale			.070**
Constant	.175	−.446	−.999**
R^2	.167	.223	.421
Adj. R^2	.144	.191	.384
N	884	884	860

Source: Authors' compilation.
[a]OLS Regression, Dependent Variable: Local Participation Scale (0–4).
Note: In this regression we also controlled for categories of education and income, "don't knows," and other nonresponses.
*t-value significant at the .1 level. **t-value significant at the .05 level.

alpha of .51). As a result, our multivariate results should have a weaker fit and weaker estimated effects of our independent variables in this model than if we had less measurement error in the dependent variable. But as the bivariate correlations show, and the multivariate results bear out, we are still able to estimate several strong relationships that are central to our analysis, and the fits of our statistical models are reasonably good, explaining 38 percent (adjusted R-square) of the variance in local participation. Moreover, to the extent that we are underestimating the effect of particular independent variables, this underestimation should be about the same for each of our measures of social and political capital and demographic variables.

Table 12.4 reports the multivariate results for our basic citywide sample. Several findings stand out. First, in interpreting the unstandardized regression coefficients, few of the coefficients appear to indicate strong substantive effects. The dependent variable represents the number of acts of participation engaged in, and its mean is only 1.3 acts, with a standard deviation of 1.1. So the overall level of local participation is not high; there is clearly ample room for enhancing political engagement. But the important question for us is: What factors have contributed to political participation in New York City? What the data clearly show is that social capital has not been enough.

In looking at social capital after controlling for the effects of education, income, other demographic variables, and political capital variables, two findings stand out. One is that memberships in purely social organizations matter independent of the other variables in our model. But this effect is not great, represented by an unstandardized coefficient of .12 (we could interpret the former to mean, technically, that nine purely social memberships on average would lead an individual to participate in one additional political activity). Second, none of the other measures of social capital have a statistically significant effect after the political capital variables are added to the regression.

In contrast, the effects of political capital are far more impressive. There are the obvious effects of citizenship and strong partisanship. The effect of memberships in organizations involved in politics is particularly impressive in that its coefficient (.25) is twice the size of that for social memberships. This reveals that while social memberships matter for political participation, memberships in organizations directly involved in politics matter much more. Union membership appears to matter above and beyond other memberships. Increasing dissatisfaction with local services is related to participation, and being directly mobilized (as measured by being contacted about voting) is a statistically significant factor as well. Discussing politics is a significant variable, but it may be endogenous, and the effect of political efficacy is larger than its standard error, but not quite statistically significant.

The one demographic variable that stands out in all our analyses is age. The question of whether this represents an aging effect or a generational or cohort effect is a classic one, but the effect we find occurs independently of our measures of social and political capital. We interpret much of the age effect as representing higher levels of participation by the generation that lived through World War II and the early postwar period. The World War II generation's political engagement remains higher than that of others because of the social and political mobilization of that period. It is clearly imperative to take age into account in estimating the effects of other variables on local participation.

Education and income and other exogenous variables were included in the equations reported, but any effects they had are clearly mediated by other variables. The fact that we find no independent effects of other demographic variables at first suggests that other bivariate demographic differences in participation levels can be explained by influences associated with variations in the social and, especially, political capital of these groups. Clearly, this is one part of the story. But it is also possible that the influences that we see at work in table 12.4 do not work to the same extent for different subgroups in the population—for whites versus blacks and Latinos in particular. Making use of our black and Latino oversamples, we estimated our model separately for whites, blacks, and Latinos. Tables 12.5 to 12.7 report the multivariate results.

What we find for whites in table 12.5 fits in much better than what we had reported thus far in terms of the relative importance of social capital. The coefficients for the effects of social versus politically oriented organizational memberships are about the same, .13 versus .20, respectively. We also find that residence clearly has a statistically significant effect for whites: simply living in the same place for twenty or more years can lead to close to one additional act of political participation, everything else

TABLE 12.5 / Influences on Local Political Participation: Whites[a]

	Unstandardized Coefficients	t-Values
Social capital measures		
Organizational memberships—social	.178**	3.427
Length of time at present address	.079**	2.113
Political capital measures		
Organizational memberships—political	.220**	3.311
Union member and union is political	.105	.665
Citizenship	.434**	2.149
Strong party identification	.341**	2.376
Recently contacted to register or vote	.296	1.920
Local services satisfaction scale	−.010	−.984
Local political efficacy scale	.031	1.430
Demographic measures		
Age	.012**	2.685
Constant	−.468	−1.145
R^2		.310
Adj. R^2		.279
N		234

Source: Authors' compilation.
[a]OLS Regression.
Dependent variable: local participation scale (0–4).
**t-value significant at the .05 level.

TABLE 12.6 / Influences on Local Political Participation: Blacks[a]

	Unstandardized Coefficients	t-Values
Social capital measures		
Organizational memberships—social	.157**	2.773
Length of time at present address	−.024	−.598
Political capital measures		
Organizational memberships—political	.286**	5.552
Union member and union is political	.235	1.519
Citizenship	.746**	3.929
Strong party identification	.365**	2.709
Recently contacted to register or vote	.369**	2.360
Local services satisfaction scale	−.023**	−2.628
Local political efficacy scale	.034	1.641
Demographic measures		
Age	.013**	2.822
Constant	−.047	−.131
R^2		.423
Adj. R^2		.396
N		225

Source: Authors' compilation.
[a]OLS Regression.
Dependent variable: local participation scale (0–4).
**t-value significant at the .05 level.

being equal. But despite these effects of social capital, the overall explained variance is slightly (.38 versus .31) less than for the larger sample reported in table 12.4, and this can be attributed to the smaller effects of the political capital variables. Clearly, the effects of these variables must be different for nonwhites, as we see in tables 12.6 and 12.7.

The estimated coefficients reported in tables 12.6 and 12.7 reveal that the effects of political capital are much greater for blacks and Latinos than for whites. The R-squares are higher than for whites, and more important, the coefficients for the political capital variables are larger and more of them are statistically significant. The social capital variables matter less as well: residence length does not have a significant effect for blacks or Latinos, and the coefficients for memberships in social organizations are smaller than for memberships in organizations involved in politics. Union membership did not make a difference in participation for whites (insignificant coefficient of .105) or for blacks (insignificant coefficient of .127), but it did make a striking and significant difference for Latinos (.434). Strong party identification also made the greatest difference for Latinos (.615 versus .355 for blacks and .398 for whites). Citizenship and mobilization efforts also made a greater difference for blacks and Latinos than for whites. The effect of dissatisfaction with local services was about the same for all three groups, but it was statistically significant only for blacks.

TABLE 12.7 / Influences on Local Political Participation: Latinos[a]

	Unstandardized Coefficients	t-Values
Social capital measures		
Organizational memberships—social	.133**	2.924
Length of time at present address	.008	.249
Political capital measures		
Organizational memberships—political	.257**	5.069
Union member and union is political	.370**	2.484
Citizenship	.588**	4.739
Strong party identification	.595**	4.284
Recently contacted to register or vote	.345**	2.674
Local services satisfaction scale	−.013	−1.955
Local political efficacy scale	.021	1.149
Demographic measures		
Age	.015**	3.640
Constant	−.324	−1.135
R^2		.446
Adj. R^2		.424
N		268

Source: Authors' compilation.
[a]OLS Regression.
Dependent variable: local participation scale (0–4).
**t-value significant at the .05 level.

CONCLUSION

Our New York City data, with its oversamples of blacks and Latinos, offer a more complex explanation of the low levels of political participation in the city. The disproportionate effects of political capital in contrast to social capital can to an extent be attributable to the behavior of blacks and Latinos, although political capital clearly has important effects on whites as well. These results also have important implications for the debate about declining levels of political participation in the United States as a result of the decline of social capital. First, the social capital explanation may be primarily part of a story about white America; it may say much less about the changing racial and ethnic American landscape as found in New York City. Second, the social capital and political participation story appears to be incomplete for cities like New York. Social capital can make a difference, but according to our data, it is a small one compared to what is more important currency—political capital. Not surprisingly, membership in political organizations is much more likely to promote political activity like contacting a local official, voting in a mayoral or school board election, or taking action on a local political issue than membership in organizations that steer clear of politics.

If foundations, not-for-profits, and government are serious about the decline of urban democracy as an issue of public concern, then we must refocus our attention on the declining institutions of political incorporation. Without the support of strong local party organizations, unions, and organizations with an explicit political agenda, the new immigrants arriving in America's large cities will not be incorporated into the political mainstream. The old party organizations provided newcomers with material incentives for participation, making the Irish, Italians, and Jews real stakeholders in American politics. The same must be done for today's immigrants from Asia and Latin America in particular. Most significantly, we need a massive campaign by government to promote citizenship, without which there is no meaningful political involvement. Finally, the New York City data indicate that for native-born black, Latino, and white Americans, engagement in politics can best be encouraged by involvement in organizations that consider political activity a part of their agenda.

In local politics, those who participate understand the value of political engagement for their day-to-day lives—they know that democracy is about making sure that the political system is responsive to their interests. Traditional forms of political participation, which are designed to engage people directly in politics, cannot be left out of the social capital conversation. The development of strong, community-based political organizations that can hold elected officials accountable for basic service delivery in their communities would be an effective beginning. But accountability will be achieved only when poor and immigrant communities become strong partners in a majority electoral coalition and have an explicit policy agenda.

Our survey of New York City residents makes it clear that political capital is critical to political incorporation for minority and immigrant residents. Yet we do not know enough about the organizations that are working effectively to build political capital in our urban communities. Examining the role of these organizations in the new immigrant communities and poor, native-born African American and Latino communities in cities like New York would be particularly informative. Our preliminary work has yielded some interesting research questions that would be appropriate for systematic and comparative study. It would be interesting to determine the extent to which communal organizations and churches actually encourage their members to engage in political activity. We know little about whether any communities are creating organizational networks for political engagement and about the extent to which the value of citizenship and voting is being taught. We need to better understand what types of institutions actually change the pattern of political incorporation. Are government-sponsored programs like Citizenship NYC and NYS Citizenship Initiative increasing citizenship rates? How are individuals who become citizens through these government programs affected by their experiences? Preliminary evidence indicates that learning English and becoming a citizen can be quite a painful process for many elderly immigrants. Has their experience had a negative impact on their families, especially the younger generation? We have very little data about why immigrants are not becoming citizens. It appears that politics has no relevance to the struggles of their daily lives. Further research into organizational networks and community concerns that reconnect politics to the day-to-day lives of ordinary people may promote political participation with a community-building focus. Without political incorporation, there will be isolated successes for small numbers of individuals in each community, but no systemic transformation.

We would like to thank Oscar Torres-Reyna, Jason Boxt, Tamar Adler, and Ilana Buterman for their expert research assistance.

NOTES

1. Interestingly, Stolle and Rochon's (1998) cross-national study, which does not focus on cities, supports our position. They find that members of associations with a political agenda are less likely to be positively associated with generalized trust, efficacy, or tolerance, but that these associations have the most politically active memberships.

2. We present most data on Miami-Dade County rather than the city of Miami because demographically, economically, and politically, the county is the more appropriate unit of analysis. We are aware of the problems related to government jurisdiction for service delivery and try to address them when necessary. Christopher Warren (1997) has an in-depth discussion of this issue.

3. Population, race, and ethnicity data are based on U.S. Bureau of the Census (1980, 1990, 1990–97, 1997a) and State of California Department of Finance (1998).

4. Per capita revenue from own sources data are based on U.S. Bureau of the Census 1987, 1992, 1993–94.

5. Citizenship data are based on U.S. Bureau of the Census (1950, 1980, 1990, 1997a). Data on voting age population are based on U.S. Bureau of the Census (1990). Registration and voting data are based on U.S. Bureau of the Census (1997b).

6. This survey was conducted between August 11 and September 8, 1997, by the Barnard-Columbia Center for Urban Policy, Columbia University/Hispanic Education and Legal Fund Opinion Research Project. The additional samples, which together with the citywide sample produced a total sample size of 350 blacks and 453 Latino New Yorkers, provide more accurate estimates of the attitudes and behavior of these two groups.

APPENDIX: DESCRIPTION OF MODEL VARIABLES AND QUESTION WORDINGS

Dependent Variable

LOCAL PARTICIPATION SCALE

Q91: "Over the past year, have you contacted a local elected official about some need or problem?" (1 = yes, 2 = no)

Q94: "Over the past year, did you participate in any kind of activity to influence a legislator's vote on rent control?" (1 = yes, 2 = no)

Q49: "In 1993, you remember that Rudolph Giuliani ran for mayor of New York City against David Dinkins. Did you vote in that election?" (1 = yes, 2 = no, 3 = not registered)

Q96: "Have you ever voted in a school board election?" (1 = yes, 2 = no)

Dummy variables were created for the above questions, where 1 = yes and 0 = no, and a scale was created by combining the scores for the four measures of local political participation, where 0 = low and 4 = high.

Independent Variables

ORGANIZATIONAL MEMBERSHIPS: SOCIAL AND POLITICAL   Respondents were asked whether they were members of the following types of organizations: a neighborhood organization, a professional association (for example, the American Medical Association, a bar association), a church or religious association, a sports club, a service club (such as Lions, Elks, or Masons), a parent-teacher association, a veterans' association, a hobby club (for example, a gardening club, a stamp-collecting club, a chess club), a civic association (such as the League of Women Voters or the Junior League), a literary or art group (such as a book or museum group), an ethnic association (the NAACP, for example, or some other group organized by people of the same nationality). All questions were coded 1 = yes and 2 = no.

All respondents who answered that they were members of any of the organizations noted here were then asked the follow-up question: "Does this organization engage in political activity?" Two dummy variables were created for each organizational membership question: one for organizational membership in a nonpolitically engaged organization, and the other for organizational membership in a politically engaged organization. Two scales, "organizational memberships: social" and "organizational memberships: political," were then created by tallying for each respondent all organizational memberships for organizations that (1) *did not* engage in political activity, and (2) *did* engage in political activity, respectively.

OTHER MEASURES OF SOCIAL CAPITAL
PLAN TO LEAVE NEW YORK CITY IN THE FUTURE

Q174: "In the future, do you plan to stay in New York City or do you plan to move somewhere else?" (1 = move, 0 = stay)

LENGTH OF TIME AT PRESENT ADDRESS

Q186: "How long have you lived at your present address?" (open-ended) (1 = less than six months, 2 = six months to one year, 3 = one to two years, 4 = three to four years, 5 = five to ten years, 6 = eleven to twenty years, 7 = twenty-one to thirty years, 8 = more than thirty years)

HOMEOWNERSHIP

Q188: "Do you live in an apartment, a single-family house, a two-family house, a row house, a co-op, a condominium, or something else?" (1 = apartment house, 2 = single-family house, 3 = multi-family house, 4 = row house, 5 = condominium/co-op, 6 = other)

All respondents who answered something other than "apartment house" were then asked:

Q189: "Do you or your family own your own home or pay rent?" (1 = rent, 2 = own, 3 = neither)

Those who answered "apartment house" were asked:

Q190: "Do you rent from a private landlord, another family member, or from the Public Housing Authority, or do you own your apartment?" (1 = private landlord, 2 = another family member, 3 = Public Housing Authority, 4 = own apartment)

Owners were identified as those who answered "own" on question 189 and "own apartment" on question 190, where 1 = yes and 0 = no.

CHURCH ATTENDANCE

Q205: "What is your religious preference, is it Protestant, Catholic, Jewish, Muslim, some other religion, or no religion?" (1 = Protestant, 2 = Catholic, 3 = Jewish, 4 = Muslim, 5 = other [specify], 6 = no religion)

Those who answered anything other than "no religion" were then asked:

Q206: "How often do you attend religious services: several times a week, every week, almost every week, once or twice a month, a few times a year, or never?" (1 = several times a week, 2 = every week, 3 = almost every week, 4 = once or twice a month, 5 = a few times a year, 6 = never)

Church attendance was created by reversing the order of the answers to question 206 and adding those who answered "no religion" to question 205 (1 = never, 2 = a few times a year, 3 = once or twice a month, 4 = every or almost every week, 5 = several times a week).

INTERNET ACCESS

Q216: "Do you or anyone in your household currently own and use a personal computer?" (1 = yes, 2 = no)

Respondents who said that there was a personal computer in the household were then asked:

Q217: "Do you have Internet access?" (1 = yes, 2 = no)

The "Internet access" variable therefore represents those respondents who have Internet access *from their homes,* where 1 = yes and 0 = no.

OTHER MEASURES OF POLITICAL CAPITAL

LOCAL POLITICAL EFFICACY SCALE

Q69: "Do you agree or disagree: 'People like me don't have any say about what the city government does.'"

Q70: "Do you agree or disagree: 'Sometimes city politics and government seem so complicated that persons like me can't really understand what's going on.'"

Q71: "Do you agree or disagree: 'I don't think local officials care much what people like me think.'"

(1 = agree, 2 = somewhat agree, 3 = somewhat disagree, 4 = disagree)

A scale was created by combining the scores for these three efficacy questions, where 3 = low efficacy and 12 = high efficacy.

UNION MEMBERSHIP

Q97: "Are you currently a member of a labor union?" (1 = yes, 0 = no)

FAMILY MEMBERS VOTE

Q62: "Do most members of your family usually vote?" (1 = yes, 0 = no)

FRIENDS VOTE

Q62: "Do most members of your friends usually vote?" (1 = yes, 0 = no)

CO-WORKERS VOTE

Q62: "Do most of your co-workers usually vote?" (1 = yes, 0 = no)

DISCUSS POLITICS SCALE

Q79: "How often do you discuss politics with family members: nearly every day, once or twice a week, less than once a week, or almost never?"

Q80: "How often do you discuss politics with friends: nearly every day, once or twice a week, less than once a week, or almost never?"

Q81: "How often do you discuss politics with co-workers: nearly every day, once or twice a week, less than once a week, or almost never?"

(1 = nearly every day, 2 = once or twice a week, 3 = less than once a week, 4 = almost never, 5 = never)

The order of the answers for each of the three "political discussion" questions was reversed, and a scale was created by combining the scores, where 1 = never, 2 = almost never, 3 = less than once a week, 4 = once or twice a week, 5 = nearly every day.

CITIZENSHIP

Q219: "Are you a United States citizen?" (1 = yes, 0 = no)

Strong Party Identification

"Strong party identification" was created by first identifying respondents who said they were registered to vote:

Q34: "Are you currently registered to vote?" (1 = yes, 2 = no);

registered in the Democratic or Republican parties:

Q38: "Are you registered as a Democrat, Republican, some other party, or are you not registered in a party?" (1 = Democrat, 2 = Republican, 3 = some other party, 4 = independent, 5 = not registered in a party);

think of themselves as Democratic or Republican:

Q176: "Generally speaking, do you usually think of yourself as Republican, Democrat, independent, or what?" (1 = Republican, 2 = Democrat, 3 = independent, 4 = other, 5 = no preference);

and call themselves strong Democrats or Republicans:

Q177: "Would you call yourself a strong (Democrat or Republican) or not a very strong (Democrat or Republican)?" (1 = strong, 2 = not very strong).

The final variable, "strong party identification," is coded 1 = yes and 0 = no.

Recently Contacted to Register or Vote

Q52: "With the election for mayor and other city elections coming up, has anyone talked to you about registering to vote or getting out to vote?" (1 = yes, 0 = no)

Local Services Satisfaction Scale

Respondents were asked to rate the quality of a range of neighborhood services as 1 = excellent, 2 = good, 3 = fair, 4 = poor, 5 = don't know/not sure. The services included garbage collection, recycling, street cleaning, pothole repair, libraries, neighborhood public schools, maintenance of parks and recreational facilities, housing code enforcement, police responsiveness to calls or complaints, and emergency medical services. The coding was reversed for all questions with "don't know/not sure" as the midrange (3), and a satisfaction scale was created by combining the scores for all services, where 9 = low and 45 = high.

DEMOGRAPHIC MEASURES
Educational Attainment

Q181: "What is the highest level of education or schooling you finished and got credit for?" (open-ended) (0 = never, 1 = less than high school, 2 = high school graduate, 3 = junior college or some college, 4 = college graduate, 5 = some graduate school, 6 = graduate school degree)

Income

Q185: "In which of the following ranges does your family income fall?" (1 = $12,000 or less, 2 = $12,001 to $20,000, 3 = $20,001 to $30,000, 4 = $30,001 to

$40,000, 5 = \$40,001$ to $\$50,000, 6 = \$50,001$ to $\$60,000, 7 = \$60,001$ to $\$80,000, 8 = \$80,001$ to $\$100,000, 9 = \$100,001$ to $\$150,000, 10 =$ over $\$150,000)$

WORK STATUS

Q183: "Are you currently working, or are you temporarily laid off, unemployed, retired, permanently disabled, a homemaker, a student, or what?" (1 = working, 2 = part-time, 3 = laid off, 4 = unemployed, 5 = retired, 6 = disabled, 7 = homemaker, 8 = student)

A dummy variable was created for "work status" by combining scores 1 and 2 (1 = yes, working) and scores 3 through 8 (0 = no, not working).

AGE

Q180: "What is your age?" (open-ended)

GENDER

Interviewers noted the gender of respondent. The variable is coded 1 = female and 0 = male.

RACE-ETHNICITY

Q202: "For statistical purposes, we'd like to ask you: Are you white, black, or some other race?" (1 = white, 2 = black, 3 = Hispanic/Latino, 4 = mixed, 5 = other)

Q222: "Are you of Hispanic origin or descent, or not?" (1 = yes, 2 = no)

The race and Hispanic origin questions were recoded into a single variable, where 1 = non-Latino white, 2 = non-Latino black, 3 = Latino, 4 = other. Dummy variables were then created for "whites," "blacks," and "Latinos."

REFERENCES

Allswang, John M. 1977. *Bosses, Machines, and Urban Voters: An American Symbiosis.* New York: Kennikat.

Baker, Susan Gonzalez, and Marilyn Espitia. 2000. "From Latin American Immigrant to 'Hispanic' Citizen: The Role of Social Capital in Seeking U.S. Citizenship." *Social Science Quarterly* 81(4): 1051–63.

Banfield, Edward, and James Q. Wilson. 1963. *City Politics.* New York: Vintage.

Berman, Sheri. 1997. "Civil Society and Political Institutionalism." *American Behavioral Scientist* 40(5): 562–586.

Berry, Jeffrey, Kent Portney, and Ken Thomson. 1993. *The Rebirth of Urban Democracy.* Washington, D.C.: Brookings Institution.

Bobo, Lawrence, and Franklin Gilliam Jr. 1990. "Race, Sociopolitical Participation, and Black Empowerment." *American Political Science Review* 84(2): 377–93.

Booth, John A., and Patricia Bayer Richard. 1998. "Civil Society, Political Capital, and Democratization in Central America." *Journal of Politics* 60(3): 780–800.

Brecher, Charles, and Raymond Horton. 1993. *Power Failure: New York Politics and Policy Since 1960.* New York: Oxford University Press.

Browning, Rufus P., Dale Rogers Marshall, and David H. Tabb, eds. 1997a. *Racial Politics in American Cities.* 2nd ed. New York: Longman.

Browning, Rufus P., Dale Rogers Marshall, and David H. Tabb. 1997b. "Can People of Color Achieve Power in City Government?: The Setting and the Issues." In *Racial Politics in American Cities,* 2nd ed., edited by Rufus P. Browning, Dale Rogers Marshall, and David H. Tabb. New York: Longman.

Casper, Lynn, and Loretta Bass. *Voting and Registration in the Election of November 1996.* Washington: U.S. Bureau of the Census.

City of Los Angeles. 1998. *1998 Economic and Demographic Information.* Los Angeles: Office of the City Administrative Officer.

Cohen, Cathy, and Michael C. Dawson. 1993. "Neighborhood Poverty and African-American Politics." *American Political Science Review* 87(2): 286–302.

Coleman, James. 1988. "Social Capital in the Creation of Human Capital." *American Journal of Sociology* 94(summer supp.): S95–120.

Edwards, Bob, and Michael Foley. 1997. "Escape from Politics?: Social Theory and the Social Capital Debate." *American Behavioral Scientist* 40(5): 549–60.

———.1998. "Civil Society and Social Capital, Beyond Putnam." *American Behavioral Scientist* 42(1): 124–39.

Erie, Steven P. 1988. *Rainbow's End: Irish-Americans and the Dilemmas of Urban Machine Politics, 1840–1985.* Berkeley: University of California Press.

Fuchs, Ester R. 1992. *Mayors and Money: Fiscal Policy in New York and Chicago.* Chicago: University of Chicago Press.

Fuchs, Ester R., Lorraine Minnite, and Robert Y. Shapiro. 1999. "Political Capital and Political Participation." Paper presented at the meeting of the Midwest Political Science Association, Chicago (April 15–17).

Goldberg, Ellis. 1996. "Thinking About How Democracy Works." *Politics and Society* 24(1): 7–18.

Hall, George E., and Courtenay M. Slater. 1994. *1994 County and City Extra: Annual Metro, City, and County Data Book.* Lanham, Md.: Bernan Press.

———. 1997. *1997 County and City Extra: Annual Metro, City, and County Data Book.* Lanham, Md.: Bernan Press.

Harris, Frederick C. 1998. "Will the Circle Be Unbroken?: The Erosion and Transformation of African-American Civic Life." In *Civil Society and Democratic Citizenship,* report from the Institute for Philosophy and Public Policy 18(3): 1–6.

Haslip-Viera, Gabriel, and Sherrie L. Baver. 1996. *Latinos in New York: Communities in Transition.* Notre Dame, Ind.: University of Notre Dame Press.

Highton, Benjamin, and Raymond Wolfinger. 1998. "Estimating the Effects of the National Voter Registration Act of 1993." *Political Behavior* 20(2): 79–104.

Huckfeldt, Robert, and John Sprague. 1987. "Networks in Context: The Social Flow of Political Information." *American Political Science Review* 81: 1197–1216.

Jones-Correa, Michael. 1998. *Between Two Nations: Immigrants, Citizenship, and Politics in New York City.* Ithaca, N.Y.: Cornell University Press.

Ladd, Everett C. 1996. "The Data Just Don't Show Erosion of America's Social Capital." *The Public Perspective* 1(June–July): 5–6.

Levi, Margaret. 1996. "Social and Unsocial Capital: A Review Essay of *Making Democracy Work.*" *Politics and Society* 24(1): 45–55.

Mansbridge, Jane. 1980. *Beyond Adversary Democracy.* New York: Basic Books.

Morone, James. 1990. *The Democratic Wish.* New York: Basic Books.

Onishi, Norimitsu. 1998. "City Now Puts Budget Surplus at Record High of $2 Billion." *New York Times,* April 23: B1.

Peterson, Paul E. 1981. *City Limits.* Chicago: University of Chicago Press.

Piven, Francis Fox, and Richard A. Cloward. 1979. *Poor People's Movements, Why They Succeed, How They Fail.* New York: Vintage.

———. 1988. *Why Americans Don't Vote.* New York: Pantheon.

Portes, Alejandro. 1998. "Social Capital: Its Origins and Applications in Modern Sociology." *Annual Review of Sociology* 24: 1–24.

Putnam, Robert. 1993. *Making Democracy Work: Civic Traditions in Modern Italy.* Princeton, N.J.: Princeton University Press.

———. 1995a. "Bowling Alone: America's Declining Social Capital." *Journal of Democracy* 6(January): 65–78.

———. 1995b. "Tuning in, Tuning out: The Strange Disappearance of Social Capital in America." *PS: Political Science and Politics* 28(December): 664–83.

———. 2000. *Bowling Alone: The Collapse and Revival of American Community.* New York: Simon & Schuster.

Reed, Adolph, Jr. 1988. "The Black Urban Regime." In *Power, Community, and the City,* edited by Michael P. Smith. New Brunswick, N.J.: Transaction Press.

Rosenstone, Steven J., and John Mark Hansen. 1993. *Mobilization, Participation, and Democracy in America.* New York: Macmillan.

Schneider, Mark, Paul Teske, Melissa Marschall, Michael Mintrom, and Christine Roch. 1997. "Institutional Arrangements and the Creation of Social Capital: The Effects of School Choice." *American Political Science Review* 91: 82–93.

Schudson, Michael. 1996. "What If Civic Life Didn't Die?" *The American Prospect* 25(March-April): 17–20.

Shingles, Richard D. 1981. "Black Consciousness and Political Participation: The Missing Link." *American Political Science Review* 75(1): 76–91.

Skocpol, Theda. 1996. "Unraveling from Above." *The American Prospect* 25(March-April): 20–25.

Smith, James P., and Barry Edmonston, eds. 1997. *The New Americans: Economic, Demographic, and Fiscal Effect of Immigration.* Washington, D.C.: National Academy Press.

Spielman, Fran. 1997. "Daley Budget Freezes Taxes." *Chicago Sun-Times,* October 5.

State of California Department of Finance. 1998. *Historical City/County Population Estimates 1991–1998 with 1990 Census Counts.* Sacramento, Calif.: Department of Finance (May).

Stolle, Dietlind, and Thomas R. Rochon. 1998. "Are All Associations Alike?: Member Diversity, Associational Type, and the Creation of Social Capital." *American Behavioral Scientist* 42(1): 47–65.

Stone, Clarence. 1989. *Regime Politics.* Lawrence: University of Kansas Press.

Sullivan, Lisa. 1997. "Hip-Hop Nation: The Undeveloped Social Capital of Black Urban America." *National Civic Review* 86(fall): 235–43.

Tarrow, Sidney. 1996. "Making Social Science Work Across Space and Time: A Critical Reflection on Robert Putnam's *Making Democracy Work.*" *American Political Science Review* 90(2): 389–97.

Tocqueville, Alexis de. 1969 [1835]. *Democracy in America.* Edited by J. P. Mayer. Translated by George Lawrence. New York: Anchor.

U.S. Bureau of the Census. 1950. *Census of Population and Housing 1950.* Washington: U.S. Bureau of the Census.

———. 1980. *Census of Population and Housing 1980.* Washington: U.S. Bureau of the Census.

———. 1987. *Census of Governments, 1987.* Washington: U.S. Bureau of the Census.

———. 1990. *Census of Population and Housing 1990.* Washington: U.S. Bureau of the Census (September).

———. 1992. *Statistical Abstract of the United States: 1992.* 112th ed. Washington: U.S. Bureau of the Census.

———. 1993–94. *Finances of Individual City Governments Having 1,000,000 Population or More: 1993–1994.* Washington: U.S. Bureau of the Census.

———. 1990–97. *Estimates of the Population of Counties by Age, Sex, and Race/Hispanic Origin: 1990 to 1997.* Washington: U.S. Bureau of the Census.

———. 1997a. *Current Population Survey March 1997, American Community Survey, 1997 Preliminary Data.* Washington: U.S. Bureau of the Census.

———. 1997b. *Voting and Registration in the Election of November 1996.* Washington: U.S. Bureau of the Census.

U.S. Department of Housing and Urban Development. 1996. *State of the Nation's Cities: America's Changing Urban Life.* Washington (April).

Verba, Sydney, and Norman Nie. 1972. *Participation in America: Political Democracy and Social Equality.* Chicago: University of Chicago Press.

Verba, Sydney, Kay L. Schlozman, and Henry Brady. 1995. *Voice and Equality.* Cambridge, Mass.: Harvard University Press.

———. 1997. "The Big Tilt: Participatory Inequality in America." *The American Prospect* 32(May-June): 74–80.

Waldinger, Roger. 1996. *Still the Promised City?: African-American and New Immigrants in Post-Industrial New York.* Cambridge, Mass.: Harvard University Press.

Warren, Christopher. 1997. "Hispanic Incorporation and Structural Reform in Miami." In *Racial Politics in American Cities,* 2nd ed., edited by Rufus P. Browning, Dale Rogers Marshall, and David H. Tabb. New York: Longman.

Warren, Mark. 1998. "Community Building and Political Power." *American Behavioral Scientist* 42(1): 78–92.

Wilson, William Julius. 1987. *The Truly Disadvantaged: The Inner City, the Underclass, and Public Policy.* Chicago: University of Chicago Press.

Wolfinger, Raymond E., and Steven J. Rosenstone. 1980. *Who Votes?* New Haven, Conn.: Yale University Press.

Wood, Richard. 1997. "Social Capital and Political Culture: God Meets Politics in the Inner City." *American Behavioral Scientist* 40(5): 595–605.

Yatrakis, Kathryn. 1981. "Electoral Demands and Political Benefits: Minority as Majority: A Case Study of Two Newark Elections 1970, 1974." Ph.D. diss., Columbia University.

Zhou, Min. 1992. *Chinatown: The Socioeconomic Potential of an Urban Enclave.* Philadelphia: Temple University Press.

Index